Reader

Trudy B. Krisher

The University of Dayton

Prentice Hall
Englewood Cliffs, New Jersey 07632

Library of Congress Cataloging-in-Publication Data

KRISHER, TRUDY.
Writing for a reader / Trudy B. Krisher.
p. cm.
Includes bibliographical references and index.
ISBN 0-13-031170-7
1. English language—Rhetoric. 2. English language—Grammar.
I. Title.
PE1408.K73 1995 94-5834
808′.042—dc20 CIP

Acquisitions editor: *Maggie Barbieri*
Editorial/production supervision: *Jean Lapidus*
Cover design: DeLuca Design
Manufacturing buyer: *Bob Anderson*

A Simon & Schuster Company
Englewood Cliffs, New Jersey 07632

Printed in the United States of America
10 9 8 7 6 5 4 3 2 1

ISBN 0-13-031170-7

Prentice-Hall International (UK) Limited, *London*
Prentice-Hall of Australia Pty. Limited, *Sydney*
Prentice-Hall Canada Inc., *Toronto*
Prentice-Hall Hispanoamericana, S.A., *Mexico*
Prentice-Hall of India Private Limited, *New Delhi*
Prentice-Hall of Japan, Inc., *Tokyo*
Simon & Schuster Asia Pte. Ltd., *Singapore*
Editora Prentice-Hall do Brasil, Ltda., *Rio de Janeiro*

Contents

Preface

TO THE STUDENT

Writing for a Reader is based on the premise that you will improve your writing not just by paying attention to your teachers and your textbooks but by paying attention to your *readers*.

Because the relationship between readers and writers is so close as to seem almost invisible, many developing writers allow this important relationship to go unexplored. Unfortunately, attempting to write without exploring the notion of who your reader is, what your reader needs, and why your reader embraces certain expectations about writing is like climbing onto a teeter-totter without thinking about who's on the other end.

Improving a skill such as writing is often a matter of improving your understanding of that all-important person for whom you write: your reader. For instance, as a child you may have created stories for yourself alone in which you were the only reader. As a youngster, you may have then come to share a piece of writing with a reader who was a trusted friend. When you reached the higher grades, you wrote largely for your teacher-reader. However, as you went out into the world, you began to write for a variety of readers in a variety of circumstances: your college admissions officer, your potential employer, your professors in a number of disciplines, and your professional colleagues. Each new reader in each of these experiences challenges you to assess each new reading-writing situation in order to communicate your message effectively. Thus, expanding the repertoire of audiences for whom you write becomes an important key to expanding your writing skills.

In many respects, the writer-reader relationship is much the same as that between host and guest. Both writer-host and reader-guest respond to an invitation to spend some time together. However, unlike a host, who generally wishes for a guest merely to have a good time, the writer may hope to achieve broader goals for the reader-guest: to enjoy, of course, but also to learn, to think, to explore, to understand. Thus, with these larger goals in mind, the writer, like a host, spreads out thoughts on a table, offering ideas for the reader to sample and consider, taking care to create a friendly atmosphere, and organizing and arranging things to accommodate the reader-guest.

Writing for a Reader is devoted to helping you, the writer, learn to relate to your reader more effectively so that you can create an experience to help your reader feel comfortable, at home, and *welcome.*

TO THE TEACHER

Because *Writing for a Reader* asks student writers to pay close attention to their readers, the traditional classroom setting in which the teacher is at the center of the learning process will need to be modified. Using *Writing for a Reader*, the teacher can implement a collaborative classroom workshop/laboratory in which the ideas of both students *and* teacher can be proposed, examined, discussed, and revised. This model, in which group critiquing and peer editing skills figure as a primary means of learning, asks teachers to become willing learners and learners to become willing teachers.

Writing for a Reader has been designed to allow teachers and students to collaborate successfully. Many features have been incorporated into the text to achieve this goal.

An Inductive Approach

Writing for a Reader recognizes that developing writers are generally unresponsive to lecture-driven teaching. Instead, they respond more readily to inductive teaching styles that encourage them to discover principles, make connections, and develop insights on their own. Such an approach helps students take responsibility for their learning.

An Attention to Process

Writing for a Reader takes students through the writing process, encouraging them to experience the recursive nature of the process itself, permitting them to learn from each unfolding stage.

An Emphasis on Prewriting and Rewriting

Writing for a Reader has been designed to emphasize the two most important stages of the writing process: the prewriting and rewriting stages. Chapter 4 deals with the prewriting stage. Chapters 6 and 7 deal with the rewriting stage.

An Emphasis on Critical Thinking

Chapter 6, which teaches responding and critiquing skills, provides techniques that can be employed throughout the course. A great number of practical techniques for developing higher–order thinking skills that can be applied to student writing have been included.

An Attention to Both Paragraph and Essay

Writing for a Reader explains the general principles of writing, particularly paragraph writing, in Chapters 1 to 7. From Chapters 8 to 16, essay writing is emphasized.

An Abundance of Student Samples

Although the work of a number of professional writers has been presented in *Writing for a Reader*, the work of student writers has been equally represented. Throughout the text and at the end of each of the chapters dealing with strategies for essay writing such as description, narration, comparison–contrast, and others, student models are offered as examples for study.

Prompts for Class Discussion and Journal Entries

Because students are encouraged to share ideas in class and to keep a journal for the course, a number of prompts for class discussion and journal entries have been included. In each chapter, class discussion topics are listed under *Talking About It* topics; journal topics are listed under *Writing About It* entries.

A Reader-Based Approach to Grammar

Although Chapter 7 on editing and proofreading and the Appendix called "A Short Course in Grammar" contain a great deal of material on grammar, throughout the text an attempt has been made to provide reader-based reasons for grammatical rules. The goal is to help students see that grammatical requirements usually operate as necessary aids rather than rigid rules. These grammatical aids enhance the ability to communicate effectively with a reader.

Emphasis on Analyzing Patterns of Error

The *Writing Assessment Profile* which appears at the end of the text invites students to record and assess the strengths and weaknesses in each of their responses to the writing assignments. Using the *Writing Assessment Profile* helps students identify their individual patterns of error as a basis for improvement and recognize that errors are opportunities to learn.

A Variety of Reading Passages and Writing Assignments That Reach Across the Disciplines

Each of the chapters in *Writing for a Reader* includes a variety of readings. Many of these readings relate to disciplines outside the humanities; these readings help students see that the principles of writing which they are learning can be applied across the curriculum. In addition, at the end of each chapter a number of writing assignments designed to complement the concepts emphasized in the chapter are suggested. Many of these assignments challenge students to write papers which relate to disciplines other than the humanities; thus, students are encouraged to think about writing across the curriculum. Furthermore, these writing assignments also incorporate instructions to help students engage more effectively in both the prewriting and rewriting stages of the writing process.

Collaborative Writing Projects

Chapter 17, devoted exclusively to collaborative writing, includes a number of innovative group assignments.

Although most composition teachers recognize that engaging in collaborative learning to develop a sense of audience is essential to progress in writing, they are often unsure about how to proceed. *Writing for a Reader* offers methods for ensuring success for both students and teachers.

Acknowledgements

I wish to thank Carol Wada, who encouraged this project from its inception; Phil Miller, who carried on; Joan Polk, who always followed through, and Jean Lapidus, who managed to pull it off.

I am also grateful to those who have engaged in thoughtful research in composition, helping composition teachers to separate the true from the false in our assumptions about teaching and learning. Researchers, teachers, and practitioners like Linda Flower, Mina Shaughnessy, Peter Elbow, Lisa Ede, Andrea Lunsford, Teresa Enos, Erika Lindemann, Barry Kroll, Joseph Williams, Bonnie Meyer, and many others have helped me become a better teacher.

I also wish to thank the following readers of this manuscript for their encouragement and insight: Elizabeth Wahlquist, Brigham Young University; Mary Carol Doyle, St. Louis Community College at Florissant Valley; Karen Standridge, Pikes Peak Community College; Joyce M. Pair, DeKalb College; Joseph I. Bommarito, C. S. Mott Community College; and Diane M. Terando, Parkland Community College.

Above all, I am indebted to my students, for they have taught me everything I know.

Trudy B. Krisher
Dayton, Ohio

1

The Challenge of Writing

Why is writing so hard?
What will help me improve?

A job applicant sits in an employer's waiting room, looking over an application form.

A nurse sits at the nurses' station, preparing to write on a patient's medical chart.

An engineer sits at a table in a trailer on a construction site, puzzling over a field report.

A secretary sits before a typewriter, wondering how to respond to a customer complaint.

A scientist sits before a computer screen, thinking about how to describe the latest research results.

Whether in an employer's waiting room, on a hospital floor, at a field site, in an office, or in a research laboratory, these different writers have one thing in common: they are all facing the challenge of writing.

People in the working world struggle with writing. Professionals like business executives, engineers, health care workers, and teachers are called on to write in the course of their everyday work. Here's what they say about the challenges of writing.

> *I wish I could write more efficiently. My boss wants his reports now. It takes me too long to write them.*
>
> —Ben Hinders, computer programmer

When I was in college, I never realized how often I would have to write in my job—or how many people would be making decisions based on what I had written. It's important for me to write well.

—Diane Rhinehart, marketing analyst

My project supervisor keeps telling me that my writing is too wordy. I don't really know how to say everything I need to say in a way that's simple and clear.

—Joseph Salamone, civil engineer

Even professional writers are often frustrated by writing. Struggling day after day on the drafts of their work, they are especially familiar with the challenges that writing presents.

My pencils outlast my erasers.

—Vladimir Nabokov

The first or second draft of everything I write reads as if it was turned out by the charwoman.

—James Thurber

(Some days) it's just awful—plodding and backing up trying to take out all the ands, ifs, tos, fors, buts, wherefores, therefores, howevers; you know, all those.

—Maya Angelou

Some writers get headaches; others get stomach aches. I get both.

—Donald Murray

In fact, like students, men and women in the workplace as well as professional writers are challenged by writing. The truth is that writing is a challenge for *everyone*.

WHAT MAKES WRITING HARD?

Although researchers aren't exactly sure *why* writing is so challenging, they do know that it *is*. By listening to writers, they have learned a lot about the writing process. One of the things researchers are finding out is that writing is difficult because writers must juggle a number of concerns as they write.

As students, you are aware of the challenges inherent in the act of writing. Understanding these challenges is useful to you as well as to people who want to learn more about the process of writing. In fact, the responses which appear below were produced by a class of composition students who were asked to come up with a list of all the things they struggled with when they sat down to write. Here are some of their observations.

When I sit down to write I struggle to

. . . come up with ideas,
. . . decide whether my ideas are worth writing about,
. . . sound interesting,
. . . pick the right words,
. . . think about what my reader needs from me,
. . . organize my ideas,
. . . write effective sentences,
. . . figure out what my purposes for writing are,
. . . begin well,
. . . end well,
. . . decide what my point is,
. . . stick to my point,
. . . get a good grade,
. . . remember all the grammar rules,
. . . think about why I'm writing,
. . . think about whom I'm writing for,
. . . figure out when I might be boring my reader,
. . . figure out when I might be interesting to my reader,
. . . spell everything correctly,
. . . try to give the teacher what he or she "wants,"
. . . think of the most effective order,
. . . keep from going off the track,
. . . figure out when I haven't written enough,
. . . figure out when I've written too much.

With all the things involved in producing an effective piece of writing, it's no wonder that developing writers sometimes feel frustrated, confused, and even overwhelmed in the face of each new writing project. Any one of the listed challenges can present difficulties. Writing well often calls on students to wrestle with all of them.

Writing About It #1

Look over the list. In your journal, respond to the following questions: Is there anything you would add to the list? Is there anything you would delete? Identify a few of the items on the list that seem to give you the most trouble when you write. Write about why they are difficult for you, and offer some solutions to make them less troubling. Then identify a few items on the list that don't usually present problems. Write about why they are less difficult for you.

Talking About It #2

Share your responses with your classmates. You might find it useful to ask another student to serve as recorder, writing the class responses about things that are hard and things that are easy on the board. Then talk about the common challenges with writing that many of you share.

WHAT IS WRITING LIKE—FOR YOU?

Students often find it helpful to use their imaginations to describe what writing is like for them. One student, for instance, described the writing process as "dumping a jigsaw puzzle on the table and trying to put it back together again piece by piece." Another said that being a writer was "like being a firefighter fighting a forest fire. You think you're making progress in one direction, and then the wind suddenly shifts, spreading the flames—and the challenges—in an entirely different direction." In the following passage, Linda Flower and John Hayes, two respected scholars and researchers, provide another imaginative description about writing. They say that a writer is someone like a very busy switchboard operator trying to juggle a number of demands on her attention and constraints on what she can do.

> She has two important calls on hold. (Don't forget that idea.)
>
> Four lights just started flashing. (They demand immediate attention or they'll be lost.)
>
> A party of five wants to be hooked up together. (They need to be connected somehow.)
>
> A party of two thinks they've been incorrectly connected. (Where do they go?)
>
> And throughout this complicated process of remembering, retrieving, and connecting, the operator's voice must project calmness, confidence, and complete control.

Writing About It #3

Use your imagination to describe in your journal what writing is *like* for you. Then share your responses with the other students in your class.

WHAT CAN HELP?

You probably already know what it takes to become a better writer. It takes hard work. It takes an ongoing investment of time. It takes an interest in learning about the techniques that make a piece of writing successful. It takes a willingness to take a hard look at your problems with writing and to learn from them.

Learning to deal with the challenges of writing is like learning to deal with any other kind of challenges you've met in your life. In fact, feeling frustrated, confused, and overwhelmed is a common reaction to challenging circumstances. These reactions are familiar to everyone.

Can you remember, for instance, the first time you sat down to a computer? If you're like most people, you probably felt overwhelmed. Perhaps you were confused by the terminology. What was a "disk drive?" A "floppy?" Was that blip you saw on the screen the "cursor?" In addition, fear lurked at the heart of much of your frustration. Would you ever be able to master this powerful tool? Could you ever learn to work with a machine that at first seemed so confusing?

One of the things you probably realized right away was that if you were ever going to master this powerful machine, you were going to need help. Eventually, of course, you wanted to use the computer alone, but you knew you couldn't possibly learn to use a computer by yourself. You would need to rely on resources, resources such as your computer manual, your teacher, or a friend.

It's likely you began to understand the skills involved in using a computer by doing three things: breaking the learning process into small, manageable parts; adjusting your fearful attitudes about your ability to use the machine; and seeking help from other sources.

When you broke up the learning process into smaller, more manageable parts, perhaps you first decided to open your computer manual and learn the names for the parts of the equipment like "keyboard," "disk drive," and "monitor." When you tried to adjust your fearful attitudes, perhaps you gave yourself a mental pep talk, cheering yourself on with encouraging statements like, "You can do it. Give yourself time. Be patient. It's only a machine."

Once you had mastered a few basic terms about the parts of the equipment, however, you were faced with another step in the process: learning more complex tasks that involved making the computer follow your commands. You needed to "edit," "save," or "retrieve" your text. At this point, you may have abandoned the computer manual and turned to a friend for help. Perhaps a friend or a teacher could advise you about what function to use or what button to push much more quickly and simply than your manual. As user friendly as your manual might have been, the friendly guidance of another person such as a teacher or classmate may have been an even more reliable resource for your learning.

Gradually, as you immersed yourself in the process of learning how to use the machine, you became more familiar with each task and what it required. You learned to move paragraphs around, to delete, and to change words. You learned that "cursor" was just a fancy name for a place marker and that "scroll" simply meant to move quickly through your text. In addition, as you became familiar with the machine, your fear began to subside. And as your fear subsided and your confidence grew, using a computer became easier each time. You were probably not ready to declare yourself a computer expert, but you were beginning to master its challenges and overcome your fear. Best of all, you were becoming the master of the computer. It was no longer the master of you!

If you look at what helped you learn to use a computer, you'll find that there were three things that aided you in learning this new skill: **breaking the process down into small parts, adjusting your attitudes, and seeking help from others.**

Learning to write is a lot like learning to use a computer—or mastering *any* skill that at first seems overwhelming. There are hundreds of examples of this. Anything you're unfamiliar with—from something as simple as scrambling an egg to something as complex as writing—can seem frustrating, confusing, and overwhelming at first. But once you've learned to break the process down into manageable parts, adjust your attitudes, and enlist the support of others, you can master almost anything—including writing!

Writing About It #4

Write in your journal about a skill you eventually mastered that seemed overwhelming at first. It might have been a simple skill like ironing a shirt or a complex skill like obtaining a job you wanted. Your goal is to reflect on the way that mastering this skill depended on three things: (1) breaking the process down into manageable parts, (2) adjusting your attitudes, (3) enlisting the support of others.

Talking About It #5

When you have finished with your reflection, discuss your ideas with your classmates. Ask a classmate to list on the board the skills discussed in the journals. As a group, review the way learning each skill was a matter of mastering the three things listed.

As the examples you have provided point out, success is not just something that happens. It is something for which you have prepared. Your school's state tennis champion didn't happen to wake up one morning with a power backhand. You didn't select the college you are happily attending by pointing randomly to a page in a college guidebook. Your artist friend didn't learn to create those lovely ceramic bowls on a single Saturday morning at the potter's wheel. Success, in fact, is not a happy accident or the result of good luck smiling on the fortunate few. Success is, instead, the good fortune that comes to those who are willing to plan, prepare, and practice.

BREAKING IT DOWN: THE WRITING PROCESS

As you have seen, the first step in learning any new skill begins with breaking it into smaller, more manageable parts. Producing an effective piece of writing works this way, too.

In the past, perhaps you thought of writing as a single, isolated act, an event that was a simple matter of writing your ideas down on a piece of paper and handing that paper in to a teacher or employer. If you did, you were not alone. Many people think that writing is a simple matter of "drafting" or "getting it down."

However, as teachers and researchers are learning more about what produces effective writing, they are discovering that "drafting" is only one step in the writing process. They are finding that learning to write effectively is a matter of working hard at *all* of the stages in the writing process—not just the drafting stage.

As you've discovered, writing is not a simple, orderly process. However, in order to discuss this process in a rational way, it's sometimes helpful to break it down into stages. These stages are commonly called, (1) *prewriting*, (2) *writing or drafting*, and (3) *rewriting*. You will study these stages in more detail later in the text. As you learn about them, you will again be reminded that writing is a dynamic, circular process rather than a neat, linear one and that the stages of the writing process reinforce and overlap each other over and over again. But you'll also discover that breaking the writing process into the stages of prewriting, writing, and rewriting provides a helpful focus for your learning.

A Student Engages in the Writing Process

Although you will need to know more about each of the stages in the writing process to become an effective writer, you might find it useful at first to get a quick overview, to take a peek at a student as he moves through the stages of the writing process.

Carlos Restrepo is an eighteen-year-old college student enrolled in a writing class to improve his writing skills. It is the beginning of the semester, and Carlos knows none of his classmates. He is somewhat apprehensive about his ability to do well in a writing course because writing has always been hard for him in the past. On the first day of class, his teacher says that most of the early class meetings will be spent on writing an introduction. Carlos's teacher says that getting to know the other students in the class will be important in this course because most of the class writings will be read and responded to by other students; therefore, their earliest writing assignment will be one in which they introduce themselves to each other.

Carlos's teacher says that a good way to look at what makes an effective introduction is to read an effective introduction by a professional writer. As Carlos's teacher hands out the essay which follows, he reminds the class that Andy Rooney is a TV "essayist" whose television essays appear regularly on CBS' *60 Minutes*.

Introducing Andy Rooney

To begin with, here are some clues to my character. It seems only fair that if you're going to read what I write, I ought to tell you how I stand:

I prefer sitting but when I stand, I stand in size 8½ EEE shoes. There have been periods in my life when wide feet were my most distinguishing characteristic.

When it comes to politics, I don't know whether I'm a Democrat or a Republican. When I was young I was under the mistaken impression that all Democrats were Catholic and all Republicans were Protestant. This turns out to be untrue, of course, and I've never decided which I am. Those of us who don't have a party affiliation ought to be able to register under the heading "Confused."

This morning the scale balanced at 203 pounds. I'm 5′9″. My mother always called me "sturdy" and said I have big bones. A little fat is what I am.

I have been arrested for speeding.

I speak French, but Frenchmen always pretend they don't understand what I'm saying.

It is my opinion that prejudice saves us all a great deal of time. I have a great many well-founded prejudices, and I have no intention of giving up any of them except for very good reasons. I don't like turnips and I don't like liver. Call it prejudice if you wish, but I have no intention of ever trying either again just to make sure I don't like them. I *am* sure.

Good ideas are overrated. It makes more difference how a writer handles an idea than what the idea was in the first place. The world is filled with people with good ideas and very short of people who can even rake a leaf. I'm tired of good ideas.

When I write, I use an Underwood #5 made in 1920. Someone gave me an electric typewriter, but there's no use pretending you can use machinery that thinks faster than you do. An electric typewriter is ready to go before I have anything to say.

Writers don't often say anything that readers don't already know, unless it's a news story. A writer's greatest pleasure is revealing to people things they knew but did not know they knew. Or did not realize everyone else knew, too. This produces a warm sense of fellow feeling and is the best a writer can do.

There's nothing mystical or magic about being a writer. A writer is just a person who writes something. There are almost no people who are not dentists who can fix teeth, but there are a lot of people who aren't professional writers who write very well. This is one of the reasons why being a writer is tougher than being a dentist.

I admire people who don't care what anyone else thinks about what they do, but I'm not one of them. I care what people think and would not want you to know how much I hope you like what I write.

Sincerely,
Andy Rooney

Writing About It #6

Think about Andy Rooney's introduction of himself as you respond to the following questions in your journal.

1. Did you find this a satisfying introduction? Why or why not?
2. What techniques or methods of providing information about himself does Andy Rooney use?
3. Having read this piece, do you have positive or negative attitudes about Mr. Rooney? Why?
4. What personal characteristics does Andy Rooney possess? What evidence from his introduction suggests these characteristics?
5. What are some opinions Rooney holds about writing? Do you agree with those opinions? Why or why not?
6. If you were to write your own introduction about yourself, in what ways would this professional writer's introduction help you?
7. Every piece of writing addresses a particular reader. What kind of reader do you think Andy Rooney had in mind as he began writing this piece?
8. Every writer has goals or purposes. What do you think Andy Rooney's goals and purposes were as he began writing this piece?
9. Every piece of writing is made up of content, organization, and language. The content of a piece of writing refers to the subject matter—what is being said. Describe what Andy Rooney's content is about and suggest how he might have gone about generating the ideas that eventually ended up in this introduction.
10. Organization refers to the order in which something is said or presented. Describe how Andy Rooney has appeared to organize this piece. Do you think this is an effective method? Why?
11. Language or expression refers to *how* something is said—the words, the sentence structures, the point of view. Describe how Andy Rooney uses language in this piece to express his ideas. Do you find his expression satisfying? Why or why not?

Talking About It #7

Discuss your journal responses with your classmates.

Carlos's teacher now says that all of the students in the class will be introducing themselves to each other by writing a paragraph.

This one-paragraph introduction, his teacher says, should focus on one single thing that is important for someone to know about them. In the Andy

Rooney introduction, Carlos's teacher points out, there are many paragraphs focusing on many different things about Mr. Rooney: the paragraph about his feet, the paragraph about his political stance, the paragraph about his prejudices. However, Carlos's teacher reminds the class that their paragraphs will focus on only *one* piece of information about themselves, not several.

In addition, Carlos's teacher says that these paragraphs will be read by every student in the class as a way of introducing themselves to each other. Carlos's teacher says that these paragraphs will be a good way for the students to get to know one another as well as a good way to immerse themselves in the writing process from the very beginning of the course.

In the section that follows, watch Carlos as he progresses through the stages of the writing process in order to complete his paragraph. As you look carefully at the material, use your journal to reflect on Carlos's experience and answer some of the questions prompted by a close look at Carlos's work.

Prewriting

Prewriting, the first step in the writing process, involves two main activities: (1) thinking about your reader and your purpose, and (2) planning strategies for content, organization, and expression. The following is Carlos's *reader profile* and *purpose statement*, important steps in the prewriting process. They will guide him while he writes his drafts.

Reader Profile: My reader is a college student like me. He is about the same age and has about the same education. My reader doesn't know anything at all about me. I will need to give him/her some important information about myself in my paragraph. Because my reader is a member of this classroom, I think he/she may be using my writing in order to learn how to be a better writer himself. My teacher says that we will be working with each other a lot in class, so my reader is someone I will be working with eventually. I don't think my reader will expect me to write in formal language. My reader will expect me to use the kind of words and sentences that any college student would know. I will be able to "be myself" for this reader.

Purpose Statement: My purpose is to introduce myself to my reader. I plan to do this by focusing on only one important piece of information about me and providing information about that. My goal is to create positive attitudes about me in my reader as I introduce myself. I'd like to sound interesting, too. My purpose will be achieved—I hope!—in one paragraph.

Talking About It #8

With your classmates, discuss Carlos's reader profile. What kind of information does it contain? Why do you think it appears as part of the prewriting stage? In what ways may it help Carlos as he moves through the other stages of the writing process?

With your classmates, discuss Carlos's purpose statement. What kind of information does it contain? Why do you think it appears as part of the prewriting stage? In what way may it help Carlos as he moves through the other stages of the writing process?

During the stage of the writing process called *prewriting*, Carlos is also planning strategies for his paragraph. These strategies are plans for dealing with *content, organization,* and *expression.* In the passage that follows, Carlos is freewriting, making use of a strategy for generating the ideas that will eventually make up the content of his paragraph.

I am really having trouble coming up with ideas. My teacher says for us to freewrite—write about just anything—for five or ten minutes. To see what we might have to say. This is my biggest problem. Coming up with something like any single trait about myself. I don't know. I never thought about it too much. I played soccer in high school. It was the only sport I took time for. I lived in New Jersey. Near the Cherry Hill Mall. I never hung out there much like some of my friends because I had to work. I always worked. When I was younger by cutting lawns, babysitting. Later on at McDonalds. I would have liked to play basketball and track, but I didn't have the time. The babysitting reminds me. I was always good with kids. Like Bobby Ferrigno. My sisters always gave this babysitting job to me. They didn't know what to do with Bobby. He had Down's syndrome, and he was always having tantrums when Lisa and Maria babysat him. He did the same with me, too, sometimes, but somehow I could handle him. Calm him down. Maybe that's what I want to do after college. Work with kids like Bobby. Right now, I'm taking Biology, Western Civilization, Introduction to Psychology, Math 102 and this English class. It's going to be a struggle. Especially keeping up with the reading in Western Civ. We sometimes have 50 pages a night. And I'm not a fast reader. One single impression of me? Pressured!

Talking About It #9

Talk to your classmates about the way in which Carlos's freewriting allows him to generate his ideas. Describe the potential ideas for writing that Carlos's freewriting presents. Describe how you think this freewriting may differ from the final paragraph which Carlos turns in.

Having developed some strategies for generating content, Carlos now begins to focus those ideas in a *working statement.* Then he turns to developing some strategies for organizing and expressing his thoughts.

Working statement:	I like working with kids with special handicaps.
Strategy for organization:	Chronology (Time sequence, Narrating a Story)
	Event 1 → Event 2 → Event 3 → Event 4
	(First) (Then) (Next) (Finally)
Strategy for expression:	tone: upbeat, positive, enthusiastic point of view: use "I" (first person) words: simple and informal

After Carlos has completed his prewriting, a significant part of the writing process, he shares what he has written with his classmates. They respond to his prewriting, offering him suggestions that can help him improve the draft which he will soon write.

Writing or Drafting

Once Carlos has thought about his reader and his purpose, engaged in some prewriting, developed some strategies for content, organization, and expression, and shared those thoughts with his fellow classmates, Carlos is prepared to enter the *writing or drafting* stage of the writing process. Here is what Carlos eventually writes for his first draft.

I like working with kids with special handicaps. I've always been a kind of people person. I feel good when I'm around these people. I used to babysit a child who acted very violent. Throwing objects and anything he had when my sister Lisa and Maria came to babysit. His parents had to be aware and always on the watch 24 hours a day. They had special gates so he couldn't hurt himself. But when I used to come to babysit, he would calm down. He learned to share with me. Some games we'd play I'd let him win. To help lift his self esteem. Winning was very important to him. But he needed to learn to accept defeat, too. Knowing Bobby has been important to me. Someday I'd like to run a camp for kids with handicaps.

Rewriting

After Carlos writes or drafts his paragraph, he enters what is arguably the most important stage of the writing process, the *rewriting* stage. This stage is made up of two related processes: (1) responding and critiquing and (2) editing and proofreading.

In the part of the rewriting stage called *responding*, Carlos asks a fellow student to respond to or comment on what he has written. You will learn more about responding in another chapter of this text; however, in the following section, you can read a fellow student's subjective response to Carlos's first draft on the left column of the page.

This is an interesting paragraph to me because I've never been a good babysitter myself. I'm too impatient. I'm sure I could never have handled a child like this.

I like working with kids with special handicaps. I've always been a kind of people person. I feel good when I'm around these people. I used to babysit a child who acted very violent. Throwing objects and anything he had when my sister Lisa and Maria came to babysit. His parents had to be aware and always on the watch 24

I find this story fascinating, but I leave it feeling incomplete. I wish the writer had told me more.

hours a day. They had special gates so he couldn't hurt himself. But when I used to come to babysit, he would calm down. He learned to share with me. Some games we'd play I'd let him win. To help lift his self-esteem. Winning was very important to him. But he needed to learn to accept defeat, too. Knowing Bobby has been important to me. Someday I'd like to run a camp for kids with handicaps.

After Carlo's classmates respond to his work, Carlos writes another draft, incorporating what he has learned from the responses to his work and then inviting his classmates to critique this new text. You will learn more about *critiquing* in another chapter of this book, but for now you can see that one of Carlos's classmates has critiqued his latest work by underlining places where he feels confused or in need of more information, by placing question marks over these sections, and by raising questions in the left margin.

Is this first sentence necessary? Doesn't the second sentence say the same thing?

?

I like working with kids with special handicaps. Babysitting for Bobby Ferrigno helped me learn that I liked working with handicapped kids. Bobby was born with Down's syndrome, and his parents loved him very much. When they had babysitters like my sisters Lisa and Maria, Bobby would throw his silverware or his

What things? Can you explain?

Do you need this phrase? Haven't you already shown *the tantrums?*

?

Matchbox cars or whatever he could get his hands on. He would have big

?

temper tantrums. My sisters' didn't know how to calm him down. When the Ferrignos asked me to babysit one time, I found that I could relate to Bobby. Bobby and me would lay on the floor together and play with his fire trucks and police cars. While we played, Bobby learned to share his fire truck ladder or his lego policeman

Can you explain this fishing game?

?

with me. Sometimes we played a fishing game. To lift his self-esteem I often let bobby win. However, this became a problem eventually. I learned that you need to teach kids with handicaps how to both win and to accept defeat ?

How did this become a problem?

I think I learned as much from Bobby as Bobby learned from me. My experience with Bobby makes me think that someday I'd like to run a camp for kids with handicaps. Working with them gives me pleasure.

What did you learn?

Talking About It #10

With your classmates, identify the specific changes in this draft that make it different from Carlos's original draft. Do you think that Carlos paid attention to the responses offered by his classmates before he redrafted the piece which appears above? What makes you think so? Do you think the draft is stronger now? Why or why not?

As Carlos begins to rewrite again, incorporating ideas from the critique offered by his classmates as well as ideas of his own, he produces another revision.

My experience as a babysitter for Bobby Ferrigno taught me that I liked working with kids with special handicaps. Bobby was born with Down's syndrome, and his parents loved him very much. However, when they hired babysitters like my sisters Lisa and Maria, Bobby would throw temper tantrums, flinging his silverware, heaving his Matchbox cars, and even tormenting Max, his favorite cat. My sisters' didn't know how to calm him down. When the Ferrignos asked me to babysit one evening, I found that I could relate to bobby. Bobby and me would lay on the floor together and play with his fire trucks and police cars. While we played, Bobby learned to share his fire truck ladder or his lego policeman with me. On other visits, sometimes we played a fishing game which involved catching metal fish with a magnetic fishing pole. To lift his self-esteem I often let bobby win. However, letting him win all the time eventually became a problem. If, on a rare occasion, I didn't let him win, Bobby would throw a tantrum, the only way he had learned to get attention from others. As a result, I learned that you need to teach kids with handicaps how to both win and to accept defeat. I think I learned as much from Bobby as Bobby learned from me. I learned that the handicapped need patience and understanding as well as communication skills and reasonable limits. My experience with Bobby makes me think that someday I'd like to run a camp for kids with handicaps. Working with these special kids gives me great pleasure.

At this point, Carlos feels ready to edit and proofread his draft. In this part of the revising process, the *editing* and *proofreading* stage, Carlos and his classmates look for surface errors. When they edit, they look closely at *how* Carlos has expressed himself in his paragraph through sentence structure, word choice, grammar, and other areas. When they proofread, they read Carlos's paper out loud to catch errors that have eluded them to this point.

Talking About It #11

With your classmates, look carefully at Carlos's text. Identify some places where Carlos needs to make editing and/or proofreading changes in his text.

Using the Writing Assessment Profile

As he has worked on his paper, Carlos has progressed through many stages in the writing process. As part of the prewriting stage, he drafted a reader profile and a purpose statement. Next, he generated and focused his ideas and planned strategies for his content, organization, and expression. As part of the drafting stage, he wrote his first draft. As part of the rewriting stage, Carlos and his classmates did some useful responding and critiquing and later some editing and proofreading.

When he has finished making the changes suggested by careful editing and proofreading, Carlos turns in the final version of his paragraph.

My experience as a babysitter for Bobby Ferrigno taught me that I liked working with children with special handicaps. Bobby was born with Down's syndrome, and his parents loved him very much. However, when they hired babysitters like my sisters Lisa and Maria, Bobby threw temper tantrums, flinging his silverware, heaving his Matchbox cars, and even tormenting Max, his favorite cat. My sisters didn't know how to calm him down. When the Ferrignos asked me to babysit one evening, I found that I could relate to Bobby. Bobby and I lay on the floor together and played with his fire trucks and police cars. While we played, Bobby learned to share his fire truck ladder or his Lego policeman with me. On other visits we played a fishing game which involved catching metal fish with a magnetic fishing pole. To lift his self-esteem, I often let Bobby win. However, letting him win all the time eventually became a problem. If, on a rare occasion, I didn't let him win, Bobby reverted to throwing temper tantrums, the only way he had learned to get attention from others. As a result, I learned that kids with handicaps need to learn both how to win and how to accept defeat. Furthermore, I think I learned as much from Bobby as Bobby learned from me. I learned that the handicapped need patience and understanding as well as communication skills and reasonable limits. My experience with Bobby makes me think that someday I'd like to run a camp for children with handicaps. Working with these children gives me great pleasure.

When Carlos has finished with his several drafts, he needs to reflect on what the writing process has taught him about his own patterns of writing.

The Writing Assessment Profile which appears at the back of this text is a useful way to record responses to your work in order to learn from them. As you progress through this course, writing a variety of different assignments and making use of your writing assessment profile, you will begin to identify your individual writing weaknesses and strengths. The profile will enable you to make realistic assessments of your progress in writing. Note Carlos's writing assessment profile and the way Carlos reflects on his work in this introduction of himself.

Writing Assessment Profile

Chapter 1: The Challenge of Writing

Writing Assignment:	*One-paragraph introduction of myself*
Responding comments:	*Interesting subject matter, but many questions about my relationship with Bobby left unanswered*
Critiquing comments:	*In the next draft, I need to answer more questions. What was wrong with Bobby? What were the games we played? How did I teach him to share? These comments revolve around the need to develop my content in more detail.*
Editing comments:	*I needed to make several changes.* *(1) Combine some sentences to condense and sharpen my ideas (sentences 1 and 2, for example).* *(2) Change some of the word choices ("children" sounds more appropriate than "kids").* *(3) Tighten up some wordy sentences.*
Proofreading comments:	*I needed to pay attention to details like apostrophes ("sisters" rather than "sisters'"), capital letters ("Bobby," "Lego"), commas ("To lift his self-esteem,"), and pronouns ("Bobby and I," not "me"). Also, in reading out loud, I caught a comma splice. I corrected it to read ". . . accept defeat. I think I learned . . .).*

Reflecting on the Writing Process

You have seen the way one student progressed through the different stages of the writing process. In the following diagram (Fig. 1.1), you can see the stages visually.

One of the things you might have noticed in reviewing Carlos's progress is that most of his work is done in two major stages of the writing process: the prewriting stage and the rewriting stage. The diagram points out that these are

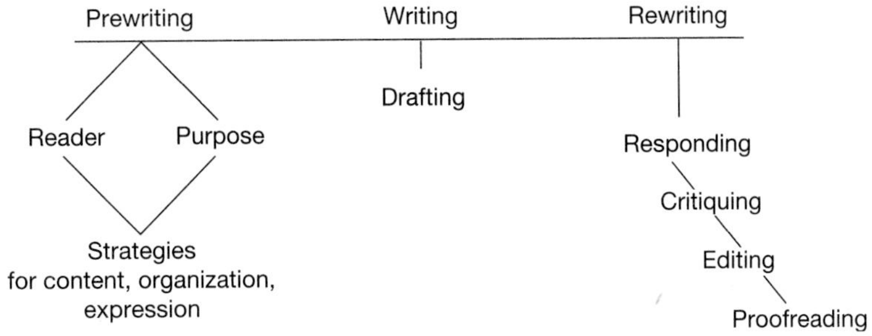

Figure 1.1

the stages in which most of the "work" of writing is done. Although in the past you might have thought that most of the work of writing takes place during the writing or drafting stage, research suggests that one of the ways you may become a more effective writer is by spending more of your time working in the prewriting and rewriting stages.

In addition, in looking over Carlos's writing experience, you may have noticed that Carlos often needed to move in and out of the various stages or back and forth between them. Although the stages of prewriting, writing, and rewriting look clear and straightforward on a chart, the reality is that the process of writing is rarely neat and orderly. In reality, every writer will often need to move in and out of the various stages of the writing process to achieve his goals because the stages typically overlap or reinforce each other.

For instance, as Carlos enters the critiquing part of the rewriting stage, he might discover that an idea—the idea about the fishing game, for example—isn't expressed fully enough. He might need to go back and prewrite some more, exploring his ideas about the fishing game in more depth. Similarly, when Carlos is proofreading, his oral reading might reveal some problems with sentence construction, problems most generally dealt with in the editing stage of the rewriting process. Although it's easy to see the stages in the writing process described in Figure 1.1, in reality the writer is constantly moving between and among the stages because the stages often overlap and reinforce each other. In a variation of the Figure 1.1 chart, Figure 1.2 can also describe the stages as follows:

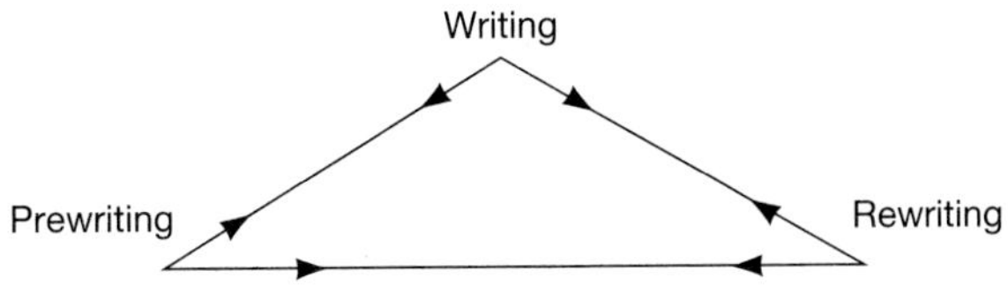

Figure 1.2

You should also note that in spite of Carlos's hard work and careful attention to the stages of the writing process, his final product is probably not perfect. There still remain many things Carlos could do to improve on his work even more. However, it is important to remember that progress, not perfection, is the goal when you are learning to become a more effective writer.

ADJUSTING YOUR ATTITUDE

As you probably know, attitude plays a key role in success. Positive attitudes followed by positive actions often lead to positive results. You may remember a storybook from elementary school about *The Little Engine That Could.* In spite of its doubts about its ability to haul a heavy load up a hill, the tiny engine succeeded after it learned to chant, "I think I can, I think I can, I think I can." Attitude held the key to the little engine's success.

On the other hand, negative attitudes are often followed by negative actions, guaranteeing negative results. It's a phenomenon called the "self-fulfilling prophecy." You tell yourself you can't write—or swim, or pass algebra, or form a lasting friendship—and then those negative attitudes lead to actions which guarantee that your negative prophecy comes true.

The important thing is to adjust your attitudes in a positive direction so that success is more likely to follow. The question is, "How do you do that?"

It's a good question.

There are several things you can do to develop positive attitudes about learning a new skill.

1. Confront your past experiences.
2. Face your situation realistically.
3. Be patient.
4. Take responsibility for your learning.
5. Keep your sense of humor.

Each of these guidelines is important. Let's take a look at them.

Confront Your Past Experiences

Everyone has past experiences that affect the present. A young child may have a fear of dogs and grow up to be fearful of all animals. A child in elementary school may have had a shorter attention span than his or her classmates and come to believe in later life that he or she can't learn. A teenager may have had a bad experience playing team sports and eventually avoids all athletic activities. These are just a few of the many examples of the way in which past experience may affect the present.

The following passage is from a short story called "Trust Me" by fiction writer John Updike. It describes a young boy's early experience at the swimming pool and suggests the effect of an early negative experience on a man's later life.

When Harold was three or four, his father and mother took him to a swimming pool. This was strange, for his family rarely went places, except to the movie house two blocks from their house. Harold has no memory of ever seeing his parents in bathing suits again, after this unhappy day. What he did remember was this:

His father, nearly naked, was in the pool, treading water. Harold was standing shivering on the wet tile edge, suspended above the abysmal odor of chlorine. . . . His mother, in a black bathing suit . . . , was off in a corner of his mind.

His father was asking him to jump. "C'mon, Hassy, jump," he was saying, in his mild, encouraging voice. "It'll be all right. Jump right into my hands." The words echoed in the flat acoustics of the water and tile and sunlight, heightening Harold's sense of exposure, his awareness of his own white skin. . . .

Then the blue-green water was all around him, dense and churning, and when he tried to take a breath a fist was shoved into his throat. He saw his own bubbles rising in front of his face, a multitude of them, rising as he sank; he sank it seemed for a very long time, until something located him in the darkening element and seized him by the arm.

He was in the air again, on his father's shoulder, still fighting for breath. They were out of the pool. His mother swiftly came up to the two of them and . . . slapped his father on the face, loudly, next to Harold's ear . . . His sense of public embarrassment amid sparkling nakedness—of every strange face turned toward him as he passed from his father's wet arms into his mother's dry ones—survived his recovery of breath. His mother's anger seemed directed at him as much as at his father. His feet now were on grass. Standing wrapped in a towel near his mother's knees while the last burning fragments of water were coughed from his lungs, Harold felt eternally disgraced.

He never knew what had happened: by the time he asked, so many years had passed that his father had forgotten. "Wasn't that a crying shame," the old man said, . . . "Sink or swim, and you sank."

Talking About It #12

With your classmates, discuss what happened to Harold in this story. Explain how the experience may have made Harold feel. Use your imagination to explain how this experience might have affected Harold's attitudes about swimming and his relationship with his parents. In what ways might this experience affect his choices about swimming again?

Writing About It #13

Think back to an early negative experience that still affects you today. Describe this situation in your journal. Try to convey not only what happened to you but how the experience made you feel. Share the experience with your class, and then discuss the strategies you might have had to adopt in order to overcome this negative situation.

Face Your Situation Realistically

Overcoming a negative experience is often a matter of facing that experience realistically. Negative experiences have a way of getting blown out of proportion, taking on much more importance than they deserve. For instance, learning to write well is admittedly difficult. But blowing those difficulties out of proportion can make you think that learning to write well is simply impossible, not merely difficult. Therefore, facing the experience realistically is one way of putting things back in perspective so that the experience can be addressed in a more effective way.

One way of facing the writing situation realistically is making sure you give yourself a realistic assessment of your problems. Sometimes students think in broad global generalities, declaring that "I just can't write" or "I've never been any good at writing. Why should things be different now?" It's important to recognize that kind of self-defeating assessment. Usually students have a number of things they do well and a number of things they do less well. It's more helpful to assess your situation with realistic phrases like this: "I sometimes have trouble supporting my ideas when I write, but I've always been a good speller"; "Organization is the thing I have to work on, but writing clear sentences has never been much of a problem for me"; "I need to spend some time writing less wordy sentences, for that way my reader can focus on the really great things I have to say." In this course, you will be given the opportunity to make up your own writing assessment profile based on feedback about what you write. Pay close attention to this profile, for it will provide you with realistic information.

Another thing that may keep you from looking realistically at writing is that the act of writing carries a mystique. The mystique says that being able to write is a gift possessed only by people of superior intelligence or talent, people like Shakespeare, William Faulkner, your last English teacher, or that brilliant girl who spoiled the curve in your creative writing class. This mystique, unfortunately, may get in the way of clear thinking about what writing actually is. Although the English language achieves great things in the hands of a Shakespeare, those achievements can set up unrealistic expectations about the effective writing which less gifted people can achieve. In the hands of most of the world—including yours—writing is simply a skill that can be practiced and learned, a skill which, when mastered, allows people to express, share, and act on their ideas in many important ways.

Another misconception that may prevent you from looking realistically at your struggles with writing is the misconception about the primacy of the final product. This myth suggests that the most important thing about your writing experience is the product—the final paper you turn in to your English teacher, the memo you lay on your boss's desk, or the letter of application you send out to graduate schools. This view suggests that every writer's goal is the letter-perfect, unsmudged submission in which no error rears its ugly head.

There's no doubt about the fact that the final product of your writing labors *is* important. That final product can influence your grade, your annual raise, or your acceptance to graduate school. However, it's important not to revere the final product so much that you ignore the process that produced it. The disorderly writing process is useful—and critical—if real learning is to occur. Think back to the last writing assignment you produced. Remember the coffee-stained pages, the scribblings and arrows, the erasure smudges, and the wadded-up fragments of paper at your feet. The fact is that this messy, experimental, disorderly process is where most of your real learning took place. In facing your writing experiences realistically, an important goal can be to value the process as much as the final product.

Closely tied to this view that the product is superior to the process is the notion that effective writing is merely a matter of following the "rules." The idea is that writing well means to punctuate properly, spell correctly, and produce complete sentences. Although each of these things is important, obsession with grammatical correctness can often work against intellectual freedom, the freedom that is so important if you are to indulge your ideas, shape your thoughts, and ultimately communicate them to a reader. Often a writer crosses out an idea or fails to follow a thought through to its conclusion because he or she is worrying about correctness: whether this word needs a capital letter, whether that verb is singular or plural, whether this sentence makes sense. The obsession with correctness often works against the writer. The writer, like a censor, vigilantly monitors in terms of right or wrong, giving orders like "don't do this" and "you can't do that" rather than encouraging herself with commands such as "try that" or "see if this works."

Most of you are familiar with this kind of rule fixing. Many common but sometimes misleading "rules" abound. They say things like this: "The first sentence of your paragraph must be the topic sentence." "Don't ever start a sentence with 'But.'" "Don't ever end a sentence with a preposition." "Your thesis statement must appear at the very end of your introductory paragraph." Some of these so-called rules may even offer good advice; the problem arises when attempts to observe these rules get in the way of thinking freely. Too much preoccupation with rules often shuts a writer down when the goal is to open the writer up.

Be Patient

Another important part of adjusting your attitudes about writing is learning to be patient. Like any important skill, effective writing skills cannot be acquired overnight. Writing, as you've probably learned, is a complex mental act in which the writer needs to be able to generate ideas, organize ideas, and express ideas to a reader. But the ability to perform a complex mental act such as writing requires more than just mental resources such as the ability to think and reason. It requires emotional resources like patience and the willingness to face frustrations head-on. Thus, writing calls not just for mental maturity; it calls for emotional maturity as well. Peter Elbow, an influential writing teacher, says, "Because there is no neat gradual way to learn to write and because progress seems so unpredictable and just plain slow, a major part of learning to write is learning to put up with this frustrating process itself."

Take Responsibility For Your Learning

One of the factors that is most likely to lead to positive results is taking responsibility for your learning. The truth is that only you can control the way you spend your time, the methods of studying you adopt, and the degree of investment in your work. Success, therefore, can come from taking control, from "owning" your work. No one else can do it for you.

However, taking responsibility is no guarantee that the task before you will be easy. There are always setbacks, obstacles, and outright failures. But don't be fooled into thinking that there is an easy way out or a way of avoiding your responsibility. There isn't.

The following passage is by John Langan, an experienced writing instructor. In this passage, Langan recounts his struggles as a college freshman and the obstacles he needed to overcome in order to succeed.

> I remember my . . . confusing first year at La Salle College in Philadelphia. I entered as a chemistry major but soon discovered that I could not deal with the mathematics course required. As hard as I tried, I couldn't pass one of the weekly quizzes given in the class. I felt the teacher was poor and the text unclear, but since other people were passing the tests, I felt the problem was in me, too. It was a terribly confusing time. Because I doubted my ability to do the work, I began questioning my own self-worth.
>
> At the same time that I doubted whether I COULD do the work in mathematics, I began to know that I did not WANT to do the work. Even if I eventually passed the course and the other mathematics courses I would have to take, I realized I did not want to spend my life working with numbers. Very quickly my career plans disintegrated. I was not going to be a chemist, and I was left in the confused and anxious vacuum of wondering what I WAS going to be.
>
> I partly responded to my general unhappiness by trying to escape. One way I did this was by resorting to games. In some respects my real major that first year at La Salle was the game room located in the student center. Before and after classes I went there to play endless games of chess and Ping-Pong. I played, I now realize, not only to find relief from my worries but also as an indirect way of trying to meet other people. For a while I had a roommate who was in college only because his parents wanted him to be; he too was desperately unhappy. We seldom talked because we had very little in common, but we would

spend entire evenings playing chess together. One day soon after midsemester grades were sent out, I came back to the dorm to find that my roommate, his clothes, chessboard—everything—had disappeared.

The games were not enough escape for me, and so I decided to get a job. I did not absolutely need a job, but I told myself I did. Not only did I need an excuse to get away from my dismal days at the college, but I also wanted to shore up my unsure self-image: If I could not be a successful student or friend . . . , I could at least be a successful wage earner. Fortunately, I did not get a full-time job but instead began working as a graphotype operator two nights a week in downtown Philadelphia. The job made me feel a little older and closer to being independent, so it helped lift my spirits.

Had I gotten a full-time job, it might have provided enough excuse for me to drop out of school, and I might have done so. As it was, I stayed, and—despite general unhappiness and partial escape through games and my part-time job—I did the work.

Mathematics was hopeless, especially because there was no tutoring program or mathematics lab at the college, so I dropped the course. But I knew I would need the chemistry course that I was taking as a basic science requirement for graduation. The course meant a massive amount of work for me, and I studied and studied and went into a test hoping to get a grade that would reflect all the studying I had done. Instead, I always came out with Ds. The grades were the more discouraging because I felt so generally displeased with myself anyway. They seemed to be saying to me, "You are a 'D' person." However, I kept studying. I read and underlined the text, took lots of notes, and studied the material as best I could. I was determined to get the course behind me and, with a final grade of low C, I did.

Talking About It #14

With your classmates, describe the ways in which John Langan avoided taking responsibility for his work. What reasons does he give for avoiding these responsibilities? Describe the ways in which John Langan accepted the responsibilities for his work. How did doing so "pay off?"

Writing About It #15

In your journal, describe the ways in which you both avoided and accepted responsibilities for your work in the past. Why did you do so?

Keep Your Sense of Humor

A sense of humor is one of those qualities that can keep you from blowing things out of proportion or focusing on the negative. When you're laughing, it's impossible to feel afraid, anxious, or worried. Laughter restores a sense of balance. As you have learned, it's important to confront your negative experiences; it's also important to laugh about them. As important as it is to remember to face your experiences realistically, be patient, and take responsibility for your learning, don't forget to take the time to laugh in the face of your own frustration.

The following passage was written by James Thurber, an American humorist and essayist. In this passage, he describes his frustration with using the microscope in his college botany lab.

I passed all the other courses that I took at my university, but I could never pass botany. This was because all botany students had to spend several hours a week in a laboratory looking through a microscope at plant cells, and I could never see through a microscope. I never once saw a cell through a microscope. This used to enrage my instructor. He would wander around the laboratory pleased with the progress all the students were making in drawing the involved and, so I am told, interesting structure of flower cells, until he came to me. I would just be standing there. "I can't see anything," I would say. He would begin patiently enough, explaining how anybody can see through a microscope, but he would always end up in a fury, claiming that I could *too* see through the microscope but just pretended that I couldn't. "It takes away from the beauty of flowers anyway," I used to tell him. "We are not concerned with beauty in this course," he would say. "We are concerned solely with what I may call the *mechanics* of flars." "Well," I'd say, "I can't see anything." "Try it just once again," he'd say, and I would put my eye to the microscope and see nothing at all, except now and again a nebulous milky substance—a phenomenon of maladjustment. You were supposed to see a vivid, restless clockwork of sharply defined plant cells. "I see what looks like a lot of milk," I would tell him. This, he claimed, was the result of my not having adjusted the microscope properly, so he would readjust it for me, or rather, for himself. And I would look again and see milk.

I finally took a deferred pass, as they called it, and waited a year and tried again. (You had to pass one of the biological sciences or you couldn't graduate.) The professor had come back from vacation brown as a berry, bright-eyed, and eager to explain cell-structure again to his classes. "Well," he said to me, cheerily, when we met in the first laboratory hour of the semester, "we're going to see cells this time, aren't we?" "Yes, sir," I said. Students to right of me and to left of me and in front of me were seeing cells; what's more, they were quietly drawing pictures of them in their notebooks. Of course, I didn't see anything.

"We'll try it," the professor said to me, grimly, "with every adjustment of the microscope known to man. As God is my witness, I'll arrange this glass so that you see cells through it or I'll give up teaching. In twenty-two years of botany, I—" He cut off abruptly for he was beginning to quiver all over, like Lionel Barrymore, and he genuinely wished to hold onto his temper; his scenes with me had taken a great deal out of him.

So we tried it with every adjustment of the microscope known to man. With only one of them did I see anything but blackness or the familiar lacteal opacity, and that time I saw, to my pleasure and amazement, a variegated constellation of flecks, specks, and dots. These I hastily drew. The instructor, noting my activity, came back from an adjoining desk, a smile on his lips and his eyebrows high in hope. He looked at my cell drawing. "What's that?" he demanded, with a hint of a squeal in his voice. "That's what I saw," I said. "You didn't, you didn't, you *didn't!*" he screamed, losing control of his temper instantly, and he bent over and squinted into the microscope. His head snapped up. "That's your eye!" he shouted. "You've fixed the lens so that it reflects! You've drawn your eye!"

Talking About It #16

With your classmates, talk about Thurber's problem. Describe his frustration—and his professor's. What strategies did Thurber make use of in facing his problem? How did his sense of humor help him through his experience? How may a sense of humor help *you* in facing your own learning challenges?

Succeeding in the face of difficulties is never easy. But there are some things that can help you adjust your attitudes in a positive direction to insure a greater likelihood of success. These involve confronting your past experiences, facing reality, taking responsibility, being patient, and maintaining your sense of humor. The same as learning to swim, using a computer, or becoming an effective listener, writing is a skill that can be learned, and it flourishes in an environment where positive attitudes exist.

ENLISTING THE SUPPORT OF OTHERS

As you've seen, learning a skill like writing is less frustrating when you break the process down into manageable parts and adjust your attitudes. In addition, learning to write is made easier when you enlist the support of others.

Traditionally, "support" has meant relying on your textbook or teacher—or both—to help you learn. Both those methods are obviously useful. Your textbook usually combines theories that help you "think" about writing with practical practice that helps you "do" writing. In addition, your teacher knows much about writing and understands how to communicate this knowledge to you, the student. Thus, both text and teacher are traditional, reliable means of support for you.

However, one important means of support has probably been underused in the traditional English classroom: your classmates. In this class, however, your classmates will become a crucial means of support for improving your writing strategies, support just as useful as your text or your teacher. In this class, your classmates will read and reflect on everything you write, and you will read and reflect on everything they write. As you learn to lean on and enlist the support of others in your class, you will be astonished by the improvement in your writing.

As you enlist the support of others, you will begin to understand that writing is, in essence, a social act. You will also see that writing improves when a writer is provided with a "real" audience.

Enlisting the support of others goes by several names. It may be called *collaborative learning, peer editing, writing groups,* or some other term. But whatever it is called, learning to work with others to improve your writing will pay off in improved attitudes and skills.

Let's look at some of the reasons why working collaboratively with others can help you become a better writer.

Providing Increased Feedback

First, perhaps the most important thing a developing writer needs is plenty of feedback. When you write, your mind dances with questions: "Does this sentence 'sound' OK?" "Have I explained this idea convincingly enough?" "Is this really the best word for what I mean?" "Is this introduction really going to 'grab' my reader?"

In the past, perhaps, your teachers answered some of these questions through comments on your papers. Perhaps they wrote "AWK" over an awkwardly constructed sentence. Perhaps they wrote "Good!" over an interesting comparison. Perhaps they circled a word, directing you to think about "word choice." Perhaps they put brackets around a paragraph, noting "more support here."

All of these comments were probably useful; however, it's likely these comments also raised even *more* questions in your mind: "How DO I make that sentence less awkward?" "What words, EXACTLY, might be better choices?" "Does 'more support' mean one more idea—or several?" In short, comments on the page, helpful though they likely were, just weren't always helpful enough.

What you probably needed was more feedback—a lot of it. This is something a teacher, working alone, is hard pressed to provide. There are too many students, too many papers; there is too little time. However, working collaboratively with other students as well as with a teacher can provide you with the abundant feedback you need.

In addition, this textbook makes use of a special feature for recording the feedback you are given about your writing. In the back of this book appears a Writing Assessment Profile which you can use every time you receive comments about your work. This profile will provide an individualized record of your strengths and weaknesses for that particular assignment. Over time, your personal writing patterns will emerge, giving you a lot of information about your writing style. The Writing Assessment Profile will enable you to chart your progress and monitor your growth as a writer.

Valuing Multiple Viewpoints

What you will find is that feedback, especially feedback representing many points of view, will benefit your writing. Each reader—including your teacher—brings his or her own unique way of looking at things to each new piece of writing. When those readers share their responses, the writer is treated to a rich menu of reactions which he can consider when he begins to revise his work. In addition, when a writer hears from several classmates that an idea was imaginative or clearly expressed, he learns about the strengths on which he can build. When he hears from several classmates that an idea was confusing or not thoroughly supported, he learns about the weaknesses on which he can improve. Finally, since reactions to writing are so often subjective, dialogue with a group can free the writer from beliefs that he is the victim of tyranny, the tyranny of a teacher's single subjective response.

Understanding Choices

Another benefit of collaborative learning in the writing classroom is that you will come to see writing for what it really is—a matter of choices, not rules. Too often students view writing as a matter of spelling correctly or writing complete sentences in order to observe the rules of grammar. This view often leads students to think of writing as a matter of right and wrong, an activity in which the participant either follows the rules or breaks them. This view also leads teachers to play the "gotcha!" role, becoming a kind of grammatical police officer handing out tickets in the form of red marks for breaking the laws.

Such a view does the written language a disservice, for it prevents students from appreciating the liberation of thought that is at the heart of all language. One of the benefits of working with others will be that you will come to see the way in which writing is not primarily about rules but about the series of choices made in the interests of clear communication with a reader. The writing may be effective or ineffective, of course, but working with others will help free you from the restrictive blinders of right and wrong.

Creating Reader Empathy

You're probably familiar with the concept of "empathy." If a person is empathetic, he or she is able to imagine how another person feels or thinks. Writing well is also a matter of developing a kind of empathy, an empathy with the reader. When a writer can be empathetic to the reader, he or she can mentally slip into the reader's mind to understand how a reader might respond to what's been written.

Developing this kind of empathy is not easy. An actor, for instance, develops a performance to move an audience and can tell whether or not it's succeeding by the audience's response. A comic, of course, wants to make the audience laugh, and the dead silence or rollicking laughter is an immediate indication of how he or she is doing. But it's not so easy for writers. A reader neither applauds nor laughs nor throws tomatoes. The silence that accompanies reading gives a writer no clue as to how he or she is doing. Because of this lack of objective response from the reader, the writer often doesn't know whether his or her work has succeeded or failed.

Talking with readers, however, can help a writer judge how he or she is doing. Talking with readers helps writers develop the kind of empathy necessary for effective writing. Fostering dialogue between reader and writer is one important way of encouraging writers and readers to stand in each others' shoes, of strengthening an already vital relationship into an even more empathetic one. Listening to readers respond to writing reminds the writer of the way readers read. When the writer listens carefully, the readers can tell him or her what they need, what they expect, and when they've been reached. Since writers and readers are involved in a collaborative relationship, a relationship involved in sharing ideas for mutual consideration, it's vital for writers to know whether that relationship is succeeding. Only readers can tell them.

Strengthening Critical Thinking

As you learn to listen to the criticisms of others, your own critical thinking skills will improve. You and the other students in your class will begin to discuss important questions: "What makes a good idea?" "What are the most effective ways of organizing that good idea?" "How can that idea be expressed most effectively?" As you learn to engage in dialogue, raise questions, and answer them, you and your classmates will begin to model the critical thinking process for each other. Talking about writing will provide you with direct experience in analyzing, discovering, inquiring, synthesizing, connecting, and evaluating, processes at the heart of critical thought. This ability to think critically is essential to success in the classroom, on the job, and in life itself.

BECOMING PART OF A COMMUNITY

When you strive to become a better writer, you are seeking entrance into a community, a community which uses language in a particular way. If you are currently taking general education classes in college, you will be learning to become part of the language community of the college graduate. As a writer seeking admission into that community, you will begin to learn about the admission requirements for initiation. You will learn that the community values certain things: lively and rigorous discussion of ideas, creative problem solving, effective communication. Becoming a member of the community means demonstrating that you also respect these values and have attempted to acquire them.

As you come to understand the generally educated reader in your writing classroom and what is expected from written communication, you prepare yourself to enter the broader community of all generally educated writers. Furthermore, you lay the groundwork for membership in the more specialized language community of your chosen profession. Eventually, you may seek to move beyond the language community of the classroom and the language community of the generally educated person to write and read as a scientist or businessperson or teacher in an even more specialized language community. If that group is a community of scientists, for instance, you will learn the admission requirements for that community. You may discover, for example, that scientists value reliable data and accurate expression. If the community you seek to join is a group of business professionals, you will learn that those colleagues have their own special language values. You may discover, perhaps, that these professionals value strong company relations and language that cuts through bureaucracy. Eventually, as you learn what membership in your particular language community requires, you will come to respect, acquire, and demonstrate the values of that more specialized language community. And, one day, you will enjoy the responsibilities and privileges of membership.

WRITING ASSIGNMENTS

Choose one or more of the suggestions from the following list as a writing assignment. Make use of the stages of the writing process—prewriting, writing, and rewriting—as you write.

A. Refer to Andy Rooney's introduction and Carlos Restrepo's introduction as you write your own introduction of yourself to your classmates. Make certain to focus on only one item of information about yourself. You may write one paragraph or several.

Before you write, engage in some prewriting activities. You may wish to create a reader profile and a purpose statement. You may wish to engage in some freewriting as part of your strategy for developing content, organization, and expression. Remind yourself that these are techniques you will learn more about in future chapters, so aim to do the best you can with the understanding you now possess. Your purpose now is to develop a sense of the prewriting stage of the writing process.

After you draft your work, share it with your classmates in order to develop a sense of the rewriting stage of the writing process. Ask your classmates to respond to and critique your work before you rewrite it. After you rewrite it, ask them to make editing and proofreading suggestions. Remind yourself that these techniques will be explored in more detail in future chapters, so aim to do the best you can with the understanding you now possess. Your purpose now is to develop a sense of the rewriting stage of the writing process.

When you are finished with your introduction of yourself, record your own and your classmates' responses in the Writing Assessment Profile that appears in the back of this textbook.

B. Interview a classmate, taking notes on what you learn about him or her. Then focus on only one item of information about that person, writing one paragraph or several as you introduce that person to your classmates. Refer to Andy Rooney's introduction and Carlos Restrepo's introduction as you write about this classmate.

Before you write, engage in some prewriting activities. You may wish to create a reader profile and a purpose statement. You may wish to engage in some freewriting as part of your strategy for developing content, organization, and expression. Remind yourself that these are techniques you will learn more about in future chapters, so aim to do the best you can with the understanding you now possess. Your purpose now is to develop a sense of the prewriting stage of the writing process.

After you draft your work, share it with your classmates in order to develop a sense of the rewriting stage of the writing process. Ask your classmates to respond to and critique your work before you rewrite it. After you rewrite it, ask them to make editing and proofreading suggestions. Remind yourself that these techniques will be explored in more detail in future chapters, so aim to do the best you can with the understanding you now possess. Your purpose now is to develop a sense of the rewriting stage of the writing process.

When you are finished with your introduction of your classmate, record your own and your classmates' responses in the Writing Assessment Profile that appears in the back of this textbook.

C. Observe one of your classmates carefully, taking notes and recording impressions of him or her. You may notice things like items of clothing, facial expressions, tone of voice, characteristic ways of speaking, gestures and mannerisms, or anything else that captures your attention. You are to observe this person without talking to him or her. Then write one or more paragraphs recording these impressions. Do *not* reveal the classmate's name. You will want to produce a piece of writing so clear that your classmates will be able to infer the identity of your subject from the observations you provide.

Before you write, engage in some prewriting activities. You may wish to create a reader profile and a purpose statement. You may wish to engage in some freewriting as part of your strategy for developing content, organization, and expression. Remind yourself that these are techniques you will learn more about in future chapters, so aim to do the best you can with the understanding you now possess. Your purpose now is to develop a sense of the prewriting stage of the writing process.

After you draft your work, share it with your classmates in order to develop a sense of the rewriting stage of the writing process. Ask your classmates to respond to and critique your work before you rewrite it. After you rewrite it, ask them to make editing and proofreading suggestions. Remind yourself that these techniques will be explored in more detail in future chapters, so aim to do the best you can with the understanding you now possess. Your purpose now is to develop a sense of the rewriting stage of the writing process.

When you are finished with your writing, record your own and your classmates' responses in the Writing Assessment Profile that appears in the back of this textbook.

D. Observe some items that characterize you and that are found in a single place. The place may be your room, house, car, or pocketbook. Those items that characterize who you are may be books on your bookshelf in your room, mementos on the refrigerator in your kitchen, music tapes kept in your car, items carried in your pocketbook, or many other things. Then write one or more paragraphs in which you use these items to suggest your personality to your classmates.

Before you write, engage in some prewriting activities. You may wish to create a reader profile and a purpose statement. You may wish to engage in some freewriting as part of your strategy for developing content, organization, and expression. Remind yourself that these are techniques you will learn more about in future chapters, so aim to do the best you can with the understanding you now possess. Your purpose now is to develop a sense of the prewriting stage of the writing process.

After you draft your work, share it with your classmates in order to develop a sense of the rewriting stage of the writing process. Ask your classmates to respond to and critique your work before you rewrite it. After you rewrite it, ask them to make editing and proofreading suggestions. Remind yourself that these techniques will be explored in more detail in future chapters, so aim to do the best you can with the understanding you now possess. Your purpose now is to develop a sense of the rewriting stage of the writing process.

When you are finished with your writing, record your own and your classmates' responses in the Writing Assessment Profile that appears in the back of this textbook.

CHAPTER ONE REVIEW

Writing About It #17

Use your journal to reflect on what you learned in this chapter.

2

Writing for a Reader

What does it mean to "write for a reader?"
How can writing for a reader help me
improve my writing?

Writing for a Reader is based on this simple premise: when writers learn to *write for a reader*, their writing improves.

But what does it mean to "write for a reader?" What are your reader's needs? What are your reader's expectations? How do you find them out? And, once you do, how do you meet those needs? How do you live up to those expectations?

The answers to these questions are not simple. But you can begin to answer them by talking to your readers and by asking your readers what they need. In this course, you will talk to your classmates about your writing over and over, again and again. In talking to these readers, you will discover what works and what doesn't, what needs to be saved and what needs to be changed. Doing this will make you—and the others in your class—better writers, for you will have learned to write for a reader.

KEEPING YOUR READER IN MIND

One of the most important things research about writing suggests is that effective writers write with a reader in mind. That's one of the reasons why this book is called *Writing for a Reader*. It will introduce you to the many ways keeping a reader in mind can help you improve your writing.

You might find it useful to think of you, the writer, as a host and your reader as a guest. A host, as you know, wants a guest to enjoy himself or herself, to have a good time while they're together. A writer has a similar but often broader purpose for the reader-guest: to enjoy, of course, but also to learn, to think, to explore, to understand. A writer, like a host, spreads out his or her thoughts on a table, offering ideas for the reader to sample and consider. Like a host, a writer takes care with his or her presentation, organizing efforts to accommodate the reader–guest. The writer strives to create an atmosphere for the guests that makes them feel comfortable, at home, welcome. When he or she succeeds, the writer, like a successful host, has created a memorable experience for both.

Although the memorable experience between host and guest is the goal, everyone is familiar with unsuccessful attempts to reach it: the toddler's birthday party at which the birthday boy cried and had to be put down for his nap; the Thanksgiving dinner featuring the turkey that just wouldn't get brown; the office party which the boss ruined by turning every conversation back to the subject everyone wanted to forget for an evening: work. Similarly, writers and readers often fail to achieve a successful experience. Perhaps the writer failed to define the reader clearly, or forgot to clarify his or her purpose. Perhaps the writer neglected to revise with care.

The world is full of examples of writing that fails to communicate. All of us have experienced writing that is confusing or misleading, writing that leaves us scratching our heads. Sometimes we pore over a passage, puzzling out the words. Sometimes we backtrack and reread, struggling to grasp a writer's meaning. Sometimes we fall asleep over long pages of type unbroken with space or illustrations. When we can't understand what a reader has said, sometimes we even wonder what's wrong with us. We easily forget that it's first the writer's responsibility to understand the reader, to *keep the reader in mind* as he or she writes. If the reader falls asleep, often it means that the writer wasn't fully awake.

One of the reasons writers might not write with a reader in mind is that they don't know how. Perhaps they haven't developed the quality of empathy, the kind of empathy with a reader that allows them to stand in the reader's shoes, looking at a text as a reader would. This ability to empathize with a reader is an important quality, a quality that is difficult to develop, but a quality that is enormously important to your success as a writer.

To understand the difference between writing that keeps the reader in mind and writing that doesn't, let's imagine the following scene:

Assume, for a moment, that you've gone to your grandmother's apartment for the first time in order to help her with her monthly chore of paying her bills. Your grandmother is looking forward to your visit. She places a plate of cookies at your elbow as you sit down to work. Not only is she happy to see you; she is grateful for your help. In the last few months, her eyesight has begun to fail, and she keeps getting notices from the power company that she's neglected to pay her bill. Your grandmother has every intention of paying her utility bill, but sometimes she forgets where she's put it, and last month she told you she thinks she got a notice from the company threatening to shut off her electricity if she missed another payment.

Munching a cookie, you rip open the envelope from the power company. Inside are some flyers with tips for saving energy, and there's a little white sheet that bears this notice:

Third Party Designation Notification Form

Customers 65 or over may voluntarily designate a third party of their own selection to whom notification of past due bills will be sent. Receipt of billing statements or disconnect notifications by a third party places no obligation on such party for payment of the bill nor does it cause deferment or prevention of disconnection of service if payment is not received as required. Completion and signing of the attached pre-addressed, postage-paid third party notification request form will provide the protection afforded by this procedure.

Talking About It #18

Talk with your classmates about the following questions:

1. What purpose did the utility company have in mind when it sent out this notice?
2. Is the notice from the power company relevant to you or your grandmother? Why or why not?
3. Is it likely that you would stop to read the notice? Would you be more likely to throw it away without reading it? Why or why not?
4. When you read the notice, was it easy for you to read? Why or why not?
5. Do you think that most of the customers who received this notice would be likely to read it? Why or why not?
6. What specific advice would you give the utility company for improving the possibility that this notice would be read?

If you concluded that few customers would either read or understand the notice sent out to them, you're probably right. And the reason why you're right is that the utility company forgot a fundamental principle of effective writing: writing with a reader in mind.

Forgetting this principle probably caused the utility company to lose thousands of dollars. When company executives noticed that no one was sending back the pre-addressed envelope, they might have decided to try again. If they did, they might have sent out something like this:

Are you 65 or older?

Would you like to name someone to get a copy of important notices we send to you?

Do you sometimes mislay your bill or forget to pay us? Would you feel more comfortable if we sent a second copy of past-due bills and other important notices to someone else like your son or daughter or a friend?

If you are 65 or over, you can ask for this special service. When we send you a notice that you are late in paying us or a notice that we are going to turn off your gas or electricity, we will also send a copy of the notice to the person you name.

You still have to pay the bill. The other person does not have to pay the bill. We can still turn off your gas or electricity if we do not get paid by the date on the notice. But you will have the protection of knowing that someone can remind you to pay us.

If you would like this service, fill out the attached card and send it to us. Our address is already on the card. We pay the postage.

Talking About It #19

Talk to your classmates about the following questions:

1. Would you be more likely to read this second notice than the first one? Why or why not?
2. What specific techniques did the writer of the second notice use that made it easier to read?
3. Do you think the second notice did a better job of keeping the reader in mind? Explain.
4. Give a short explanation of what you think "writing for a reader" means. Give some examples of writing you may be asked to do—now and in the future—which will improve if you learn to "write for a reader."

THE WRITING–READING SITUATION

The writer of the second letter to the power company's customers was more successful because a more effective job of analyzing the writing-reading situation was done.

Analyzing a writing–reading situation effectively is a lot like taking a successful photograph. Although it's possible to take a stunning picture without much thought or planning, success is more likely if the photographer thinks about a number of things before beginning: the purpose of the photograph, the goals of the photographer, the elements of composition, the choice of lens, the type of film, even the choice of a camera. The fact is that a successful photograph is less a matter of luck and more a matter of skill. The photographer needs not merely to trip the shutter, but to aim, focus, plan, and think—before tripping the shutter.

Analyzing the writing–reading situation works in much the same way as taking an effective picture. Taking a successful photograph requires the photographer to understand the elements of the photographic situation: composition, lighting, perspective, focus, and lens. Producing a successful piece of writing requires the writer to understand the elements of the writing-reading situation as well.

ELEMENTS OF THE WRITING–READING SITUATION

Every successful piece of written communication is the result of the satisfying interaction among four elements: *the reader, the writer, the work,* and *the language.*

As you begin to learn more about writing for a reader, you will come to appreciate that analyzing the elements of your writing situation is important to your success. You will begin to see that effective writing can be achieved when you become comfortable with answering many of the following questions in order to size up your writing–reading situation—before you begin to write.

1. The Reader

Who is your reader? How would you define the reader? Can you "picture" your reader? What does the picture tell you? What are the reader's attitudes—about you the writer, about the work, and about the language community which you share?

What kinds of appeals might be effective with this reader? Appeals to emotion? Appeals to reasons or facts? Appeals to your expertise as a writer?

What are the reader's needs and expectations? From the writer? From the work? From the language itself?

2. The Writer

Who are you as a writer? How would you define yourself? What are your purposes and goals? What techniques will be most likely to achieve them?

What are your attitudes—about the reader, about the work, and about the language community which you share?

What are your needs and expectations? From the reader? About the work? From the language itself?

3. The Work

What is the purpose of the work? What techniques will be employed to achieve that purpose?

Is this work appropriate for this reader?

What content or information should the work contain? What content or information can this work leave out?

What type of organizational form will best communicate that information?

4. The Language

What language community will the writer and reader be members of for the purposes of this piece of writing? Is it a general language community? A specific language community? How do you know?

What are the goals and values of this language community? How will those goals and values be reflected in your writing?

What language choices or expressions will make the work more successful? Choices about tone? Choices about sentences? Choices about words? Other language choices?

The following passage appeared in *The Washington Post*, a newspaper known for its in-depth coverage of the government and its workings. The subscribers who make up the newspaper's audience probably include thousands of government workers and public servants. Read the passage carefully, and then respond to the questions which follow it in your journal.

Input to Output, 35 minutes

Total Lead Time: 35 minutes

Inputs:

1 cup packed brown sugar

½ cup granulated sugar

½ cup softened butter

½ cup shortening

2 eggs

1½ teaspoons vanilla

2½ cups all-purpose flour

1 teaspoon baking soda

½ teaspoon salt

12-ounce package semi-sweet chocolate pieces

1 cup walnuts or pecans

Guidance:

After procurement actions, decontainerize inputs. Perform measurement tasks on a case-by-case basis. In a mixing-type bowl, impact heavily on brown sugar, granulated sugar, softened butter and shortening. Coordinate the interface of eggs and vanilla, avoiding an overrun scenario to the best of your skills and abilities.

At this point in time, leverage flour, baking soda, and salt into a bowl and aggregate. Equalize with prior mixture and develop intense and continuous liaison among inputs until well coordinated. Associate key chocolate and nut subsystems and execute stirring operations.

Within this time frame, take action to prepare the heating environment for throughput by manually setting the oven baking unit by hand to temperature of 375 degrees Fahrenheit (190 Celsius). Drop mixture in an ongoing fashion from a teaspoon implement onto an ungreased cookie sheet at intervals sufficient enough apart to permit total and permanent separation of throughputs to the maximum extent practicable under operating conditions.

Position cookie sheet in a bake situation and surveil for 8 to 10 minutes or until cooking action terminates. Initiate coordination of outputs within the cooling rack function. Containerize, wrap in red tape, and disseminate to authorized staff personnel on a timely and expeditious basis.

Output:

Six dozen official government chocolate-chip cookie units.

(c. 1982, *The Washington Post*)

Talking About It #20

With your classmates, analyze the writing-reading situation which resulted in the chocolate-chip cookie recipe. Imagine that you were the writer of the recipe. Use the questions from page 36 to guide you as you attempt to describe the **reader**, the **writer**, the **work**, and the **language community** involved in this writing-reading situation. Decide whether you felt this piece of writing successfully met the goals represented by your writing-reading analysis.

Writing About It #21

Imagine that you are going to rewrite this recipe. Choose a reader with specific attitudes about cooking with which you are familiar (your mother who is a gourmet cook, your sister who can't scramble an egg, your brother who loves cookies, etc.). Then use the questions from page 36 to guide you as you attempt to describe the reader, the writer, the work, and the language community involved in this new writing-reading situation. Finally, rewrite the recipe for this new reader. When you have finished, share your rewritten recipes with the classmates. Discuss the way the change in reader changes the writing-reading situation.

CONSTRAINTS AND THE WRITING SITUATION

As you have seen in the examples mentioned, your writing situation is profoundly influenced by your reader, often called your *audience*. What you write is critically affected by who your reader is. As a result, each new writing situation is different because each new writing situation addresses a new and different reader.

In addition, every writing situation operates under a certain number of constraints or limitations. A history professor may assign a paper, stating that it should be 8 to 10 pages long. That page length requirement, therefore, operates as a constraint on the writing situation. Later on in the course, that same professor might ask you to write a paper in which you compare and contrast General Grant and General Lee. The directive to compare and contrast is another constraint on your writing situation. You will not be rewarded for describing, narrating, or illustrating material about the two Civil War generals, for the situation limits you to comparisons and contrasts. Thus, constraints are at work in this writing situation as well.

The fact is that constraints or limitations are present in every writing situation. These constraints may be informational or situational or cultural. An informational constraint, for example, refers to limits on the information with which you are working. Sometimes information is simply unavailable to you, the writer. You may be writing a science paper on the electrical stimulation of paralyzed muscles and its success in helping paralyzed people to walk, but you may find that information about the latest studies has not been published or that the most significant research is still in progress. Another example of an informational constraint occurs when you choose *not* to discuss certain information or decide to downplay its importance. In a job application, for instance, you might choose to omit references to being laid off from the job in the department store where you once worked, believing that such information might harm your chances for securing new work. On the other hand, you might decide to mention that information and include an explanation to minimize its negative impact. You might reveal, for instance, that the department store was taken over by a national chain, a situation which led to company reorganization and employee layoffs. Such considerations are examples of informational constraints on the writing situation.

Other constraints on the writing situation can be situation or cultural. Restrictions about page length or instructions to compare and contrast are example of situational constraints. Letters to the editor of a newspaper cannot run on for pages because newspaper pages do not offer unlimited space. Research or library papers cannot be presented without bibliographies because the information they contain must be credibly documented. In addition, cultural constraints place limits on the writing situation as well. American culture values politeness and consideration of others. Generally, writers are discouraged from being rude or outrageous in print. The writer given to rudeness can be dismissed as a boor, and the writer given to outrageous falsehoods can be sued for libel. Such cultural constraints are also at work in writing situations.

LETTERS: AUDIENCE CONSTRAINTS

One way of exploring the needs of a reader or audience and of recognizing the constraints at work in every writing situation is to practice writing letters. In this age of instant communication by means of telephone or electronic mail, we often forget that letters can be important and personal way of keeping in touch. Stationary, ink, and sealing wax still possess the power for pleasing, and most of us have known the pleasure of tearing open the envelope on a letter written for our eyes only.

Imagine the letters you have written in your life: a thank-you note to Aunt Agnes who crocheted that blue afghan for your birthday; a letter of complaint about that *Popular Mechanics* subscription which you paid for but which never came; letters of inquiry sent out to colleges you were interested in attending; a love letter, doused in perfume, composed when you first started dating your boyfriend or girlfriend; a "Dear John" or "Dear Jane" letter sent when you broke up.

If you'll think for a moment about those letters, you'll notice that who your reader was greatly influenced what you wrote. You will also notice that you operated under certain constraints. You may have recognized the constraint of thanking Aunt Agnes in a timely fashion. You may have adopted a reasonable, patient tone in your letter of complaint to *Popular Mechanics*, in spite of your anger. You may have carefully checked your letters of inquiry to colleges, recognizing their potential for making an important first impression of you. You may have felt either less or more restrained about revealing your feelings to your boyfriend or girlfriend, depending on whether you were writing an earlier love letter or a later "Dear John" or "Dear Jane."

Letters are also an efficient means of communicating information. Most magazines offer regular features called *letters* columns where readers can solicit brief information or advice on topics that concern them: the best time to plant trees, the proper dress for an evening wedding, the standard amount for a tip at a business lunch. Most newspapers feature advice columns, for example, Ann Landers's popular column; these are simply informal replies to letters received by the columnist on topics of concern to the writers. Newspapers also regularly feature popular Letters to the Editor sections where community members can voice their opinions on critical issues.

Because writing a letter is often a less formal writing situation than writing a research paper or a college essay, the informality of the letter form offers writers a great deal of freedom. In a letter, writers are free to explore critical questions about their readers: Who is my reader? What constraints are at work in this reading–writing situation? What attitudes do this reader and I already share? What opinions are the reader and I likely to disagree about? What appeals will be most effective with this reader? What information does my reader need from me? What is the best way for me to supply it? What kind of language or style will be most appealing to this reader?

In the section which follows, you will read some humorous but "unsent" letters from Andy Rooney, the writer who introduced himself to you in Chapter 1. They originally appeared under the title "Letters Not Sent" in Rooney's collection of essays called *Pieces of my Mind*. Read them carefully and then respond to the reflection questions which follow.

Mr. Michael Vishniac
Acme Plumbing Co.

Dear Mr. Vishniac:

I know what a busy man you are and I hate to bother you but I am writing in the hopes of being able to make an appointment with you to fix the faucet in our downstairs bathroom. It has been dripping for five months. I have called your plumbing company but all I get is an answering service. I understand you have been wintering in the Bahamas.

If it isn't convenient for you to make a house call to fix the faucet, would it be possible to make an appointment for me to bring the sink over to you to be fixed?

Sincerely,
Andrew A. Rooney

Leslie Cartwright
Abraham Lincoln Grade School

Dear Mrs. Cartwright:

How wonderful it was of you to ask all thirty-one students in your fourth grade English class to write me individually for details on how I got started writing, how I get my ideas, who has influenced me most as a writer, and what a young person who wants to be a writer should study.

I was so touched that I'm going to set aside the other work I had planned to do in the next three or four days and answer all thirty-one of your students.

I have to go now because many of the students told me to please get my answers back to them quickly as you told them their assignment was due next Thursday.

Sincerely,
Andrew A. Rooney

Mrs. Franklin Z. Welles
Glenmont Library Charity Assn.

Dear Mrs. Welles:

I would like to contribute an article of old clothing for your auction to raise money for the new sidewalk in front of the Glenmont Library but am unable to do so. I wear my old clothes.

Sincerely,
Andrew A. Rooney

Talking About It #22

The Andy Rooney letters were "unsent." For each of the letters, talk with your classmates about why you believe Andy Rooney did not send them.

Writing About It #23

In order to explore the way letters can help you define your reader as well as the constraints of the writing situation, imagine that you are Andy Rooney, writing a letter to Michael Vishniac, Leslie Cartwright, and Mrs. Franklin Z. Welles. The letters you write, however, *will* be sent. After you have written these to-be-sent letters in your journal, share them with your classmates, discussing what was left out or added to your new letters that made them different from Andy Rooney's letters. Try to explain what writing constraints prompted you to write your letters the way you did, discussing your view of your readers and the constraints at work in this letter-writing situation.

Student Mary Lynn Taylor has written two letters in the section which follows. They demonstrate the many ways in which a piece of writing is critically influenced by how the writer defines the reader and the constraints inherent in that definition. Read them carefully and then use your journal to reflect on the questions which follow the letters.

1.

Sun. nite—late!!

Dear Juan,

Finally, I got up enough courage to do it! I quit !!%$#@

You'd be proud of me. I know you've been telling me to do it for months now, but I never had the nerve. That is, until last night.

It was our busiest Saturday night ever (and the hottest). The guests were all lined up in the lobby and out the door. I was frantic in the kitchen, trying to get all the main courses ready.

I had worked all evening on getting the sauce just right. Fettucini Alfredo was the special, and you have to be careful with the sauce or it burns. I was proud of my hard work—*and* my sauce. I could barely see into the pot I was stirring because the steam was so thick (the Grovers are too cheap to buy a proper ventilation system). . . .

Well, then in comes the grand Mr. Grover with his chest stuck out so far I was surprised there was still room in the kitchen for the rest of us. He walks over to my station and peers over my shoulder to see what I was doing and said, " Janet can finish up with that, Miss Taylor. Why don't you go clean the back restrooms? One of the guests complained."

I was furious! I was hired as a cook, Juan, not a housekeeper. It wouldn't be so bad if cleaning the restrooms hadn't been their son's job. Mr. and Mrs. Grover let Henry get away with murder—and then they pay him the same as the rest of us, even though he's not yet sixteen. And Janet is a sweetheart, but she's there to do the salad making. She doesn't know anything about sauce. In fact, when I came back from restroom duty, it was beginning to stick to the bottom of the pot.

I could handle all this, Juan, if this was just the first time. Or the second. But the Grovers have shown me that they're impossible to work for over and over again. So I wrote them tonight. To quit. I need the work, Juan, but working for considerate employers is more important to me than the money. Besides, I can work for my brother's landscaping business for the few weeks until college starts. Thanks for all your letters and your encouragement. It's meant a lot to me, and I think I'm making the right decision.

Your friend,
M. L.

2.

Mary Lynn Taylor
13 Center Street, Apt. D
New Brunswick, New Jersey 08903

Ethel and Harold Grover
Villa Italia Restaurant
1551 Harbor Isle Drive
Brunswick, New Jersey 07674

August 6, 1994

Dear Mr. and Mrs. Grover,

Thank you for giving me the opportunity to work in your restaurant this summer. Working as a cook in an Italian restaurant has provided me with many useful skills. I find, however, that I must resign my position effective immediately. I will be starting college in a few weeks and need time to prepare and reflect on this new experience in my life.

I wish you continued success at the Villa Italia.

Sincerely yours,
Mary Lynn Taylor

Talking About It #24

Talk to your classmates about Mary Lynn's letter to Juan. Use the following questions to guide your discussion.

1. How do you think Mary Lynn defined Juan, her reader, before she wrote this letter?
2. What was Mary Lynn's purpose in writing this letter to Juan?
3. Why does Mary Lynn explain her "real" reasons for quitting to Juan?
4. Describe the tone or style of this letter. Do you feel it was an appropriate tone, given her reader and her purpose? Explain.

Jennifer Ricci is another student who, like Mary Lynn Taylor, has used letter–writing as a means of exploring the reader-writer situation and its constraints. Jennifer wrote two letters about an important decision in her life: one to her parents and one to her friend. Jennifer's letters, which follow, allowed her to explore a situation that could create deep conflicts in her family, conflicts that could possibly damage her important relationship with her parents.

Read Jennifer's letters carefully, noticing the way she approached her parents about her problem and the way she approached her friend Gretchen about her problem.

1.

Dear Mom and Dad,

I am not really sure how to start this off. I know this is something that you are not going to be happy with, and I also know that you will try to talk me out of this decision. It won't work this time. I have been considering what I am about to say for a long time, and I have finally made my decision. I will not change my mind.

This University is not for me. I don't feel comfortable here. I am not making any good friends. I hate the campus, and I am not enjoying my classes at all. I know you were so proud of John when he graduated from here last year, but my brother was always a top student, and school is a place where he shines. I am telling you all this, Mom and Dad, because I want to drop out of school.

Before you jump to the phone to call me, let me tell you that I promise to pay back every cent you paid for my tuition. I know how hard you both worked to save the money to send me to school. I will always be grateful for that. I will prove my gratitude by paying back every penny. I also promise to get a good job as soon as I come home. I know what you will say. What kind of a job could I get with just a high school degree? How do you expect to compete in today's economy? Dad, when I come home, I could work with you at the warehouse while I was looking for a job. You are always needing extra help, and at the warehouse I could begin paying back my debt to you right away. Also, you and Mom both know how hard I work. I can type nearly 80 words a minute, and I'm good with computers. More important, I am always friendly with customers, and my employers always say I'm a good worker. You both know that once I find a job, I have no trouble doing good work.

I realize how much I have disappointed you. That is what makes this decision so hard. You were so proud of John, and then you were so proud to have me, your daughter, in college. Everyone says that these are the best years of your life, but they haven't been for me. These have been the eight most miserable months of my life.

Please understand what I am asking of you both. I want you at least to accept my decision even if you don't agree with it. You both have always told me that all you ever wanted was for me to be happy. Well, I'm not. I can't force myself to like something that would take up four years of my life just to make you both proud.

Dad, I can just imagine what you are saying with that frown you get that runs deep between your eyes. Mom, I can picture you settling him down like you always do, trying to keep him calm, trying to get him to listen. But I can also picture how much you both love me and want what's best for my life. I'll be home next weekend, and we can talk some more. In the meantime, remember that I love you both,

Jennifer

2.

Dear Gretchen,

We have been best friends for many years, and I feel I can tell you anything. I really need your help now because I am doing something that I am really unsure about. I am dropping out of school. Please write back right away and tell me what you think.

Ever since I started here at the University, I have been miserable. At first, it was so hard getting used to the campus and finding my way around. Then it was hard adjusting to my roommate. Laura is a very social girl, and she was always going out. But Laura can make good grades without studying very hard. Not me. In fact, I'm having a terrible time keeping up. I'm working hard, but the hard work just isn't paying off. I'm not the best student in the world, and I'm a slow reader. The professors give tons of reading, and I can't keep up with it. I just keep falling farther and farther behind. I think I'd just better quit now before I flunk out. What do you think?

I'm so scared, Gretchen. Tonight I wrote Mom and Dad telling them about my decision. I don't feel like it's the wrong decision for me, but I'm not as sure about this decision as I made it sound to them. But I *am* sure of one thing. I feel very bad for wasting my parents' money. And I feel bad because they were so proud of the fact that their daughter was going to college. It feels awful to disappoint them, especially since John graduated from here with practically straight As.

I offered in my letter to pay Mom and Dad back for every cent they spent on my tuition and to get a job right away. I also reminded them that I'm a hard worker who can hold down a job. Do you think I'm right when I say that school's just not the right kind of work for me?

I am afraid of how Mom and Dad will react, Gretchen, especially my Dad. He is going to be furious and tell me that I am not going to get anywhere in life without a college diploma. He is going to tell me at least to finish out this semester. But my Mom will try to settle him down and convince him to listen to me. I will be going home next weekend to talk to them face to face. I feel ashamed and disappointed. I really hope this is the right decision for me.

But I can't live my life trying to live up to Mom and Dad's expectations. I want them to be proud of me, but I don't want to be unhappy myself. I guess that I always felt attending college would make *them* happy, but I know now that attending college won't make *me* happy. My confidence is so shaky about doing the work here, I think that quitting is my only way out.

I am really glad for a friend like you to trust and confide in. Thank you for listening and understanding. Please write back and let me know what you think. You always give me good advice. Wish me luck, and WRITE BACK RIGHT AWAY!

Love,
Jennifer

Talking About It #25

With your classmates, discuss the following questions about Jennifer's letter to her parents:

1. How does Jennifer define her readers? What characteristics do they possess that Jennifer will have to deal with in her letter?

2. What concerns does she think her parents will have about her decision? How does she address those concerns? Use specific references to her letter to support your answer.
3. What appeals does she use in the letters? Appeals to reason? Emotions? A combination of both? Use specific references to her letters to support your answer.
4. What is Jennifer's purpose in writing these letters? What techniques does she use to achieve her purpose? Do you think her purpose has been achieved? Explain.
5. What constraints were in operation in this writing-reading situation? Situational? Informational? Cultural? Explain.
6. Describe the tone or style of Jennifer's letters. Given her readers and her purpose, do you think it is effective? Why or why not?

UNDERSTANDING WRITER-BASED AND READER-BASED PROSE

In this chapter, you have been looking carefully at the writer–reader relationship. Researchers in recent years have been looking carefully at the writer–reader relationship, too. One of the things they have found out is that skillful writers write with a reader in mind, producing what researchers have come to call *reader-based prose*. Reader-based prose communicates clearly with a reader, providing three important things: (1) effective content, (2) effective organization, and (3) effective expression. Content refers to information that is satisfying and complete. Organization means a structure that is appropriate and efficient. Expression refers to choices about the way in which language is used and includes matters such as word choice and sentence structure. You will learn much more about content, organization, and expression in chapters to come, but it is important for you to be aware that effective content, organization, and expression help create reader-based prose.

Writer-based prose, on the other hand, is writer-centered, not reader-centered. Writer-based writing remains understood largely to the writer; there is much in this kind of writing that leaves a reader unsatisfied or sometimes downright confused. Writing that fails to provide satisfying content, organization, or expression is what is meant by writer-based prose.

Learning to improve your writing is a matter of learning how to turn writer-based prose into reader-based prose. You will learn many techniques for doing this as you read this textbook. However, you may profit from watching other students as they attempt to turn their writer-based writing into reader-based writing.

The paired passages which follow show developing writers hard at work writing and then revising their drafts in an attempt to keep their readers in mind and produce reader-based prose. As you read these passages, think about which one of the pair best keeps the reader in mind. Note that these student revisions are not "perfect"; they may still need more work. However, each revised example in the pair was an honest effort on the part of the student to revise with a reader in mind in order to produce reader-based prose.

1. Writing is a growing process that begins as something physical and becomes mental. I remember how hard it was to use my pencil to create the strange figures. My tongue would hang out of the corner of my mouth as I strained to write the alphabet. Once I had the printing mastered, I needed to learn cursive. Conditioning my hand to make new letters and to be able to write them for pages was somewhat difficult. I would shake my hand after every so many lines to help the cramps. I later on learned to appreciate writing as something more than mindlessly moving a pen across paper. Reading more books gave me a respect for other people's stories that they had written. It was not until I started writing papers or stories and took a creative writing class that I really started to see where the stories and songs that I really enjoyed came from. They came from the knowledge and understanding of the authors. The authors need understanding and knowledge to be able to take experiences and their understanding for life and put them into print. Just as artists need to be able to take what they have seen and be able to recreate what they've seen onto canvas or paper.

—Chris Maggini

2. Writing is a process that begins as something physical and ends as something mental.

In first grade, I remember how hard it was to use my pencil to create the strange letters. My tongue would hang out of the corner of my mouth as I strained to write the alphabet. However, once I had the printing mastered, then I needed to learn cursive. Conditioning my hand to make the new letters flow together in one fluid line seemed difficult. Writing them for pages on end seemed impossible. I would shake my hand after every so many lines to help the cramps.

In high school, I learned to appreciate writing as something more than mindlessly moving a pen across paper. Finally, I began to see writing as more of a mental act. Reading more books, I gained new respect for other people's stories. Taking a creative writing class, I began to write stories and papers of my own. I began to realize that the stories I loved came from the creative minds of their authors. These authors sifted their life experiences through their minds and then put the most interesting ones into print. Like all artists, they took what they saw and shared it with others.

It's taken me many years to appreciate what writing creates. Not something with the hand. But something with the mind.

—Chris Maggini

Talking About It #26

With your classmates, compare Chris's two passages. In which one did he attempt to keep the reader in mind? How do you know? In revising this piece, what changes resulted in the greatest gains—changes in **content**, changes in **organization**, or changes in **expression**?

1. Living in a boarding house was very interesting, but I would not stretch it to the word "pleasant." Because my parents worked for the military and traveled the Far East as part of their jobs, I attended the Hartford American Boarding School in Cyprus, and I went to school with children from all over the world. It might sound like a lovely life, but I didn't think so. We were usually crowded, cold, and hungry.

Ten girls lived in one enormous room under a corrugated iron roof that kept them awake all night when it rained. All we had to ourselves was a tiny little space consisting of a hard bed, two cupboards, and a desk. In addition, whether day or night, it was always cold. When it rained, the walls leaked. When the wind blew, it fought its way through the cracks so that huddling up to the radiator in search of warmth was hopeless. At bedtime it was hard to sleep, for the sheets were starched and cold. The worst indignity was that we were always hungry. No food was allowed in the dorms. The reason was simple: MICE! Because of this rule, it was difficult to sneak food into the dorm, and the matron searched our rooms when we were off to classes, handing out demerits for no-food violations. Even when we went down to meals, everything the kitchen cooked was drowned in oil, and some things were simply inedible.

In spite of the difficulties I faced, boarding at Hartford American taught me to appreciate the simple things in life that most people take for granted: space, warmth, and food.

—Julia Hurley

2. Living in a boarding house was very interesting, but I would not stretch it to the word "pleasant." At my boarding house in Cyprus, I went to school with children from all over the world, and we were usually crowded, cold, and hungry. There were ten people to one room. It was cold day and night, and huddling up to the radiators was useless when the wind was blowing. Finally, there was no food in the dorm, and if we tried to sneak food in, the matron gave us demerits. "Pleasant" was not the word for my boarding house experience.

—Julia Hurley

Talking About It #27

With your classmates, compare Julia's two passages. In which one did she attempt to keep the reader in mind? How do you know? In revising this piece, what changes resulted in the greatest gains—changes in **content**, changes in **organization**, or changes in **expression**?

1. If someone were to first meet me and gather their first impressions about me, I would want them to notice my good leadership qualities. I am a very people-oriented person with good fluent communication skills. I figure I can learn something from everyone I meet. I want to express myself in a manner that when people come in contact with me, I will be remembered. My strong and demanding voice, which I got from my Dad, helps me in this. I like to feel like I'm in command not only with people but with life in general.

—Jason Mudd

2. The first thing people notice about me is that I'm a leader. I think this is because I'm a "people person" who enjoys talking and listening. It's usually easy for me to become a leader in a group—even a group of new people—because I have good communication skills. Most of the time I know what I want to say and how I want to say it. My voice is strong and commanding, like my father's. My Dad was foreman at General Motors for 36 years. His big, deep bass voice carries like mine. I think I learned about listening and speaking and leading from watching him deal with union problems over the years. In high school, I was in many leadership positions like football captain, President of Teen Board, and Vice-President of Student Council. I like being in command. I like leading.

—Jason Mudd

Talking About It #28

With your classmates, compare Jason's two passages. In which one did he attempt to keep the reader in mind? How do you know? In revising this piece, what changes resulted in the greatest gains—changes in **content**, changes in **organization**, or changes in **expression**?

WRITING ASSIGNMENTS

Choose one or more of the suggestions from the following list as a writing assignment. Make use of the things you have learned in this chapter about keeping your reader in mind, analyzing the writing–reading situation, and creating reader-based prose as you write.

A. Imagine that you have decided to drop a course in the middle of the quarter or semester. In order to gain permission to do so, you need to get your professor's permission. Write two letters, one to your professor requesting permission to drop the course, the other to your best friend explaining your decision for doing so. Remember that your goal is to write for your reader.

Share your two letters with other students in your class and note their general responses to your work in these three areas: (1) effectiveness of content, (2) effectiveness of organization, and (3) effectiveness of expression. Record their responses in the Writing Assessment Profile which appears in the back of this text.

B. Choose two pages of class notes from a course in which you are currently enrolled. Then rewrite those notes for either a real or imaginary elementary school age brother or sister who understands little about the subject. Remember that your goal is to write for your reader.

Share your rewritten class notes with other students in your class and note their general responses to your work in these three areas: (1) effectiveness of content, (2) effectiveness of organization, and (3) effectiveness of expression. Record their responses in the Writing Assessment Profile which appears in the back of this text.

C. Copy a favorite passage or several passages that run at least 30 lines long from a Shakespearian play. Then rewrite those passages into modern English so that your classmates can easily understand them. Remember that your goal is to write for your reader.

Share your rewritten passage or passages with other students in your class and note their general responses to your work in these three areas: (1) effectiveness of content, (2) effectiveness of organization, and (3) effectiveness of expression. Record their responses in the Writing Assessment Profile which appears in the back of this text.

D. Write out two different sets of directions on how to get from your home to the closest grocery store. The first set of directions is for your aunt, an experienced driver of 40 years. The second set of directions is for a younger brother or sister who has only recently learned to ride a bike. Remember that your goal is to write for your reader.

Share your two sets of directions with other students in your class and note their general responses to your work in these three areas: (1) effectiveness of content, (2) effectiveness of organization, and (3) effectiveness of expression. Record their responses in the Writing Assessment Profile which appears in the back of this text.

CHAPTER TWO REVIEW

Writing About It #29

Use your journal to reflect on what you learned in this chapter.

3

Prewriting: Your Reader and Your Purpose

What is prewriting?
How can it help my writing?

WHAT IS PREWRITING?

Most of you are familiar with the Latin prefix "pre-." It means "before," "prior to," "in advance." The weatherman tries to "pre"-dict the weather—*before* it strikes. Conference planners hold "pre"-liminary discussions to set an agenda *prior to* a meeting. Broadway musicals often include a musical "pre"-lude, setting the theme or mood *in advance* of the performance.

You are also familiar with the importance of advance preparation. You preview your textbook before you go into the lecture hall. You warm up your muscles before you exercise. You have your car checked out before you go on vacation. But how much advance preparation do you give your writing assignments? What do you do to get ready to write? How much prewriting do you actually do?

If you're like most writers, the answer is probably "not enough." Many people equate "writing" with "drafting," or "getting it down." They confuse various parts of the writing process, thinking that writing means things such as complete sentences, organized paragraphs, proper spelling, and manuscript form. Such writers profit from an understanding of the stages of the writing process and the roles that each stage plays in the successful completion of a piece of writing. They benefit from an understanding of prewriting and the way in which focusing early attention on the beginning stages of the writing process is more likely to insure success at the end.

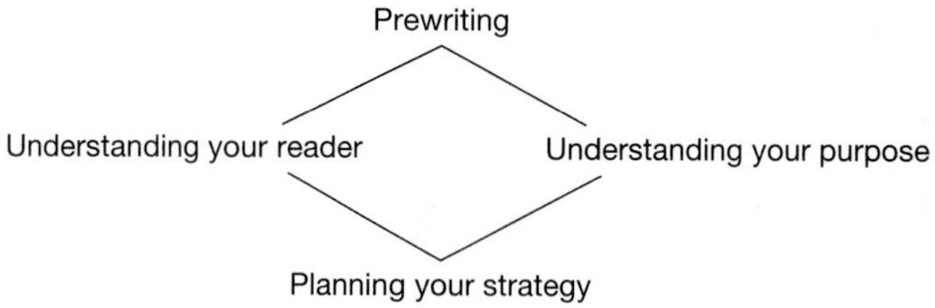

Figure 3.1

Many things—not just writing—profit from this kind of early attention. Previewing your textbook before your history class will help you understand the professor's lecture. Stretching before exercising will help prevent unnecessary muscle strains. Checking out your car before you take off on vacation will ward off the possibility of your being stranded along the interstate, fuming over a dead battery.

Prewriting works that way, too. It takes place *before* you begin to draft your work, *prior to* and *in advance* of the actual drafting.

Prewriting offers writers many benefits. It helps them "warm up" to the writing task. It encourages them to think about their reader. It helps them formulate their purposes and goals. It helps them think through strategies about their content, their organization, and their expression without locking them into an early commitment to any of these considerations. It frees them from the pressures of drafting and revising.

Prewriting is also fun. It's like splashing around in the water before the formality of swimming lessons. It's like wandering the backroads instead of the main drag. It's like frolicking on summer vacation before the routine of school sets in. Prewriting is the place where skillful writers spend much of their time.

You'll remember that the writing process itself is made up of three parts: (1) prewriting, (2) writing or drafting, and (3) rewriting. The prewriting stage of the writing process is made up of three parts as well. These stages involve (1) understanding your reader, (2) understanding your purpose, and (3) planning your strategy. If you were to diagram the prewriting part of the writing process, it might look like Figure 3.1.

PREWRITING: UNDERSTANDING YOUR READER

Because understanding your reader is so important to your success as a writer, it's useful to make sure you have a clear idea in your mind about just who your reader is before you begin to write. You already know that skillfully focusing and pointing a camera prior to snapping the shutter can assure you of taking a more effective picture, and you will learn that defining your reader through prewriting—before you put words on a page—results in a more successful piece of writing as well.

However, as important as your reader is, defining your reader is not easy. Many of you are familiar with instructors who have given you writing assignments with directions that advise you to "consider your audience" before you write. That, of course, is good advice. But it's also something of an empty generality. Who, exactly, *is* your audience? Is your audience made up of one reader—or several? Is your audience a "real one"—a newspaper editor, a potential employer, a college admissions committee? Or is your audience an "imagined" one—an audience whose role seems more hypothetical than real? Or will your teacher or instructor make up your "audience?"

The issue of audience is complex. For instance, when you're writing a letter to a friend or loved one, the audience may seem safe and thus the words may come easily. On the other hand, when you're writing to a stranger, like a prospective employer, the audience may seem threatening because it's largely unknown; in this case, you may find your thoughts shutting down, your mind a blank. When you're writing in a situation where the consequences of failure seem serious—a college application essay or an essay exam for a college course—you might find it increasingly difficult to generate ideas; in a panic, you feel yourself freezing up. In every writing situation, the issue of audience is an issue you will need to confront.

Talking About It #30

Talk to your classmates about some of the following situations involving a sense of audience.

1. Which do you find easier—talking in front of a large audience or talking in front of a small group? Why? What are the challenges that face you when you talk before a large audience? a small group? Can you draw any parallels with writing?
2. Describe some experiences in which you had to tell a story or a joke to a small group. What was your audience's reaction as you talked? In what way did your audience's reaction or response help you or hinder you in telling your joke or story? Can you draw any parallels with writing?
3. Does a certain kind of audience cause you to be "not yourself?" For example, are there situations involving audiences in which you find yourself sounding more self-important or pretentious than you really feel? Or are there situations in which you find yourself sounding shy or ingratiating or unsure? Explain these situations.
4. Talk to your classmates about how it makes you feel when you write something for each of the following audiences: yourself, as when you're writing in a journal; a person you know very well like a friend or relative; an unknown audience like a potential employer or a committee of some kind; a teacher who is

grading your work. Discuss what it is like to write for audiences which are ever more distant from you. In what way can skill as a writer be developed by learning to write for a variety of audiences?

Because learning to write for a reader involves developing a reliable sense of audience, let's look at a student faced with a writing situation and examine how she handles its challenges. Mary Bapu, an international student from India studying engineering in the United States, is enrolled in a civil engineering lab. She is asked to write a laboratory report in which she examines the differences between certain fine and coarse substances in order to determine their proper proportion in a concrete mixture.

While writing her report, Mary experiences difficulties related to her understanding of her "reader" or "audience." What, for instance, can Mary assume about the amount of explanation her teacher/reader expects? Although Mary will be investigating certain types of Portland cement during the lab, must her lab report begin by defining "Portland cement," a substance so commonly used in civil engineering projects that even beginning engineers are familiar with it? Although during the lab, Mary and her lab partners perform a lab procedure known as "sieve analysis," must Mary, in the course of her lab report, offer any explanation of this common procedure, a procedure with which her teacher/reader is unquestionably familiar? If Mary decides she must offer at least some information about the process of sieve analysis, what information will she leave in and what information will she take out? Also, as Mary begins to write her report, she also wonders what "tone" or "voice" she needs to adopt for purposes of this report. Should she attempt to sound like a professional scientist? A competent technician? An earnest, if struggling, student?

These are difficult questions to answer. But they are the kinds of questions most writers face in any writing situation. And learning to write reader-based prose requires that you attempt to answer them by getting to know your reader. Let's try to find out how.

Similar to Mary Bapu, one of the things you've learned so far is that it's important to keep your reader in mind when you write. When your reader is familiar to you, the task is much easier. Your mother, who is worried about how you will adjust to your college roommate, will expect your first letter home to say something about your budding relationship. Your English teacher, who appreciates a keen sense of observation, will expect your next composition to be filled with some unique and specific details. If you know your reader well, if the reader is *familiar* to you, keeping the reader's needs in mind as you write will not be too difficult.

However, keeping the reader's needs in mind is especially challenging when the reader is *unfamiliar* to you—even though the experience of writing for an unfamiliar reader is a common one. For instance, at the beginning of every new writing course you have ever taken, you've probably experienced the "first paper" syndrome, that queasy feeling that accompanies the writing of your first draft. The reason for at least some of your anxiety is that you're not yet sure about what your unfamiliar teacher wants. Perhaps you've experienced writing a resume to accompany a job application and worried about what experience to emphasize or what people to list as your references because you don't know who, exactly, will be reading your application. Maybe you've experienced writing a letter of inquiry or complaint to a company, addressing your unknown reader awkwardly as "To Whom It May Concern." One of the reasons why these choices are so difficult for you is that the reader is *unfamiliar*; you're being challenged to figure out what this unknown reader wants.

Although the unfamiliar reader is someone who's not well known to you yet, you can get to know him or her better by making some educated guesses about this reader and using those guesses to analyze your writing-reading situation. Those guesses—called your *reader profile*—make up an important part of your prewriting strategy.

The following passage is from an essay called *Simplicity* by William Zinsser. In it, he offers some assumptions about his reader that guide him when he writes. Read the passage carefully, and then reflect on this passage in your next journal entry.

> Who is this elusive creature the reader? The reader is someone with an attention span of about sixty seconds—a person assailed by forces competing for the minutes that might otherwise be spent on a magazine or a book. At one time these forces weren't so numerous or so possessive: newspapers, radio, spouse, home, children. Today they also include a "home entertainment center" (TV, VCR, video camera, tapes and CDs), pets, a fitness program, a lawn and a garden and all the gadgets that have been bought to keep them spruce, and that most potent of competitors, sleep. The person snoozing in a chair, holding a magazine or a book, is a person who was being given too much unnecessary trouble by the writer.
>
> It won't do to say that the snoozing reader is too dumb or too lazy to keep pace with the train of thought. If the reader is lost, it's usually because the writer hasn't been careful enough. The carelessness can take any number of forms. Perhaps a sentence is so excessively cluttered that the reader, hacking thorough the verbiage, simply doesn't know what it means. Perhaps a sentence has been so shoddily constructed that the reader could read it in any of several ways. Perhaps the writer has switched pronouns in mid-sentence, or has switched tenses, so the reader loses track of who is talking or when the action took place. Perhaps Sentence B is not a logical sequel to Sentence A—the writer, in whose head the connection is clear, has not bothered to provide the missing link.
>
> Faced with such obstacles, readers are at first remarkably tenacious. They blame themselves—they obviously missed something, and they go back over the mystifying sentence, or over the whole paragraph, piecing it out like an ancient rune, making guesses and moving on.

But they won't do this for long. The writer is making them work too hard, and they will look for one who is better at his craft.

Writing About It #31

Reflect on William Zinsser's essay in our journal by writing about the following questions:

1. What are a few of the characteristics of Zinsser's readers? What evidence from the passage supports your view?
2. What implications do these characteristics have for Zinsser when he is faced with a writing situation?
3. How do you feel about Zinsser's essay? Do you agree or disagree with his characterizations about readers? Why?
4. If you had written this essay, would you have added any other characteristics? How would those characteristics have affected your writing?

When you have finished your journal entry, share your responses with your classmates.

One good way of learning to think about readers is to study magazines and newspapers. Magazine and newspaper publishers spend a lot of time—and money—thinking about their audiences or readers. That kind of thinking is critical. If publishers don't think about the needs of their audience, they're out of business. Getting to know their readers makes good business sense.

If you take some time to wander in a bookstore with a well-stocked magazine section, you'll find that there are literally hundreds of publications designed to capture the attention of a nation of readers with diverse interests: *Working Mother, Muscle and Fitness, Skin Diver, Christmas Crafts, Backpacker, Railroad Model Craftsman.*

If you study a special-interest magazine with care, you'll discover that its editors have spent a great deal of time profiling its readers. Everything about the magazine, in fact, has been designed to pique the reader's interest. The articles, the advertising, the photography, the layout, the headlines, the cover, and the writing style have all been designed with one goal: meeting the needs of the reader.

Students who are learning about readers and beginning to profile them often profit from studying the techniques which magazines and newspapers use to appeal to readers. Following is a paper written by student Matt Hahn which shows the way *Hot Rod* magazine appeals to its readers.

Are your T-shirts coated with motor oil? Is the thought of improving the exhaust system on your car more appealing than the thought of a movie and dinner with your friends? Would you like to learn the latest techniques on how to modify your car? If you're a hot rod fanatic, rev up your engines and speed on over to the closest magazine rack because *Hot Rod* magazine is the magazine for you.

You can turn to almost any article in *Hot Rod* for advice about how to modify a car. An article called "Framed" gives you step-by-step instructions on how to install a ProStreet frame onto a 1956 or 1957 Chevy. If you're looking to improve the exhaust system on your car, "Collector Science," using pictures and bold-face print, tells you how. If it's improvements to the engine you want, "Heads Up" will tell you about the new aluminum heads built by the ARAO company that can improve your engine's horsepower.

Like the articles, the advertisements in *Hot Rod* give the reader information about how to modify a car. An advertisement for the Edelbrock company recommends its exhaust manifolds, carburetors, and camshaft kits. It even offers the reader a toll-free number to find out where the nearest Edelbrock company is located. Other ads by other companies promote gear shifters, molded carpets, tires, custom wheels, and fuel system cleaners.

In addition to the articles and advertisements, the photographs in *Hot Rod* spark the interest of the reader interested in modifying cars. There are pictures of the "Super Sano," a big block Chevelle that puts out 450 horsepower. There are shots of a 1970 GTX, a Pontiac GTO, and a 1990 Ford Probe that was modified into a ProStreet dragster. The bold photographs—in both black-and-white and color—dramatize the excitement that accompanies modifying a car and whet the interest of the *Hot Rod* reader.

If working all day Saturday to turn your fast car into something even faster is your idea of heaven, then you're the reader that *Hot Rod* wants to interest, and *Hot Rod* is the magazine that you'll want to buy.

Talking About It #32

Bring a few special-interest magazines and newspapers to class. Share them with your classmates. Discuss the special audiences or readers the magazine is seeking to interest. Note the way advertising, articles, photography, and other aspects of the magazine are designed to appeal to this reader.

Take a popular newspaper or magazine like *The National Enquirer* whose appeals are outrageous or outlandish and discuss the ways in which the articles, photography, language choices, and other aspects of the magazine appeal to a reader who is looking to be entertained. Then take a popular, respected newspaper or magazine like *The New York Times*, whose readers are seeking responsible information, and note the way this newspaper or magazine treats the news for these readers.

Discuss the way in which different assumptions about readers result in differing publications.

Writing About It #33

In your journal, write several paragraphs that compare and contrast the readers of both *The National Enquirer* and *The New York Times*. Use evidence from the newspapers such as articles, photography, language choices, and other elements to support your ideas about these two readerships. Share your writing with your classmates.

Creating a Reader Profile

Creating a reader profile is a good way to begin to get to know your reader or audience and a good way to begin to achieve focus in the early stages of writing. Creating a reader profile is also a good first step in the prewriting stage of the writing process because a reader profile will help you see that readers have *personal characteristics* and *situational factors* that can help you develop a clearer picture of your reader, turning an unfamiliar reader into a familiar one.

Identifying Personal Characteristics

Everyone has personal characteristics. Your sister or brother has a temper that flares instantly but dies out just as quickly. Your boss is a stickler for punctuality. Your mother never forgets a birthday. Readers are human, too. They can be skeptical, curious, bored, or busy. William Zinsser gave his imagined readers some personal characteristics when he described their short attention span and the many activities competing for their attention. You can identify your readers' personal characteristics, too.

The things that characterize your readers are as various as readers themselves. They are things like this.

Name
Title
Age
Sex
Occupation
Educational background
Economic status
Religious preference
Political affiliation
Family
School
General attitudes about reading

Writing About It #34

Try to identify some of your own characteristics as a reader by responding to each of the topics in your journal. Profile yourself in each of the topics listed from name and age to political affiliation and general attitudes about reading. Then share your personal profile with several of your classmates.

In order to discover the general attitudes about reading that apply to you in more detail, explore the following questions in your journal.

1. What kind of reader are you? Do you typically feel positive or negative about reading? Are you similar to or different from the reader portrayed in William Zinsser's essay? Explain.
2. Think of three adjectives that would describe you as a reader. Explain.
3. What advice would you give to a writer who was writing something for you? Explain.
4. For what purposes do you usually read? General purposes? Specific purposes? For pleasure? For information? Explain.
5. What kinds of subjects appeal to you as a reader? Explain.
6. What have you read in the past that you enjoyed? What have you read in the past that you didn't enjoy? Explain.
7. What usually frustrates you about what you're reading? What usually gives you satisfaction about what you're reading? Explain.
8. What are your earliest memories about reading? In preschool? In elementary school? In high school? Explain.
9. What kind of language appeals to you when you're reading?

Advertisements and Personal Characteristics

Advertisements abound in the world today. We see them on billboards, on television, in magazines, on automobile bumpers. Flip through the pages of any popular magazine and look at the ads. You won't have to look hard to notice that they are targeted to specific audiences or readers. An automobile advertisement, for instance, is designed with a specific reader or audience in mind when it appeals to the consumer who values gas mileage or the vacationer who needs a lot of storage space or the driver who likes flashy sports cars. Marketing research executives spend a great deal of time and money discovering their target audiences and profiling their personal characteristics. In the world of advertising, reader or audience "profiles" cannot be left to the imagination.

Newspapers are also in the business of profiling audiences or readers. A large part of a newspaper's revenue is generated by the regularly featured classified advertising section as well as by individual advertisements scattered throughout the paper. The classified ads contain columns detailing employment opportunities and items for sale ranging from houses and cars to puppies and kittens. Each of these ads is designed to appeal to the personal characteristics of a reader. A person with a love for vintage cars stops to read the ad that says, "Souped Up '57 Chevy. Mint Condition." A prospective home buyer with an interest in nature is intrigued by the ad which reads, "15-Acre Wooded Lot with Babbling Brook." A father interested in buying a well-behaved dog for the family pauses over the ad which says, "Buff Cocker Spaniel. Housebroken. Good with children." Furthermore, because space is limited and newspapers charge for each word of advertising, people placing ads must choose their words carefully. Their ads must reach their intended readers effectively and economically.

One of the liveliest features of many classified advertising sections in magazines and newspapers today is the regular appearance of the "Personals" ad. These advertisements, which run under a variety of titles such as "Dating Opportunities" and "Heartlines" are a type of friendship service, designed to link Ms. Right with an appropriate Mr., or Mr. Right with an appropriate Ms. These advertisements, often funny and appealing, can instruct the writing student about techniques for profiling the personal characteristics of readers. In the passage which follows, from "Advertisements for Oneself," Lance Morrow, a distinguished writer and *Time* columnist, takes a look at the popular form in which a writer hopes that his or her personal traits will ultimately attract a reader.

It is an odd and compact art form, and somewhat unnatural. A person feels quite uncomfortable composing a little song of himself for the classifieds. The personal ad is like a haiku of self-celebration, a brief solo played on one's own horn. Someone else should be saying these things. It is for others to pile up the extravagant adjectives ("sensitive, warm, witty, vibrant, successful, handsome, accomplished, incredibly beautiful, cerebral, and sultry") while we stand demurely by. But someone has to do it. One competes for attention. One must advertise. One must chum the waters and bait the hook, and go trolling for love and laughter, for caring and sharing, for long walks and quiet talks, for Bach and brie. Nonsmokers only. Photo a must.

There are poetic conventions and cliches and codes in composing a personal ad. One specifies DWF (divorced white female), SBM (single black male), GWM (gay white male) and so on, to describe marital status, race, sex. Readers should understand the euphemisms. "Zaftig" or "Rubenesque," for example, usually means fat. "Unpretentious" is liable to mean boring. "Sensuous" means the party likes sex.

The sociology of personals has changed in recent years. One reason that people still feel uncomfortable with the form is that during the sixties and early seventies personal ads had a slightly sleazy connotation. They showed up in the back of underground newspapers and sex magazines, the little billboards through which wife swappers and odd sexual specialists communicated. In the past several years, however, personal ads have become a popular and reputable way of shopping for new relationships. The *Chicago Tribune* publishes them. So does the conservative *National Review*, although a note from the publisher advises, "*NR* extends maximum freedom in this column, but *NR*'s maximum freedom may be another man's straitjacket. *NR* reserves the right to reject any copy deemed unsuitable." *National Review* would likely have turned down a West Coast entreaty: "Kinky Boy Scout seeks Kinky Girl Scout to practice knots. Your rope or mine?" *National Review's* personals are notably chaste, but so are those in most other magazines. The emphasis is on "traditional values," on "long-term relationships" and "nest building."

Anyone composing a personal ad faces an inherent credibility problem. While we are accustomed to the self-promotions of politicians, say, we sense something bizarre when ordinary people erupt in small rhapsodies of self-celebration that are occasioned by loneliness and longing. One is haunted by almost piteous cries that come with post-office-box number attached: Is there anyone out there? Anyone for me?"

Composing an ad with oneself as the product is an interesting psychological exercise, and probably good training in self-assertion. Truth will endure a little decorative writing, perhaps. The personals are a form of courtship that is more efficient, and easier on the liver, than sitting in bars night after night, hoping for a lucky encounter. Yet one feels sometimes a slightly disturbed and forlorn vibration in those columns of chirpy pleading. It is inorganic courtship. There is something severed, a lost connection. One may harbor a buried resentment that there are not parents and aunts and churches and cotillions to arrange the meetings in more seemly style.

That, of course, may be mere sentimentalism. Whatever works. Loneliness is the Great Satan. Jane Austen, who knew everything about courtship, would have understood the personals columns perfectly. Her novel *Emma*, in fact, begins, "Emma Woodhouse, handsome, happy, clever, and rich, with a comfortable home and happy disposition." The line might go right into the *New York Review of Books.*

Talking About It #35

With your classmates, respond to the following questions about "Advertisements for Oneself."

1. How do you feel about the "Personals" ads? Would you ever place one? Why or why not?
2. What are some things about the personals ads that make Lance Morrow "quite uncomfortable?" Would these things make you uncomfortable as well?
3. What are the "cliches" and "codes" of the personals ads? What are the "euphemisms?"
4. What evidence does Morrow offer that the personals ads are becoming more "popular and reputable?"
5. What about the ads does Morrow find "slightly disturbed and forlorn?"
6. Overall, does Morrow approve or disapprove of the personals ads? Why?

Studying the personals ads is a good way of learning to understand the personal characteristics of readers. People "advertising" themselves from the columns of a newspaper or magazine are looking for a reader who represents that "certain someone," someone with intelligence, humor, or a gift for friendship, depending on the requirements of the writer. Take a few moments to study the following ads, and then respond to the journal entry which follows.

1. Berkshires, Attractive, Charming travel writer, author, and Francophile seeks middle-aged, intelligent, lively and caring man for companionship and romance.

2. Large, Irritable woman, 47 at least, nonetheless seeks agreeable man, for conversation. Boston.

3. Japanese Graduate Student from Tokyo, 20, studying theoretical physics at large Midwestern university. Fairly fluent in English, better with numbers. Seeks Japanese female of similar interest who also needs companionship.

4. Fortysomething, Tall, Slim, Attractive Redhead and mom, writer, and creative director. Love the arts, tennis, family, friends, and having one special man. A cosmopolitan Protestant. Send note, phone, photo.

5. SWM, Age 61, Previously Married, 5′10″, 164 lbs., bearded. Enjoys wilderness exploration, hiking, foreign travel, log cabins, and luxury. Savors good wine, pre-dinner martini, and an occasional cigar. Career, profession, status, and prestige irrelevant. Humor, zest for life, spontaneity, and earthiness essential.

6. Fetching, Blue-Eyed Blonde, 31, 5′10″, animal lover, old-movie buff, reader of mystery novels, focused, warm, and independent. Seeks monogamous relationship with tall, stable, affectionate, intelligent man to 44. Letter/photo.

7. Warm, Funny, Literate Scientist turned Doctor, 33. Fervent government-hater, hopeless coffee addict. 5′4″. A lover of mountain trails and brownstone streets. Note and photo appreciated.

Writing About It #36

Refer to the list of Personal Characteristics of readers which appears on page 58. Use the items on the list to describe the writers of each of the seven ad entries mentioned. Much of what you put down will be guesses or hunches about these largely unknown readers, but be bold in your attempts to profile each of them. Be prepared to defend your hunches as you discuss your seven profiles with your class.

Read each of the ads carefully, paying close attention to your description of Personal Characteristics from the previous entry. Imagine that you are a reader who believes he or she possesses the characteristics desired by the writer of the ad. Then write a letter in response to *one* of the ads. When you craft your letter, emphasize and highlight the desired characteristics to make yourself appealing to the writer of the ad.

Compose a short creative "advertisement" for yourself for the Personals columns, omitting your name. Then see if your classmates can identify you from your description. Finally, write a paragraph related to your self-descriptions on any of these topics.

1. Explain why you described yourself the way you did. What traits did you emphasize? Why? What traits did you neglect or leave out? Why?
2. Explain whether you were comfortable or uncomfortable composing a personal ad. What aspects of the experience made you feel comfortable? Uncomfortable? Why?
3. Write an "advertisement" for your "ideal" companion. Then write a paragraph explaining why the personal characteristics you included are important to you.

Identifying Situational Factors

As you have seen, part of preparing a reader profile consists of thinking about the reader's personal characteristics such as age, sex, or educational status. The other part consists of thinking about a number of situational factors that affect the reading situation. These factors which affect the reader and the reading situation include the following:

1. purpose,
2. requirements,
3. environment,
4. use,
5. attitudes toward the writer, the work, and the language.

Part of understanding who your reader is comes from understanding the *purposes* for which readers read. Readers read to be informed, entertained, and stimulated. But purposes vary from situation to situation. The purposes of a reader looking for an explanation of the town's new traffic regulations in the local newspaper are different from the purposes of a reader laughing over an Erma Bombeck magazine column in the waiting room of the dentist's office. Thus, the reader's purpose for reading is a significant factor in the reading–writing situation.

Typically, however, readers read for either general or specific purposes. For example, a reader of *USA Today*, the national newspaper, is probably seeking general information about the latest news. On the other hand, a reader of the *The Chronicle of Higher Education,* a newspaper for college teachers, may be seeking more specific information about the latest news in his or her specific field of interest, college teaching. In addition, the same reader often reads for different purposes at different times. Sometimes the same reader may pursue general goals, scanning a newspaper such as *USA Today*; at other times he may pursue specific goals, reading the articles in *The Chronicle of Higher Education*.

Another important situational factor is the *requirements* of the reading situation. Your Aunt Martha, who believes that thank-yous for gifts should be sent immediately, will not have a positive attitude toward your thank-you note which arrives three months after Christmas. Your late reply does not honor the situational requirement of promptness. Professor Thompson, your Western Civilization teacher, will not be receptive to your 20-page research paper when the situational requirement was a 5-page book review.

A third factor that influences a reader's situation is the *environment* in which the reading is done. A busy office manager, juggling many people and responsibilities, will require your memo to be clear and concise; she hasn't the time to waste on figuring out your main point. A college student trying to read John Locke's philosophy in a quiet library has a more promising situational environment than a college student reading that same assignment in a crowded dormitory room. The reader, therefore, is affected by the situational environment.

Another important situational factor is the *use* to which the reader plans to put what he or she is reading. A marketing manager, for example, may use a market analysis report in order to decide which new products to develop in the coming year. A college admissions officer may use a high school teacher's letter of recommendation as a basis for deciding whether or not to admit a prospective student. An employee on vacation may use a spy novel as a way of relaxing on the beach. A consumer may use an article in *Consumer Reports* as a way of deciding what type of running shoe to buy. All these are examples of the varied uses influencing the reading situation and the reader.

Finally, your reader holds certain *attitudes* about this reading situation. He or she holds attitudes about the writer and the work itself. In addition, your reader is a member of a language community, and the values of this community make up some of the attitudes your reader brings to the reading situation. For example, a chemistry professor reading your final lab report of the semester holds certain attitudes about you. Over the course of the semester, he has come to respect the hard work you put into your reports and your willingness to learn from your mistakes. For that reason, his attitude toward you, the reader, may be one of positive interest. But your chemistry professor also holds certain attitudes about the work itself. He expects a lab report to contain certain formal requirements, for example, an Abstract or a Discussion section, and he expects that the abstract will be no more than 100 words and that the Discussion will offer specific explanations for your laboratory findings. If he receives an overlong Abstract or a Discussion section that glosses over the laboratory findings, he will be a keenly disappointed reader. Finally, the language community in which your chemistry professor works values objectivity, clarity, conciseness, and accuracy. If your report is objective, clear, concise, and accurate, you will have gone a long way toward honoring the situational factor called the reader's attitude.

The Reader Profile: Personal Characteristics and Situational Factors

Let's think more concretely about the personal characteristics and situational factors that affect your reader profile by using an actual writing situation.

Imagine that you are a mother majoring in Health and Recreation at your local community college and that you are interested in re-entering the job market now that your two small children are in school. You have been reading the Employment Opportunities section of the newspaper, and an ad for a recreation director in one of the city parks has caught your attention. The ad says that you must apply to the Personnel Director for the City of Dayton, Mr. Walter E. Styron, and attach a cover letter and resume by May 30.

You are worried. You're not sure what to say in your cover letter or what to put in your resume because you don't know anything about your reader. Other than his name and his job title, he is totally unfamiliar to you.

You can help make this unfamiliar reader more familiar by compiling a reader profile as part of your prewriting activities. You might then refer to the list of personal characteristics that often characterize readers and begin to check off the items on the list.

As you work on fleshing out the personal characteristics of your unfamiliar potential employer, you realize you are engaged in some educated guesswork. You're unsure about his economic status, political affiliation, or religious preference. You make an educated "guess" about his age, writing, "I don't think this person would be very young because I guess it would take many years of hard work to be promoted to this position." You jot down another "hunch" about his educational background, writing, "probably well educated to serve as personnel director for the entire city."

You look at the notes you have made, somewhat discouraged. You've tried hard to characterize this reader by listing his personal traits, but because this reader is largely unknown, there's still not much in your reader profile.

In cases like this, when your reader is unfamiliar to you and attempts to make him more familiar by making guesses about personal characteristics don't offer enough information, you can often turn to the situational factors in the reading situation for help. You can look at the five situational factors to help you profile your reader more accurately: purpose, requirements, environment, use, and attitudes toward the writer, the work, and the language community.

The work of Sonja Faruki follows. She is the community college student and mother who is seeking work as a recreation director at a city park. Sonja has worked hard on her reader profile as part of her prewriting activities. She is attempting to flesh out the personal characteristics and situational factors affecting the needs of Mr. Walter E. Styron, the reader of her application for employment.

Reader Profile Sheet

Personal Characteristics	
Reader's name	Mr. Walter E. Styron
Reader's title	Personnel Director, City of Dayton
Reader's age	I don't think this person would be very young because I guess it would take many years of hard work to be promoted to this position.
Reader's sex	M
Reader's occupation	Professional Personnel Director
Reader's educational background	probably well-educated to serve as personnel director for the entire city
Reader's economic status	?
Reader's religious preference	?
Reader's political affiliation	?
Reader's family	?
Reader's school	?
General attitudes about reading	?

Situational Factors

Requirements: cover letter
resumé
due date, May 30

Environment: I picture this reader in a very busy office. I imagine the phones ringing, a secretary coming in with appointment calendars, a lot of meetings with hopeful employees. The environment I'm imagining tells me that this busy person would not have time to read a long cover letter telling the story of my life. Mr. Styron might want something that was concise and simple and got right to the point.

Purpose: General _____ Specific __X__ Mr. Styron would have a very specific purpose for reading my application. He is reading in order to make a hiring decision. He would be looking for specific information about my qualifications for this particular job. He probably would only be interested in information that related to my capabilities as a recreation director.

Uses: Mr. Styron has a very definite use for my application. He'll use it to decide whether I get the job!

Attitudes toward the writer, the work, the language community: Because Mr. Styron doesn't know me, I have an opportunity to create positive attitudes in my application and a good "first impression." My hunch is that he may, however, hold certain attitudes toward the work itself and the language community. I think Mr. Styron would expect the application to be neat and well written. This reader will expect the cover letter and resumé to be clear and to contain information that relates to the position of recreation director. I believe the language community in which he works—the busy business environment—would cause him to hold attitudes valuing clarity and conciseness. He would probably be interested in language that gets the message across quickly and clearly.

Reader Profile Sheet

Personal Characteristics

Reader's name
Reader's title
Reader's age
Reader's sex
Reader's occupation
Reader's educational background
Reader's economic status
Reader's political affiliation
Reader's family
Reader's school
General attitudes about reading

Situational Factors

Requirements
Environment
Purpose General—— Specific——
Uses
Attitudes toward the writer, the work, and the language community

Profiling Your Classroom Teacher

A student was once overheard giving advice to his fellow classmates about how to get a high mark on a certain history professor's essay assignment. "Say something about Napoleon," advised the student. "Napoleon's his field of study." Although this student's advice may smack of cynicism, it also rings of truth. Students through the decades have understood that giving the teacher what he or she "wants" often leads to a better grade.

The fact is that who your teacher is, what her experience has been, and how she views the writing situation can profoundly affect the way your writing is received. English teachers, for example, often differ from science teachers in their view about writing and language use. Although it's important not to stereotype people and to recognize that individual differences abound, in general, the English teacher values subjectivity while the science teacher values objectivity. This means that the English teacher often appreciates personal responses displayed in poetic language whereas the science teacher values impersonal responses displayed in to-the-point, no-nonsense prose. It's not that either the English teacher or the science teacher has the "right" point of view; it's that each teacher holds different values about writing and the language choices writing implies.

But even English teachers, with their general belief in individual response and poetic language, differ greatly. In your own experience, you undoubtedly came across a variety of teachers with a variety of different values. Maybe one was a stickler for grammar or another was indifferent to spelling errors while another insisted on imaginative interpretations to reading assignments. Each year, it was important for you as a student to discover not just what English teachers in general valued, but what this English teacher in particular held dear.

Writing About It #37

Discuss with your classroom teacher his or her values about writing. Then fill out a Reader Profile Sheet on your teacher based on that discussion. If filling out the Reader Profile Sheet is made easier by proposing a "real" writing situation, ask your teacher to supply that "real" writing situation for you.

Fill out a Reader Profile Sheet on a teacher you have had in the past. Discuss with your classmates the variety of teachers and requirements which you have profiled. If filling out the Reader Profile Sheet is made easier by proposing a "real" writing situation, supply a "real" writing situation for purposes of this journal entry.

Write a paragraph in which you compare and contrast your present teacher with a teacher you have had in the past. Use your reader profile sheets to guide you in your writing. Then share these paragraphs with other students in your class.

Profiling Your Classroom Reader

In many ways, your classroom reader, like your teacher, is a kind of unfamiliar reader, too. Because much of what you are writing in this class is read by your fellow classmates, however, it's important that you get to know your classroom readers and ready yourself for writing by preparing an accurate reader profile of them. When you write in this class, as in any writing–reading situation, you need to know many things about your readers: What are their characteristics? What are their expectations? How will this information affect what you write?

Learning to understand your classroom readers will be good experience for learning to understand many different kinds of readers—not only in the classroom, but in the larger campus community, and, ultimately, in the larger world where you will be a practicing member of a writing-reading community.

Talking About It #38

Choose one of your classmates to act as recorder. Then refer back to the personal characteristics of yourself as a reader which you recorded from page 58. These are characteristics ranging from name and age to general attitudes about reading. Ask your recorder to make a chart of your classroom characteristics as a group based on your individual responses. After the recorder has charted your responses, attempt to notice any trends or patterns in this information, and discuss the implications of these trends or patterns for the writing you will do in this course.

Now ask that same recorder or a different recorder to explore the general attitudes about reading you explored earlier in the chapter on page 59. Although these responses will often be highly individual, attempt to notice any trends or patterns in this information as well. Record those trends or patterns in your chart of classroom characteristics. After you have charted these responses, discuss their implications for the writing you will do in this course.

PREWRITING: UNDERSTANDING YOUR PURPOSE

Although an understanding of your reader is crucial to the success of any piece of writing, it's important to remember that the reader makes up only one half of the reader–writer relationship. The important *other* half is the writer.

Perhaps at this point you've begun to realize that readers and writers are engaged in a vital relationship. Like a dancer and her partner or a nursing child and its mother, writers and readers are similarly interdependent. The writer, like a spider, spins and weaves the strands of his thought, hoping to lure the reader into the web of his meaning. The process requires a collaboration in which both writer and reader mutually entertain, persuade, enrich, and inform each other. The writer-reader relationship is a classic example of the buddy system: neither can go it alone.

You'll remember from earlier chapters that there are four elements to the writing– reading situation: (1) the reader, (2) the writer, (3) the work, and (4) the language community. You've looked closely at the first element—the reader. Now let's turn to element number two—the writer.

The section entitled "Elements of the Writing Situation," which you studied earlier, suggested several questions you can ask yourself as you begin to examine your role as a writer in the writing–reading situation.

1. Who are you as a writer? How would you define yourself?

2. What are your purposes and goals? What techniques will be most likely to achieve them?

3. What are your attitudes—about the reader, about the work, and about the language community which you share?

4. What are your needs and expectations? From the reader? About the work? From the language itself?

If you'll look closely at these four questions, you'll see that Question 1 is a general question designed to get you to think about yourself as a writer in broad terms. Questions 2, 3, and 4 are specific questions designed to get you to think about yourself as a writer when you are working on a particular piece of writing.

Because it's as important for you to think about yourself as a writer when you adopt the role of writer as it is for you to think about yourself as a reader when you adopt the role of reader, let's take some time to think about what kind of writer you are.

Although it's obviously simplistic to reduce a complex perspective such as an attitude toward writing to a one-word adjective, sometimes it's instructive to do so. Writers can be "enthusiastic" or "bored" or "thoughtful" or "inhibited"; the list of adjectives which can describe a writer's attitudes is endless. However, many writers across the decades have thought it worth their time to share how they feel about writing. One of them is Ray Bradbury, a well-known American science fiction writer. In the passage which follows, called "The Impulse to Write," Bradbury lets you into his attitudes about writing.

> If you are writing without zest, without gusto, without love, without fun, you are only half a writer. . . . For the first thing a writer should be is—excited. He should be a thing of fevers and enthusiasms. Without such vigor, he might as well be out picking peaches or digging ditches. God knows it'd be better for his health.
>
> How long is it since you wrote a story where your real love or your real hatred somehow got onto the paper? When was the last time you dared release a cherished prejudice so it slammed the page like a lightning bolt? What are the best things and the worst things in your life, and when are you going to get around to whispering or shouting them?
>
> Wouldn't it be wonderful, for instance, to throw down a copy of Harper's *Bazaar* you happened to be leafing through at the dentist's, and leap to your typewriter and ride off with hilarious anger, attacking their silly and sometimes shocking snobbishness?
>
> I did that a few years back. I came across an issue where the *Bazaar* photographers, with their perverted sense of equality, once again utilized natives in a Puerto Rican back-street as props in front of which their starved-looking mannikins postured for the benefit of yet more emaciated half-women in the best salons in the country. The photographs so enraged me I ran, did not walk, to my machine and wrote "Sun and Shadow," the story of an old Puerto Rican who ruins the *Bazaar* photographer's afternoon by sneaking into each picture and dropping his pants.
>
> I dare say there are a few of you who would like to have done this job. I had the fun of doing it; the cleansing after-effects of the hoot, the holler, and the great horselaugh. Probably the editors at the *Bazaar* never heard. But a lot of readers did and cried, "Go it, *Bazaar*; go it Bradbury!" I claim no victory. But there was blood on my gloves when I hung them up.

Talking About It #39

With your classmates, respond to "The Impulse to Write." Use the following questions to guide you in your discussion.

1. Did you enjoy reading Ray Bradbury's account of his impulses about writing? Why or why not?
2. What one-word adjective or adjectives describe Bradbury's attitudes about writing? Why?

Writing About It #40

In your journal, describe your attitudes as a writer. What one-word adjective best describes your attitudes about writing? Why?

In the passage by Ray Bradbury, you've read a professional writer's account of his attitudes toward writing. But people who don't write professionally also hold attitudes about writing, and these attitudes can influence the way they approach the writing situation. One student, Heather Vermillion, used the one-word adjective "struggling" to describe her attitudes toward writing. A passage in which Heather attempted to trace the reasons for her struggles appears below.

Writing well has always been very difficult for me, and my experiences with writing are a continual struggle to express myself the way I want to.

I remember my grade school teachers saying that I did not have a vivid imagination and that I had a hard time expressing myself. I was also told that I did not have any sense of creativity. All of my teachers knew from the beginning that I had a problem, but no one offered any assistance. I continued to work hard, but the hard work just didn't seem to pay off. As a result, I felt that I was destined to write poorly from an early age.

In high school, I seemed to improve a great deal, and I give a lot of that credit to Mr. Ahlm, my English teacher. He spent many days helping me write and rewrite the papers that were due. I did better under his supervision, but often I found myself forgetting what he said or failing to perform the way I hoped I could perform. I still struggled to make the kinds of grades I wanted in writing.

In college, I was shocked to find that my best grade came from College Composition I. Because the course was required and I was aware of my weaknesses as a writer, I worked especially hard. In fact, I had never worked so hard in any course in my life! I went from a "D minus" on my first paper all the way up to a "B." Mr. Jackson, my professor, wrote a note on my final paper that made me feel good. He said my achievements made teaching worthwhile.

I still struggle with writing, however. I think I always will. I am glad that there are others in the world who can write for entertainment, and I enjoy reading their works. But I believe that there were people put on this earth to write and others put on this earth—like me—to struggle with writing!

Writing About It #41

Use your journal and the questions below to explore your attitudes as a writer.

1. What one-word adjective would describe your attitudes as a writer? Why?
2. Are your writing experiences more like Ray Bradbury's or more like Heather Vermillion's? Explain.
3. What things frustrate you when you write? What things please you when you write? Explain.
4. Who were some of your memorable writing teachers and why were they memorable? Explain.
5. Do you ever write for pleasure? Or do you only write when required to? Explain.
6. Where do you do most of your writing? Explain this setting in detail.
7. What are your earliest memories about writing? What emotions or feelings do these early memories call up? Explain.
8. What emotions are associated with your elementary school writing experiences? Your junior high experiences? Your high school experiences? Explain.
9. If you were to give yourself some advice about writing, what would you tell yourself? Explain.
10. Are there any attitudes you hold about writing that you would like to change? Why? What would you be willing to do in order to change them?

Share your journal responses to the questions which appear with other students in your class.

Defining your general attitudes as a writer will offer you insight into yourself, insight about your own composing processes and practices. But attitudes also come into play when you are faced with a specific writing–reading situation. Just as writers hold general attitudes about writing, they also hold specific attitudes about the memo, the letter, or the essay that makes up the particular writing–reading situation facing them.

For instance, it's possible for a writer to hold an indifferent or lukewarm attitude about the act of writing in general but to hold strong, even passionate attitudes about subjects such as her town's leadership vacuum or her company's hiring policies, attitudes that may find their way into a letter to the editor or an office memo that she writes.

In cases like this, as in most writing situations, the writer's attitudes greatly influence an important aspect of the writing process: the writer's *purposes* or *goals*. In fact, this writer's purposes and goals may be driven by her attitude about the subjects on which she is writing. Her letter to the editor of the town newspaper or the petition she circulates to the town council may be driven by the goal of putting a qualified candidate on the ballot, thereby ending the leadership vacuum that disturbs her. Or the memo that she writes to her boss or company personnel director offering new policy suggestions concerning her company's hiring practices may be driven by the purpose of effecting widespread changes in company hiring practices.

In such cases, attitudes affect a writer's purposes and goals. These cases offer you the opportunity to examine in more detail the specific questions that affect you, the writer, when you are immersed in the writing–reading situation:

What are your purposes and goals? What techniques will be most likely to achieve them?

What are your attitudes—about the reader, about the work, and about the language community which you share?

What are your needs and expectations? From the reader? About the work? From the language itself?

What Is Your Purpose?

A *purpose* is a goal or an aim or an intent.

In one sense, purposes seem easy because purposes are about what you want to do or what you want to accomplish in a piece of writing. On the other hand, purposes are complex because they are multifaceted and because they are continually changing.

For instance, the woman who is concerned about the hiring practices at work may have many purposes or goals when she sits down to write. One goal may be to have someone—for instance, her boss—take notice of the problem. Another goal may be to articulate the hiring issue for herself so that she fully understands the policies and their ramifications. The writer may also intend to fashion an airtight argument for her view, one that will withstand the controversy and debate that is likely to ensue once she airs her concerns publicly. In addition, an important goal or purpose may be to effect a major change in company policy. Thus, this writer's purposes are multifaceted.

But once she immerses herself in the writing situation, this writer will likely find that her purposes are not just multifaceted: they are constantly changing as well. As she sits at her desk, pen in hand, she may decide that her company's personnel director might be more likely to effect a change than her boss, so she may change the target of her memo from her boss to the personnel director. As she begins to write her articulation of the policy issues, she may discover that her goal of a carefully reasoned airtight argument may be less effective than a more emotional appeal that cites specific instances in which several of her coworkers had been victims of the current company policy. As she writes, she might also find that a memo, which is often a public and formal method of office communication, may not be the most effective form in which a serious problem can first be aired. Perhaps she decides to write a letter instead, attempting to accomplish her goal in a more private, confidential form of writing shared between herself and her company's personnel director. Finally, as she writes, facing the complexity of the writing situation on paper, she may refocus her original goal: to change only one aspect of the hiring policy, not the entire policy as a whole. Thus, purposes are constantly changing.

Purposes, multifaceted and constantly changing, are the same as trying to shake hands with the eight-limbed octopus: do you shake one limb or do you shake them all?

General Purposes

In spite of the fact that the goals or aims of writing are multifaceted and that they often shift when a writer is immersed in the writing process, every piece of writing can generally be characterized in terms of purpose. These kinds of "all-purpose" purposes are

1. to express yourself,
2. to entertain,

3. to inform,
4. to persuade.

A reader scanning the pages of a diary of his or her senior year in high school is reading material written for the purpose of personal expression. A reader chuckling over a passage by Mark Twain or H.L. Mencken is likely being treated to a writer whose purpose is largely to entertain. A reader scanning the headlines for the outcome of last-night's baseball game is searching for writing that informs. A reader concentrating on an article in a medical journal about the safety of mammograms is exposed to a writer with the purpose of persuading her about the relative safety of these screening procedures.

The passages which follow offer you an opportunity to determine their authors' general purposes. Read each of them carefully, and then answer the questions which follow.

1. Recently, I played lead guitar in a rock band, and the rhythm guitarist was—not that I wish to drop names—Stephen King. This actually happened. It was the idea of a woman named Kathi Goldmark, who formed a band consisting mostly of writers to raise money for literacy by putting on a concert at the American Booksellers Association convention in Anaheim, California.

So she called a bunch of writers who were sincerely interested in literacy and making an unbelievable amount of noise. I think we all said "yes" for the same reason. If you're a writer, you sit all day alone in a quiet room trying to craft sentences on a word processor, which makes weenie little clickety-click sounds. After years and years of crafting and clicking, you are naturally attracted to the idea of arming yourself with an amplified instrument powerful enough to be used for building demolition, then getting up on a stage with other authors and screaming out songs such as *Land of 1,000 Dances*, the lyrics to which express the following literary theme:

"Na, na, na, na, na, na na na na
Na na na, na na na, na na na na."

—Dave Barry

2. The wild turkey is truly a North American bird. This unique animal once thrived in our land, but, like the bison, wild turkeys all but died out by the turn of the century. Today, however, the wild turkey is alive and well and thriving in Ohio.

Before European settlement, wild turkeys on this continent numbered millions. A thousand birds in a day were seen by two hunters in New England in 1632. After this date, with increased hunting and forest destruction, turkeys began to disappear. By 1672 in New England, John Jossely wrote, "I have also seen threescore broods of young Turkies on the side of a marsh, sunning themselves in a morning betimes, so that 'tis very rare to meet with a wild Turkie in the Woods."

Wild turkeys originally thrived in all of forested Ohio. In 1880, however, they had been reduced to a remnant and, according to the records, the last wild turkey in Ohio was killed in Adams County in 1904.

Today, wild turkeys are back in good number. The Ohio Division of Wildlife transplanted wild turkeys from surrounding states in the 1950s and 1960s, and this has allowed for the return of the turkey to a majority of Ohio's counties. With this increase there is now a huntable population. During recent years, 3,000–4,000 turkeys have been harvested each spring. Alive and well, the turkeys are thriving in the forested areas of southern and eastern Ohio and in Shawnee State Forest and Wayne National Forest.

—*Paul Knoop*

3. Television-watching constitutes a deprivational experience for the child of formative years. A pre-school child who watched but 20 hours a week, which is well below the national average, will have spent 4000 plus hours staring at television by the time he enters first grade. Four thousand hours of not exercising any competency skill has got to have negative impact on the child's learning abilities.

During the first seven years of life, the environment imprints enduring patterns into the central nervous system. If a young child spends significant time staring at a fixed and flickering electronic field, is it not reasonable to assume that this experience is interfering with the establishment of key neural skills, including a long attention span and certain reasoning abilities? Might this not also go a long way toward explaining the epidemics of learning disabilities (LDs) and attention deficit disorder (ADD)?

Parents have, for the most part, ignored the alarm I've sounded. Those with LD and ADD children have been outraged. For obvious reasons, they prefer a genetic "it couldn't be helped" explanation over a developmental one. By and large the professional community has dismissed my arguments. I've been called an iconoclast and even threatened with charges of unethical conduct. "There's no research to support what you're saying," they've said.

Well, now there is. Psychologist Jane Healy, author of *Endangered Minds: Why Our Children Don't Think*, proposes that television's electronic environment is actually altering the brains of children, both functionally (how the brain works) and structurally (its construction). She sees a connection between the increase in learning disabilities (and lower reading scores in general), hyperactivity, and ADD and the time American children spend splotched in front of television sets during the most critical years of brain development.

I've said children should not be allowed to watch any television until they are completely literate, which translates to no television until age eight or so. So, now that the choice is clear, will parents opt for smart kids or the convenience of an electronic baby-sitter? And will school administrations put their money where their mouth is and remove television sets from elementary classrooms? And will

Action for Children's Television stop playing footsie with the networks and demand they do the right thing: stop producing programs targeted to formative-years children and begin warning their parents of the dangers of letting them watch any television at all?

We'll see.

—John Rosemond

4. Everything that exists in the present has come out of the past, and no matter how new and unique it seems to be, it carries some of the past with it. The latest hit recording by the newest group is the result of the evolution of that group's musical style and of the trends in music and society that have influenced them. Perhaps their style developed from earlier rock styles associated with the Beatles or perhaps they are taking off from even older folk themes used by Bob Dylan. Well, Dylan was influenced by Woody Guthrie, who wrote his songs in the 1930s and whose music grew out of his contact with the heritage of American folk music from the nineteenth century, which in turn had come in great measure from earlier music in England and Scotland, some of which has its origins in the Middle Ages. Modern jazz music, such as that of Billie Holiday or Louis Armstrong, evolved from the music of black communities in the United States and the Caribbean. Enslaved black people brought the earlier forms of that music with them from Africa in the eighteenth and nineteenth centuries. So you can see that the house of the present is filled with windows into the past.

—Jules R. Benjamin

5. I like writing in my journal. It is a kind of secret place where I can write down my private thoughts, my cruel impulses, my unacceptable desires. My journal represents safety to me. I can lock it up and hide it away without fear of public embarrassment. This security gives me the sweet taste of complete freedom.

—Mylene Muceno

Talking About It #42

Get together with a group of your classmates and decide whether the purpose or purposes of each of the writers was to express themselves, to entertain, to inform, or to persuade. Explain your answer by referring specifically to the passages themselves.

Sometimes a piece of writing fulfills more than one purpose. For instance, it may both inform *and* entertain. A sports story which recounts last night's baseball game in an entertaining fashion would be an example of a piece of writing that fulfills more than one purpose. Try to read several current magazines or newspapers and then Xerox a copy of at least one article that manages to fulfill more than one purpose. Share these articles with your classmates.

Specific Purposes

Although writers aim to accomplish general purposes, for example, entertaining, informing, persuading, and expressing themselves, they aim to accomplish specific purposes as well. Such specific purposes can best be understood in the context of specific writing situations, writing situations in which a writer has thought about the reader as he or she formulates the purpose. Examples of these kinds of specific writing situations follow.

Writer: a staff nurse

Reader: parents whose children are inpatients in a children's hospital

Purpose: to create a handout for the bulletin board in every room that teaches parents about the importance of hand washing as a preventive against the spread of germs

Writer: a big brother

Reader: a little brother

Purpose: to write a note to be read by the little brother when he comes home after school explaining the chores that need to be done by supper

Writer: an office manager

Reader: the office secretaries

Purpose: to write a memo scheduling a meeting to address the issue of covering the phones at lunchtime

Writer: head of the local arts organization

Reader: former corporate contributors to the arts fund

Purpose: to write a letter that generates an increase in company contributions to the arts fund

As the examples which appear make clear, the purpose of a piece of writing is closely tied to the relationship of writer and reader.

Writer's Purposes and Reader's Needs

As you have seen from the examples listed and from the chapters you have read thus far, the writer–reader relationship is an interdependent one, one in which the reader's needs and writer's purposes challenge and shape the written text.

In addition, many writing situations challenge a writer because not just one reader is faced, but several. The woman who wanted to effect a change in her company's hiring policies would ultimately be challenged to create documents that addressed a variety of readers with a variety of perspectives: her boss, the company personnel director, employees who were victims of the current system, local newspaper reporters, a lawyer, or the members of a labor relations board. In these cases, the subject matter remains the same, but the approach to it differs because the writer reassesses her purpose in light of her reader's needs. In addition, writers often need to draft a single text which may itself have several readers. If the woman in this example were drafting an office memo to be shared among secretaries, the office manager, her personnel director, and the company president, the needs of these multiple readers would all have to be served in the context of a single memo. Thus purposes and readers are highly interdependent.

A good way of learning how writers accomplish multiple purposes with different readers is to watch them at work. The following material treats the same general subject—the juvenile justice system's growing reliance on Teen Courts. But each writer approaches the subject with a different goal, aim, or *purpose*, depending on what reader he or she is trying to reach. Read each passage carefully with an eye to the writer's purpose and the reader's needs.

1. A Jury of Their Peers

"This court," the judge says, banging down her gavel, "has decided to suspend your license for 10 days."

The young man and his father look at each other, disappointed. As the father bends over a court form and begins to sign a paper, the young man hesitantly steps up to the judge's bench. "Well, can I at least drive to school, your honor?" asks the tall young man who has just had his license suspended.

The judge turns the question over to the jury.

"How far do you live?" a juror inquires. She has long blonde hair pulled back in a ponytail.

"About a mile," the young man says, hopefully.

The judge asks the young man and his father to step outside the chamber so that the court can discuss the issue.

"Well?" asks the judge, turning to the jury. She has a page boy haircut and a sunburned nose. The jury begins to deliberate. They wear glasses and braces and class rings as well as serious, deliberate expressions. Neither judge nor jury members look a day over 17. "What do you think?" the judge asks.

"I think we should make him walk," says a curly-haired youth in a white shirt with a buttoned-down collar.

Another juror, the young girl sitting next to him, says, "It's not like Oakwood's that big. You can walk almost anywhere here."

"I agree," says another boy. "And it's not like 10 days is forever."

The judge listens attentively, nods her head, and then calls the young boy and his father back into the chamber. "I'm afraid," she says, "that your request is denied."

This kind of dispensation of justice is all in a Saturday morning's work for the 10 teenagers who serve as judge and jury as members of Oakwood's Teen Court, a unique and successful method for administering juvenile justice.

Oakwood's Teen Court, in which teens judge other teens, began back in 1966 as a way of relieving the increasing load on the Montgomery County Common Pleas Court, the official dispenser of juvenile justice in the county. But Teen Court—made up exclusively of high school juniors and seniors—operates under clear guidelines. It decides only misdemeanors, not felonies. It hears only first-time offenses. Since those who appear before it do not contest their charges, Teen Court rules on neither guilt nor innocence. It does, however, set penalties for the wide range of charges brought before it.

Offenders are brought before Teen Court on a number of charges, usually minor. Typical charges range from failure to stop at a traffic light to jaywalking to driving without a license. However, more serious charges also appear before the court. Oakwood's teen jurors have deliberated charges like criminal damaging, receiving stolen property, possession of criminal tools, and possession of a deadly weapon.

And Teen Court members—made up of equal numbers of junior and seniors at Oakwood High School—do set penalties. Sometimes the court may order a certain number of hours of community service as penalty for an offense. A common penalty for a common charge—driving over the speed limit—is a suspended license of one day for every mile per hour over the speed limit.

Tom Talbot, Jr., a lawyer and the adult referee/advisor to the teens on the court, says, "Kids don't necessarily get off any easier in Teen Court. Teen jurors are sometimes more harsh in terms of punishments than Juvenile Court judges."

On the other hand, a decision to go before the Teen Court rather than before a Juvenile Court judge offers some advantages. At Juvenile Court, the offender may be given points that can remain permanently on the driver's license; or, in the case of a nondriving offense, a fine or sentence to the county workhouse can be imposed. At Teen Court, decisions stay off an offender's record, and car insurance is not raised because of points earned on a license.

Teen Court works much like a municipal court. A judge is selected as well as a bailiff and a court reporter. The rest of the students serve as jurors. Court is held about every 6 weeks on a Saturday morning in regular court chambers at the Oakwood City Building. Typically, a dozen or more cases appear on the docket.

Teen Court members, recommended by teachers and selected by the previous year's teen jurors, cite many benefits of serving on a jury of teen peers. "Some of these cases are really interesting," says Pat Graham, 17. "Being a juror on Teen Court has really whet my interest in becoming a lawyer." Carole Stoops says, "We take the penalties seriously because we know we're doing students a favor by letting them show up here. We're serious about doing a good job and proud of the good job we do." Says senior Tim Lentz, "It's a great little introduction to the law."

The young man given the 10-day license suspension pulls his wallet from the pocket of his jeans. He fumbles for his driver's license and passes it across the bench to the judge, a young woman whom he knows from his high school Spanish class. As he turns to leave the chamber, she says, "You should be aware that if you're cited again for speeding, you'll have to appear before the Montgomery County Juvenile Court." The young man grimaces and nods. He leaves the courtroom license-less.

The judge raps her gravel. "Case closed," she says.

2. Memo

To: Mike Kelly, Chief of Police, City of Oakwood
From: Sharon Woods, Teen Court Judge
Re: Request of Travel Funds
Date: March 12, 1993

This memo is a request for travel funds for three Teen Court members. Sharon Woods, Tim Lentz, and Pat Graham have been invited to speak at the Toledo, Ohio Juvenile Justice Forum about the operation of Oakwood's Teen Court.

Expenses cover gas mileage of $30 (150 miles at 20 cents a mile), motel expenses of $120 (one night, two rooms at $60 a room), and food costs of $90 (three meals at approximately $10 a meal). Total expenses for the trip are estimated at $240.

I understand that you and Jay Weisman, City Administrator, are in favor of this trip and that approval of funds will be made by the city Budget Director upon receipt of this memo.

3. Dilution of Justice: The Teen Court System
The Journal of Juvenile Justice

The Teen Court system, the practice of permitting teenage jurists to decide certain juvenile cases, does little to dispense justice but much to dilute it. The elements of this system, which vary somewhat from district to district, generally include a panel of teen judges, a jury, a bailiff, and a court reporter; an advisor/referee who is usually a lawyer; court dates held approximately eight times a year; and a courtroom meeting place. Although the Teen Court system is catching on, adding approximately 40 new Teen Courts in America each year, the system is not to be encouraged. Teen Courts weaken America's juvenile justice system.

First of all, Teen Courts, but their very existence, send a message to offenders that considerations of economy take precedence over considerations of justice. Most juvenile courts decide to set up Teen Courts for reasons of judicial economy: they have too many cases and too little time to process them. Thus, Teen Courts are designed to promote a presumably swifter and more timely administration of justice. Although the rules of most Teen Courts limit offenses to misdemeanors, deciding appropriate punishment for those misdemeanors is often a weighty matter. How many teenagers would be capable of distinguishing appropriate punishments in offenses as different as failure to stop at a traffic signal and possession of a deadly weapon? Therefore, just as raising the speed limit promotes the flow of traffic but fails to improve the highway death record, sending offenders to Teen Court may speed up the court docket but slow down the public perception that justice is actually being done. Administrative considerations should not be allowed to dictate what amounts to an alternative justice system.

An alternative justice system like Teen Court lacks the tough kind of accountability that the established system of Juvenile Courts can provide. First of all, by offering the alternative of appearance before a Teen Court, guilty pleas are encouraged. The offender who believes he or she is innocent will often forego his right of appearance before a Juvenile Court judge because he or she is afraid to take the risk of a potentially tougher sentence should the judge fail to believe his claim of innocence. In addition, the whole notion of "crime" requires the social consequences of "punishment," and meaningful punishment is not something a Teen Court can provide. Instead, teenagers offer peers who stand accused "community service" punishments, everything from planting flowers in front of the YMCA to mowing grass in front of the nursing home. Such "punishments" trivialize the notion that the punishment must fit the crime, They are slaps on the wrist, not serious consequences.

Even worse, Teen Courts teach our nation's young people, clearly our most important national resource, about a kind of judicial tyranny. America's justice system is built on the notion of a fair and impartial jury administering justice objectively. No such objectivity is possible when a jury member is someone one knows from Plane Geometry class or runs formations with out on the football field. No self-respecting judge would allow even a mere acquaintance of an accused to serve on the jury that judges him. Furthermore, review of dozens of Teen Court records by the Council on Judicial Accountability reveals that inconsistency in sentencing by Teen Courts is rampant, strongly suggesting that Teen Courts play favorites, offering lighter sentences to those who are "friends" of the court. Teenagers cannot be the kind of impartial judges a successful justice system requires.

Thus, Teen Courts dilute justice; they don't dispense it. Reasons of judicial economy should not drive the creation of Teen Courts which lack the teeth to administer meaningful punishment and the objectivity to provide fair and impartial administration of justice by a jury of unbiased "peers."

Writing About It #43

For each of the three Teen Court documents that appear, complete a Writer/Reader/Purpose chart similar to the charts you have completed earlier.

1. Writer:
Reader or readers:
Purpose or purposes:

2. Writer:
Reader or readers:
Purpose or purposes:

3. Writer:
Reader or readers:
Purpose or purposes:

Were the purposes you created general or specific purposes? What general purposes did you identify? What specific purposes did you identify?

Prewriting and Purpose

As you have learned, the prewriting part of the writing process consists of (1) understanding your reader, (2) understanding your purpose, and (3) planning your strategy. You have already studied how to create a reader profile as a means of understanding your reader, and you will soon learn how to plan a writing strategy. For now, then, let's focus attention on understanding your purpose by creating a purpose statement.

Purposes are important. They give your writing a sense of direction. If producing a written work is like taking a trip, then discovering your purpose is a lot like deciding where you want to go. Will you head north or south? Visit the mountains or the seashore? Purpose gives your writing a sense of direction.

Thinking about your purpose is an important part of your prewriting effort. The details of the trip can be filled in later, but when you start out, it's important to carry with you a developing sense of where you're going and the direction in which you're headed. That developing sense called your purpose is most useful to you in the early stages of the writing process when it's embodied in a *purpose statement.*

You've already experienced the general purposes that guide a work, purposes that entertain or inform or persuade. You've also experienced the specific purposes that guide you to "write a memo to the office secretaries scheduling a meeting to address the issue of covering the phones at lunchtime" or to "write a letter that generates an increase in company contributions to the arts fund." Now let's experience the way in which a developing sense of purpose in the prewriting stage of the writing process can be translated into a purpose statement to guide your writing efforts.

Purposes can generally be divided into two types: "thinking" purposes and "doing" purposes. A thinking purpose suggests mental activity on the part of the reader: *understanding* an idea, *reflecting* on a concept, *considering* an argument. A doing purpose suggests action on the part of the reader: *instituting* a new policy, *presenting* a new product at a sales conference, *requesting* a favor.

The list of purposes that follows is divided into "thinking" and "doing" goals.

Thinking Purposes	**Doing Purposes**
understanding	instituting
reflecting	presenting
considering	requesting
informing	authorizing
entertaining	recommending
describing	persuading
evaluating	

Thinking and doing classifications of purpose are not watertight compartments, but they can do much to help you formulate a purpose statement to guide you through the writing process. In the purpose statements which follow, decide whether they ask their readers to *think about* something or to *do* something.

Purpose statement: to describe the current system of wastewater treatment in the county

Purpose statement: to recommend a new wastewater treatment system reflecting the latest technological developments

Purpose statement: to outline the new financial aid guidelines for incoming students

Purpose statement: to authorize monies to be used to implement the new financial aid guidelines for incoming students

Purpose statement: to explain the writing strategies in Dr. Martin Luther King, Jr.'s "I Have a Dream" speech

Purpose statement: to write a policy statement for the English department requiring that all freshman composition students study the writing strategies employed in Dr. Martin Luther King, Jr.'s "I Have a Dream" speech.

Writing About It #44

Study the examples and write a few guidelines explaining to your fellow classmates some hints for writing clear purpose statements. Share your guidelines with your classmates.

Write purpose statements to describe the three Teen Court pieces you studied earlier. Label them as either (1) thinking purpose statements or (2) doing purpose statements.

In this chapter, you learned how to profile a reader and articulate a purpose as an early part of your prewriting effort. In the next chapter, you will extend those prewriting efforts as you learn to plan other strategies effectively.

WRITING ASSIGNMENTS

Choose one or several of the following writing assignments. Before you write, develop a reader profile and a purpose statement. Assume for purposes of this assignment that your reader is a classmate. After you have finished writing, share your work with your classmates. Ask them to comment on it, and then record their comments in the Writing Assessment Profile which appears in the back of your textbook.

A. Pick a special-interest magazine or newspaper that appeals to you, and write a paper explaining the way that magazine or newspaper uses elements such as articles, headlines, photography, layout, advertisements, language, and other aspects of the publication to meet the needs of the readers. Use Matt Hahn's paper on *Hot Rod* magazine, which appears on pages 56–57, to guide you. Ask your classmates to respond to several drafts of your writing.

B. Study the information you compiled on the characteristics of your classroom readers from page 68. Then write a paper in which you profile your classroom readers, supporting your ideas with reference to the chart of characteristics which appeared either on the board or in your classmates' descriptions of themselves as readers. Ask your classmates to respond to several drafts of your writing.

C. Look over your responses to the questions on page 71, which help you identify your attitudes or experiences about writing. Write an essay of at least four paragraphs which describes those attitudes or experiences. Make sure you develop a reader profile and a purpose statement before you begin.

D. Choose a single subject to explore from the perspective of four different purposes. Write four paragraphs on the subject—one which demonstrates a purpose to express yourself, one which demonstrates a purpose to entertain, one which demonstrates a purpose to inform, and one which demonstrates a purpose to persuade.

For example, if you choose the topic of athletic shoes, one of your paragraphs might be a personal statement expressing how you feel about athletic shoes. A second paragraph might be an entertaining look at the choices of athletic shoes available on the market. Another of your paragraphs might try to inform the reader about some aspect of athletic shoes. A fourth paragraph might try to persuade your reader to buy a particular brand or argue that the purchase of athletic shoes represents an unnecessary expense.

Before you write each of your paragraphs, create a reader profile and purpose statement. A list of possible topics follows.

athletic shoes

children

political advertisements

medical tests

computers

college teachers

E. Write two paragraphs in which the purpose remains the same but the *reader* changes. For instance, assume that your purpose is to write two paragraphs. The purpose of both paragraphs is to attract new students to your university. In the first paragraph, your readers will be students who have completed high school and who will be attending college for the first time. In the second paragraph, your readers will be adult women students who are coming back to school to get their college degrees after having raised a family.

Before you write your paragraphs, write a purpose statement which will apply to both, and write a reader profile which will characterize each new reader differently. You may wish to write your two paragraphs on the topic of coming to the university as suggested or you may wish to write your two paragraphs on a topic of your own creation. Remember to keep the purpose the same but change the readers.

CHAPTER THREE REVIEW

Writing About It #45

Use your journal to reflect on what you learned in this chapter.

4

Prewriting: Planning Your Strategy

How can I develop my ideas more effectively? How can I begin to organize what I want to write? What strategies can I use to improve what I want to say and how I want to say it?

Although there are a few who strike it rich by winning a lottery or inheriting a prime piece of real estate from a long-lost relative, the fact remains that most successes are built on strategy, not luck. A successful neighborhood clean-up campaign, a successful novel on the best-seller lists, a successful campaign for the presidency all have one thing in common: they are the result of strategic planning. Strategies are a dependable way of meeting a goal.

Strategies are also important to successful writing. You'll remember from Chapter 1 that writing is often a matter of juggling a number of complex tasks that cry out for your attention. When you write, you must deal with a great number of competing factors, for example, articulating purposes, understanding readers, composing sentences, and even remembering the rules of punctuation. Because there are so many factors to consider and it is so easy to be overwhelmed by them, planning a strategy is not just important: it is essential. Competent plans enable you to achieve a measure of control in the face of complexity. They assist you in taking careful aim at your targeted readers and purposes. In fact, the difference between writing with a strategy and writing without one is often the difference between firing scattered shots and hitting the bull's-eye.

Because successful planning is the foundation for successful writing, it is important to understand what planning is. First, planning is different from writing. Planning is a way of producing *ideas*; writing is a way of producing *texts*. Many people struggle to understand this distinction, and often they dismiss the kind of idea-producing that goes with planning as less important than what they consider the "real" business of writing: producing the words, sentences, and paragraphs that make up texts.

Second, successful plans have an open, fluid quality about them. Good plans are flexible. They allow for change. They can even be discarded in favor of newer, better plans that emerge during the writing process. Often a short but clear plan suggesting the basic structure and content of a projected text is preferable to an intricate plan that runs to several pages. If a plan is too detailed, sometimes the writer can feel hemmed in by the plan, its slave rather than its master.

Finally, planning is a broad rather than a narrow process. Many writers think that planning reduces to something quick and easy like "make an outline." Although outlining can be an effective way of planning part of a piece of writing, equating planning with outlining obscures the fact that planning a successful strategy is a matter of making plans in three broad areas: *content, organization,* and *expression.*

As you saw in "Introducing Andy Rooney" in Chapter 1, every piece of writing is made up of three elements: content, organization, and expression. Content generally refers to the subject matter or topic, organization to the structure in which the subject matter is arranged or presented, and expression to the ways in which language is used to express the writer's ideas.

To use an analogy, writing is a kind of journey. In the course of that journey, you will travel through a particular landscape. It may be a landscape as familiar as your backyard or as unfamiliar as a pocket of rain forest. But this landscape represents your content. You will also explore the landscape in a certain way. For example, you might take the backroads, an interstate highway, a hot air balloon, or some other route. The route you take on your explorations, however, represents your organization or structure. Finally, you will conduct your journey in a particular style. You may travel by luxury liner, by birchbark canoe, or by foot, but the style in which you travel represents your expression. Although the journey itself will undoubtedly accommodate changes and adjustments as it unfolds, there's little point in setting out if you haven't settled on three things beforehand: where you're going, how you're going to get there, and what style you plan to travel in. Plans about those three things make up your strategy.

STRATEGIES AND CONTENT

One of the most universal reactions students experience when they begin to immerse themselves in a writing assignment is, "What am I going to say?" This question is often accompanied by a rising feeling of panic, a sinking feeling of despair—or both. These are common feelings. There are many reasons for these feelings. However, one of the main reasons why content—the what-I'm-going-to-say part of writing—troubles students so much is that they often focus too early on the challenge of producing a *text*; they either ignore or shortchange the important and essential challenge of first producing *ideas*. It's something like starting up the car before you've decided where you want to go. As the material that follows points out, producing ideas is a matter of using effective strategies for generating content—before you begin to produce a draft.

CONTENT: GENERATING AND FOCUSING

When you plan the content of a paper as part of your prewriting strategies, you are attempting to do two things: (1) generate content and (2) focus content. When you *generate* content, you produce a number of ideas which you can later develop as you write. When you *focus* content, you begin to shape and form these ideas.

The questions that follow will help guide you as you make plans for the content of your texts.

Generating content

How can I discover what I know?
How can I discover what I need to know?

Focusing content

Will the content I have discovered satisfy my reader and my purpose as reflected in my reader profile and my purpose statement?
Can I shape this content into a working statement?

Generating

Generating ideas can be fun. In fact, this is the freewheeling, let-yourself-go part of the writing process. It can be a creative, mind-expanding activity. One of the reasons why it's so enjoyable is that you can—and should—generate ideas free of any constraints. That is, when you generate ideas, you forget entirely about any of the other challenges of writing. You ignore the requirements of "correctness." You send grammar off into the stratosphere. You stash concerns about your reader and your purpose into the attic for safekeeping. You banish any idea of "making sense" to the dungeon where it belongs—for now.

When you generate ideas, you indulge yourself. You fool around. You play. Generating ideas is like fiddling around on the piano, looking for a musical theme. It's like sketching on an artist's tablet before you've settled on the definite shape of the drawing. It's like looking over the buffet table before you pick up your plate. And there are many dependable methods for helping you generate content. Several of them are explained. They are talking, freewriting, looping, brainstorming, sketching, and questioning.

Talking

A time-honored method for generating ideas is so common that it is often undervalued. It shouldn't be. Talking to others about your topic or exploring potential subjects in search of a topic with others is one of the most productive methods you can use.

If your attitude toward conversation is one of genuine interest and you are willing to be honest and open in your responses to others, talking can offer you new ideas, new perspectives, and new energy for the task at hand.

Talking About It #46

Choose a partner and spend some time "just talking" to him or her. The goal of your conversation is to generate as many topics as possible on the subject of "college life." As you talk, jot down some notes on these potential topics. Then put check marks next to the ideas you would not have come up with without the help of a conversation partner.

Choose a different partner and spend some time "just talking" to him or her. The goal of your conversation is to generate as many subtopics as possible on a subject for a sociology, psychology, religion, music, art, or philosophy class. You and your partner must together decide on an appropriate subject and then explore that subject together, generating as many subtopics as possible on your chosen subject. As you talk, jot down some notes on these potential ideas. Then put check marks next to the ideas you would not have come up with without the help of a conversation partner.

Freewriting

Freewriting, a powerful idea-generating technique developed by teacher and writer Peter Elbow, is an excellent way of discovering what you know and what you might need to know in order to produce a written work. Freewriting will help you generate ideas more effectively; it is based on the following simple guidelines.

1. When you freewrite, you write on anything at all—just as it occurs to you—for at least 10 minutes.

2. When you freewrite, you write continually without stopping.

3. When you freewrite, you turn off the editor in your head that concerns itself with grammar or any of the other traditional conventions of writing.

In the passage that follows, student Sean Gorman shares his freewriting with you. His preliminary reader profile and purpose statement appear as well. Although Sean can generally downplay concerns about readers and purposes as he freewrites, this material has been provided to orient you, Sean's reader, to the nature of his writing task.

Sean's reader profile: Professor Spears, who teaches Biology 101, a freshman biology class, has stated his interest in developing our powers to "observe like a scientist" and to "write like a scientist" in this assignment. He has also stated that our observations are to "raise scientific questions." Although he is only asking us to write one paragraph, this is my first written assignment for Professor Spears. In class, he is very demanding. He is a stickler for details and encourages questioning.

Sean's purpose statement: to describe a common piece of fruit through careful observation that raises scientific questions in a 250-word paragraph for which no outside sources are to be used.

Sean's Freewriting: A piece of fruit. A common piece of fruit. Professor Spears wants me to describe a common piece of fruit. Through careful observation. That raises scientific questions. Common piece of fruit. I'm thinking of my kitchen table at home. My mother always had a basket on that table filled with fruit. I grabbed a piece almost every day after school. Peaches in the summer. Plums. Almost always apples and bananas. A common piece of fruit would be something like that. An apple. A banana. Would a kiwi be a common piece of fruit? A nectarine? No way. So what will I pick? A banana? A banana might be interesting. That funny skin that you peel just like a monkey. Or maybe I could write about a peach. It's got a pretty color and the skin is fussy. Or do you spell that "fuzzy?" Can't think about that now. Turn off the editor, Sean. Maybe I'll use an apple. An apple. Describe it. Professor Spears wants me to describe it. O.K. What's the big deal.? O.K. Describe it, Sean. Red, of course. I'm thinking of an apple that's red. It's got a stem sticking out of the top, doesn't it? The stem is brown. Maybe there's a leaf still attached to the stem. What color is the leaf? Dark green? Brown and shriveled? I'm wondering if I have to describe this apple on both the inside and the out. Hmmm. I'm still just on the outside. In my mind I see that funny little thing on the bottom that it sits on. Sort of like an apple seat. What's that called? I'll have to look it up. Oops, can't do that. Professor Spears says no outside sources. I can't think of enough to say here. I'm going to have to stop. But when I freewrite I'm supposed to keep going for at least ten minutes. This is hard. I see that I'm going to need some more ideas. I'm running out of steam. I think I'm going to have to get a real apple. I think I'll need to hold it in my hand, feel its weight, look at it more closely. Maybe that's what Professor Spears means by "careful observation." It seems like such a simple assignment. At least it seemed like that at first. Maybe it's not. Maybe it's not so simple.

Talking About It #47

With your classmates, look closely at Sean's freewriting and the characteristics of freewriting which have been explained to you. Use examples from Sean's freewriting to discuss how he has (1) written down his ideas just as they occurred to him, (2) written continually without stopping, and (3) turned off the editor in his head.

Writing About It #48

It is often said that freewriting is a powerful method for *choosing* a topic when an assignment is open-ended. In your journal, write a paragraph that explains how Sean's freewriting helped him choose a topic for his paragraph for Professor Spears.

Choose a topic from the following list. Then freewrite about it for 10 minutes. Possible topics for freewriting include the following:

Money
Roommates
Household chores
Sports

When you have finished, share your freewritings with other members of your class. Note the way the different freewritings you read (1) took up ideas just as they occurred to the writers, (2) demonstrated a willingness to write continually without stopping, and (3) turned off the editors in the writers' heads.

Looping

Looping is another way of generating ideas. It grows out of a piece of freewriting and is a way of deepening and strengthening the ideas you have begun to develop. It is a kind of *focused* freewriting.

Here is the way looping works. You freewrite about your topic for 5 minutes or so and then look back over what you have written to find an idea that you'd like to develop in more detail. This idea is called your "center of gravity." Typically this idea will be something that interests you or appears important to you or in some other way stimulates your thinking.

This center-of-gravity idea then becomes the jumping off point for your first "loop." You write this center of gravity idea as a single sentence and you then begin to freewrite again, focusing on that sentence only, remembering to write down things as they come into your mind and remembering to turn off the editor in your head.

After you have written about this center of gravity idea for a while, look back over what you have now written, and try to generate a second loop from a second center of gravity sentence. Keep looking over your work, finding centers of gravity, and then using centers of gravity sentences as jumping off points into your loops. Many writers find that this is a helpful way of generating ideas. Sean's looping efforts follow.

Freewriting: *Maybe I'll use an apple. An apple. Describe it. Professor Spears wants me to describe it. O.K. What's the big deal.? O.K. Describe it, Sean. Red, of course. I'm thinking of an apple that's red. It's got a stem sticking out of the top, doesn't it? The stem is brown. Maybe there's a leaf still attached to the stem. What color is the leaf? Dark green? Brown and shriveled?*

Center-of-gravity sentence: *I can describe the apple sitting on the table before me in terms of its colors.*

Loop one: *The outside of this apple is a warm shade of red. But the color yellow also appears on its skin. Some tiny yellowish streaks on the skin move down the surface like latitude lines on a globe. The color of the stem at the top of the apple is brown, and there's also a tiny brown shriveled leaf attached to the stem. This apple is a funny-looking shape. Kind of lopsided. One side larger than the other. I wonder why. This apple fits firmly in the palm of my hand. It's a perfect shape for holding in my hand.*

Center-of-gravity sentence: *I can also describe an apple in terms of its shape.*

Loop two: *The top of the apple is wider and fuller than the bottom, but the middle or "waist" is the widest, fullest part of all. The bottom or base of this apple sits on a kind of "seat" that makes me think of a fat lady perched on a tiny stool. This apple tilts to one side. It is lopsided. One side is fatter than the other. Is "lopsided" one word or hyphenated? Would it be "lop-sided?" Just as with freewriting, I'm going to have to worry about that later. But I haven't written anything about the inside of this apple yet. The flesh. Or the core. Maybe that's going to be my next idea.*

Center-of-gravity sentence: *The inside of this apple is very interesting.*

Loop three: *It is made up of the familiar flesh and core. The flesh is white and firm, sweet-tasting and juicy. It makes a crunchy sound when bitten into. The core runs through the middle of the apple. Surrounding the core are five chambers that are shaped like a five-pointed star. The chambers contain some dark brown seeds.*

Writing About It #49

Look closely at Sean's looping and the characteristics of looping and freewriting which have been explained to you. Then choose one of the following subjects. Freewrite on it for about 5 minutes. Then create at least three centers-of-gravity sentences and the looping that flows from them. Choose your subject from this list of suggestions.

School
Music
Nature
Cars

When you have finished your looping, make sure you have labeled your center-of-gravity sentences. Then share your looping with other members of your class.

Write a paragraph in which you explain whether you preferred freewriting or looping as a means of generating ideas. Give reasons for your preference.

Brainstorming

Brainstorming is another powerful tool for generating ideas. Brainstorming, sometimes called *listing,* is a matter of taking down all the ideas that pop into your head as you think about a topic. It is an effective way of thinking of a great number of ideas that relate to your subject. Brainstorming frees you up in the same way that freewriting does. When you brainstorm, you don't worry about the order of your ideas or their relationships. You simply free associate, jotting down anything that comes to mind. You also don't worry about putting those ideas into complete sentences.

It's also productive to brainstorm with other people. When the members of a group put their heads together to brainstorm a problem, they can almost always generate more ideas than each member alone. In fact, brainstorming during an office meeting is a well known way of generating solutions in the workplace. In the brainstorming example that follows, note how student Margaret Donnelly uses this technique as a way of generating ideas for her paper. The reader and purpose of her paper are also explained for you.

Margaret's reader profile: Anita Waycross is a graduate assistant in the English department, teaching Composition 101, freshman composition, for the first time. On previous papers throughout the semester, Ms. Waycross has shown more concern for the use of specific detail than for consideration of grammar. When she gave this assignment, a paper on "Apples as a Symbol in Literature," she repeated her desire to see "abundant support for ideas." She has stressed the importance of research all semester as well, and for this paper she required the use of at least three outside resources. She also encouraged us to discuss the topic and resources among ourselves.

Margaret's purpose statement: to explain how the apple has been used as a symbol in literature in an essay which makes use of at least three outside resources and which may benefit from discussion among students about both the topic and the resources.

Margaret's brainstorming:

The Apple as Symbol

1. *Adam and Eve—symbol of knowledge*
2. *The story of Johnny Appleseed—symbol of productivity, fertility*
3. *Snow White and the Seven Dwarves—symbolizes magic*

After Margaret has jotted down these three stories, the result of her brainstorming, she realizes that she will need more information than she has to write an effective paper. She then decides to brainstorm her topic—"The Apple as a Symbol in Literature"—with a few of her English classmates over lunch. After the group meets, Margaret's extended brainstorming list now looks like this.

1. *Adam and Eve—symbol of knowledge or immortality*
2. *The Story of Johnny Appleseed—symbol of productivity, fertility*
3. *Snow White and the Seven Dwarves—symbolizes magic/transformation*
4. *"The White Snake"—Grimm Brothers' fairy tale—symbol ???*
5. *The story of William Tell, national hero of Switzerland—symbol of courage*
6. *Hercules and the Golden Apples of the Sun—not sure of symbol ??*
7. *The apple and the Judgement of Paris—symbol of discord*
8. *Idunn and the apples of immortality—Norse myth—symbol of immortality*
9. *Avalon, the "Isle of Apples"—Welsh legend symbolizes ???*
10. *"The Princess of the Garden of Eden"—Irish tale—symbolizes life/immortality*
11. *Anasindhu and the apple of immortality—Persian myth—???symbol*
12. *"The Princess on the Glass Hill"—Norwegian tale—???symbol of immortality*
13. *Saint Dorothea—Christian legend—symbolizes ???*

As you can see from the examples which now appear on Margaret's list, using other people as resources for brainstorming ideas is an effective technique. Although Margaret will now need to narrow her focus and select and shape her ideas in more detail, Margaret's brainstorming efforts have provided her with a wealth of potential material for her paper.

Writing About It #50

Think of a campus problem that bothers you. Describe the problem in a sentence or two. Then brainstorm solutions to the problem, listing as many solutions to the problem as come to mind. Next, ask a recorder to write several of the campus problems on the board and, with your classmates, brainstorm even more solutions to the problems than appear on your original lists. Does this exercise help you see the way in which brainstorming ideas with others can help you generate a number of ideas?

Sketching: Branching and Mapping

People dress differently; they have different learning styles, too. Some people are verbal learners, learning easily whenever words are involved. Some people are kinesthetic learners, learning best in a hands-on, tactile environment. Some people are visual learners, responding to pictures or graphics as a way of learning. When it comes to generating content, these visual learners often plan what they want to say through two useful sketching techniques: branching and mapping.

Branching

Branching encourages you to make use of branches—just like three branches—in order to generate and classify ideas. The topic, then, is the main idea or trunk of the tree; the ideas supporting the main idea lead off from it like sturdy supporting branches; and the ideas related to those supporting ideas fan out from them like twigs. What emerges is a sketch of your ideas visually represented as the trunk, branches, and twigs of a kind of "idea" tree (see Fig. 4.1).

Jose Carmenella, the student whose content plan is represented by the branching scheme that follows was working out some strategies for a paragraph on "Problems Facing Apple Growers" for a special seminar on Planting and Propagation offered by the Agricultural Science Department at his community college. Jose's reader and purpose are given.

Jose's reader profile: Professor Armenio Morales, chairman of the Orchard Propagation Program of the Agricultural Science Department, will be my reader. He has a special interest in the propagation problems of orchard farmers. Professor Morales says this one-paragraph assignment is to be written after we have examined several varieties of apples in order to identify problems that face their growers. Professor Morales's assignment sheet asks me to write a paragraph that "contrasts the problems facing growers of two varieties of orchard fruit and that suggests directions for research on the part of biologists."

Jose's purpose statement: to examine the propagation problems of a variety of apples and then to select two varieties to contrast in a paragraph which suggests directions for further research.

Notice that a branching structure does not have to take the same form as in Fig. 4.1. Your branching structure can also be produced top-down; in this structure, the main idea "trunk" is at the top, and the related ideas spread down like roots rather than branches. Or a branching structure can be turned on its side with the main idea at the far side of the paper and the ideas fanning out from it horizontally. On the page, this branching structure would look something like Figure 4.2.

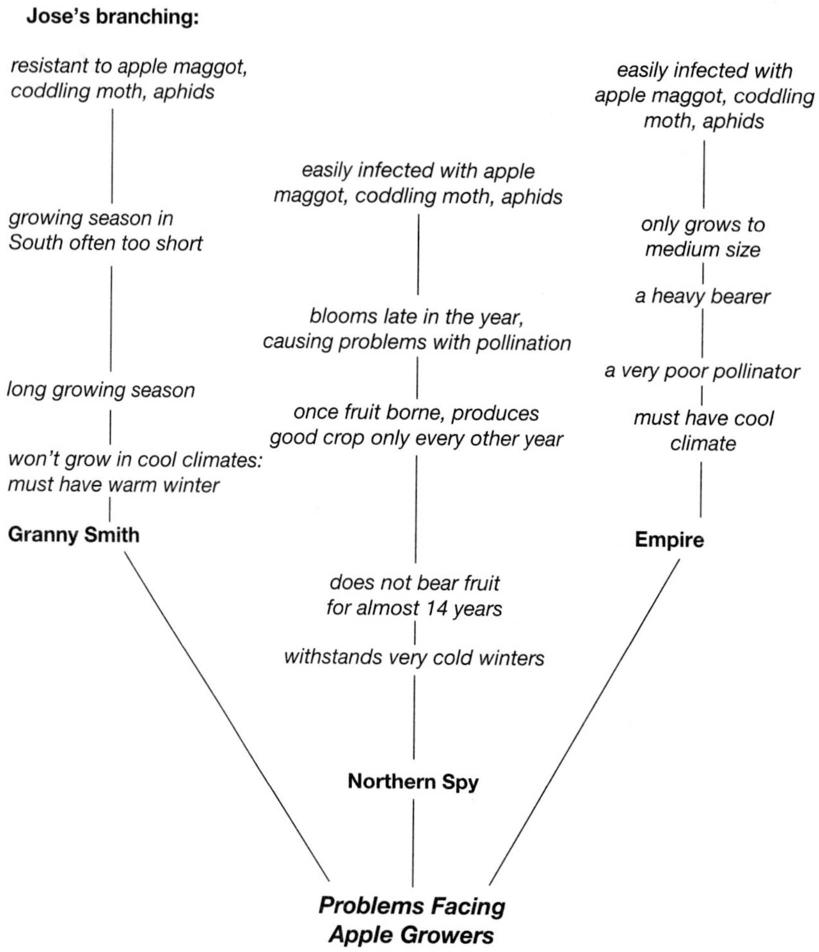

Figure 4.1

Mapping

Another visual strategy for generating content is a technique called mapping. When you "map" the content for a paper, you put your central idea in the center of the map. Then, as ideas related to the central topic occur to you, you place them on the map, too. Each new idea can then be used to produce other new ideas. The important thing about mapping is to be sure to draw lines connecting the related ideas to each other; this will help make the relationships

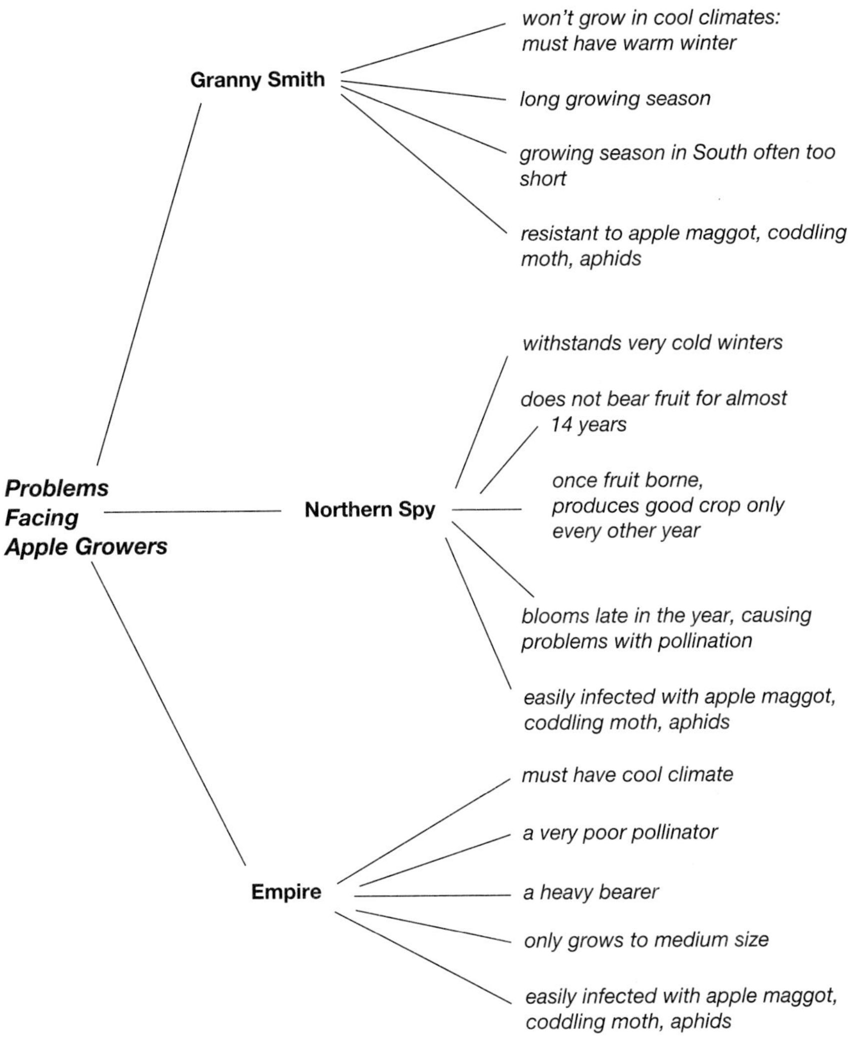

Figure 4.2

among the ideas clear to you. After you have finished with your mapped diagram, areas of thought that produce more fruitful ideas will become clear to you.

If Sean—the student who was writing the description of his apple for his Biology 101 paper—decided to use mapping instead of freewriting or looping as a technique for generating ideas, his mapped sketch might look something like Figure 4.3.

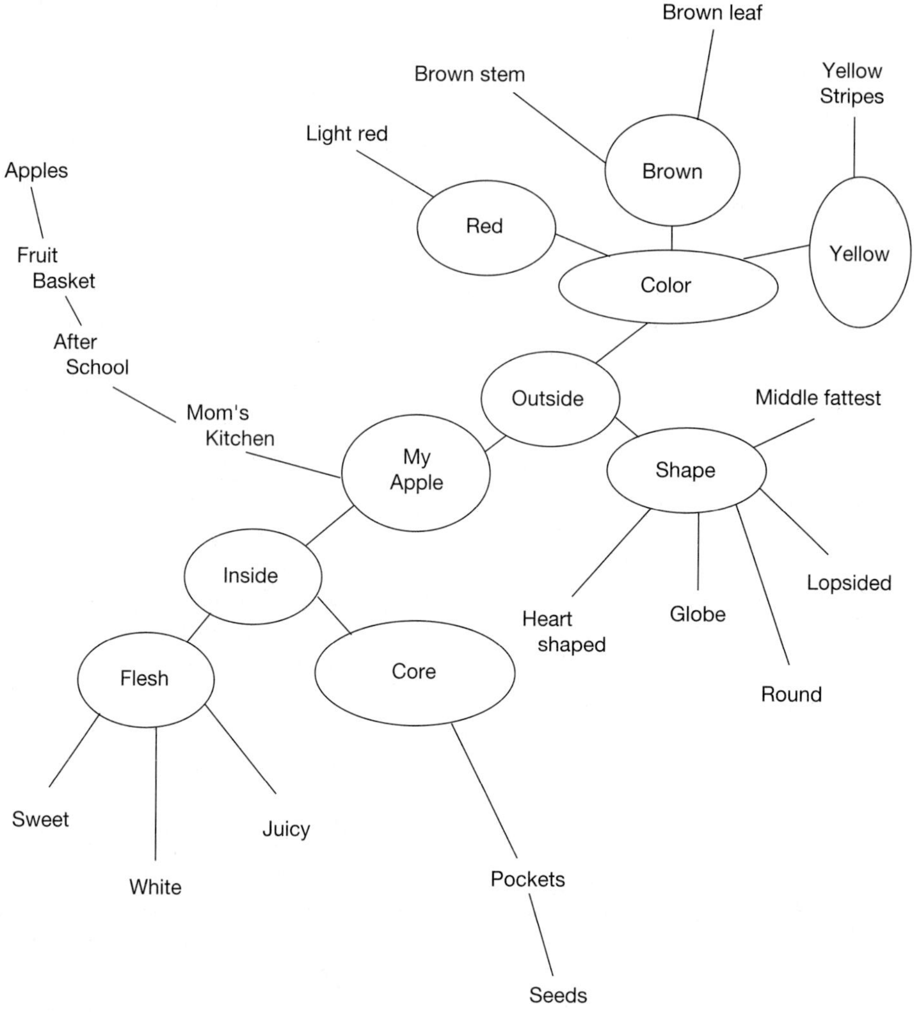

Figure 4.3

Writing About It #51

Choose one of the following topics—or a topic of your own. Then generate ideas for it using a branching technique and a mapping technique.

Pizza
Children's television programming
Choosing a college
Video games
The value of extracurricular activities

After you have finished generating your branches and your maps, write a paragraph discussing which technique—branching or mapping—appealed to you more and why.

Share your branches and maps with the other students in your class.

Questioning

Questions are a time-honored method for generating the thoughts that lead to interesting content. Think back to the two-year-olds you have known and the provocative question they ask over and over again: "Why?" Think of the popular advice columns that proliferate in magazines and newspapers; many of them take the question and answer or Q-and-A format. Think of the press conferences given by the president when journalists press the national leader with questions, questions, questions. Indeed, questions are one of the best—and easiest—ways of generating information or content.

Questions can be used to generate content by making use of six common questions. They are **Who? What? When? Where? Why? How?** These are questions commonly asked by journalists when they write their news stories. These questions are particularly good at yielding information when chronology, or a sequence of events, is important. As you work with this method on a particular piece of writing, you will come to discover that one or two questions will stand out as critical, depending on the purpose of the writer and the needs of the reader. For instance, a police report on a local arson case may simply report the incident, explaining **what** happened. A newspaper editor, however, seeking to explain the reason for several outbreaks of arson in the community, may focus on **why** the incidents occurred. Thus, a piece of writing may be built around the answer to either one or several of the journalist's key questions.

Donna Hannah is a student at a branch campus of a state university. As a member of the campus Human Ecology Club, she is serving on a committee that is responsible for writing a process description on "How to Bake an Apple Pie." The text of this process description will be reviewed by Dr. Roberta Gates, the club sponsor and a Human Ecology professor on Donna's campus. Once the text is approved, the process description will be copied and handed out to local junior high school students and faculty members as part of the Human Ecology Club's college-in-the-high-school community service project. Notice the way Donna makes use of the questioning technique as she produces ideas for her process description. Notice also that this writing project must satisfy the needs of two different readers.

Donna's reader profile #1: Dr. Roberta Gates, Human Ecology Professor and Human Ecology Club sponsor, has told my committee that this chronological process description must explicitly state every step in the process, contain language that can be understood by 7th or 8th grade students, and reflect positively on the quality of writing produced at the university level.

Donna's reader profile #2: The junior high school students who will receive this description are largely unknown to me. However, these students will be using this process description to bake an apple pie during one 50-minute class period.

Donna's purpose statement: to describe the process of baking an apple pie as part of the Human Ecology Club's college-in-the-high-school community service project and as a basis for a 50-minute classroom session.

Donna's Questioning:

Who? junior high school students

What? baking an apple pie

When? 50-minute classroom session

Where? John F. Kennedy Junior High School; the Human Ecology lab

Why? to learn how to bake a fruit pie as part of the Human Ecology curriculum

How? steps in the process

- making the crust
- filling the crust
- baking
- preparing materials
    - equipment
    - preheating
    - helpful hints
        - choosing the apples
        - choosing the crusts
            - fluted edges
            - braided edges
            - scalloped edges

Writing About It #52

Pick one of the topics which appears—or a topic of your own choosing. Then follow Donna Hannah's method of generating ideas by responding to the questions **Who? What? When? Where? Why?** and **How?** Suggested topics include the following:

Fertilizing your lawn
Packing for a trip
Writing a research paper for a class you are currently taking
Bathing a dog

Focusing

You'll recall from the beginning of the chapter that developing strategies about content is made up of two parts: (1) generating content and (2) focusing content. Now that you're familiar with effective techniques for generating content like talking, freewriting, looping, brainstorming, branching, mapping, and questioning, you're ready to concentrate on focusing the content you've developed. You're ready to discover the answer to this question, raised in an earlier section of this chapter: Will the content I have discovered satisfy my reader and my purpose as reflected in my reader profile and my purpose statement?

If you look closely at the content—the what-I'm-going-to-say—created by Sean, Margaret, Jose, and Donna, you'll see that at this point in the writing process, the ideas they have generated are still largely unfocused. Sean's freewriting contains a lot of useless information, Margaret's list of symbols is very long, Jose needs to choose among Granny Smiths, Northern Spys, and Empires for his contrast paragraph, and Donna needs to think some more about the order of presentation of her pie-baking steps.

However, if these four students were photographers, not writers, they would, at this point, have decided generally what scene they'd be photographing—a view of the park, some children at play, or a group of friends shooting baskets. But at this point, their cameras are simply aimed at the scene. They are not *focused* yet.

Focus is important. It's what allows a photograph—or a piece of writing—to become a satisfying, effective, unified whole. A properly focused photograph banishes shadows and blurred edges. Similarly, a properly focused piece of writing banishes fuzzy thinking or gaps in content.

But focusing—an important part of your strategic content planning—is not the same thing as writing. Focusing is what you do just before you trip the shutter. It's what you do just before you write a first draft. But it's not a process that's cast in bronze, for focusing—like planning itself—is fluid and flexible. Your focus can always be reconsidered and changed. For example, as you're training your camera on the park scene, preparing to focus, you might notice that you can't get the entire park bench in the frame, so you move back to refocus for a wider angle shot. Or perhaps you decide on an entirely new angle of focus; instead of shooting the entire group of basketball players at play, perhaps you try to capture several pairs of hands and arms battling at the net. When you make these kinds of changes, you are making decisions about focus, decisions that will ultimately determine the success of your photograph—or your piece of writing.

Two important techniques exist for helping you keep your focus clear. These techniques are (1) *reconsidering your reader and purpose* and (2) *formulating a working statement.*

Focusing: Reconsidering Your Reader and Purpose

Of course, if you're like Sean, Margaret, Juan, and Donna and you've immersed yourself in the writing process already, you have a reader profile and a purpose statement on hand. But while you freewrote or brainstormed or mapped your content, you kept those reader/purpose considerations largely in the background. Now it's time to consider readers and purposes again.

Sean, you'll remember, had identified the following reader and purpose characteristics for his descriptive paragraph about the apple. Following you'll see that he's jotted down key points about his reader and purpose in order to reconsider them again.

Reader:	**Purpose:**
wants me to observe like a scientist	to write a paragraph of 250 words
wants me to write like a scientist	to describe a common fruit
can be demanding	to raise scientific questions
can be a stickler for details	to use no outside sources
encourages questions	

As Sean begins to think about how to focus the content he has generated, he reconsiders his reader's needs and his own purposes. As he reads over his looping, he crosses out some material and adds other material in light of his reader and his purpose. His looping activity now looks like this.

Freewriting:

~~*Maybe I'll use an apple. An apple. Describe it. Professor Spears wants me to describe it. O.K. What's the big deal.? O.K. Describe it, Sean. Red, of course. I'm thinking of an apple that's red. It's got a stem sticking out of the top, doesn't it? The stem is brown. Maybe there's a leaf still attached to the stem. What color is the leaf? Dark green? Brown and shriveled?*~~

Center-of-gravity sentence:

I can describe the apple sitting on the table before me in terms of its colors.

Loop one:

The outside of this apple is a warm shade of red. But the color yellow also appears on its skin. Some tiny yellowish streaks on the skin move down the sur-

face like latitude lines on a globe. ***What makes the different colors of red and yellow? What causes the streaking effect???*** *The color of the stem at the top of the apple is brown, and there's also a tiny brown shriveled leaf attached to the stem. This apple is a funny-looking shape. Kind of lopsided. One side larger than the other.* ***I wonder why.*** ~~*This apple fits firmly in the palm of my hand. It's a perfect shape for holding in my hand.*~~

Center-of-gravity sentence:

I can also describe an apple in terms of its shape.

Loop two:

The top of the apple is wider and fuller than the bottom, but the middle or "waist" is the widest, fullest part of all. The bottom or base of this apple sits on a kind of "seat." ~~*that makes me think of a fat lady perched on a tiny stool.*~~ ***When you turn the apple over to examine the seat, you see a dried brownish kind of pod. I wonder what this is.*** *This apple tilts to one side. It is lopsided. One side is fatter than the other.* ~~*Is "lopsided" one word or hyphenated? Would it be "lop sided?" Just as with freewriting, I'm going to have to worry about that later. But I haven't written anything about the inside of this apple yet. The flesh. Or the core. Maybe that's going to be my next idea.*~~

Center-of-gravity sentence:

The inside of this apple is very interesting.

Loop three:

It is made up of the familiar flesh and core. The flesh is white and firm, sweet tasting and juicy. It makes a crunchy sound when bitten into. ***I wonder what makes the apple taste so sweet.*** *The core runs through the middle of the apple. Surrounding the core are five chambers that are shaped like a five-pointed star. The chambers contain some dark brown seeds.* ***But when I looked closely into the seed chambers, I saw five dark seeds on one side of the chamber and no dark seeds of this type on the other side of the chamber. I noticed that the dark seeds were on the side of the apple that was full and swollen. The empty chambers were on the side of the apple that was shrunken and lopsided. Could this in some way relate to the presence or absence of dark seeds??!!!##*****

Talking About It #53

Work with groups of three or four other students. Choose one student to be the recorder or secretary. Imagine that you are Sean, reconsidering your looping in light of your reader and your purpose. Discuss the following questions with your group. In answering them, you will have to refer over and over again to Sean's characterizations of his reader and his purpose. Ask your recorder to write down your answers.

1. What specific considerations about reader and/or purpose made Sean cross out lines 1–5 and 21–24?
2. What specific considerations about reader and/or purpose made Sean add the boldfaced material in lines 9–10, 13, 19–20, 27–28, and 30–36?
3. Do you think these changes have brought Sean's content into better focus? Why or why not?

Look back over Margaret's reader profile and purpose statement on page 93. Then turn to her brainstorming list on page 94 to review the ideas she generated about apples as symbols in literature. In light of Margaret's reader and purpose, what does she need to do now to achieve a clearer focus about her work? Why? You'll remember that Margaret was required to use three outside references and encouraged to consult other students in preparing her paper. Will consulting outside references help her at this point? Will consulting other students? Why or why not?

Look back over Jose's reader profile and purpose statement on page 95. Then turn to Jose's branching structure on page 96 to review the ideas he generated about the propagation problems of apple farmers. In light of Jose's reader and purpose, what does he need to do now to achieve a clearer focus about his work? Why?

Look back over Donna's reader profile and purpose statement on page 100. Then look at Donna's questioning techniques on page 100 to review the ideas she generated about how to bake an apple pie. In light of Donna's readers and purpose, what does she need to do now to achieve a clearer focus about her work? Why?

Focusing: Formulating a Working Statement

You have learned that after you generate some of your content it is helpful to focus that content by reconsidering it in light of your reader and your purpose. It's also helpful to focus your ideas about that content by formulating a *working statement*. This working statement is a sentence that guides your efforts as you begin your actual writing.

Think of your working statement as a kind of polestar, like the North Star. You have probably heard stories about the way the North Star was used in the days of the Underground Railroad. When slaves, determined to head to freedom in the North, tried to escape from their masters, they began on a journey through territory that was largely unknown to them, sleeping by day and traveling by night under the cover of darkness. They knew that if they got lost—as they invariably did—they could look for the North Star in the sky and follow its lead. To do so guaranteed that they'd be heading in the right direction, heading North.

A working statement for a writing task works that way, too. You can use a working statement as a guiding light or focus for your journey through the writing process. As you begin to falter or lose your way in a piece of writing—as you undoubtedly will—you can return to your working statement again and again. It will help you find your path. It will help you focus your efforts in the right direction again.

Working statements are sentences that provide the guiding focus for your writing efforts, whether your writing efforts involve something as short as a paragraph, or something longer such as an essay or research paper. The key thing to remember about them, however, is that at this stage of the writing process they operate not as final, definitive statements but as tentative, flexible statements. They are something similar to a scientist's working hypothesis which serves to guide the research efforts but which can be revised or changed as new information appears. Similarly, a writer's working statement guides the writing efforts, but it can be changed or even discarded as the writing evolves.

Working statements are easy to characterize. They have four distinctive characteristics.

1. Working statements are sentences.
2. Working statements are not too broad.
3. Working statements make a point.
4. The point serves as the guiding focus for the writing.

Sean, the student who is writing the descriptive piece about the apple for his biology teacher, is now attempting to shape his content into a working statement. But Sean understands that the key word is *working*. He knows he can change or modify his working statement as his paper evolves. For now, however, he needs to have a working statement to guide him as he begins to write. He tries out several potential working statements, statements in sentence form of the point he will be trying to make in his paragraph. Here are several of the sentences Sean writes as he attempts to formulate his working statement.

The ins and outs of apples.

An apple is easily observed.

An apple a day may keep the doctor away, but an apple invites a scientist to observe.

The apple before me on the table is fascinating on the outside and on the inside.

The apple before me on the table can be described from the outside in.

Sean decides, finally, that the sentence on line 7 will serve as the most appropriate working statement for his paragraph.

Talking About It #54

With your classmates, discuss why you think each potential working statement was ultimately rejected by Sean. Refer to the characteristics of working statements previously listed to help you support your ideas. Finally, discuss why Sean thought the last sentence would serve as the best working statement.

Talking About It #55

Turn to the work of Jose, the student writing about the problems of growing apples. As a group, attempt to write several working statements that might serve to guide his writing efforts. Refer to Jose's reader profile and purpose statement as well as to the characteristics of working statements previously listed to help you. As you write down potential working statements, discuss what is strong and what is weak in each of them. Then pick your best working statement to share with the class.

Margaret and Donna, unlike Sean and Jose, are each writing longer papers. Margaret's essay about the apple as a literary symbol and Donna's process description will probably be at least several paragraphs in length. Both are currently struggling to write a working statement that will serve as a guiding focus for their writing efforts. They are attempting to write a sentence which explains their point, a point which they will try to explain and develop through several paragraphs in their essays. Following you can see Margaret trying out several potential working statements.

The symbolic apple.

Many stories in literature contain apples.

Apples are symbols in literature.

The apple is a symbol in Norse, Irish, and Biblical literature.

Apples are often discovered to be symbols of immortality.

In the Biblical story of Adam and Eve, the Norse myth of Idunn, and the Irish tale of "The Princess and the Garden of Eden," the apple is used as a symbol of immortality.

Margaret decides, finally, that the sentence on lines 6 to 8 will serve as the most appropriate working statement for her essay.

Talking About It #56

With your classmates, discuss why you think each of the potential working statements mentioned was ultimately rejected by Margaret. Refer to the characteristics of working statements to help you. Then discuss why you think Margaret thought the last sentence would serve as the best working statement.

Writing About It #57

Like Margaret, Donna—the student writing about how to make an apple pie—also is writing an essay. With your group, attempt to write several working statements that might serve to guide her writing efforts. Refer to Donna's reader profile and purpose statement as well as to the characteristics of working statements previously listed. As you write your working statements down, discuss what is strong and what is weak in each of them. Then pick your best working statement to share with the class.

STRATEGIES AND ORGANIZATION

You will remember that strategies are plans for effective writing and that strategies need to be developed in three areas: (1) content, (2) organization, and (3) expression. You've learned that strategies about content are developed through generating ideas and focusing them. Now it's time to learn about the ways you can develop strategies for organizing your work.

Organization lends structure to things. Batter is formless until you pour it into a cake pan, a loaf pan, or a muffin tin to give it shape. A beautiful piece of silk is only a bolt of cloth until it is stitched into a scarf, a jacket, or a blouse. A semester at college is only a formless period of time until a student begins to structure that time, blocking in classes, study sessions, and extracurricular activities. A piece of clay is a heavy wet slab on a potter's wheel until the potter shapes and forms it under his fingers. Similarly, organization is what lends structure to the content a writer has begun to develop. Until that content is organized in some meaningful way, pounded and shaped to meet the reader's needs and the writer's purposes, content—like the batter, the silk cloth, the unstructured time, or the unshaped clay—remains formless, of little use to anyone.

There are, of course, many different types of writing you are already familiar with: letters, memos, paragraphs, essays, articles, journal entries, and so forth. There are also many types of writing which you may grow more familiar with as you continue your education: abstracts, memos, summaries, editorials, proposals, research papers, and others. Often, different types of writing offer clues about organization. For instance, most people are familiar with the organizing principles for a business letter: the salutation, the body, and the closing. They are familiar, too, with the general organizing principles of an essay: introduction, body, and conclusion.

However, although general guidelines about organizational form do exist, each writing situation is unique. It suggests a unique set of readers, a distinctive purpose, a specific content, and a special style or expression, and each writing situation requires a unique organizational structure as well. When a contractor builds a house, for instance, general ideas about how houses are constructed are kept in mind. But the challenge is to bring that general structural plan to life for a specific homeowner who likely has his or her own individual needs and preferences. The same kind of challenge exists for people attempting to organize what they write. They may possess a few underlying ideas about how to organize an essay, for instance, but what they're really struggling to do each time they face a new writing situation is to figure out an organizational plan to meet the needs for this unique and particular set of ideas.

Figuring out an organizational plan for the content you've begun to develop is critical. Such plans give you a structure that can guide you as you write. They can also be adapted to new ideas or approaches that occur to you as you immerse yourself in your draft. Furthermore, they are useful when you revise, for you can use plans to check what you've written against what you intended to write, and you can restructure your drafts in response to that information.

ORGANIZATIONAL PLANS

Plans for organizing a piece of writing are usually one of three types: collections, chronologies, or connections.

A *collection* plan uses facts, examples, reasons, descriptions, and other material developed by the writer to support a working statement. The success of these plans often depends on the writer's ability to provide the reader with satisfying, convincing detail. A collection plan could be diagrammed as illustrated in Figure 4.4.

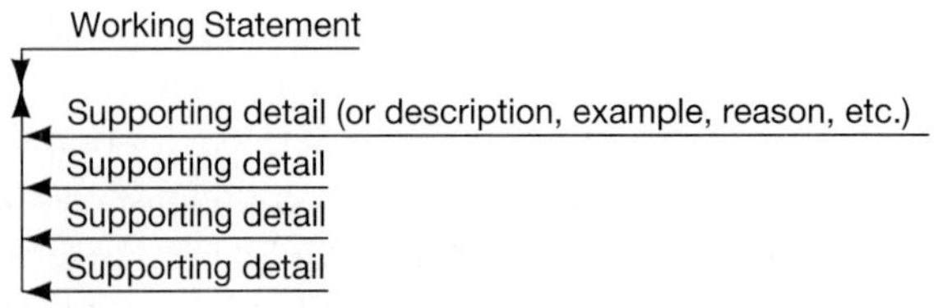

Figure 4.4

A second common plan, a *chronology*, structures content by presenting events as they occur through time in order to support a working statement. Often the success of this type of plan depends on the writer's ability to arrange the sequence of events in an effective order. A diagram of a chronology plan might look something like Figure 4.5.

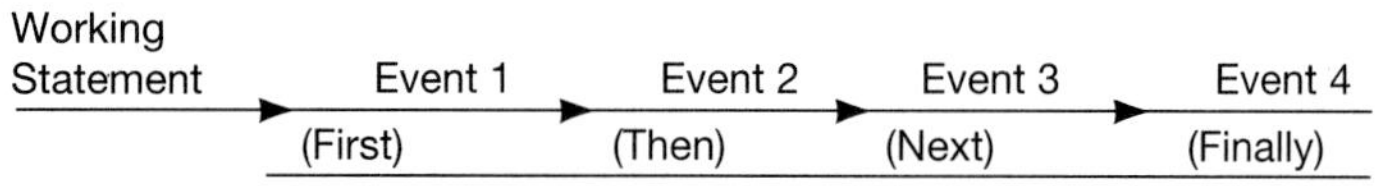

Figure 4.5

The third common plan, the *connection* plan, supports a working statement by explaining the relationships among ideas. Such plans deal with relationships by comparing and contrasting ideas or by suggesting solutions to problems or by examining causes and their effects or by raising questions and providing answers. The connection plan could be diagrammed as in Figure 4.6.

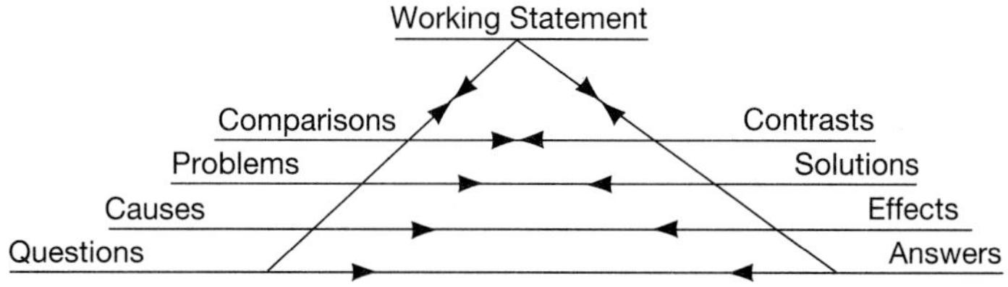

Figure 4.6

An interesting way of developing your understanding of writing plans is to look at advertisements in newspapers and magazines. These advertisements also make use of the organizational plans called collections, chronologies, and connections to persuade their readers to buy their products. In the advertisements which appear in the following pages, (Exhibits 4.1 through 4.5), can you tell which ones appeal to their readers with collections of reasons or descriptions or examples? Can you tell which ones appeal to their readers through chronology? Can you tell which ones appeal to their readers by making connections through developing relationships?

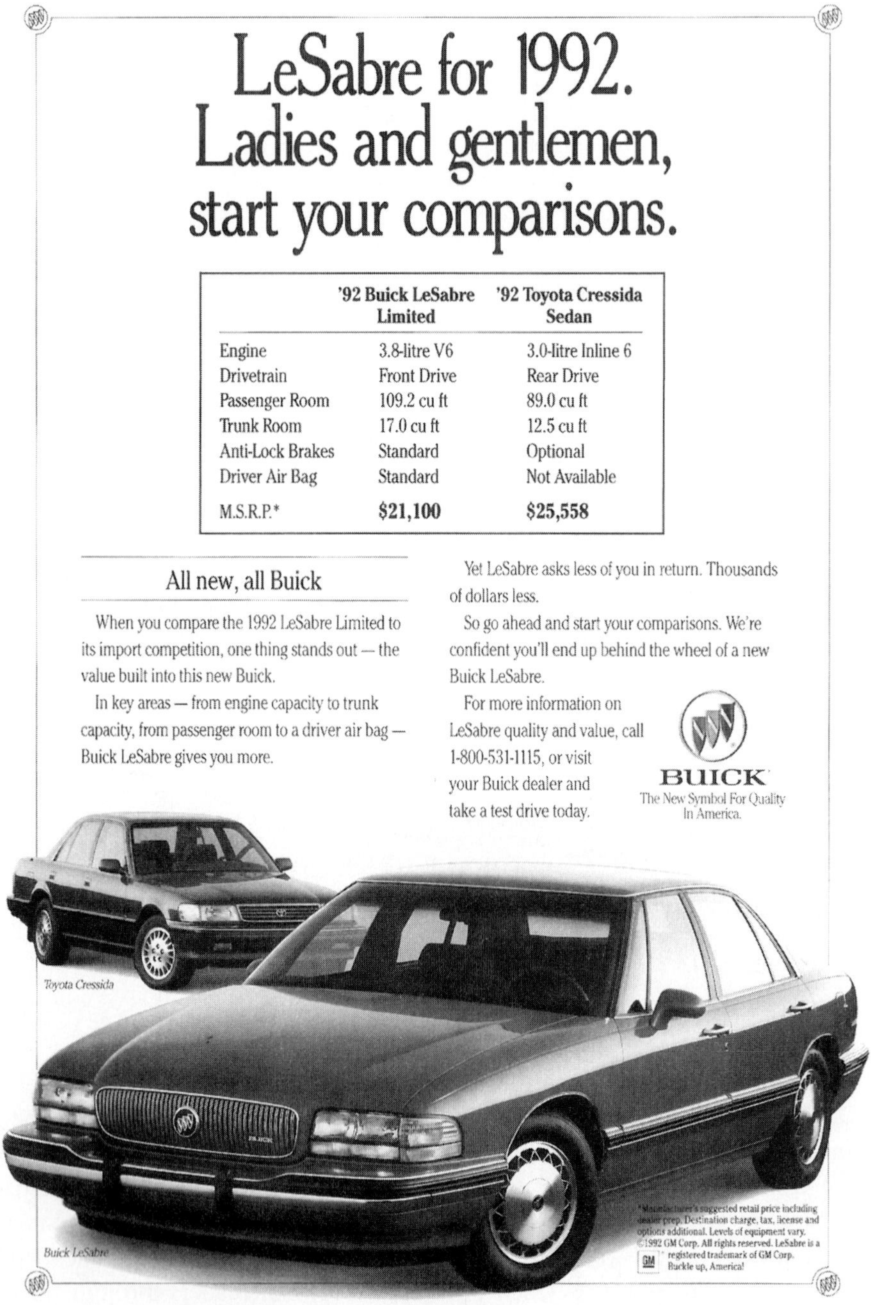
LeSabre for 1992.
Ladies and gentlemen,
start your comparisons.
'92 Buick LeSabre Limited
'92 Toyota Cressida Sedan
Engine 3.8-litre V6 3.0-litre Inline 6
Drivetrain Front Drive Rear Drive
Passenger Room 109.2 cu ft 89.0 cu ft
Trunk Room 17.0 cu ft 12.5 cu ft
Anti-Lock Brakes Standard Optional
Driver Air Bag Standard Not Available
M.S.R.P.* $21,100 $25,558
All new, all Buick
When you compare the 1992 LeSabre Limited to its import competition, one thing stands out — the value built into this new Buick.
In key areas — from engine capacity to trunk capacity, from passenger room to a driver air bag — Buick LeSabre gives you more.
Yet LeSabre asks less of you in return. Thousands of dollars less.
So go ahead and start your comparisons. We're confident you'll end up behind the wheel of a new Buick LeSabre.
For more information on LeSabre quality and value, call 1-800-531-1115, or visit your Buick dealer and take a test drive today.
BUICK
The New Symbol For Quality In America.
Toyota Cressida
Buick LeSabre
suggested retail price including
prep. Destination charge, tax, license and
options additional. Levels of equipment vary.
1992 GM Corp. All rights reserved. LeSabre is a
GM
registered trademark of GM Corp.
Buckle up, America!

Exhibit 4.1

Nouvelle Avocado Half Shell
California Avocado Chicken Salad
California Avocado Club Sandwich
Super.
Something phenomenal happens when a California Avocado lands on your favorite dish. Seafood takes on a delicious new dimension. Barbecued chicken is elevated to greater heights. And pasta gains a spirit all its own. ¶ But its powers don't stop there.
¶ The California Avocado is also a great addition to a tuna salad or turkey sandwich. And sliced into a BLT, it's out of this world. ¶ Inspire your next culinary creation with a California Avocado. Its only limit is your own imagination.
Natural.
California
AVOCADOS
Ripe With Possibilities.

Exhibit 4.2

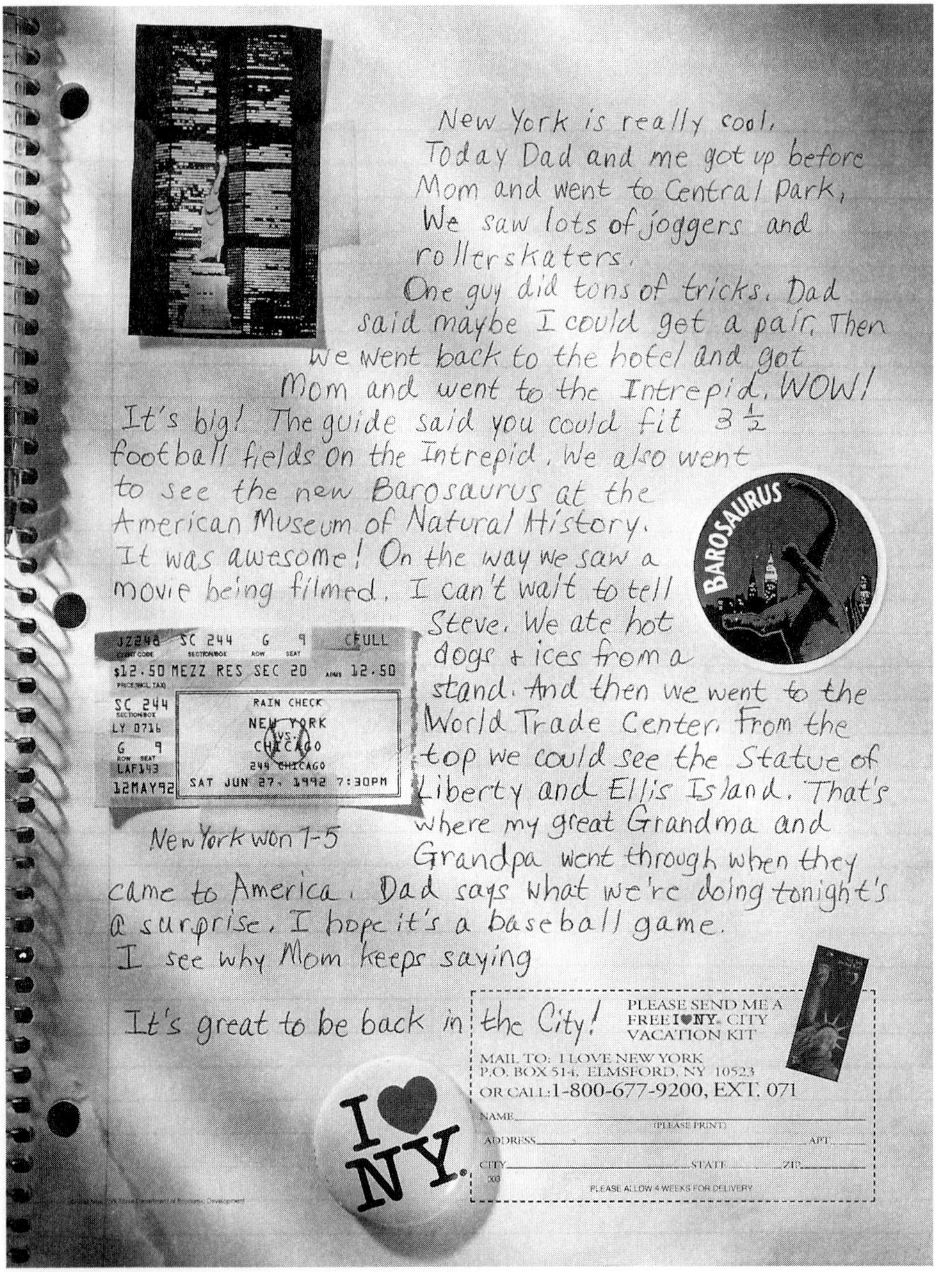
New York is really cool.
Today Dad and me got up before Mom and went to Central Park.
We saw lots of joggers and rollerskaters.
One guy did tons of tricks. Dad said maybe I could get a pair. Then we went back to the hotel and got Mom and went to the Intrepid. WOW!
It's big! The guide said you could fit 3 1/2 football fields on the Intrepid. We also went to see the new Barosaurus at the American Museum of Natural History.
It was awesome! On the way we saw a movie being filmed. I can't wait to tell Steve. We ate hot dogs + ices from a stand. And then we went to the World Trade Center. From the top we could see the Statue of Liberty and Ellis Island. That's where my great Grandma and Grandpa went through when they came to America. Dad says what we're doing tonight's a surprise. I hope it's a baseball game.
I see why Mom keeps saying
It's great to be back in the City!
BAROSAURUS
JZ248 SC 244 G 9 FULL
$12.50 MEZZ RES SEC 20 12.50
SC 244
LY 0716
G 9
LAF143
12MAY92
RAIN CHECK
NEW YORK VS. CHICAGO
244 CHICAGO
SAT JUN 27, 1992 7:30PM
New York won 7-5
PLEASE SEND ME A FREE I ♥ NY CITY VACATION KIT
MAIL TO: I LOVE NEW YORK P.O. BOX 514, ELMSFORD, NY 10523
OR CALL: 1-800-677-9200, EXT. 071
NAME (PLEASE PRINT)
ADDRESS APT.
CITY STATE ZIP
PLEASE ALLOW 4 WEEKS FOR DELIVERY
I ♥ NY

Exhibit 4.3

extra
extra
extra
care
NEW!
condition
BY CLAIROL®
3-in-1
Shampoo Plus
NEW!
·Shampoo
·Conditioner
·Protectant
In One!
condition 3-in-1
Shampoo Plus!
CLEANS Advanced balanced cleansing system.
CONDITIONS 99% oil-free, moisturizing conditioners.
PROTECTS Exclusive paba-free sunscreen formula.
We take extra care of your hair
CLAIROL®

Exhibit 4.4

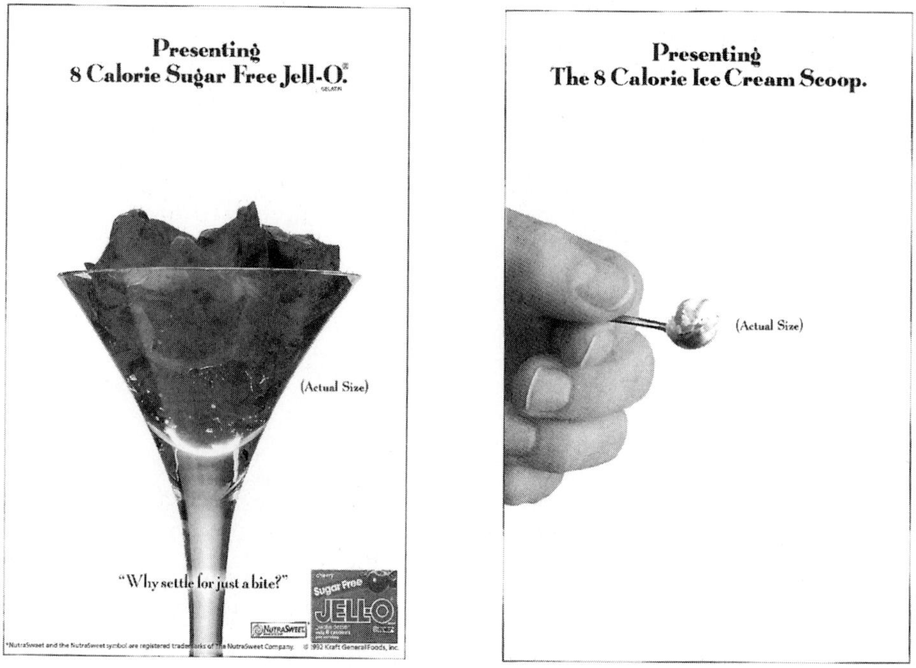

Exhibit 4.5

Let's turn to the students we've just studied—Sean, Jose, Margaret, and Donna—and watch the way they make use of plans as part of their organizing strategies. Look carefully at their working statements and organizational plans, Figures 4.7 through 4.10. Then in the space provided, label the plan as either a collection, a chronology, or a connection.

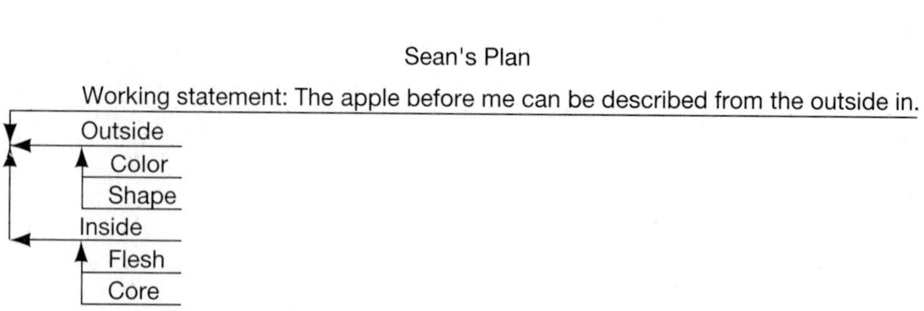

Figure 4.7

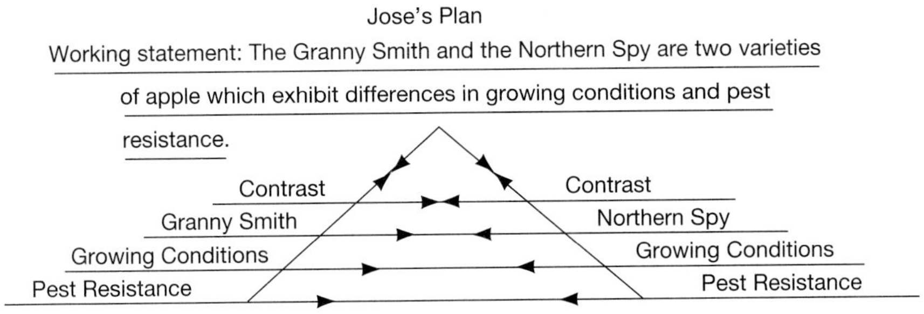

Jose's Plan
Working statement: The Granny Smith and the Northern Spy are two varieties of apple which exhibit differences in growing conditions and pest resistance.

Type of Plan ______________________

Figure 4.8

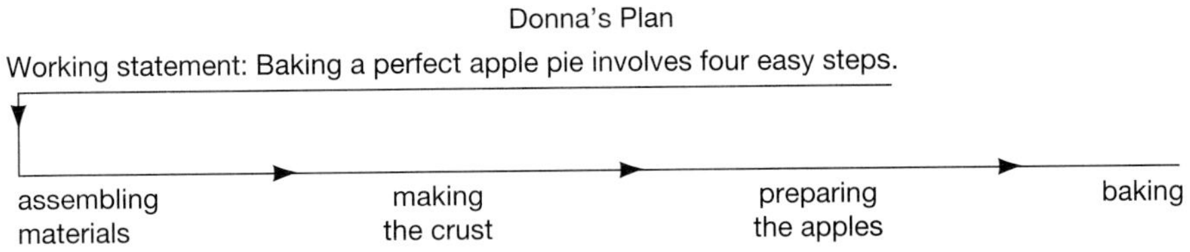

Donna's Plan

assembling materials

preparing the apples

Type of Plan ______________________

Figure 4.9

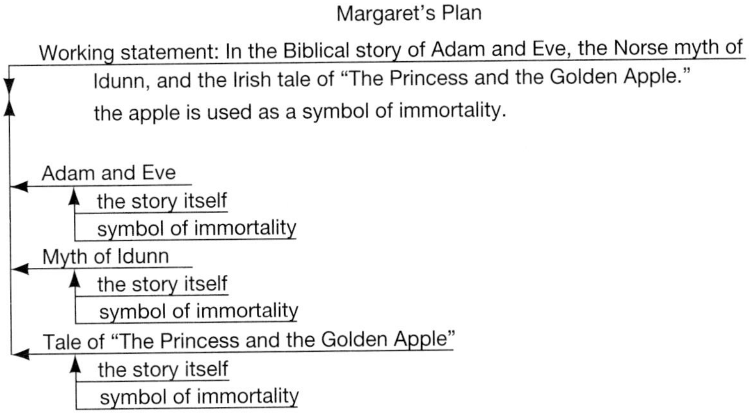

Margaret's Plan
Working statement: In the Biblical story of Adam and Eve, the Norse myth of Idunn, and the Irish tale of "The Princess and the Golden Apple." the apple is used as a symbol of immortality.
Adam and Eve
the story itself
symbol of immortality
Myth of Idunn
the story itself
symbol of immortality
Tale of "The Princess and the Golden Apple"
the story itself
symbol of immortality

Type of Plan ______________________

Figure 4.10

STRATEGIES AND LANGUAGE

As you'll recall from earlier chapters, each writing situation involves four elements: the reader, the writer, the work, and the language. You've looked thus far at the needs of the reader, the purposes of the writer, and the content and organization of the work. Now it's time to turn your attention to the last element in the writing situation: the language.

Take a moment to read back the following sentences, sentences you have already read in this text.

1. I speak French, but Frenchmen always pretend they don't understand what I'm saying.

2. Harold was standing shivering on the wet tile edge, suspended above the abysmal odor of chlorine.

3. Customers 65 or over may voluntarily designate a third party of their own selection to whom notification of past due bills will be sent.

4. Are your T-shirts coated with motor oil? Is the thought of improving the exhaust system on your car more appealing than the thought of a movie and dinner with your friends? Would you like to learn the latest techniques on how to modify your car?

5. The personal ad is like a haiku of self-celebration, a brief solo played on one's own horn.

6. Within this time frame, take action to prepare the heating environment for thoroughput by manually setting the oven baking unit by hand to temperature of 375 degrees Fahrenheit (190 Celsius).

7. If you are writing without zest, without gusto, without love, without fun, you are only half a writer.

8. Wild turkeys originally thrived on all of forested Ohio. By 1880, however, they had been reduced to a remnant and, according to the records, the last wild turkey in Ohio was killed in Adams County in 1904.

If you have read carefully, you probably detected differences among these different passages, differences in the way they "sounded," differences in the way the authors presented themselves in writing. One author may have sounded "funny," another "pompous," a third "poetic" or "friendly" or "matter-of-fact." Part of the strategic planning process for any piece of writing involves preliminary thinking about how you want to "sound" in the text. Prewriting, as you have seen, involves planning strategies about content and strategies about organization. It also involves strategies about *expression*—the style in which you'll express yourself. Each text is different because each text involves a unique presentation of content and organization. But each text is also different because it involves a unique use of language as well.

Writing About It #58

In your journal, characterize each of the eight passages in a one-word description. Then explain why you gave each passage the one-word description that you did. Share your descriptions with other members of the class.

In your journal, write the dictionary definition for the word "ambience," sometimes spelled "ambiance." Then list several restaurants or places to eat with which you are familiar. In one word, characterize the "ambience" of each. Share your one-word descriptions with your classmates, explaining why you characterized the ambience this way.

In your journal, write the first dictionary definition of the word "mood." Then list several pieces of music with which you are familiar. In one word, characterize the "mood" of each of these pieces of music. Share your one-word descriptions with your classmates, explaining why you characterized the mood this way.

In your journal, write the nonscientific definition for the word "atmosphere." Then list several movies with which you are familiar. In one word, characterize the "atmosphere" of each of these movies. Share your one-word descriptions with your classmates, explaining why you characterized the atmosphere this way.

Write a paragraph in which you offer some ideas about how a writer establishes an "ambience" or "atmosphere" or "mood" in a piece of writing. Choose a classmate to act as a recorder and list those ideas on the board. Compare and contrast your ideas in a class discussion.

Expression and the Language Community

One of the reasons why different pieces of writing "sound" different is that different pieces of writing are written for different language communities. A citizen may write a letter to the editor of her local newspaper, using language for the general newspaper reading public. A nuclear physicist may submit an article to a professional journal, writing for the specialized needs of other nuclear physicists. In fact, every piece of writing is designed to meet the needs of a language community, either a general or a specific readership.

In addition, every language community shares certain goals and values, translating those values into practices about writing. The scientific community, for example, values objectivity and impartiality, translating those values into writing practices that urge writers to write from the third person point of view, avoiding the pronoun "I." The arts and humanities community, on the other hand, values personal insight and creative expression. These values translate into writing practices that urge writers to embrace subjectivity and poetic language. Thus, the language community, whether general or specific, holds certain values about writing, and those values determine the kinds of choices about language which you as a writer will make.

You are now familiar with the process of planning strategies for the content and the organization of your writing. You can also begin to plan strategies for the language you will use by thinking about the answers to the following questions:

What language community will the writer and reader be members of for the purposes of this piece of writing? Is it a general language community? A specific language community? How do you know?

What are the goals and values of this language community? How will those goals and values be reflected in your writing?

What language choices or expressions will make the work more successful? Choices about tone? Choices about sentences? Choices about words? Other language choices?

Talking About It #59

Choose someone to be the recorder for your small group. As your group discusses the following questions about the writing assignments of Sean, Margaret, Jose, and Donna, ask the recorder to write down your answers. Then share your answers with the class.

1. *Sean's paper*
   What language community do Sean and his reader share? Is it a general language community? A specific language community? What are the goals and values of this language community? How will these goals and values affect Sean's choices about language?
2. *Margaret's paper*
   What language community do Margaret and her reader share? Is it a general language community? A specific language community? What are the goals and values of this language community? How will these goals and values affect Margaret's choices about language?
3. *Jose's paper*
   What language community do Jose and his reader share? Is it a general language community? A specific language community? What are the goals and values of this language community? How will these goals and values affect Jose's choices about language?
4. *Donna's paper*
   What language community do Donna and her reader share? Is it a general language community? A specific language community? What are the goals and values of this language community? How will these goals and values affect Donna's choices about language?

Expression and Tone

Once you have determined the language community to which your writing belongs and the values that community holds, you can begin to make choices about how you will express yourself in language. Those choices will help give your writing its "tone," that unique "sound" that characterizes your style or manner of writing and which comes across as "concerned," "poetic," "cautious," "passionate," or any number of other adjectives. Tone refers to the *ambience*, the *atmosphere*, or *mood* of a piece of writing. Tone is a reflection of several things: (1) the reader's needs and the writer's purposes, (2) the writer's attitudes toward subject and reader, (3) the writer's distance from the reader, and (4) the writer's diction.

The Reader's Needs/The Writer's Purposes

Readers come to a piece of writing with various expectations. Readers have needs. They may need to be informed. They may need to be entertained. They may need to be persuaded about a certain idea or belief. But readers don't approach a piece of writing as a blank slate on which the writer scribbles a message. Readers approach writing with their own attitudes, attitudes about the writer, the work, or the language community which reader and writer share.

Writers approach a piece of writing with their own purposes and goals, too. They define those goals and purposes and then develop strategies for meeting them. Writers, like readers, don't approach a piece of writing with an empty head. Like readers, they too hold attitudes about the reader, the work, and the language community which they share.

For instance, let's say that you're the editor of a monthly newsletter called *Survivor*. The newsletter resulted from the concerns of three cancer survivors who became friends through a support group in their local area. As they met and talked, the three friends perceived a need for a means of communicating with other cancer survivors about issues such as understanding the long-term effects of treatment, maintaining a positive attitude, obtaining affordable and appropriate health-care coverage, and keeping informed about the latest research. Out of these concerns, the newsletter *Survivor* was born. Current subscribers number in the thousands.

Talking About It #60

With your classmates, discuss issues relating to *Survivor* magazine by using the following questions to help you.

1. What needs and expectations would readers of *Survivor* be likely to have?
2. What attitudes would readers be likely to share?
3. In light of the needs/expectations of readers and their attitudes, what tone would the editor of the newsletter want to project? How would the newsletter manage to project that tone?
4. What purposes and goals would the writer of a *Survivor* newsletter article be likely to have?
5. What attitudes would the writer be likely to hold?
6. In light of the purposes/goals of the writer, what tone would the writer want to project? How would the writer manage to project that tone?
7. Are the concerns of the readers of *Survivor* newsletter likely to be the same as the concerns of the writers of articles for the newsletter? Why or why not? What would happen to *Survivor* newsletter if the concerns of the readers were not the same as the concerns of the writers or vice versa?

Think back to Sean, the student who was writing the description of the apple. What were his reader's needs and expectations? What were Sean's own purposes and goals? Are they closely related? Explain. How successful would Sean's description be if his concerns and his reader's concerns were not the same? Explain.

The Writer's Attitudes toward Subject and Reader

Writers hold various attitudes about their subjects and their readers, and these attitudes are also reflected in the *tone* of their writing.

For instance, a writer sending the state senator a letter supporting a ban on the chemical Alar, a chemical used to treat apple crops, may adopt a tone of reasonableness, urgency, or outrage, depending on his or her attitude toward the subject. If this writer has been informed about the dangers of the chemical through his or her work, by reading or studying about it, a tone a reasonableness may be adopted in his or her letter as the reasons in favor of a ban are outlined. If this writer has recently heard alarming television news reports that the heat process used to make apple juice or sauce from apples sprayed with Alar produces a chemical even more carcinogenic than Alar itself and that young children, major consumers of these apple products, are greatly at risk, the writer may adopt a tone of urgency in his or her letter. If this writer is the father of a child recently diagnosed with cancer who suspects that living beside orchards which are regularly sprayed with Alar may have caused his child's disease, the tone of his letter may be one of outrage.

Similarly, a writer's attitude toward his or her reader—like his or her attitude toward the subject—can affect the tone of the work. If the letter writer in the example mentioned believes his or her reader—the state senator—can generally be counted on to respond favorably to environmental issues, the tone will likely reflect that positive attitude. On the other hand, if the senator has a record of opposing nearly all environmental causes, the writer may adopt a tone that is greatly different. Thus, the writer's attitude toward the reader will greatly affect the tone of his or her work.

The Writer's Distance from the Reader

People interact at different distances from one another. A convocation speaker often talks from behind a podium, at a distance from the graduates listening to him or her in the auditorium. Lovers, on the other hand, speak to their beloveds up close, comfortable with whispering messages in their ears. Both situations are examples of the distances that may exist between people when they communicate.

When people write, they choose a certain distance from their readers, too. Such distances are often referred to as *point of view*. Writers need to consider point of view as part of their tone and overall writing strategy during the prewriting stage of the writing process.

A more distant point of view is represented when a writer chooses to write in the third person, making use of the pronouns "he," "she," "it," "one," "they," or "them." The third person point of view is considered more objective and formal than other points of view as in the sentence which follows:

> Writers must try to consider their readers when they compose their texts.

The second person point of view is represented by the pronoun "you." Second person point of view operates at a much closer distance to the reader than the third person point of view. The second person point of view is more intimate, more familiar, more "user friendly" as in this sentence.

> You need to consider your reader when you write.

Sometimes, especially when the writer is giving directions or commands to the reader, the second person subject pronoun is omitted. In such cases, the sentence is still said to be in second person.

> Consider your reader when you write.

The first person point of view makes use of the pronoun "I." It is more personal and subjective than either of the other points of view. First person point of view does not hold the reader at a distance; it creates intimacy with the reader, bringing the reader up close to the writer. The following sentence makes use of the first person "I" point of view.

> I always try to think about my reader when I write.

The following chart will help you remember the various points of view available when you write, the signal words that characterize them, and the degree of formality and level of intimacy which they represent.

Point of View	*Signal Words*	*Degree of Formality*	*Level of Intimacy*
First	I, we, my, mine us, our	subjective	intimate personal
Second	you	informal	friendly
Third	he, she, it, they, them his, him, her, its their	objective, formal	distant

It's important to remember that there is no "right" or "wrong" point of view, but it's also important to remember that choice of point of view greatly affects the tone of a piece of writing.

Talking About It #61

Think back to the work of Sean, Margaret, Jose, and Donna whose work you came to know in the earlier parts of this chapter. Given their purposes and their readers, what point of view should each of them adopt in their papers? Why do you think so?

The Writer's Diction

Diction refers to the words a writer chooses. As you write, you are constantly choosing words. You decide whether a character "walks," "ambles," or "stumbles." You decide whether an idea is "important," "pressing," or "critical." You decide whether an event was "pleasant," "memorable," or "record-breaking." You decide whether something "can't" or "cannot" be expressed in a certain way. You make choices about words—your diction—all the time.

Diction is related to words in the same way that style is related to dress. For instance, you may decide to wear black tie and tails in attending a formal event. Or you may dress in a coat and tie, adopting a more informal style for a business meeting or professional conference. Or you may put on shorts and sandals, adopting a casual manner for a party with friends. Diction works in this way, too. You may choose words that are (1) formal, (2) informal, or (3) casual.

Formal diction is recognized by its formal tone and elevated style. Laws, treaties, ceremonies, and formal speeches make use of formal diction. Formal diction never makes use of slang terms and is scrupulously grammatical. Informal diction is adopted in business, academic, and professional settings in which people choose their words carefully and take care with their grammar. Most writing usually makes use of informal diction. Casual diction is adopted with friends, family, and intimates in situations where slang words and ungrammatical expressions are readily accepted. Whether you decide to use formal, informal, or casual diction, the important thing to remember is that you choose words like dress, based on their appropriateness for the occasion.

The passage that follows is an example of informal diction. Read it carefully, paying close attention to the writer's choice of words.

Earth Covenant
A Citizen's Treaty for Common Ecological Security

Principles and Commitments

In covenant with each other and on behalf of the whole Earth community, we commit ourselves to the following principles and actions:

Relationship with the Earth: All life forms are sacred. Each human being is a unique and integral part of the Earth's community of life and has a special responsibility to care for life in all its diverse forms. Therefore, we will act and live in a way that preserves the natural life processes of the Earth and respects all species and their habitats. We will work to prevent ecological degradation.

Relationship with Each Other: Each human being has the right to a healthful environment and to access to the fruits of the Earth. Each also has a continual duty to work for the realization of these rights for present and future generations.

Therefore, concerned that every person has food, shelter, pure air, potable water, education, employment, and all that is necessary to enjoy the full measure of human rights—we will work for more equitable access to the Earth's resources.

Relationship Between Economic and Ecological Security: Since human life is rooted in the natural processes of the Earth, economic development, to be sustainable, must preserve the life-support systems of the Earth.

Therefore, we will use environmentally protective technologies and promote their availability to people in all parts of the Earth. When doubtful about the consequences of economic goals and technologies on the environment, we will allow an extra margin of protection for nature.

Governance and Ecological Security: The protection and enhancement of life on Earth demand adequate legislative, administrative, and judicial systems at appropriate local, national, regional, and international levels. In order to be effective, these systems must be empowering, participatory, and based on openness of information.

Therefore, we will work for the enactment of laws that protect the environment and promote their observance through educational, political, and legal action. We shall advance policies of prevention rather than only reacting to ecological harm.

Declaring our partnership with one another and with our Earth, we give our word of honor to be faithful to the above commitments.

Sincerely,

(Signature)

Talking About It #62

After you have read the passage, imagine that you are a student teacher in an elementary school teaching a science unit on the environment. You want to raise your students' awareness of the importance of protecting the environment. Therefore, as part of this teaching unit, you want your students to read and understand this Earth Covenant. However, you realize you will have to change much of the diction so that your elementary children can understand the words, and you begin to make these changes by going back through the text and circling any words or phrases that might cause confusion or misunderstanding. With your classmates, suggest which words or phrases might need to be changed and what words or phrases might be suitable substitutes for them in order to achieve informal diction appropriate to elementary school children.

Think back to Donna, the student who was writing the how-to process description on how to bake an apple pie. Given her purpose and her audience, why will diction be a special concern in Donna's paper?

STRATEGIES ABOUT EXPRESSION/LANGUAGE

As you have seen, strategies about language or expression make up part of your prewriting planning process just the same as strategies about content or organization. As they begin to think about drafting, many students find it helpful to write a one-word description of their tone, informally articulating the atmosphere they wish their writing to achieve as they begin to write their first draft. They may also find that they need to answer questions about language, defining their language community, their tone, their point of view, and their diction before they begin to write. Whatever their approach, they know they must start to think about how they will use language as they turn their attention to their first draft.

As Sean begins to plan his strategy for using language in his description of the apple, he makes these notes to himself.

Strategies about expression/language

Language Community: *scientific community*

Tone: *scientific objective*

Point of view: *third person*

Diction: *informal diction; use precise words to suggest scientific precision*

Think about the other students whose prewriting you have followed. Would their strategies about language and expression be the same as Sean's? Why or why not? In what way would they differ?

Talking About It #63

The following passage will help you think about the language strategies involved in a piece of writing. The passage represents a California law which attempts to deter government employees from engaging in corruption. After you read the passage, try to answer the questions which appear below it with your classmates. The law reads as follows:

> No one who holds, or who is seeking election or appointment to, any office or employment in a state or local agency shall, directly or indirectly, use, promise, threaten or attempt to use, any office, authority, or influence, whether then possessed or merely anticipated, to confer upon or secure for any individual person, or to aid or obstruct any individual person in securing, or to prevent any individual person from securing, any position, nomination, confirmation, promotion, or change in compensation or position, within the state or local agency, upon consideration or condition that the vote or political influence or action of such person or another shall be given or used in behalf of, or withheld from, any candidate, officer, or party, or upon any other corrupt condition or consideration. This prohibition shall apply to urging or discouraging the individual employee's action.

Try to suggest a one-word description of the tone of this passage. Then discuss the elements of tone reflected in this passage by answering the following questions: (1) What do you think are the reader's needs and the writer's purpose? Why? (2) What do you think is the writer's attitude toward the reader? Why? Toward the subject? Why? (3) What is the writer's point of view? Why was this point of view chosen? (4) Is the writer's diction formal, informal, or casual? How do you know?

In the following passage, the California law has been rewritten. Read it carefully and then answer the questions which follow.

Important Notice—Jobs and Politics

If You

• Have a job	) in a
• Want a job	) state or local
• Hold office	) agency
• Want to hold office	)

READ THIS:

It is against the law to use your influence over a job or an office

1. To buy votes or other political action. or to try to.
2. To make any other corrupt deal. or to try to.

Now try to suggest a one-word description of the tone of this rewritten passage. Then discuss the elements of tone reflected in this passage by answering the following questions: (1) What do you think are the reader's needs and the writer's purpose? Why? (2) What do you think is the writer's attitude toward the reader? Why? Toward the subject? Why? (3) What is the writer's point of view? Why was this point of view chosen? (4) Is the writer's diction formal, informal, or casual? How do you know?

Compare the first passage and the rewritten passage in order to answer the following questions. (1) What elements of tone were changed when the first passage was rewritten? How do you know? Point to evidence from the rewritten passage to support your answer. (2) Why do you think the writer made these changes? Do you think these reasons are valid ones? (3) Which passage do you prefer? Why? (4) As a citizen of California, which passage would be more likely to keep you from engaging in political corruption? Why?

DRAFTING

As you have seen, an important part of the writing process is called prewriting. If you've followed carefully along in this text and made an earnest effort to understand prewriting, you have grasped the many steps that prepare you for writing. Like Sean, Margaret, Jose, and Donna, you are probably ready to write a preliminary draft of your paper. If you'll look back at all you and they have done and learned, you will notice that you have accomplished quite a bit during your prewriting efforts. At this point, you and the students you've been following have come to understand the connections among the reader, the writer, the work, and the language, and you have studied all of the following prewriting steps:

Profiling your reader and writing a reader profile,
Understanding your purpose and writing a purpose statement,
Planning your strategy for content by generating ideas and focusing ideas in a working statement,
Planning your strategy for organization,
Planning your strategy for expression in language.

As you move from prewriting to the second major stage in the writing process—Writing or Drafting—a few points will guide you as you begin.

1. *Get comfortable.* Only you can know the conditions that make drafting a paper efficient and effective for you. Some writers need undisturbed quiet. Others need a place where they can spread out all their papers. Still others need a comfortable chair, bed, or desk. Do whatever it takes to get yourself comfortably focused on the job at hand. It will make that job go more quickly and smoothly.

2. *Take heart from the prewriting efforts you have already made.* Preview your notes about reader and purpose. Picture your reader in your mind. Imagine that you, the writer, are engaging in conversation with your reader. Those imaginary efforts will help make your reader "real" to you. Go over your strategies for content, organization, and expression before you begin writing. Remind yourself that you have the most important part—prewriting—behind you and that effective writers spend a large part of their time in this stage of the writing process—just as you have.

3. *Share your prewriting with a fellow classmate or friend.* An impartial observer can, at this point in the writing process, provide you with a fresh eye, offering reactions to your topic, your organization strategies, and other aspects of prewriting. Take advantage of the opportunity that talking over your prewriting offers you.

4. *When you feel yourself getting "lost" as you write—and you invariably will—try returning to your working statement as a way of regaining focus.* If returning to your working statement doesn't help, however, and you feel you're getting hopelessly lost, take 5 or 10 minutes to do some more freewriting, or spend that time rethinking your organizational plan, or your working statement, or your choices about tone and expression.

5. *Keep going.* Develop a system for keeping yourself moving. Offer yourself words of encouragement. Push yourself and then reward yourself with a short break. Try out a method of notation that will keep you from diverting your efforts from your goals by circling things you can come back to later or putting a big question mark over problem areas you can return to at another time.

6. *Understand and respect your own writing processes.* If you feel you're most effective writing the entire preliminary draft at one sitting, do so. If, on the other hand, you're a writer who can only work on one or two sections of your paper at a time, give yourself permission to follow your own instincts. Don't be undermined by watching that fellow down the hall who can crank out a paper in the hour before class or your best friend who can draft a paper in the midst of a crowded dormitory room. Respect yourself and your own writing needs.

7. *Remind yourself frequently that your preliminary draft is tentative.* If it helps you to call the preliminary draft a "working draft" or "discovery draft," or "zero draft," do so. Try to avoid the self-created pressure of writing things perfectly the first time through. Remember that you can—and should—go back over your work many times before it is ready to be handed in.

WRITING ASSIGNMENTS

Choose one or several of the following suggestions to write about in a paper. Make sure that you invest a good deal of time and effort engaging in the prewriting process. Before you begin your draft, write a profile of your reader, a statement of your purpose, and show that you have developed strategic plans in the areas of content, organization, and expression. In the area of content, for instance, be certain to generate your ideas through talking, freewriting, looping, brainstorming, branching, mapping, or questioning. Then reconsider your ideas by refocusing on your reader and purpose and writing a working statement. Choose a preliminary method of organization such as a collection plan, a chronology plan, or a connection plan. Make some early decisions about your language and expression by jotting down ideas about the language community, your tone, the distance between writer and reader you wish to establish, and your diction. For purposes of these writing assignments, you can assume that your reader will be your classroom teacher. When you have finished, share your writing with the other students in your class. Be sure to record their comments on the Writing Assignment Profile which appears in the back of this text.

A. Write a paper in which the purpose is for you to examine your own writing processes. This paper might describe your writing habits or give examples of various types of writing you've done over the years. It might explain how you go about writing a paper, providing the steps in your writing process, or it might compare your writing habits as a child with your writing habits now. You may examine your writing processes from any angle that interests you.

B. Look back over some of the journal entries you wrote when you were learning to generate content. Earlier in this chapter, for example, you generated content by talking, freewriting, looping, brainstorming, branching, mapping, and questioning some ideas. Choose one of these content-generating entries that please you, and then plan the organizational strategy and the language strategy for that same content. After you have planned your strategies, write your draft from those plans.

C. Choose an advertisement from a magazine or newspaper that you find effective. Describe the ad and then explain the ways in which the content, the organization, and the language/expression of the ad work together to make the advertisement effective. Remember to plan your own strategies for content, organization, and expression before you write.

D. Create a product for sale in the marketplace. Think of an appropriate audience for the product, and then create an advertisement for the product. Decide on the appropriate language/expression considerations of the ad, and write a paper explaining your ad to your reader. Your paper should describe the content you chose for your ad, the organizational plan, and the language expressions you will be using. In each case, explain why you made the choices you did.

CHAPTER FOUR REVIEW

Writing About It #64

Use your journal to reflect on what you learned in this chapter.

5

From Speaking to Writing

Why is writing so different from talking? How can learning about those differences make me a better writer?

It is often said that communication takes place in one of four ways: by reading, by writing, by speaking, and by listening. You are now familiar with the way in which reading and writing are interdependent acts, and you also probably understand the way in which speaking and listening depend on each other. But have you ever thought about what the act of speaking and listening can tell you about the act of writing and reading?

In this chapter, you will spend some time learning about the act of speaking and listening in order to understand some important things about writing and reading. In order to do some thinking about the act of speaking and listening, take a minute to listen in on the following conversation between some part-time community college students who have met in the student center during a break between classes.

Joe: Hey, Mary! Have a seat over here.

Mary: Oh, hi, Joe! Good to see you. Sure, be glad to. Could you just watch my stuff for a minute? I've got to make a phone call. Rachel's got an ear infection, and I just want to give the sitter a quick call to see how she's doing. Be right back.

Ben: (comes over) Say, aren't you in the Speech class? Seven to ten tonight?

Joe: Sure. I recognize you. I'm Joe Bellino. (They shake hands.) Mary over there's in the class, too. Want to join us?

Ben: Sounds good. Oh, yeah. I think I recognize her from the speech she gave the other night. Pretty good job, I'd say.

Joe: (nods in agreement) So how're you doing in that class anyway?

Ben: The class is fine. Mrs. Wolfe's a great teacher, and she really knows her stuff. It's kind of a fun class, too. Hearing what everybody has to say and all.

Joe: I like it, too. Only the class is the easy part. The hard part's finding the time for the reading and then preparing the speeches and then wondering how you're ever gonna get free to practice them. I've got a full-time job in Domestic Relations Court.

Ben: Sounds interesting. Whatcha do?

Joe: Bailiff. It's a great job. But it's tough going to school this quarter in addition to 40 hours at work. I'm only taking 6 hours now. Don't have the time—or the money—for much more. But I'm lucky, I guess. My boss sometimes gives me release time when I've got a big exam coming up.

Ben: I know what you mean. I'm at the Packard plant. Just got promoted. I'm doing more administrative-type things now. Never done 'em before. My job takes a lot of time. That plus school. Even so, I manage to squeeze in some study time at lunch or during my break. It's a killer, though, know what I mean?

Joe: (nods) Um-humm. Only too well. Say, want some coffee?

Ben: Sure. Here's a quarter. Just black.

Joe: Thanks.

Mary: (comes over) Whew! (shrugs her shoulders) Thank goodness everything's O.K. The sitter says Rachel's asleep. I was afraid her ear might still be bothering her and I might have to miss class tonight. I'd hate to cut it. I had to miss early in the semester when Anna had the chicken pox. A 3-hour class is just too important to miss. Mrs. Wolfe covers everything pretty fast.

Joe: Glad everything's all right. Mary, this is Ben. He's in our class, too. Sits in the back. I'll be back with some coffee. One cream, Mary, right?

Mary: Right. Thanks, Joe. So, Ben, what do you think of Mrs. Wolfe's class?

Ben: I think it's pretty good. The chapter on listening was the best so far. I found that it's really helping me at work. I've just been promoted. Have to listen to people a lot more now in order to make decisions. The listening stuff Mrs. Wolfe taught us about really helps.

Mary: I liked it, too. Don't have a job just yet, though. My girls are still little. Taking care of them is my full-time job. But I'm hoping this degree will help me get a good paid position once they're in school.

Joe: Here's the coffee. Nothing like machine coffee to keep you awake in class, folks.

Mary: Thanks, Joe. Tastes a little like brewed gasoline, doesn't it?

Ben: (laughs) Sure does. I live on the stuff when I'm up late studying. By the way, Mary, that was a great speech you gave last class.

Mary: (smiles) Thanks, Ben. It was a relief to have it over with. The only time I had to practice was when Rachel was down for a nap.

Ben: I know what you mean. The first speech I gave was practiced at my son's little league baseball game. Between innings I stole a few seconds to look at my notecards. Then slipped 'em in my pocket when Ryan was up to bat.

Joe: (blowing on his coffee) Wow, this stuff's hot! I'll bet I've got you guys beat in the study skills department. Made a tape of my talk. Then played it on the way in and out to work. Tried to talk right along with myself while it played. The other drivers on the beltway kept giving me funny looks. Must've thought I was crazy.

Mary: (laughs) I did get to practice my speech. While the baby was asleep. But I never spoke it louder than a whisper before I gave it in class. Afraid of waking the baby up.

Joe: (gathering up his books and laughing) Let's go, guys. Almost seven.

Now that you're familiar with this conversation among Mary, Ben and Joe, take a look at the following written account produced by Ben. It is a written perspective covering much of the same information in the students' conversation.

Although college students who hold jobs while going to school are challenged by many problems, they also develop solutions for handling these problems well. The first challenge is the demand of work. In addition to serving as an effective employee for a typical 40-hour week, worker–students are often required to attend professional development workshops, put in overtime, and make after-hours meetings related to their jobs. However, these worker–students learn to meet those challenges by becoming effective managers of time, turning breaks into study sessions or lunch hours into reading periods. If they have an understanding boss, they can often finagle release time to study for important exams. The second challenge is the challenge of school. At school, the student–worker faces challenges like reading the textbook, attending and participating in class, studying for tests, writing papers, preparing speeches and presentations, and monitoring the dozens of details that go into being a successful student. However, the demands of a 40-hour work week in addition to the demands of college attendance sometimes cause problems with attending class, meeting deadlines for schoolwork, or even staying awake in class. To meet those demands, college students who hold full-time jobs develop survival strategies like studying in the car on the way to work or practicing for a speech while the baby is taking a nap or learning to drink strong coffee in between classes. Finally, attempting to maintain a quality home life is also difficult when a college student needs to work as well as study. Sometimes family life is neglected in the press for time. More often than not, however, a family member balancing college and work develops innovative ways of coping with this problem. Such students learn to slip in a few minutes of study while attending a little league game or review notes for a test while sitting in the pediatrician's office. Thus, although college students who also hold jobs are usually challenged by many problems, they are resourceful enough to develop successful solutions for them as well.

—Ben Blumenshied

Talking About It #65

With your classmates, compare and contrast characteristics of the spoken dialogue among Ben, Joe, and Mary with the written account produced by Ben.

Refer to the dialogue among Ben, Joe, and Mary and the written account produced by Ben as you and your classmates together attempt to fill in the blanks on the following chart which contrasts speaking/listening with writing/reading.

Differences Between Speaking/Listening and Writing/Reading

can move around	
	results in a product
involves two or more participants	
spontaneous	
	permanent
makes use of gesture, facial expression, and vocal tone to assist the listener	
	dependent on the eye
audience is present	
unplanned	
	writer must supply the context or experience
speakers/listeners can ask for clarification	
	focuses on a text
collaborative	

Writing About It #66

Use the chart to pick out three of the most significant differences between speaking/listening and writing/reading. Then write a short essay explaining the ways in which those three differences are apparent in the spoken dialogue among Ben, Joe, and Mary and in the written account by Ben which previously appears. Use specific examples from the dialogue and written account in explaining your answer. When you have finished, share your short essay with the other students in your class.

It has been said that "writing is merely the habit of talking with the pen instead of the tongue." Do you agree or disagree with this statement? Explain your opinion in a paragraph.

As you have seen, writing and speaking share some similarities. They are both forms of communication so common to us that we often take their importance for granted. They both use the basic rules of English grammar to communicate their messages. They are both used for a variety of purposes as part of daily life. However, as you have also seen, there are important differences between them as well. Perhaps the most important difference is the fact that the reader is not physically present when the writer is writing. The reader, unlike the listener, is unavailable to the writer in that the reader cannot indicate to the writer when he or she is puzzled or bored. The writer cannot ask the reader questions or gesture to the reader or indicate meaning by facial expressions; conversely, the reader cannot question, gesture, or grimace in response. The reader cannot indicate satisfaction or comprehension, and the writer cannot know whether his or her silent partner is satisfied or understood. Because of these and other reasons, writing is governed by special conventions, conventions which you must become familiar with if you are to become a better writer.

A *convention* is a general agreement about the way things are done. In the world of commerce, it is generally agreed that you can only acquire something that you have paid for. In the world of government, it is generally agreed that officials will be elected by a vote of the people. In the world of industry, it is generally agreed that minor children will not be permitted to hold a job until they reach an established age. Thus, a convention is a general agreement about the way things are done in a certain sphere of activity.

Conventions apply to writing as well. A child learning to write his or her first report will struggle to master the conventions for organizing paragraphs. A young person who relies on speaking more than writing for communicating will need to learn the written conventions that satisfy a reader when he or she writes. A foreigner learning English for the first time needs to become acquainted with the conve[...]ns for constructing English sentences. Thus, improving writing is often a ma[...]roving your understanding of the conventions that govern it.

[...]bout writing exist in three major areas, areas with which you [...]. These areas are organization, content, and language/ exp[...] the conventions that govern these major areas of wri[...]

CONVENTIONS ABOUT ORGANIZATION

Many conventions exist about organizing a piece of writing so that a writer is able to communicate effectively with the reader. These conventions teach a writer to make use of paragraphs, topic sentences, unity, and coherence as ways of reaching the reader. The following sections will take up these conventions one by one.

Paragraphs

Have you ever caught yourself dozing over a page of text? Have you ever tried to read long, unbroken lines on a page, forcing yourself to backtrack and reread after you've become hopelessly lost? Sometimes these acts of confusion occur because you have difficulty concentrating: you're tired or you're uncomfortable or your mind's distracted by some personal problem. Sometimes you'll experience a comprehension problem because your reading skills need improvement or you need to build up your vocabulary. However, confusion sometimes occurs because the writer hasn't bothered to think about the reader, particularly the way in which paragraphs can be constructed as an *aid* to comprehension. In the following paper, student Carl Herman has neglected to use paragraph indentation as a method for helping his reader understand his message.

At the beginning of September, while still a student at the University of Denver, I found a job in a travel agency called "Travel Travel." The pay is excellent; I am becoming more familiar with the city and the businesses of Denver, and I am gaining valuable training in my interpersonal relationships. As a result, working for Travel Travel has been a good experience. First, the salary and fringe benefits I receive are excellent. I work every Monday, Wednesday, and Friday from 12:30 to 5:30, and I am paid $7.50 an hour. I was even paid for a five-hour training course required by my employer. In addition, when I am working, I am given the office car, a four-door white Honda Civic. I use the car to deliver airline tickets around the city of Denver, and I am paid 60 cents for every mile I travel. This money is added to my base salary. Second, I am becoming very familiar with the city and businesses of Denver while a Travel Travel employee. I have delivered airline tickets to big and small businesses. I have found myself inside the corporate offices of the Denver Broncos as well as the smoke-filled basement of the City Saloon. While I am in the offices of these businesses, I get a first-hand view of how offices are run. In addition, my job with Travel Travel is helping me improve my interpersonal relationships. In the office, I am learning how to accept constructive criticism when my boss teaches me how to improve my techniques at invoicing and handling files. When I work the receptionist's desk at lunch, I am learning how to talk to and handle a wide variety of clients. Outside of the office, as I deliver tickets to area businesses, I am learning to be flexible and adaptable, important characteristics for working with others. Because of the salary I'm receiving, th[illegible]sinesses I am coming to know, and the training in interpersonal relatio[illegible]ve been given, working for Travel Travel has been a positive worki[illegible]for me.

Talking About It #67

With your classmates, discuss some of the following questions about the essay which appears above.

1. What is your physical reaction to a long, unbroken column of text like Carl's paper? Explain.
2. What is your mental reaction to a long, unbroken column of text like Carl's paper? Explain.
3. Study Carl's paper carefully, and then decide where appropriate paragraphs might appear. Use the numbered lines to help you explain where you believe a new paragraph should start. Share your conclusions about where new paragraphs should begin. Examine your reasons for choosing where to insert paragraphs in Carl's essay. Do these reasons offer sound general principles for the convention of paragraphing? Why?

At the Beginnings of Paragraphs: Topic Sentences

You have seen the way paragraphs, acting as a visual clue to a writer's meaning, can help readers make their way mentally through a piece of writing. In addition, an effective paragraph also contains an orienting statement, a statement that gives a reader clues about what the paragraph will be about. Such orienting statements are called *topic sentences.*

As a reader, you require information from the writer. As you begin each new paragraph, you rightfully ask yourself the following questions as you read: What is this new paragraph going to be about? What is its topic? How is it similar to or different from the paragraphs which have come before or the paragraphs which are to follow? Answers to these questions will likely be satisfied by a clear, effective topic sentence.

In fact, some researchers believe that topic sentences are so important that information cannot be understood without them. For instance, the information which appears below has been presented without a topic sentence. Read it carefully, trying to understand what the paragraph is about.

> The procedure is actually quite simple. First you arrange things into different groups depending on their makeup. Of course, one pile may be sufficient, depending on how much there is to do. If you have to go somewhere else due to lack of facilities, that is the next step: otherwise, you are pretty well set . . .

J.D. Bransford and M.K. Johnson, who investigated this paragraph and its effect on readers, concluded that readers could not make sense of it without being first given the topic: washing clothes. The same passage—with the addition of a topic sentence—appears again on page 136. Read it carefully and decide whether or not the orienting sentence called the topic sentence really does aid communication.

The process of washing clothes is very simple. First you arrange things into different groups depending on their makeup. Of course, one pile may be sufficient, depending on how much there is to do. If you have to go somewhere else due to lack of facilities, that is the next step: otherwise, you are pretty well set . . .

Writing About It #68

Choose a simple process to describe—like making breakfast, walking a dog, or growing a plant from seed. Write a short paragraph describing the steps in this process, but *do not write* an orienting topic sentence. After you have written your paragraphs, share them with the other members of the class and see if they can figure out what process you're describing. Then write a topic sentence that begins the paragraph and orients the reader to your topic. Share these revised paragraphs with your classmates and decide whether or not the addition of a topic sentence aids communication.

Talking About It #69

Go back to the essay written by Carl about working for a travel agency. Underline the topic sentences for his paragraphs. Discuss your choices with your classmates. Read the paragraphs out loud—first *without* the topic sentences and then *with* them. Are your classmates as readers more satisfied with the paragraphs that begin with topic sentences? Why or why not?

Having studied topic sentences, do you feel that topic sentences are more effective when placed at the beginning of a paragraph? Do you think they could be just as effective when placed at the end of the paragraph or somewhere in the middle? Explain.

In the Middles of Paragraphs: Unity and Coherence

Creating Unity

You are already familiar with the idea of "unity" in everyday life. You know that if a football team fails to act as a unit, a losing game is likely to result. You know that if an office fails to adhere to unified policies and procedures, office efficiency can slump. You know that if a parent fails to practice unified disciplinary techniques, children are often confused about expectations.

This idea of *unity*—a sense of consistency and wholeness—applies to writing as well. One good way of learning about unity is by focusing on paragraphs. Since readers already think of paragraphs as representing units of thought, it's only natural for them to expect paragraphs to be unified. But what makes paragraphs—and longer pieces of writing—unified? How do you achieve unity or a sense of wholeness in a piece of writing? You can begin to answer those questions by looking at topic sentences and controlling ideas.

You have already learned that topic sentences help orient the reader to the subject matter in a paragraph. But topic sentences are made up of two things: (1) a subject or topic and (2) a point to be made about that subject or topic called the *controlling idea*.

In the topic sentences from Carl Herman's essay which follow, you can see the difference between the topic or subject and the controlling idea or point.

First, the salary and fringe benefits I receive are **excellent**.
(topic) (controlling idea)

Second, I am becoming very **familiar with the city and businesses** of
(controlling idea)
Denver while a Travel Travel employee.
(topic)

In addition, my job with Travel Travel is helping me **improve my**
(topic)
interpersonal relationships.
(controlling idea)

As Carl's topic sentences show, the controlling idea is a word or phrase that appears in the topic sentence and serves as the guiding focus for the paragraph. In short, the controlling idea is the **point** you are trying to make in the paragraph about your subject or topic. Unity in a paragraph is thus achieved by focusing on the controlling idea throughout the entire paragraph.

Talking About It #70

You should recognize some of the topic sentences which follow because they have already appeared in your text. As you read them carefully, identify the subject or topic of the topic sentence and identify the controlling idea or point by placing them in the chart provided. The first example has been done for you.

1. Let's face it: writing is challenging.
2. Prewriting, the first stage in the writing process, involves two main activities.
3. Readers and writers are engaged in a vital relationship.
4. Every successful piece of written communication results from the interaction among four elements: the reader, the writer, the work, and the language.
5. As you have seen, writing and speaking share some similarities.

	Topic or Subject	*Point or Controlling Idea*
1.	writing	challenging
2.		
3.		
4.		
5.		

In the paragraphs which follow, written by student Marc Gilardi, one is more unified than the other. Can you tell which one offers the reader that sense of consistency and wholeness called unity?

1.

Modern houses are of poorer quality than houses built in the past. More time and work went into the houses of yesteryear because they were built by craftsmen who took pride in the quality of their materials and the workmanship they provided as master carpenters, plumbers, and bricklayers. Today, houses are prefabricated on an assembly line; all a workman has to do is slap them together at the site. One of the most common building materials used today is soft yellow pine, but homeowners building decks and other outside structures often prefer redwood or cedar. In addition, older homes offer a quality of detail rarely found in a modern home. For instance, hand-carved English mahogany woodwork often dressed the door frames and windows and baseboards of an older house. In newer houses, however, builders are satisfied with straight machine-cut running boards used in an all-purpose fashion for doors, windows, and baseboards. Doors themselves demonstrate the decline in quality of the modern dwelling. In the past, doors were beautifully carved from one-and-a-half-inch thick wood; in the present, doors are finished pieces of plywood laid over two-by-four-inch studs. Older homes often have attics; these special places are filled with unexpected treasures like rare editions of old newspapers or the love letters between great-grandmother and great-grandfather. Modern homes are filled with gleaming appliances like refrigerators, dishwashers, and microwaves—unlike great-grandma's house which had an ice chest, a sink, and a wood-fired stove. Most of all, older houses were built to last. They often survived floods, fires, and natural disasters. In 1992, when Hurricane Andrew slammed into Miami, Florida, a community filled with prefabricated modern houses, the structures disintegrated like toothpicks under the hammering winds. Thus, older houses offer an abundance of what modern houses lack: old-fashioned quality.

2.

Modern houses are of poorer quality than houses built in the past. More time and work went into the houses of yesteryear because they were built by craftsmen who took pride in the quality of their materials and the workmanship they provided as master carpenters, plumbers, and bricklayers. Today, houses are prefabricated on an assembly line; all a workman has to do is slap them together at the site. In addition, older homes offer a quality of detail rarely found in a modern home. For instance, hand-carved English mahogany woodwork often dressed the door frames and windows and baseboards of an older house. In newer houses, however, builders are satisfied with straight machine-cut running boards used in an all-purpose fashion for doors, windows, and baseboards. Doors themselves demonstrate the decline in quality of the modern dwelling. In the past, doors were beautifully carved from one-and-a-half-inch thick wood; in the present, doors are finished pieces of plywood laid over two-by-four-inch studs. Most of all, older houses were built to last. They often survived floods, fires, and natural disasters. In 1992, when Hurricane Andrew slammed into Miami, Florida, a community filled with prefabricated modern houses, the structures disintegrated like toothpicks under the hammering winds. Thus, older houses offer an abundance of what modern houses lack: old-fashioned quality.

Talking About It #71

Discuss with your classmates the two paragraphs which appear above. Identify the topic sentences, and circle the controlling idea. Then decide which of the two paragraphs demonstrates unity—a satisfying sense of wholeness. In the paragraph that you felt was less unified, use the numbers provided to help you locate the sentences which need to be removed from that paragraph in order to strengthen the unity of it.

Checking for Unity

You have seen from these examples that unity is important to the success of a paragraph. You will also see that it is easy to check your paragraphs for unity. In the example that follows, student Katie Harbin is performing a "unity check" on her paragraph. Study it carefully and examine what she has done.

I have an easygoing personality.

1. Little things rarely upset me.

2. For instance, I can wait calmly in long lines at the grocery store or at the bus stop without getting upset.

3. If bad weather threatens to spoil my picnic, I'll bring the picnic basket inside and plan to have just as much fun indoors.

4. My carefree attitude allows me to shrug off things that might bother another person.

5. My dog, for example, once chewed up one of my Italian leather sandals; I took it very calmly, figuring that I could always buy other shoes but that Oscar was irreplaceable—and more important.

* **6.** When it comes to classwork, however, I'm not easygoing at all.

* **7.** I study like a maniac, rewriting class notes, outlining the reading material, and preparing for tests several days in advance.

* **8.** I'm obsessive when it comes to school.

9. My parents often wonder what makes me so relaxed.

10. Because my father has a quick temper and my mother is a constant worrier, they wonder how they had a daughter who takes life as it comes in her own easygoing style.

11. But they've lived with me long enough to accept who I am—a girl who travels life's highway without honking her horn or passing others at breakneck speed, a girl who lives life in the laid-back lane.

Talking About It #72

Look carefully at Katie's "unity check." Describe with your classmates the steps in the process Katie uses to check on the unity of her paragraph. Will she have a stronger paragraph after she has performed her unity check? Why or why not?

As you have seen, unity is an important organizational aid to the reader. A writer keeps the needs of his or her reader in mind when every sentence in a paragraph supports the controlling idea. Supporting the controlling idea helps the reader stay focused on the writer's main point. Thus, unity is an organizational aid that helps you, the writer, produce reader-based prose.

Coherence

Coherence is another organizational convention of effective writing. Remembering the principles of coherence, like remembering the principles of unity, will help you keep your reader in mind as you write the middle portions of your paragraphs and essays.

Coherence refers to the way a paragraph or longer work "holds together." Readers expect that the ideas in a paragraph or longer work will be connected and related to each other in a logical, satisfying way. If a paragraph or longer work exhibits coherence, it is consistently logical and connected; it "makes sense" to the reader.

An analogy might help you understand the concept of coherence. Let's say you're watching two dancers attempting a new dance step in the ballroom dancing class they're taking. They get the logical progression of steps confused, making their moves in an improper order or forgetting to repeat the steps that need to be repeated. They step on each other's feet regularly. They bump into each other occasionally. They look awkward and ungainly. The dance demonstrates little sense of relatedness or connection.

On the other hand, let's say that you're watching an old movie on TV. It features the famous dancing team of Fred Astaire and Ginger Rogers. As you watch, you marvel at the way they glide smoothly across the floor, the logical progression of steps both organized and satisfying. You observe the way Fred Astaire "leads" Ginger Rogers around the room, his hand pressed elegantly to her back, gently moving her here or smoothly maneuvering her over there. You applaud the way they move together, never missing a beat, "flowing" across the room as a unified team. You are enchanted by their achievement of grace.

Coherence in writing refers to that same kind of satisfaction. Observing the principles of coherence keeps a reader from stumbling or tripping as he or she moves from idea to idea. Like a well-placed hand guiding a dancer through her steps, coherence helps a writer move the reader through his or her ideas with assurance and grace, confident that the reader is being given a sense of relatedness and connection.

In the two paragraphs which follow, one of them offers the sense of relatedness and connection called *coherence*; the other one does not. Read them carefully and determine which paragraph appears to be more coherent.

1.

Student evaluation of teachers is a good idea. Students are the learners; teachers are the teachers. Shouldn't they evaluate how well they are doing their job? Teachers grade students all the time; it's only fair that students get to do the same. Students are struggling to improve their learning all the time. Teachers tell them to study harder, to organize their time more wisely, to take careful notes, or to review their coursework in study sessions. Teachers need to be told that they should plan their lessons more carefully, incorporate more relevant material in class, choose a more interesting textbook, or respond more directly to student needs.

2.

Student evaluation of teachers is a good idea. The job of a student is to learn; the job of a teacher is to teach. Therefore, shouldn't both sets of workers, struggling to give and receive an education, have a chance to find out how they're doing their jobs? The fact is that the evaluation process has been one-sided for too long. Instructors throughout history have evaluated their charges by passing out smiles, gold stars, grades, and report cards. As a result, students are urged to improve their learning all the time. For instance, their teachers tell them to study harder, to organize their time more wisely, to take careful notes, or to review their coursework in study sessions. Similarly, teachers could profit from the same kinds of evaluations if students are given the opportunity to award their teachers a "grade." When students tell teachers that they should plan their lessons more carefully, incorporate more relevant material in class, choose a more interesting textbook, or respond more directly to student needs, both teacher and learner benefit. Therefore, student evaluations of teachers is an A+ idea.

Talking About It #73

Discuss whether you think paragraph 1 or 2 conveys a better sense of coherence or relatedness. Then refer to the numbered lines in the paragraphs to suggest the differences between paragraph 1 and 2, noting the specific ways in which the more coherent paragraph conveys a more satisfying sense of relatedness.

Like unity, coherence is a convention of writing well worth mastering, and it is achieved in the following three ways: (1) by establishing a logical order, (2) by repeating key terms or their synonyms, and (3) by using transitions. Let's see how each one of these methods helps a writer achieve coherence.

Establishing a Logical Order

Have you ever overheard a child explaining to a young friend about how to play a new board game? Sometimes those explanatory directions can be confusing because, in the child's haste and inexperience, he or she can easily get the directions out of order and hopelessly confuse his or her young friend. Or have you ever experienced that sinking feeling that comes in the middle of telling a joke when you realize you've told the story in the wrong order? Have you ever tried to give a passing motorist directions, offering an explanation that you've had to revise once you've thought of a new and better way of helping him or her arrive at his or her destination? If you have, then you've experienced the same problem that besets all writers: the problem of establishing a logical order.

Logical order is important. To try to provide your reader with ideas without arranging them in their proper logical place is to invite confusion.

Talking About It #74

A few examples of paragraphs follow which have not been written with the necessary attention to order. Study them carefully and then decide on an orderly arrangement that best satisfies the reader's need for a logical presentation of ideas. The sentences have been numbered to make referring to them easier.

1. (1) Benjamin Franklin was an inveterate reader. (2) As a child, he taught himself to read, borrowing books from everywhere and escaping into the hayloft to read them. (3) As a grown man, Benjamin Franklin turned his love of reading into an act of significance for his fellow Philadelphians, founding the city's first lending library. (4) As a young man, he took an apprenticeship to his brother James, a printer. (5) In the print shop, he avidly read the stories that were being set in type, arranging and rearranging them until they satisfied his own exacting standards for a good story. (6) As a youth, he would spend long hours on the banks of the Schuykill River, an open book in his hand.

2. (1) The young child's sweet face was irresistible. (2) The pink lips were pushed into a pucker. (3) The wispy strands of pale blonde hair curled down the forehead and across the eyes like intricate strands of lace. (4) The chin ended in a tender point like the tip of a valentine. (5) The tiny nose tilted up sweetly at the end as if poised for a kiss. (6) In the center was a deep dimple like the indentation made in the mashed potatoes before the gravy is slipped in. (7) When she turned her face to me, her eyes locked into mine, and something turned a key in my heart.

3. (1) Earning my college degree is very important to me. (2) In addition, I think that college will teach me independence. (3) At college, I will meet a number of people with different backgrounds and be exposed to ideas that will help me stretch and grow. (4) At college I will have to make my own independent decisions: about how to spend my money, about how to organize my time, about how to succeed in my courses. (5) Most of all, college will prepare me for my life's work. (6) First, I think that going to college will help broaden my experiences. (7) At college, as I learn to be an accountant or a teacher or an engineer or an office manager, I will take the first step that will lead me into the rest of my life.

The three paragraphs show you the importance of a logical arrangement of ideas. They are also examples of the *types* of logical order available to you as an organizational aid to coherence. In general, you can arrange your paragraphs and essays using any of these three types of logical order:

1. time order,
2. space order,
3. order of importance.

Look back over the paragraph examples which previously appeared. Which one makes use of the logical order called *time* or *chronological order*? Can you think of other kinds of writing which rely on chronological order? Which one makes use of a logical arrangement of details in space? Can you think of other kinds of writing which make use of *spatial order*? Which one uses the logical order which ranks the presentations of ideas in the order of their importance? Can you think of other kinds of writing which make use of the method of logical presentation called *order of importance*?

Writing About It #75

Use your journal to tell a joke. Make sure that you use the logical order called time or chronological order to tell your joke accurately. Share your journal responses with your classmates.

Use your journal to describe a person or place you know well. Make sure that you use the logical order called *space order* to describe your person or place effectively. Share your journal responses with your classmates.

Use your journal to write a paragraph in which you try to convince someone of something. Use the logical order called *order of importance* to arrange your ideas. Share your journal responses with your classmates.

Repeating Key Terms or Their Synonyms

Your past experiences have made you familiar with the way in which repeating things helps you to understand and to remember them. For instance, when you begin reading a chapter in a textbook, often you need to go back and repeat or reread the material in order to understand and remember it. You've probably listened to a keynote speaker on several occasions, noting the way he or she repeated the main points in order to impress them on his or her audience and help the audience remember them. You've probably taken care of younger children, repeating advice such as "Don't touch the hot stove!" or "Look all ways before you cross the street!" in order to help them understand and remember that important information.

Repetition can also help your writing. Repeating key terms or their synonyms can help you achieve coherence by reminding your reader of the points you are trying to make and helping your reader to remember them. In the previous example on pages 172–173, about the superiority of older homes, note the way the writer used the key term "house." At many points during his discussion he repeated the key term "house" in order to remind his readers of the importance of this term and to help them keep this important term in mind as they read.

Sometimes, however, repeating the same word over and over again can seem boring or dull; when this is the case, often writers replace key terms with synonyms for them. That way, they can still help the reader keep the key ideas in mind; they just use different words in order to do so. In the paragraph about the superiority of older homes, notice the way the writer used synonyms for the key term "house." Sometimes Marc used the word "home," "dwelling," or "structure" to help keep his key idea in mind without repeating the word "house" over and over again. In the paragraph by Katie Harbin, in which she described her "easygoing" personality, she used several synonyms for the key term "easygoing." These synonyms were "carefree," "laid-back," and other appropriate phrases. Thus, repeating key terms or using synonyms for them helps your reader keep your key ideas in mind throughout the middle of a text. Using this method helps your reader follow your main idea and enables you to write more reader-based prose.

Writing About It #76

Look back over the paragraphs you wrote earlier—the joke, the description of a person or scene, and the paragraph in which you convince someone of something using order of importance. Underline the key term or terms in this paragraph. Then circle each place where you repeat this key term or use a substituting synonym for it. After you have finished circling these terms, pass your paragraphs to a fellow classmate. Ask your fellow classmate if he or she is satisfied with the number of key terms or synonym substitutions for them that appear in the paragraphs. Are there places where your reader feels that additional repetition of key terms or their substitutes might be helpful? If so, write them into your paragraphs at this time.

Write a paragraph in which you describe something that is either very large or very small. After you have written this paragraph, note the number of times you either repeated your key term or used a synonym for it. Pass your paragraphs to a classmate and ask whether or not the key term of largeness or smallness was kept sufficiently in the reader's mind. If it was not, repeat key terms or substitutes for them as you revise your paragraph.

Using Transitions

You'll recall from the material you read earlier that coherence is the quality of connectedness or relatedness. One of the best ways of achieving this sense of connection and relation is by using transitions. Transitions are *words that help link one idea to another.* They can point out the way in which one idea is similar to another. They can point out the way in which one idea is different from another. They can point out the way in which one idea results from another. As the connections or links between your ideas, transitions can do many useful things. Like a partner's hand pressed to your back and guiding you through a dance routine, transitions are a helping hand to your readers, guiding them through your prose, signaling turns of thought here or repeated ideas there.

Transitional expressions are easy to use if you remember that they are used to serve a purpose, the purpose of guiding your reader. Similar to a scout forging a trail, transitions help keep your readers on the path you want them to follow. It's important, therefore, that you choose your transitions carefully, linking them to the appropriate purpose. For this reason, the following list of transitions shows not just the transitional word but the purpose for which it may be used as well.

Purpose	**Transitional Expressions**
to add	also, and, and then, as well, besides, beyond that, first (second, third, last), for one thing, furthermore, in addition, moreover, next, what is more
to compare	also, as well, both (neither), in the same way, likewise, similarly
to contrast	although, be that as it may, but, even though, however, in contrast, nevertheless, on the contrary, on the other hand, whereas, yet
to concede (a point)	certainly, granted that, no doubt, of course, to be sure
to emphasize	above all, especially, in fact, in particular, indeed, most important, most of all, surely
to illustrate	as a case in point, as an illustration, for example, for instance, in particular, one such, yet another
to place in space	above, beside, below, beyond, further, here, inside, nearby, next to, on the far side, outside, to the east (south, north, west)

to place in time	after a while, afterward, at last, at present, briefly, currently, during, eventually, finally, first (second, third, last, etc.), gradually, immediately, in the future, later, meanwhile, now, recently, soon, suddenly, today, yesterday
to qualify	perhaps
to give a reason	as, because, for, since
to show a result	and so, as a consequence, as a result, because of this, consequently, for this reason, hence, so, therefore, thus
to summarize	all in all, finally, in brief, in conclusion, in other words, lastly, on the whole, to sum up

Writing About It #77

Look back at the previous paragraph you studied by Marc Gilardi on the superiority of older houses. Circle the transition words in this paragraph and indicate the purpose for which they are being used in order to aid the understanding of the reader.

Look back at your own three paragraphs—the joke, the description of a person or place, the paragraph attempting to convince someone of something using order of importance. Circle the transitional expressions you used in each of these paragraphs and write down the purpose each of them is designed to achieve for the reader. Do you think you have used enough transitions so that your meaning is clear to your reader? If not, add transitions where necessary. Now share your paragraphs with a classmate. Does your classmate feel you have used enough transitions to make your meaning clear? Your classmate should indicate where you might profit from using additional transactions. Discuss these suggestions to decide whether additional transitions are needed. In each place where you have added a new transition, indicate the purpose that each new transition word serves.

Checking for Coherence

Earlier in this chapter, you learned to check a paragraph for unity by making use of a unity check. Now you can learn to check a paragraph for coherence by making use of a *coherence check*. The process is a simple one in which you read the paragraph sentence by sentence from the title to the conclusion. The key difference between checking for coherence and reading a paragraph as you normally would, however, is that when you're checking for coherence, you stop after you read each sentence, writing down a prediction about what you expect to read about in the sentence to come. When you do this, you are making guesses about the coherence that exists between the sentences you are reading. Then, when you read the following sentence, you can check to see whether that sentence matches your prediction. If it does match your prediction, you can read on. If it doesn't match your prediction, you know you will have to make changes in the sentence to meet your reader's expectations.

A simple example will help you see how this kind of predicting can help you check for coherence. Read the following short poem, noting the place where your expectation was not met.

> This little piggie went to market,
> This little piggie stayed home,
> This little piggie had roast beef,
> And bacon is on sale this week for $1.99 a pound.

Although this is a simple example, lack of coherence in a paper will give you a similar sense of being jarred by the text when your expectations or predictions about what you are reading are unfulfilled. When you are first learning to perform a coherence check, it is helpful to actually write each sentence separately or to use a piece of paper to cover all of the sentences except for the sentence you are currently examining. Because you learn to perform coherence checks on your own work with more skill after you have practiced performing coherence checks on the work of others, the paragraph below on time management by student Darnell Hahn will give you practice in understanding coherence checks. Read it through once, and then notice the way Darnell's classmate performed a coherence check by writing down predictions about what he expected to read.

My Troubles with Time

Time management is a problem for me in my school life, my athletic life, and my personal life. I have poor time management, mainly because I never manage my time properly. I usually am late for meetings. When I have to pick my mom up at the mall, I am usually late because I've been driving around with my friends, unaware of the time. Often I'm tired the next day. This year, I've missed the bus for college four times already. I have to walk into my Biology lab late and watch the professor frown and make a mark with his pencil next to my name in his grade book. I have a group project in my Marketing class due at the end of the semester. I'm late for most of our group meetings, too. I often don't know what's going on. I have a college basketball scholarship. My time management is a problem. I sometimes show up late to practice. My coach benched me for a week. I even was late to an important meeting between my coach and the athletic director about my scholarship. I may lose my scholarship because of my poor time management skills.

My Troubles with Time

Based on the title, I predict this paragraph will be about Darnell's problems with time.

1. Time management is a problem for me in my school life, my athletic life, and my personal life.

> *Based on this topic sentence, I predict the next sentence will talk about Darnell's problems with school life.*

2. I have poor time management, mainly because I never manage my time properly.

> *I'm not sure why this sentence was in here. It seems to say just what he's said in sentence one, only in different words. I'm still expecting Darnell to say something about his problems with school life.*

3. I usually am late for meetings.

> *I'm glad to see an example of Darnell's time management problems, but I'm not sure if this has fulfilled my prediction. I was expecting something on time management problems relating to school life. I'm not sure if being "late for meetings" is a personal problem, an athletic problem, or a school problem. I predict that Darnell's next sentence will have something to do with meetings or will perhaps list another time management problem.*

4. When I have to pick my mom up at the mall, I am usually late because I've been driving around with my friends, unaware of the time.

> *I'm predicting another example of a time management problem in the next sentence.*

5. Often I'm tired the next day.

> *This may be another time management problem, but it's not explained very fully. And I'm not sure if it's a personal or a school or an athletic time management problem. I predict either more explanation of why Darnell is tired or another example of a time management difficulty in the next sentence.*

6. This year, I've missed the bus for college four times already.

> *Yes! This is another time management example. Because he mentions "college," I'll guess this is a problem with time that relates to his schoolwork. I'm predicting another school-related example in the next sentence.*

7. I have to walk into my Biology lab late and watch the professor frown and make a mark with his pencil next to my name in his grade book.

> *Yes! This a school-related example. I'm predicting another school-related example or else another new example of Darnell's time management problem in the next sentence.*

8. I have a group project in my Marketing class due at the end of the semester.

> *This is a school-related example. I predict an explanation of Darnell's time problems as they relate to this group project.*

9. I'm late for most of our group meetings, too.

> *I'm predicting either an elaboration of how being late to the group meetings affects Darnell's Marketing project or else an entirely new example of his time management struggles.*

10. I often don't know what's going on.

> *I guess he's still talking about the Marketing group project, but I'm not sure. I predict he'll either explain about his confusion or go on to another new example next.*

11. I have a college basketball scholarship.

> *I expect he will explain how the basketball scholarship is related to his time management problem somehow.*

12. My time management is a problem.

> *Although I don't see the relationship between the problem with time management and basketball, I expect he'll explain it in the next sentence.*

13. I sometimes show up late to practice.

> *Perhaps he will show the consequence of being late to practice. Or maybe he will give another new example of his time problems in the sentence to come.*

14. My coach benched me for a week.

> *Yes! We have a relationship here. I'm expecting another consequence of his lateness or else a new example of how his poor time management relates to another athletic difficulty.*

15. I even was late to an important meeting between my coach and the athletic director about my scholarship.

> *Yes! We have another athletic difficulty. I'm expecting more about either the consequence of that meeting or a new example.*

16. I may lose my scholarship because of my poor time management skills.

> *Yes! A consequence is discussed here. I'm expecting it's about time for a conclusion next as this seems the most serious example of Darnell's problem with time management so far. I'm predicting that he'll end his paragraph soon.*

This material shows Darnell's classmate attempting to assess the coherence of the paragraph by making predictions about the relationships among the ideas in it. Darnell has listened carefully to the coherence checks from a variety of his classmates, and, after careful thought, he has revised his paragraph again. Darnell's revision follows.

Time management is a problem for me in my personal life, my school life, and my athletic life. In my personal life, my poor time management causes me to be late to meetings with my friends. Often my three buddies and I meet for lunch at McDonald's, and because I'm usually late, we don't ever have enough time to really talk. In addition, when I have to pick my mom up at the mall, I am usually late because I've been driving around, unaware of the time. Because of poor time management, I don't get enough sleep at night; as a result, I'm often tired the next day. My school life also suffers because I don't manage my time well. This year, I've missed the bus for college four times already. Consequently, I have to walk in to my Biology lab late and watch my professor frown and make a mark with his pencil next to my name in his grade book. Another example of my problem with time involves the group project I need to do in my Marketing class. Because I'm late for most of our group meetings, my part of the project will be weak, and I feel bad about letting the other group members down. Worst of all, my poor time management habits are affecting the part of my life that is most important to me—athletics. I am very proud of the college basketball scholarship I was given, but my time management problem is getting in the way of my success in this area of my life, too. Sometimes I show up late to practice. After that had happened five times, my coach benched me for a week. Because of my struggle with time management, my coach called an important meeting with me to discuss my problem. Believe it or not, I was even late to that! As a result, it is very clear to me that I need a solution to my problem with time in order to succeed in my personal life, my school life, and my athletic life.

Talking About It #78

With your classmates, think about the following questions about Darnell's rewritten paragraph.

1. In what specific ways has Darnell now made use of his topic sentence to provide a more logical order to his paragraph? How has he grouped his ideas to make his presentation more logical?
2. What key terms or their synonyms does Darnell now repeat for his reader? Does repeating these key terms or synonyms help you follow his thoughts more easily?
3. Look at each of the transitions listed. Then describe what purpose the transitions actually serve in Darnell's paragraph.
   a. *"In my personal life," line 2*
   b. *"In addition," line 5*
   c. *"as a result," line 8*
   d. *"also," line 9*
   e. *"Consequently," line 10*

f. *"Another," line 13*
g. *"Worst of all," line 16*
h. *"too," line 20*
i. *"After," line 21*
j. *"As a result," line 24*

4. Do you find Darnell's concluding sentence effective? Why or why not?

At the Ends of Paragraphs: Conclusions

Paragraphs and longer pieces of writing need to be organized in three key places: the beginning, the middle, and the end. You've learned the way topic sentences organize the beginning of a paragraph and the way unity and coherence organize the middle section of a paragraph. Now it's time to learn about conclusions and the way in which they organize the ending of a paragraph.

One of the easiest ways to establish a satisfying ending to a piece of writing is to restate your topic sentence in different words. Notice the way in which the following concluding sentences use different words to restate the topic sentence.

Topic Sentence: Modern houses are of poorer quality than houses built in the past.

Concluding Sentence: Thus, older houses offer an abundance of what modern houses lack: old-fashioned quality.

Topic Sentence: I have an easygoing personality.

Concluding Sentence: But they've lived with me long enough to accept who I am—a girl who travels life's highway without honking her horn or passing others at breakneck speed, a girl who lives life in the laid-back lane.

Topic Sentence: Student evaluation of teachers is a good idea.

Concluding Sentence: Therefore, student evaluations of teachers is an A+ idea.

Thus, concluding sentences, by restating the topic sentence in different words, help convey to your reader the sense of finality and closure your reader needs. A strong concluding sentence is evidence that you are writing for your reader.

In this section, you have seen the ways in which speaking and listening are different from reading and writing. As a result, writing requires special conventions for organizing such as paragraphing, unity, and coherence. These are conventions that help keep a reader on track from the beginning, through the middle, and at the end of a piece of your writing.

CONVENTIONS ABOUT CONTENT

Because writing and reading are different from speaking and listening, many conventions also govern the information or **content** in a piece of writing. If you'll recall the conversation between the three community college students—Joe, Mary, and Ben—you'll remember that the information they discussed ranged freely from topic to topic. They talked about their speech class; they talked about their jobs; they talked about the challenges of balancing school and work.

Ben's written paragraph, which developed out of this conversation, however, used this information—or content—in a different way. Instead of ranging from topic to topic and subject to subject, Ben's writing used content in a specific way: to make *connections* between his personal observations about the problems of being a working college student and the solutions he and his friends developed for coping with them. As Ben drew connections between problem and solution, expressing them on paper, he was making use of a convention of writing, the convention of using content to make a specific point.

In addition, as you've learned in Chapter 4, three broad strategies exist for organizing the presentation of your content, for using your content to make a specific point. These are *collections, chronologies*, and *connections*. Ben's paragraph about community college students, for instance, draws connections between the problems of balancing work, school, and home and solutions like studying during lunch hour, listening to tapes on the way to work, and practicing while the baby is napping. Carl's paper about his job in a travel agency makes use of *collections* of reasons to support his view that his job has been a satisfying experience. Marc's essay about the differences in quality between older and newer homes draws connections between past and present home construction by comparing and contrasting ideas, for example, materials and workmanship.

Collections, chronologies, and connections are broad, general ways of thinking about content and the way it can be developed. Underneath these broad categories, in fact, are more specific ways for collecting ideas or detailing chronologies or making connections. The following chart will acquaint you with these specific methods which can be used alone or combined with each other in order to flesh out your content.

Collections	*Chronologies*	*Connections*
facts	narratives	problem/solution
descriptions		comparison/contrast
examples/illustrations		cause/effect
reasons		question/answer
		classification
		analysis

Talking About It #79

In the following passages, you will notice the different methods or combinations of methods the writers are using to develop their content. Refer to the chart as you discuss with your classmates which broad method—collection, chronology, connection—and which specific method or combination of methods you feel the writer is using.

1. Why is marking up a book indispensable to reading? First, it keeps you awake. (And I don't mean merely conscious; I mean wide awake.) In the second place, reading, if it is active, is thinking, and thinking tends to express itself in words, spoken or written. The marked book is usually the thought-through book. Finally, writing helps you remember the thoughts you had, or the thoughts the author expressed.

—*Mortimer J. Adler, "How to Mark a Book"*

2. Doing the laundry in my mother's day was a whole day's performance. First we boiled the white clothes, transferring them to the washing machine dripping on a broom handle. Then we ran them through the machine and then through a wringer into the rinse tub. Next, they went through the wringer a second time and into the bluing water. They ran through the wringer a third time as they left the bluing water and went into the laundry basket for toting to the back yard. There they were shaken out and hung on the clothesline to dry. The colored clothes went through the same process as the whites, except that they were not boiled because they would fade. If clothes were to be starched, they even received a third rinsing, and they were then wrung out by hand before they went into the laundry basket.

—*Roz Young, "History Repeats Itself with Major Improvements"*

3. English has not had a coherent and consistent spelling system in 1000 years and has not been reformed in 300, according to Bob Brown, President of the Simplifyd Spelng Society. The Society believes that the English language has evolved into a maddening complexity of words that have letters that serve no purpose. English, the Society says, is confusing to native children trying to learn it and is hellish for foreigners. The solution, according to Brown, is Cut Spelng, which purges many redundant letters from English words. Cut Spelng merely eliminates superfluous letters and substitutes letters closer to the actual sounds. The following sentence is an example of the Simplifyd Spelng Society's solution to the problems of English spelling: "Ecnomic and social problms in Britn and America ar increasingly being linkd to educationl standrds."

—*Richard O'Mara, "Society sels Simplifyd Spelng"*

4. . . . The dictionary has been a particular disappointment to me as a basic reference work, and the fact that it's usually more my fault than the dictionary's doesn't make it any easier on me. I have at least twenty words that I look up ten times a year. I didn't know how to spell them in high school and I still don't. Is it "further" or "farther" if I'm talking about distance? I always go to the dictionary for further details. I have several dictionaries, and I avoid the one farthest from me. Furthest from me? . . . There are still some words I look up in the dictionary because I'm too embarrassed to ask anyone how they're spelled. I've probably looked up "embarrassed" nine times within the last few years as a more natural way to spell the word."

—*Andy Rooney, "Dictionaries"*

5. Art depends heavily on feeling. It is feeling, not some rule, that tells the abstract painter to put his yellow here and there, not there, and may later tell him that it should have been brown or purple or pea-green. It's feeling that makes the composer break surprisingly from his key, feeling that gives the writer the rhythms of his sentences, the pattern of rise and fall in his episodes, the proportions of alternating elements, so that dialogue goes on only so long before a shift to description or narrative summary or some physical action. The great writer has an instinct for these things.

—John Gardner, The Art of Fiction: Notes on Craft for Young Writers

6. The school bus is a yellow submarine, parting the gray churning sea of morning. It steers its way through the flotilla of traffic, sounding its foghorn, flashing signals like a lighthouse beacon, heading out into the open asphalt sea. The young salts fill the tin can with blarney. They brag and roister, swaggering like seadogs. They cheat on homework as shamelessly as pirates at cards. The air is salty with the smell of potato chips and pretzel rods, and their shrieks slice through it like swords. It is a motley crew: gum stuck up under the bunks, jackets crushed under fannies, ribbons and barrettes slipped from their moorings. Finally, the captain docks. She weighs anchor, disgorging her catch at the harbor of spelling tests, the pep band, equal opportunity for all, and the republic for which it stands. Orange, yellow, autumn-colored, the school bus slips across the pavements of our imagination, dropping into the season like the first turned leaf, harbinger of fall.

—Trudy Krisher, Ohio magazine

7. We have written *The New Vegetarians* for several reasons. First, the topic of vegetarianism is a timely and important one. Recent medical research indicates that a high-fat, low-fiber diet centered on meat is a contributing factor in cardiovascular disease—the leading cause of death in the United States today. Second, we find vegetarianism to be an intriguing personal and social phenomenon. Although there are many books available on meatless cooking and vegetarian issues, we know of no other work that shows why people become vegetarians and how this affects their psychological functioning, private lives, and social relationships.

—Paul R. Amato and Sonia A. Partridge, The New Vegetarians

8. Dear Ann Landers:

I'm dictating this letter to the nurse because I'm not yet able to sit up and hold a pencil. Please print my letter for other executives who think they can't possibly spare the time to take a vacation. Suddenly I have plenty of time, but all I can do is lie flat on my back and look at the ceiling. The doctor won't even let me make a phone call. He says I'm lucky to be alive after that massive heart attack.

I thought my company would collapse if I didn't get to the office every morning at 8 a.m. At night I always lugged work home. I never took time to have lunch with a friend. I used to grab a sandwich at my desk and dictate to my secretary between bites. I drove my associates crazy, telephoning them at crazy hours and on

Sundays. I could never spare the time to see a movie or a play or just sit around with friends. I had too much to do. For the last five years, my wife has been begging me to go to a doctor and get a physical, but I couldn't spare the time.

Now I discover the business is doing fine without me—in fact, the figures are up. If God gives me a few more years, I'll know how to use them. Strange that a man has to look death in the face before he learns how to live.

—Ann Landers, Truth Is Stranger

9. In a gallery off the rue Dauphine . . . , I happened upon an exhibit of medieval torture instruments. It made me think that pain must be as great a challenge to the human imagination as pleasure. Otherwise there's no accounting for the number of torture instruments. One would be quite enough. The simple pincer, let's say, which rips out flesh. Or the head crusher, which breaks first your tooth sockets, then your skull. But in addition I saw tongs, thumb-screws, a rack, a ladder, ropes and pulleys, a grill, a garrote, a Spanish horse, a Judas cradle, an iron maiden, a cage, a gag, a strappado, a stretching table, a saw, a wheel, a twisting stork, an inquisitor's chair, a breast breaker, and a scourge.

—Phyllis Rose, "Tools of Torture: An Essay on Beauty and Pain"

10. If you observe a person conversing, you'll notice that he indicates he's listening by nodding his head. He also makes little "Hmm" noises. If he agrees with what's being said, he may give a vigorous nod. To show pleasure or affirmation, he smiles; if he has some reservations, he looks skeptical by raising an eyebrow or pulling down the corners of his mouth. If a participant wants to terminate the conversation, he may start shifting his body position, stretching his legs, crossing or uncrossing them, bobbing his foot or diverting his gaze from the speaker. The more he fidgets, the more the speaker becomes aware that he has lost his audience. As a last measure, the listener may look at his watch to indicate the imminent end of the conversation.

—Edward T. Hall and Mildred Reed Hall, "The Sounds of Silence"

Quantity and Quality: Issues About Content

As you've seen in these passages, there are many specific ways of developing content. Students, however, struggle not only with the methods for developing content but also with questions about how much information to include and how they can make that information interesting to their reader.

At different stages in the writing process, students ask themselves questions like, "Have I offered enough reasons to convince my reader of my point?" "Have any steps in my narrative been left out?" "Have I included enough points of comparison to satisfy my reader?" "Have I written *enough*?" In other words, they worry about the amount or *quantity* of their content.

Another struggle students often voice about content is a concern about the interest level of what they are writing. They ask, "Would a reader really be interested in what I've written?" "What can I do to capture the attention of my reader?" "How can I make sure that my reader isn't bored?" These questions underlie worries about the *quality* of their content.

Questions about quantity and quality are difficult to answer. Like many other questions about writing, the answer is that "it depends." Whether or not a piece of writing is satisfying in terms of quantity and quality depends on many things: the needs of the reader, the purposes of the writer, the nature of the work, and the language community for which the work is written.

In dealing with the issues of quantity and quality, let's imagine that a student has been given an assignment to choose a city and then write a paragraph that conveys a sense of the *uniqueness* of that city. Here is a student paragraph written in response to that assignment.

> New York is an interesting place to visit. It has the Statue of Liberty and the Empire State Building. It has its famous streets like Wall Street and Broadway and Fifth Avenue. It has parks like Central Park and ferries like the Staten Island Ferry. Mostly it has people, rich and poor, happy and depressed, bums and billionaires. New York is an interesting place.

Talking About It #80

Discuss the following questions in response to the paragraph on New York.

1. What was the assignment?
2. What was the writer's purpose?
3. What is the topic sentence of the paragraph? the controlling idea?
4. What general method did the writer use to develop content—collection, chronology, or connection?
5. What specific method or methods did the writer use to develop content?
6. Is the amount or quantity of content provided sufficient to achieve the writer's purpose and meet the reader's needs? Explain.
7. Is the content provided interesting to you? Is the quality of the content high? Explain.
8. What suggestions would you make to this writer as he or she begins to revise this draft?

The following paragraphs are from an essay on New York by writer Gay Talese. The essay first appeared in *Esquire* in 1960.

1. New York is a . . . center for odd bits of information. New Yorkers blink twenty-eight times a minute, but forty when tense. Most popcorn chewers at Yankee Stadium stop chewing momentarily just before the pitch. Gumchewers on Macy's escalators stop chewing momentarily just before they get off—to concentrate on the last step. Coins, paper clips, ball-point pens, and little girls' pocketbooks are found by workmen when they clean the sea lion's pool at the Bronx Zoo.

2. New York is a city of 38,000 cabdrivers, 10,000 bus drivers, but only one chauffeur who has a chauffeur. The wealthy chauffeur can be seen driving up Fifth Avenue each morning, and his name is Roosevelt Zanders. He earns $100,000 a year, is a gentleman of impeccable taste and, although he owns a $23,000 Rolls-Royce, does not scorn his friends who own Bentleys. For $150 a day, Mr. Zanders will drive anyone anywhere in his big, silver Rolls. Diplomats patronize him, models pose next to him, and each day he receives cables from around the world urging that he be waiting at Idlewild, on the docks, or outside the Plaza Hotel. Sometimes at night, however, he is too tired to drive anymore. So Bob Clarke, his chauffeur, takes over, and Mr. Zanders relaxes in the back.

3. Shortly after seven-thirty each morning hundreds of people are lined along Forty-second Street waiting for the eight A.M. opening of the ten movie houses that stand almost shoulder-to-shoulder between Times Square and Eighth Avenue. Who are these people who go to the movies at eight A.M.? They are the city's insomniacs, night watchmen, and people who can't go home, do not want to go home, or have no home. They are derelicts, homosexuals, cops, hacks, truck drivers, cleaning ladies and restaurant men who have worked all night. They are also alcoholics who are waiting at eight A.M. to pay forty cents for a soft seat and to sleep in the dark, smoky theatre. And yet, aside from being smoky, each of Times Square's theatres has a special quality, or lack of quality, about it. At the Victory Theatre one finds horror films, while at the Times Square Theatre they feature only cowboy films. There are first-run films for forty cents at the Lyric, while at the Selwyn there are always second-run films for thirty cents. But if you go to the Apollo Theatre you will see, in addition to foreign films, people in the lobby talking with their hands. These are deaf-and-dumb movie fans who patronize the Apollo because they read the subtitles. The Apollo probably has the biggest deaf-and-dumb movie audience in the world.

Talking About It #81

With your classmates, discuss the questions which follow.

1. Assuming that Gay Talese's purpose was to suggest the uniqueness of New York City, do you feel his purpose was achieved? Explain.
2. What is the topic sentence of each of the paragraphs? What is the controlling idea of each of the paragraphs?
3. What general method did the writer use to develop content—collection, chronology, or connection?
4. What specific method or methods of developing content did Talese use in developing the content of each of the paragraphs?
5. Was the amount or quantity of content provided sufficient to achieve the writer's purpose and meet the reader's needs? Explain with reference to each of the paragraphs.

6. Was the content provided interesting to you? Was the quality of the content high? Explain with reference to each of the paragraphs.
7. Compare Gay Talese's three paragraphs on New York with the student draft of the paragraph on New York. Which paragraphs are more satisfying in terms of amount or quantity of content? Explain. Which paragraphs are more satisfying in terms of quality of content? Explain.

Writing About It #82

Write a paragraph in which you formulate your own explanation for what makes the content of a piece of writing both sufficient and interesting. Share your responses to this question with your classmates.

Developing the Quantity and Quality of Your Content

As you've seen, writing is different from conversation because the reader does not talk to the writer; the writer communicates with him or her in silence. As a result, you cannot ask your reader if the amount of content is sufficient or if your content is interesting because the reader is not there. You must, then, develop methods of your own for determining how much content is "enough" and whether the content is "interesting."

Sources for Developing Content

As you've seen in the previous example, you develop sufficient and interesting content in two ways: through yourself and through others.

Some of the methods of developing ideas yourself include the following:

personal experience,
journal reflections,
careful observation,
invention techniques (freewriting, looping, brainstorming, mapping/branching, questioning).

Some of the methods of developing ideas through others include the following:

conversations,
interviews,
documents,
brochures,
journal articles,
newspapers,

magazines,
books,
other sources.

Let's say, for example, that you're attending a state university and have been asked to write a paper for your English teacher on a campus problem that concerns you. You're not required to offer a solution to the problem or provide reasons for the existence of the problem. For this paper, you are simply being asked to establish that a problem exists and is worthy of your concern.

As you begin thinking of a campus problem for your paper, you remember that just this week you had your stereo system stolen from your dormitory room, so you decide that the problem of campus theft is an issue you're interested in investigating, and you want to make sure that you have sufficient information in your report to convince your reader/teacher of the importance of this topic.

You begin developing the content for your paper by turning inward, probing yourself and your own experience with campus theft. You make notes about your own personal situation, recalling several of the prewriting techniques you learned about in Chapter 4, deciding to generate some ideas through brainstorming. You begin to list your ideas, recording the time, date, and circumstances of the theft of your stereo system and your reaction to it. Next, you thumb back through your journal from last year because you remember that your boyfriend had his bicycle stolen from the bike rack outside his dorm last spring. Sure enough, as you consult your journal, you see that Bob's bike—even though it was locked and chained—was stolen last April. Therefore, through personal experience, journal reflections, careful observation, and invention techniques, you begin to collect information that can provide content for your paper.

As your curiosity about your topic grows, you begin to turn to others for information you can use in your paper. You listen carefully to your friends as you bring up the topic of campus theft. As they report different occurrences of theft to you, you begin to take careful notes about what they've said, compiling information for future reference.

You then decide that you need to consult outside sources for even more convincing information. You call the Campus Security office and set up interviews with the Director of Campus Security and a campus police officer. You meet with both of them, interviewing them about their knowledge of campus theft. While you are meeting with the Director of Campus Security, he provides you with a brochure that recounts the latest crime statistics, including statistics on campus theft. While you are there, he tells you that the term "theft" actually describes three separate crimes: petty theft, theft, and grand theft. While you are interviewing the police officer, he shows you incident reports describing various cases of theft that have taken place on campus during the past year. He also refers you to the campus newspaper series about crime on campus, published just last month. After your interview, you head to the campus newspaper office and read the newspaper article about campus crime, gathering even more information for your report. Finally, you go to the library and consult the journals available on criminal justice, picking out an article called "Campus Crime: Felons and Friends" from the September issue of the *Journal of Juvenile Justice*. As a result, you have used outside sources of information—interviews, documents, newspaper articles, and journal articles—as rich sources to develop the content of your paper.

Writing About It #83

Imagine that you have been given the same assignment as the student above: to establish the existence of a problem on your campus that concerns you. Choose any problem that comes to mind, and then make two columns on a piece of paper. Label one "Self" and the other "Others." Then list the specific resources—yourself and others—which you could use in order to generate sufficient content for this paper. Be as specific as possible about the nature and sources for developing your content.

An early draft of the first paragraph of Susan Pierce's paper on the problem of campus theft follows. In it, she begins to study the problem by examining her own personal experience.

I first began to think about the problem of campus theft when my stereo system was stolen this year. When I got back to my room after a hall meeting, my stereo system was gone. I was furious. I then decided that theft on campus was a serious problem.

Talking About It #84

With your classmates, discuss the questions which follow.

1. Are you satisfied with the amount or quantity of information/content Susan provides in this paragraph? Explain.
2. Are you satisfied with the quality or interest level of the information/content Susan provides in this paragraph? Explain.
3. Use the numbers which appear on the lines of Susan's paper to indicate places where you as a reader need either more information or better quality information.
4. As a group, write down some questions you would like Susan to answer in her second draft.
5. Is Susan's paragraph an example of writer-based prose or reader-based prose? Explain.

Writing About It #85

Return to the campus problem you identified for yourself. Begin to explore the problem by writing a paragraph about your own experience with this problem. Share your paragraph with your classmates and ask them to comment on the quantity and quality of the information/content you provided. Ask them to write down some questions they would like answered as you begin your second draft.

The paragraph which follows is Susan's redraft of the paragraph which previously appeared.

I first began to think seriously about the problem of campus theft when my stereo system was stolen this year. It was a Monday night in October, the Monday before Halloween. We were making plans for a Halloween door decorating contest, deciding whether to put up pictures of witches or pumpkins or ghosts. When my roommate and I got back to our room, scissors and construction paper in hand, we were ready to get to work decorating our door with yellow-eyed black cats. Deciding to put on some music while we cut and pasted, I reached over to turn on the stereo, and the table on which it had rested was empty! At first I thought perhaps someone had borrowed my stereo. But why would anyone borrow a stereo without asking? Then I thought maybe someone was playing a practical joke. But what could possibly be funny about stealing someone's stereo? After the campus security officer interviewed me, taking down information about my Sano X-47 stereo system, I was angry and confused. I began to think that campus theft might be a serious problem.

Talking About It #86

With your classmates, discuss the following questions.

1. Is Susan's second version of this paragraph more satisfying to you as a reader? Why or why not?
2. Did Susan answer some or all of the questions you hoped she would answer for you?
3. Is Susan's paragraph an example of writer-based prose or reader-based prose? Explain.

Writing About It #87

Consider the feedback from your classmates as you revise your own paragraph on your experiences with a campus problem. After you have rewritten it, ask your fellow classmates whether this redraft is more satisfying and why. Find out whether you answered the questions they wanted answered.

After Susan explored her own experiences, you'll remember that she turned to outside sources—like her friends—to add to and develop her ideas about campus theft. She talked informally with the students she knows and took notes on what they told her. In the following paragraph Susan records that expanded information on campus theft.

As I began to talk to my friends about what had happened to me, I found that many of them had experienced similar incidents of theft and were equally concerned about the problem. Mary had a common experience. Julie had a bizarre one. I remembered that my boyfriend Bob had a bicycle stolen last year.

Talking About It #88

With your classmates, discuss the following questions.

1. Are you satisfied with the amount or quantity of information/content Susan provides in this paragraph? Explain.
2. Are you satisfied with the quality or interest level of the information/content Susan provides in this paragraph? Explain.
3. Use the numbers which appear on the lines of Susan's paper to indicate places where you as readers need either more information or better quality information.
4. Write down some questions you would like Susan to answer in her second draft.
5. Is Susan's paragraph an example of writer-based or reader-based prose? Explain.

Writing About It #89

Return to the campus problem you identified for yourself. Begin to explore your problem in greater depth and expand your knowledge base by talking to other students about the problem. Then write a paragraph in which you develop those ideas. After you have written your paragraph, share it with your classmates and ask them to comment on the amount and quality of the information/content you provided.

The paragraph which follows is Susan's redraft of the paragraph that recounts the experiences of her friends with campus theft.

As I began to talk to my friends about what had happened to me, I found that many of them had experienced similar incidents of theft and were equally concerned about the problem. I remembered back to last spring when my boyfriend Bob had his bicycle stolen even though it had been both locked and chained to the bicycle rack behind his dorm. My friend Mary experienced a common kind of theft at the beginning of the semester. She had gone down the hall to take a shower, leaving her rings and watch on the bench outside the stall while she washed. When she got out of the shower, the jewelry was gone. My friend Shandra experienced a more bizarre incident. She had left her clothes circulating in the dryer in the downstairs laundry room, and when she returned, one favorite item was missing—her only pair of designer jeans. Furthermore, the "thief" had left the rest of the clothes on the counter, in neatly folded piles.

Talking About It #90

With your classmates, discuss whether you think Susan's second version of this paragraph is more satisfying to you as a reader.

Writing About It #91

Consider the feedback from your classmates as you revise your own paragraph on your experiences with a campus problem. After you have rewritten it, ask your fellow classmates whether this redraft is more satisfying and why. Find out whether you answered the questions they wanted to have answered.

You may recall that Susan developed information on the topic of campus theft by talking to the University of Greenwich's Director of Campus Security and a campus police officer. Here is the paragraph she wrote in an attempt to communicate what she learned.

In investigating the problem of theft on campus, I decided to talk to two adults likely to know something about campus crime: a police officer and the Director of Campus Security. Both talked to me freely during the interviews, confirming that theft is not only common on the University of Greenwich campus but that it is also increasing.

Talking About It #92

With your classmates, discuss the following questions.

1. Are you satisfied with the amount or quantity of information/content Susan provides in this paragraph? Explain.
2. Are you satisfied with the quality or interest level of the information/content Susan provides in this paragraph? Explain.
3. Use the numbers which appear on the lines of Susan's paper to indicate places where you as readers need either more information or better quality information.
4. Write down some questions you would like Susan to answer in her second draft.
5. Is Susan's paragraph an example of writer-based prose or reader-based prose? Explain.

Writing About It #93

Return to the campus problem you identified for yourself. Begin to explore the problem in even more depth by interviewing two or more people in positions of authority who are likely to add to your store of information about the problem. Then write a paragraph or two incorporating this additional information. When you have finished, share your paragraph with your classmates and ask them to comment on the amount and quality of the information/content you provided.

The paragraphs which follow represent Susan's revision of her previous paragraph.

In separate interviews, campus police officer Randy Groesbeck and John Delamer, Director of Campus Security, confirmed that campus theft is both common and increasing.

Officer Groesbeck reported that campus theft was quite common. He said that the majority of thefts involve personal belongings like bicycles or stereo sets. In addition, he stated that wallets and purses and jewelry are also commonly stolen. Looking back over a stack of incident reports, Officer Groesbeck even recounted bizarre or unusual reports of theft. One student, for example, reported the theft of a bag of dirty laundry. Another reported a stolen textbook, recovered, in fact, when the thief tried to resell it in another semester. Finally, Officer Groesbeck remembered the most unusual theft report of his police career: a report on a stolen Reese cup.

Director of Campus Security, John Delamer, explained that theft on campus is generally increasing. He noted that most students are negligent about securing their property. He said they typically forget to lock the doors to their room or their car or fail to purchase and use locks for their bikes; therefore, such negligence, Delamer says, does not "lead to" theft but "invites theft." He pointed out that the University of Greenwich recognizes three types of theft: petty theft, theft, and grand theft. Petty theft, Delamer explained, refers to the theft of items of $299 or less. Theft refers to the theft of items from $300 to less than $5000. Grand theft refers to items valued at more than $5000 but less than $100,000. Furthermore, Delamer referred to the publication entitled Crime Statistics, 1993: University of Greenwich, *a publication that is updated every year. The statistics in this publication clearly show that although incidents of grand theft are on the decline, incidents of both theft and petty theft continue to rise. Theft reports are at 29 for 1993 as compared to 27 for 1992 and 21 for 1991. Petty theft reports are at 76 for 1993 as compared to 65 for 1992 and 49 for 1991.*

Talking About It #94

With your classmates, discuss the following questions.

1. Is Susan's second version of this paragraph more satisfying to you as readers? Why or why not? Is this second version an example of writer-based prose or reader-based prose? Explain.
2. Note the way Susan's information is organized.
   a. *Examine Susan's paragraphs. Why does she use three paragraphs? What is the purpose of each paragraph? Does the one-sentence paragraph which begins the section serve a special purpose?*
   b. *What are Susan's topic sentences? her controlling ideas? Are her paragraphs unified? Explain.*
   c. *Take note of the coherence in these paragraphs. Has she made use of a logical order? Explain. Does Susan repeat key terms or synonyms for them? Explain. Does she make use of transitions? Explain.*
3. Take note of Susan's content.
   a. *What techniques does she use to give credit to her sources of information?*
   b. *Is the amount of information satisfying? Is the information interesting? Explain.*

Writing About It #95

Consider the feedback from your classmates as you revise your own paragraph on your experiences with a campus problem. After you have rewritten it, ask your fellow classmates whether this redraft is more satisfying and why. Find out whether you answered the questions they wanted to have answered. Make sure your classmates comment on the organization and the content.

After Susan has examined her own experience, contacted her friends, and interviewed some campus authorities about the problem of theft, she now turns to some outside sources—*The Greenwich Weekly*, the campus newspaper, and the *Journal of Juvenile Justice*, a professional journal—to add to her store of information about campus theft. Her first draft of a paragraph discussing what she learned follows.

In 1991, The Greenwich Weekly*, the campus newspaper, began a weekly "Crime Log" feature. This feature showed that campus theft was a recurring problem. A special issue of* The Greenwich Weekly *also focused on the problem of campus crime, citing statistics documenting the increase in theft. An article in the* Journal of Juvenile Justice *explained that campus security departments are growing increasingly alarmed about campus theft. The article cited efforts underway on several campuses for fighting this serious problem.*

Talking About It #96

With your classmates, discuss the following questions.

1. Are you satisfied with the amount or quantity of information/content Susan provides in this paragraph? Explain.

2. Are you satisfied with the quality or interest level of the information/content Susan provides in this paragraph? Explain.
3. Use the numbers which appear on the lines of Susan's paper to indicate places where you as readers need either more information or better quality information.
4. Write down some questions you would like Susan to answer in her second draft.
5. Is Susan's paragraph an example of writer-based prose or reader-based prose? Explain.

Writing About It #97

Return to the campus problem you identified for yourself. Consult at least two outside sources that can help you develop more information about the campus problem you have chosen. Then write a paragraph incorporating this additional information. When you have finished, share your paragraph with your classmates and ask them to comment on the quantity and quality of the information/content you provided. Find out what questions they would like you to answer in your second draft.

Susan rewrites the paragraph which incorporates the information she developed by consulting outside sources. Here is her revision.

Both local and national publications cite growing concerns about campus theft.

In 1991, The Greenwich Weekly, *the campus newspaper, began to take a more serious look at campus crime. First, the newspaper began a weekly "Crime Log" feature. This feature, a small box at the right hand corner of page 2, reported many incidents of campus crime as a way of calling attention to this special problem. Specific incidents of theft were regularly reported. For instance, the Crime Log for April 8, 1991 stated, "Blue Schwinn Frontier 10-speed BMX bicycle, Serial Number 347839LE, stolen from the rack behind Kettering Dorm." On May 24, 1991, the Crime Log stated, "One pair of Guess jeans, size 10, stolen from the laundry room of Marycrest dorm." Second, the September 14, 1992 issue of* The Greenwich Weekly *made campus theft a front-page story. A rash of incidents of theft, which included 13 theft reports following the Homecoming football game, prompted this special story. The article emphasized the importance of securing dorm rooms, particularly on weekends when large groups of students were known for being away for long periods of time.*

In addition to local concerns about campus theft, an article in the November 1993 issue of the Journal of Juvenile Justice *points out national concerns about this problem. The author, Thomas Forster, Director of Campus Security at Northeastern College, writes: "Sensational campus crimes like rape take up increasing attention in the campus press. Unfortunately, more common crimes like theft continue to grow while they are at the same time almost completely ignored." Forster cited a new educational program called "Friends and Felons," designed to educate students about techniques for preventing theft. He also explained Northeastern's new and successful efforts to identify valued property for students. In this program, security officers brand stereos and bicycles and other property with a student's social security number. In the event of a theft, therefore, identification and recovery of the property is made easier.*

In conclusion, students and campus security officers as well as the local and national media are voicing concerns about campus theft. It is a growing problem: one not to be feared but to be faced.

Talking About It #98

With your classmates, discuss the following questions.

1. Is Susan's second version of her paragraph more satisfying to you as a reader? Why or why not? Is this second version an example of writer-based prose or reader-based prose? Explain.
2. Note the way Susan's information is organized.
   a. *Examine Susan's paragraphs. Why does she use four paragraphs? What is the purpose of each paragraph? Does the one-sentence paragraph which begins the section serve a special purpose?*
   b. *What are Susan's topic sentences? her controlling ideas? Are her paragraphs unified? Explain.*
   c. *Take note of the coherence in these paragraphs. Has she made use of a logical order? Explain. Does Susan repeat key terms or synonyms for them? Explain. Does she make use of transitions? Explain.*
3. Take note of Susan's content.
   a. *What techniques does she use to give credit to her sources of information?*
   b. *Is the amount of information satisfying? Is the information interesting? Explain.*

Writing About It #99

Consider the feedback from your classmates as you revise your own paragraph on your experiences with a campus problem. After you have rewritten it, ask your fellow classmates whether this redraft is more satisfying and why. Find out whether you answered the questions they wanted to have answered. Make sure your classmates comment on the organization and the content.

FROM PARAGRAPH TO ESSAY

As Susan begins to look over what she has written about campus theft, she sees that her many paragraphs about campus crime and the many sources that informed them can be arranged to make up a longer piece of writing called an *essay*. An essay, sometimes called a theme or composition, is simply a series of paragraphs developing a single point contained in a *thesis statement*.

A thesis statement for an essay grows out of the working statement you learned about in Chapter 4. Just as the topic sentence provides the orienting focus for a short paragraph, so does the thesis statement provide the orienting focus for a longer work—an essay—which is made up of a series of paragraphs. Just as a topic sentence contains a *controlling idea* or *point* which is developed in the course of the paragraph, so does a thesis statement contain a *controlling idea* or *point* developed in the course of the essay.

As Susan begins to arrange her various paragraphs on campus crime into an essay, she reads back over all that she has written and decides that her thesis statement will be the following sentence:

> I began to think that campus theft might be a serious problem.
> (subject/topic) (controlling idea)

As you read Susan's essay, which follows, note the way all of the paragraphs focus on her controlling idea: the seriousness of campus theft.

I first began to think seriously about the problem of campus theft when my stereo system was stolen this year. It was a Monday night in October, the Monday before Halloween. We were making plans for a Halloween door decorating contest, deciding whether to put up pictures of witches or pumpkins or ghosts. When my roommate and I got back to our room, scissors and construction paper in hand, we were ready to get to work decorating our door with yellow-eyed black cats. Deciding to put on some music while we cut and pasted, I reached over to turn on the stereo, and the table on which it had rested was empty! At first I thought perhaps someone had borrowed my stereo. But why would anyone borrow a stereo without asking? Then I thought maybe someone was playing a practical joke. But what could possibly be funny about stealing someone's stereo? After the campus security officer interviewed me, taking down information about my Sano X-47 stereo system, I was angry and confused. I began to think that campus theft might be a serious problem. As I began to talk to my friends about what had happened to me, I found that many of them had experienced similar incidents of theft and were equally concerned about the problem. I remembered back to last spring when my boyfriend Bob had his bicycle stolen even though it had been both locked and chained to the bicycle rack behind his dorm. My friend Mary experienced a common kind of theft at the beginning of the semester. She had gone down the hall to take a shower, leaving her rings and watch on the bench outside the stall while she washed. When she got out of the shower, the jewelry was gone. My friend Shandra experienced a more bizarre incident. She had left her clothes circulating in the dryer in the downstairs laundry room, and when she returned, one favorite item was missing—her only pair of designer jeans. Furthermore, the "thief" had left the rest of the clothes on the counter, in neatly folded piles.

In separate interviews, campus police officer Randy Groesbeck and John Delamer, Director of Campus Security, confirmed that campus theft is both common and increasing.

Officer Groesbeck reported that campus theft was quite common. He said that the majority of thefts involve personal belongings like bicycles or stereo sets. In addition, he stated that wallets and purses and jewelry are also commonly stolen. Looking back over a stack of incident reports, Officer Groesbeck even recounted bizarre or unusual reports of theft. One student, for example, reported the theft of a bag of dirty laundry. Another reported a stolen textbook, recovered, in fact, when the thief tried to resell it in another semester. Finally, Officer Groesbeck remembered the most unusual theft report of his police career: a report on a stolen Reese cup.

Director of Campus Security, John Delamer, explained that theft on campus is generally increasing. He noted that most students are negligent about securing their property. He said they typically forget to lock the doors to their room or their car or fail to purchase and use locks for their bikes; therefore, such negligence, Delamer says, does not "lead to" theft but "invites theft." He pointed out that the University of Greenwich recognizes three types of theft: petty theft, theft, and grand theft. Petty theft, Delamer explained, refers to the theft of items of $299 or less. Theft refers to the theft of items from $300 to less than $5000. Grand theft refers to items valued at more than $5000 but less than $100,000. Furthermore, Delamer referred to the publication entitled Crime Statistics, 1993: University of Greenwich, a publication that is updated every year. The statistics in this publication clearly show that although incidents of grand theft are on the decline, incidents of both theft and petty theft continue to rise. Theft reports are at 29 for 1993 as compared to 27 for 1992 and 21 for 1991. Petty theft reports are at 76 for 1993 as compared to 65 for 1992 and 49 for 1991.

Both local and national publications cite growing concerns about campus theft.

In 1991, The Greenwich Weekly, the campus newspaper, began to take a more serious look at campus crime. First, the newspaper began a weekly "Crime Log" feature. This feature, a small box at the right hand corner of page 2, reported many incidents of campus crime as a way of calling attention to this special problem. Specific incidents of theft were regularly reported. For instance, the Crime Log for April 8, 1991 stated, "Blue Schwinn Frontier 10-speed BMX bicycle, Serial Number 347839LE, stolen from the rack behind Kettering Dorm." On May 24, 1991, the Crime Log stated, "One pair of Guess jeans, size 10, stolen from the laundry room of Marycrest dorm." Second, the September 14, 1992 issue of The Greenwich Weekly made campus theft a front-page story. A rash of incidents of theft, which included 13 theft reports following the Homecoming football game, prompted this special story. The article emphasized the importance of securing dorm rooms, particularly on weekends when large groups of students were known for being away for long periods of time.

In addition to local concerns about campus theft, an article in the November 1993 issue of the Journal of Juvenile Justice points out national concerns *about this problem. The author, Thomas Forster, Director of Campus Security at Northeastern College, writes: "Sensational campus crimes like rape take up increasing attention in the campus press. Unfortunately, more common crimes like theft continue to grow while they are at the same time almost completely ignored." Forster cited a new educational program called "Friends and Felons," designed to educate students about techniques for preventing theft. He also explained Northeastern's new and successful efforts to identify valued property for students. In this program, security officers brand stereos and bicycles and other property with a student's social security number. In the event of a theft, therefore, identification and recovery of the property is made easier.*

In conclusion, students and campus security officers and the local and national media are voicing concerns about campus theft. It is a growing problem: one not to be feared but to be faced.

Paragraphing and the Essay

You'll remember from the early part of this chapter that paragraphing, an organizational tool for conveying meaning to your reader, is an important convention of writing. In addition, longer pieces of writing—essays and research papers or magazine articles—often make use of special kinds of paragraphs for conveying meaning. These paragraphs are called introductory paragraphs, concluding paragraphs, and transitional paragraphs.

Introductory Paragraphs

You probably know that first impressions are important. You're likely familiar with the situation of meeting someone for the first time, hoping to make a good impression. You recognize that first impressions are opportunities for making a friend, cementing a business partnership, or establishing a relationship. Because you never get a second chance to make a first impression, it's important that the first impression you make is a good one.

First impressions are important in writing, too. As a reader, you've probably experienced the difference between a novel that grips you in the first line and one that puts you to sleep before you've reached the second page. As a writer, because you want to make sure your writing grabs your reader from the very first line, you want to write a good *introductory paragraph*, a paragraph that makes the reader want to read on, a paragraph that makes a good first impression.

A good introductory paragraph or series of paragraphs will do two things: (1) announce the thesis statement and (2) interest the reader. The introductory paragraph announces the thesis so that the reader knows, early in the piece, what point the writer will be making. The introductory paragraph interests the reader so that the reader will become involved in following the point the writer is trying to make. In order to make the introduction interesting, the writer can make use of a number of techniques. The writer can

1. ask questions,
2. cite facts,
3. use quotations,
4. set a scene,
5. tell a story.

In the following paragraphs, Susan Pierce is experimenting with different techniques for writing an introductory paragraph for her essay on campus theft. Notice that she is attempting to achieve two goals in these introductory paragraphs: announcing her thesis and attempting to interest her reader.

1. Have you ever locked and chained your bicycle to the bike rack behind your dorm only to discover it missing in the morning? Have you ever put your watch and ring outside the stall when you went down the hall for a shower and found them missing while you were drying off? Have you ever had a pair of fashion jeans stolen from the laundry room? Is the experience of having something stolen familiar to you? If so, you are undoubtedly concerned about the problem of theft on college campuses.

2. The National Association of Campus Security Officers recently published some alarming statistics. Among the 350 college campuses which were part of a national survey of crime on campus, theft was classified as the most rapidly growing type of campus crime. The NACSO study broke the crime of theft down into three categories: petty theft, theft, and grand theft. NACSO defined petty theft as the theft of items of \$300 or less, theft as the theft of items of more than \$300 but less than \$5000, and grand theft as the theft of items of more than \$5000 but less than \$100,000. However, the alarming fact about theft as reported by NACSO is that it is growing on college campuses at a rapid pace. In 1993, grand thefts were up by 24%, thefts were up by 36%, and petty thefts were up by 57%. Thus, campus theft is a serious problem on college campuses.

3. Many people are familiar with the line from the Bible, written by Luke, about "a certain man (who) went down from Jerusalem to Jericho and fell among thieves." Few college students, however, would imagine that such a famous line might have implications for their college experience. When they travel from their home to a college campus, they would be unlikely to expect that they had fallen "among thieves." The fact is, however, that campus theft is a serious problem on college campuses today.

4. I first began to think seriously about the problem of campus theft when my stereo system was stolen this year. It was a Monday night in October, the Monday before Halloween. We were making plans for a Halloween door decorating contest, deciding whether to put up pictures of witches or pumpkins or ghosts. When my roommate and I got back to our room, scissors and construction paper in hand, we were ready to get to work decorating our door with yellow-eyed black cats. Deciding to put on some music while we cut and pasted, I reached over to turn on the stereo, and the table on which it had rested was empty! At first I thought perhaps someone had borrowed my stereo. But why would anyone borrow a stereo without asking? Then I thought maybe someone was playing a practical joke. But what could possibly be funny about stealing someone's stereo? After the campus security officer interviewed me, taking down information about my Sano X-47 stereo system, I was angry and confused. I began to think that campus theft might be a serious problem.

Talking About It #100

In each of the four introductory paragraphs, identify with your classmates the thesis statement and the method for creating an interesting introduction. Discuss the effectiveness of these different introductions.

One-Sentence Paragraphs

A paragraph is a signal to a reader which carries visual impact. A new paragraph says, "New idea here" or "Pay attention, reader." For this reason, writers often like to make use of the impact inherent in new paragraphs. When you read the Andy Rooney piece in Chapter 1 in which Andy Rooney introduced himself to you, you saw a writer using short or one-sentence paragraphs to suggest different aspects of his personality and create an impression on his reader.

In addition to using short paragraphs in special circumstances like Rooney does, writers sometimes use short one-sentence paragraphs to indicate transitions between sections of an essay or a report. Such paragraphs are called *transitional paragraphs*. Often transitional paragraphs are very short; frequently they are no more than one sentence. But they are an important marker indicating a new idea, a shift in thought, or an organizational signal for the reader.

Talking About It #101

Susan Pierce's essay appears on pages 168–170. In it appear two transitional paragraphs. With your classmates, use the numbered lines to identify these two transitional paragraphs. Then indicate the reason why Susan used each transitional paragraph.

Concluding Paragraphs

Concluding paragraphs, like introductory and transitional paragraphs, are paragraphs which are used for special purposes. A moviegoer, for instance, likes to feel satisfied at the end of a movie. Likewise, readers need to feel a sense of satisfaction at the end of a piece of writing. A concluding paragraph provides that sense of satisfaction or completion for them. A writer who takes care to provide a satisfying ending is probably thinking about his reader and striving to create reader-based prose.

Concluding well is a matter of summing up, of tying up the various strands of thought developed in a paper. In fact, writers often use summarizing transitions to signal that their conclusion has begun, choosing words and phrases such as "finally," "in conclusion," "in the final analysis," "in other words," "on the whole," "to sum up," and other choices. In addition, writers can choose from several methods for writing good summations or conclusions. These methods include the following techniques:

1. restating the thesis statement,
2. answering a question raised in the paper,
3. providing a summarizing quotation,
4. providing a summarizing fact or facts,
5. providing a summarizing situation or story.

In the following examples, student Susan Pierce is trying out several methods of writing a conclusion to her paper on campus theft.

1. In conclusion, students and campus security officers and the local and national media are voicing concerns about campus theft. It is a growing problem: one not to be feared but to be faced.

2. Are you concerned about the stereo system stolen from your dorm room? Are you worried about the rings and wallets missing from student dressers? Are you outraged when you hear of locked bicycles stolen from bike racks? If so, you are among the growing number of college students who are beginning to take the crime called campus theft seriously.

3. In the Bible, the book of Luke recounts the story of the unsuspecting man who "fell among thieves." This unfortunate soul experienced first-hand the unexpected consequences of theft. Unsuspecting college students are often like that Biblical man who fell among thieves. However, today they are quickly learning—the hard way—that campus theft is a crime not to be taken lightly.

4. To sum up, the statistics are alarming. The National Association of Campus Security Officers reports that, in 1993, grand thefts were up by 24%, thefts were up by 36%, and petty thefts were up by 57%. Thus, campus theft is a serious problem on college campuses.

5. Last week Mary Akers, a freshman living in Harper Hall, discovered that the credit card she had accidentally laid on the top of her bureau was missing. Fortunately, Mary had participated in the new campus identification program. As a result, her credit card was immediately canceled after she contacted campus police. But Mary Akers was one of the lucky ones. Unlike many college students, she was aware of the seriousness of the problem of theft on campus.

Talking About It #102

For each of the concluding paragraphs that appear, make note of the method of concluding that Susan Pierce used. In addition, identify any transitional words or phrases used to signal the concluding paragraph.

Unity and the Essay

As she begins to organize her essay, Susan reminds herself that the topic or subject of her paper, found in her thesis statement, is campus theft and that her controlling idea or point is that it is a serious problem. Just as in writing a paragraph, Susan will strive for unity, a sense of wholeness, in her essay. To achieve unity, Susan will make sure that all of her topic sentences support her controlling idea.

Susan remembers that when she writes a paragraph, she makes use of a unity check to keep her from going off the track and to ensure a sense of satisfying wholeness. Now Susan makes use of a unity check to ensure that same sense of satisfying wholeness for her essay. This is what she writes.

Thesis statement: I began to think that **campus theft** (topic) might be **a serious problem** (controlling idea).

Topic sentence, Paragraph 1: As I began to talk to my friends about what had happened to me, I found that many of them had experienced similar incidents of **theft** and were equally **concerned about the problem.**

Topic sentence, Paragraph 2: In separate interviews, campus police officer Randy Groesbeck and John Delamer, Director of Campus Security, confirmed that **campus theft** is both **common and increasing.**

Topic sentence, Paragraph 3: Officer Groesbeck reported that **campus theft** was quite **common.**

Topic sentence, Paragraph 4: Director of Campus Security, John Delamer, explained that **theft** on campus is generally **increasing.**

Topic sentence, Paragraph 5: Both local and national publications cite **growing concerns** about campus **theft.**

Topic sentence, Paragraph 6: In 1991, *The Greenwich Weekly*, the campus newspaper, began to take a more **serious look** at campus **crime.**

Topic sentence, Paragraph 7: In addition to local concerns about **campus theft,** an article in the November 1993 issue of the *Journal of Juvenile Justice* points out **national concerns** about this problem.

Writing About It #103

Take a few moments to write in your journal and create your own definition of "unity." Compare the unity check Susan performed on her essay with the unity check Katie Harbin performed on her paragraph which you read on pages 173–174. How are these unity checks similar or different? Explain.

Coherence and the Essay

You'll remember from the earlier part of this chapter that coherence is an important convention of writing and refers to a sense of connectedness or relatedness. You learned that effective paragraphs exhibit a sense of coherence; in this section of the text, you will learn that effective essays and longer works exhibit coherence as well.

Achieving coherence in an essay is similar to achieving coherence in a paragraph. It is a matter of

1. establishing a logical order like time order, space order, or order of importance,
2. repeating key terms or their synonyms,
3. using transitions.

Talking About It #104

Discuss the full essay written by Susan Pierce on pages 168–170 as you examine it for that sense of connectedness or relatedness called coherence. Use the following questions to guide you:

1. What is the logical order Susan has chosen for this essay. Is it time order? space order? order of importance? Give reasons for your answer.
2. What key terms or synonyms for them does Susan use in this essay?
3. List some of the transitions Susan uses in this essay.
4. Divide into groups and ask each group to perform a coherence check on a different one of Susan's paragraphs. Refer to pages 146–150 to recall the steps involved in a coherence check which you have studied.
5. Do you think Susan's essay achieves a sense of coherence? Why?

CONVENTIONS ABOUT EXPRESSION

As you have seen, a lot of what you need to learn about writing grows out of the fact that the reading/writing situation is very different from the speaking/listening situation. Although a listener is present to a speaker, a reader is not physically present to a writer. As a result, a writer needs to provide enough interesting content to communicate his or her ideas effectively. A writer must also strive for a sense of unity or wholeness and a sense of coherence or relatedness. If the reader were physically present to the writer, the reader could ask questions about the content or tell the writer where he or she has veered off the subject or suggest how to make explicit connections between ideas. Because he or she is not present, however, the writer must develop a personal sense of how to accomplish these things.

You have learned in previous chapters that a writer must develop certain strategies about his or her work as he or she plans it and immerses in its development. These strategies involve plans about *content, organization*, and *expression*. Conventions or established ways of doing things are also at work in each of these areas. You have seen the way in which conventions about content require sufficient quantity and interesting quality of ideas in a piece of writing. You have seen the way in which organization is developed in terms of conventions like topic sentences, thesis statements, controlling ideas, unity, and coherence. Now let's turn to the concept of expression and see how the reading/writing situation is different from the speaking/listening situation in order to understand the conventions that govern good choices in this area.

Talking is different from writing. When you talk to people, you interact with them. There's a lot of give and take in talking. When you talk with someone, you cooperate with someone else and someone else cooperates with you. It's what is meant by "holding up your end of a conversation." If you didn't hold up your end or if your partner didn't hold his or her end up, the whole conversation would come tumbling down. In fact, without this mutual cooperation, it would be impossible even to have a conversation with another person.

When you move from expressing yourself in speech to expressing yourself in writing, however, problems often occur. Writers, forgetting that their reader is not physically present, sometimes write the way they talk—as if they're expecting their reader to cooperate with them by finishing their words, adding to the dialogue, or otherwise holding up their end of the conversation. When writers write the way they talk, expecting their readers to act in ways that only speakers or listeners can act, they run into trouble. Generally this kind of trouble with expression leads to two main problems:

1. problems understanding conventions about content,
2. problems understanding conventions about grammar.

Student Kyle Bishop is struggling with problems in expression in the draft of a paragraph about his summer job that follows. Read it carefully and then respond to the journal questions.

I really enjoyed my job this summer. At the Foodtown in Oregonia. That's a town in Ohio. The people I worked with really made my job exciting. Never a dull moment, let me tell you. We'd keep our manager happy with our announcements over the P.A. system. Man, was it fun to get to know the people who'd come into the store all the time!

Talking About It #105

With your classmates, discuss the paragraph by Kyle by referring to the following questions.

1. Do you think that, in this paragraph, Kyle writes like he talks? Why or why not? Give specific examples to support your opinion.
2. Do you think this paragraph is an example of writer-based prose or reader-based prose? Why?
3. Does this paragraph suggest that Kyle might expect for the reader to help him in the same way that a conversational partner might help him hold up his end of a conversation in which they were engaged? Why do you think so?
4. In this paragraph, Kyle struggles to express himself clearly. One of his challenges is to understand the conventions about content in a piece of writing. If you were in a speaking/listening situation with Kyle rather than in a reading/writing situation with him, what questions would you ask Kyle to answer for you in order for him to make the content clearer?
5. In this paragraph, as Kyle struggles to express himself clearly, another of his challenges is to make use of the grammatical conventions that govern a piece of writing. If you were in a speaking/listening situation with Kyle rather than in a reading/writing situation with him, what grammatical conventions could Kyle ignore? Explain. Because Kyle is in a reading/writing situation with you, what grammatical conventions must he pay attention to? Explain.

In the paragraph which follows, Kyle has rewritten his original paragraph, reminding himself that in the reading/writing situation, unlike the speaking/listening situation, certain conventions govern the expression of his ideas. The convention about content says that the writer owes the reader a full and detailed elaboration of content. The convention about grammar says that, in the act of writing as opposed to the act of speaking, ideas about grammatical correctness can be very different and must be carefully observed.

I really enjoyed my job this summer as a deli clerk at the Foodtown in Oregonia, Ohio. The people I worked with—usually Mary Jo Hattick and Fred Boreshevski—kept both workers and customers entertained. For example, often Mary Jo and Fred and I took the ham salad spread and shaped it like a pig, adding a green pepper slice for a mouth, salami for ears, and black olives for its nose. We completed the little porker's outfit with a tiny straw hat and a corncob pipe. My manager loved the announcements we made over the public address system. Some of the workers sang "Bake, Bake, Bake Your Bread" to the tune of "Row, Row, Row Your Boat"; the singing really brought customers scrambling to the deli department. Finally, it was fun getting to know all the people who came into the store. The "regulars" included Kim and Karl who came in at least once a day for something small—a quarter pound of cheese or a few slices of roast beef. Mr. Nachman came about every other day and bought the same thing: two fat kosher pickles. Often Mrs. Light brought her two-year-old, and I loved passing pieces of cheese across the counter to her daughter. The people both inside and outside the deli department at Foodtown helped make work an interesting experience for me.

Talking About It #106

With your classmates, reflect on Kyle's revisions by referring to the following questions.

1. Use the numbered lines to indicate where Kyle has expressed his content/ideas more completely. Be specific.
2. Give examples of the conventions of grammar that Kyle honors as he expresses himself in this second draft.
3. Is this revised paragraph an example of writer-based prose or reader-based prose? Why?

WRITING ASSIGNMENTS

Choose one or several of the writing assignments which follow as a way of understanding the differences between reading/writing and listening/speaking.

A. Follow the steps provided as you work on this assignment.

1. *Find an interview in a magazine, newspaper, or journal. The interview may be with someone famous like a celebrity or a political leader or the interview may be with someone who's an expert at something like scuba diving or jewelry making.*
2. *As you read the interview, take notes on the content or information the interviewee provides during the interview. Look over your notes and decide on at least three aspects of the content which you could develop as topics for three separate paragraphs. Write those three paragraphs, making sure you write for a reader by including a topic sentence, focusing on the controlling idea, and striving for unity and coherence. For instance, if you read a interview with a famous rock musician, you might write three paragraphs on the following topics discussed in the interview: (1) Producing rock music is hard work. (2) The life of a rock musician is often unstable. (3) Competition in the rock music field is fierce.*
3. *Look over your three separate paragraphs and decide how you might combine them into a longer essay. Write that longer essay, making sure you write for a reader by including a thesis statement, focusing on the controlling idea, and striving for unity and coherence. Because this is a longer essay, you will need to write an interesting introduction and a satisfying conclusion.*
4. *Share your essay with the students in your class. Elicit their comments on your content, your organization, and your expression. Record their comments in the Writing Assessment Profile and then rewrite your essay.*

B. Follow the steps provided as you work on this assignment.

1. *Learn about a special interest or talent of one of your classmates or one of your professors. Interview that person, asking detailed and probing questions designed to elicit as much information as possible about the person's special interest or talent. Take careful notes and tape record the interview.*
2. *Look over your interview notes and play back the tape. Then decide on at least three aspects of the content which you could develop as topics for three separate paragraphs. Write those three paragraphs, making sure you write for a reader by including a topic sentence, focusing on the controlling idea, and striving for unity and coherence.*
3. *Look over your three separate paragraphs and decide how you might combine them into a longer essay. Write that longer essay, making sure you write for a reader by*

including a thesis statement, focusing on the controlling idea, and striving for unity and coherence. Because this is a longer essay, you will need to write an interesting introduction and a satisfying conclusion.

4. *Share your essay with the students in your class. Elicit their comments on your content, your organization, and your expression. Record their comments in the Writing Assessment Profile and then rewrite your essay.*

C. Follow the steps provided as you work on this assignment.

1. *Review the differences between speaking/listening and reading/writing which you charted on page 132 in this chapter.*
2. *Tape record a conversation with a friend. The conversation can be a dialogue on any subject that comes to mind, but you should try to stick with one general topic as you converse. Suitable general topics might be the difference between high school and college, the experiences which led to your friend's choice of a major, or reasons why your friend is attending the college or pursuing the job in which he or she is currently employed. Even though the presence of a tape recorder introduces an artificial element into the writing situation, you should strive for a conversation that is as natural as possible. The conversation must last at least 10 minutes.*
3. *Write down the main points of the conversation in several paragraphs. Refer to the paragraph which Ben Blumensheid wrote about holding a job and going to school to help you (page 131).*
4. *Play back the tape, taking notes about the conversation that point out the differences between the speaking/listening and reading/writing situation. Read over the written paragraph or paragraphs you composed for #3. Refer to the chart on page 132 about the differences between speaking and writing as you produce specific details from the spoken conversation and the written account to point out the differences between the speaking/listening and reading/writing situation.*
5. *Write an essay in which you refer specifically to the spoken dialogue and written account you produced as you compare and contrast the differences between the speaking/listening and reading/writing situation. As you write this essay, make sure you write for a reader by including a thesis statement, focusing on the controlling idea, and striving for unity and coherence. Because this is a longer essay, you will need to write an interesting introduction and a satisfying conclusion.*
6. *Share your essay with the students in your class. Elicit their comments on your content, your organization, and your expression. Record their comments in the Writing Assessment Profile and then rewrite your essay.*

CHAPTER FIVE REVIEW

Writing About It #107

Use your journal to reflect on what you learned in this chapter.

6

Rewriting: Responding and Critiquing

What does rewriting involve?
How can I learn to rewrite more effectively?
Can learning to respond to the work of others help me with my own rewriting?

An old expression reminds us that "the expert in any field was once a beginner." It's an expression worth remembering, particularly for the struggling writer. Often we are so captivated by the final product—the bronze sculpture, the mahogany chair, the violin solo—that we forget that the impressive creation once began as a piece of writing begins: with a scrap of an idea, a glimpse of a thought, a momentary flash of inspiration. In fact, most creations—like writing—begin with not very much at all. Creations are made, not born.

The difference between the product of an expert and a beginner, however, is more likely reflected in the amount of work and the quality of craftsmanship which the creator brings to the task. The expert has studied hard. The expert has made an investment of time. The expert has committed himself or herself. The expert has learned his or her craft. Time, energy, interest, patience, and knowledge have enabled the beginner to move to the level of expert.

It might be useful for you as a developing writer to look at the processes behind the products you admire. Think of a favorite movie scene and then imagine the hundreds of takes and retakes required to film it effectively. Think of a favorite popular song and imagine the song-writing sessions, the recording sessions, and the innumerable details that resulted in this successful piece of music. Think of a favorite item of furniture such as a chair or a desk that you like and then imagine the planning, designing, and crafting that went into its final production. You will quickly discover that what appears to be easy and effortless is often difficult and challenging.

Of course, writing is the same as that, too. A skilled writer makes work look easy and effortless. What never appears on the page, however, is the arrows and erasures, the rearranged paragraphs, the false starts and shaky conclusions behind the surface of this prose. The truth is that a piece of writing is really the result of *re*-writing, that often awkward process of rethinking, rearranging, and reassessing what a writer has originally scribbled across the page. It's impossible to get it right the first time. The expert must start out as a beginner.

As you've learned in the earlier chapters of this book, practiced writers spend most of their time in two stages of the writing process: prewriting and rewriting. You've looked at the way in which prewriting can improve your final product by helping you profile your reader, define your purpose, and develop strategies for content, organization, and expression. Now let's look at the way in which rewriting can improve your final product as well.

Rewriting, often called *revision*, occurs every time you **rethink** something you have written. Whether you are aware of it or not, rewriting or rethinking goes on through all the stages of the writing process. Sometimes it helps to understand the rewriting process if you think of a writer as a person who alternately wears two hats. The first hat is the creative hat, the hat the writer wears when being his or her creative self, producing ideas, developing details, creating the things he or she wants to say. The second hat is the critical hat, the hat the writer wears when being his or her critical self, rethinking ideas, reassessing details, and responding to and critiquing what he or she has written. As he or she writes, the writer constantly switches back and forth between these two hats, now the creator, then the critic.

Donald Murray, a writer and professor of English, uses other terms to describe these two hats. He calls them "the self" and "the other self." He writes: "The act of writing might be described as a conversation between two workmen muttering to each other at the workbench. The self speaks, the other self listens and responds. The self proposes, the other self considers. The self makes, the other self evaluates. The two selves collaborate: a problem is spotted, discussed, defined; solutions are proposed, rejected, suggested, attempted, tested, discarded, accepted."

The reason why prewriting and rewriting—the two most important parts of the writing process—are so important is that these processes help develop these different "selves." Prewriting helps sharpen the creative self; rewriting helps sharpen the critical self. However, both the creative and the critical selves must be sharp if the development of a satisfying piece of writing is to result.

As you turn your attention to rewriting in this chapter, you will begin to learn how to sharpen your critical eye, to "re-see" your work as you revise it and to improve your conversation with your "other self."

YOUR PEERS AND REWRITING

Writing can often seem like a pretty lonely business. You develop your thoughts. Alone. You labor at your writing desk. Alone. You write your draft. Alone. Your only companion seems to be your well-worn dictionary. In fact, after you've written your first draft, you often find yourself *rewriting* your draft alone, changing the order of what you've just written, crossing out and substituting words, adding new thoughts, and wondering what all solitary rewriters have wondered, "Is this change really any better? Why? Am I really improving on my original? How can I know?"

It's almost impossible for inexperienced writers to develop the kind of critical eye they need for successful rewriting by themselves. Knowing how to reassess and rethink what you've already written is not a skill you can learn on your own. Developing the critical self or "other self" depends on the quality of the conversation between the two parts of the writer—the self which creates and the other self which reads, reflects, and rethinks what has been created. Eventually a writer may reach the level of maturity or experience at which he or she can have a predictably satisfying dialogue between these two selves when working alone. Until then, however, a writer can work at developing a critical skill by sharpening a critical dialogue with others.

Other people, teachers and classroom peers, can serve as critical readers, responding as a kind of "critical self" or "other self" and providing feedback on what you have written. By listening to others provide this feedback as they respond to your work, you can engage in a dialogue with them to find out how they reacted, what they liked, where they were confused, or what they would have you change in revisions to come. After all, if the purpose of your writing is to write for a reader, who is better able to comment on your success than the reader himself?

PEER RESPONSES: SOME GUIDELINES

Although you may be interested in what your peers have to say about your writing and you may recognize that those comments can help you become a better writer, it's more likely that you don't like the idea of putting your work on public display, not only inviting but welcoming the criticisms of others.

There's no doubt about the fact that criticisms of your work can make you uneasy. Most writers—yourself included—have invested their "selves" in their writing. Often it's important to them. Sometimes it's personal. Always it's a reflection of who they are and what they think. One student remarked that having others criticize his work felt like being thrown in a cold shower without a towel.

Writing About It #108

Take a few moments to reflect in your journal on the following question: Does the thought of sharing your work with other students make you uncomfortable? Why or why not?

Because responses to their writing can make students uncomfortable, it's important to establish some guidelines for making sure the responding and critiquing process goes smoothly. Try to put these guidelines into practice as you begin to talk together about the work of your fellow students.

1. *Find something positive to say.* The more you read the work of others, the more you will see that every piece of writing generally has something positive about it. For instance, you may find that a work of one of your peers is disorganized, but you may also find the tone of that work to be sincere and earnest. At some point in your evaluation, make sure that those positive reactions are voiced.

2. *Focus only on what is actually in the text.* If you are the writer, resist the common temptation to explain "what you meant" or to see things that are not actually in the text. As writers listen to others talk about their work, they are often tempted to interrupt with comments like "But that's not what I meant" or "Let me explain what I was trying to say." In reality, such explanations take the group's mind off the issue at hand: the text. As a reader, resist the tendency to fill in the gaps in the text by assuming the writer's intention or meaning. Pay attention to what you actually experienced as a reader and ignore the impulse to guess what the writer may have intended. Focusing only on the text makes for more productive review sessions.

3. *Be aware of the common problems that affect many student response groups.* Students in response groups often experience two problems: (1) focusing on editing too early in the response process and (2) focusing on the writer rather than the text. The first problem, focusing on editing too early, causes students to tinker with surface details of the text like word choices, sentence structure, comma placement, or other concerns. You will learn some techniques for responding and critiquing in this chapter, and these techniques should help you resist the tendency to edit too soon. The second problem, focusing on the writer rather than the text, appears as group members begin to express curiosity about the writer—motivations, personal history, attitudes, and personality traits. This kind of curiosity deflects from the primary purpose of response groups: focusing on the text in order to improve it.

4. *Use "I" statements to take responsibility for your comments and to create a positive tone in your critical discussions.* An "I" statement allows you, the reader, to "own" your response and create an atmosphere free of blaming and negativity. For instance, saying "*I* found this section confusing" allows you to take responsibility for your criticism and promote a positive atmosphere in a way that "*You* don't make any sense at all in this section" doesn't. In addition, if you use "I" statements, you'll resist the temptation to tell the writer what to do.

5. *After you offer a response, ask the writer to restate your response to make sure what you've said is understood.* Often students don't understand the comments others make about their work. Nearly everyone shares the experience of reading teacher comments on papers that confuse rather than enlighten. In order to make certain that the writer understands the comments made about his or her work, allow him or her to restate those comments briefly.

6. *Back up criticisms with specifics.* Vague, unsupported critical comments are of little use to anyone. On the other hand, comments bolstered by specifics are of great help to the writer. Try to say "I sense a lack of connection between the idea about vegetarian meals in your first sentence and the idea of healthy eating at the end of the paragraph" rather than "This paragraph doesn't make any sense to me."

7. *Invite the writer as well as the reader to offer solutions to the problems uncovered by the comments, and allow the writer the freedom to reject any of the problems or solutions offered by readers.* In the final analysis, you are the author of your paper. Criticisms are merely feedback for you to consider when you return to revising your work. Criticisms freely given can be just as freely rejected.

8. *Monitor the performance of the group itself at regular intervals.* Groups are productive when they achieve their goals, and goals are only achieved when the group is functioning well. Take care to monitor the group to make sure it is paying attention, focusing on the text, drawing out responses, and making appropriate connections and suggestions.

9. *Number the lines of the text you are working on.* When you respond to the works of others, particularly when you get to the editing stage of the rewriting process, you will often have to refer to a particular idea or phrase or example in the text before you. Referring to specifics in a text is much easier when the lines of the text are numbered. Numbers can help your peers find the passage to which you are referring quickly and easily.

10. *Take notes on the advice you're being offered.* Your classmates will be offering you a great deal of advice that you can use when you begin to rewrite your early draft. Because it's important to remember what they say and because, in the heat of discussion, it's all too easy to forget the many points being made, do yourself a favor and write your classmates' comments down.

Talking About It #109

The following statements were made in a classroom engaged in peer responses to student papers. Refer to the list of guidelines as you respond as a group to each of the three following points. (1) Is the comment appropriate or effective? Why or why not? (2) What guideline or guidelines are illustrated by the comment? (3) If the comment was inappropriate or if the comment was ineffective, reword the comment in a more appropriate or effective way.

1. "You've got to change the ending in your next draft. It's just not any good."
2. "There's just not enough specific detail in this paragraph."

3. "I think you're trying to tell me that my paragraph would be more unified if I had stuck to my controlling idea."
4. "I think your story about helping your grandfather build his boat is really neat, even though I think you got the order a little mixed up in that third paragraph."
5. "A lot of us have said we'd like to see you focus your paper on one central person—like your mother—in your next draft rather than trying to say so many things about so many other relatives. What do you think?"
6. "You don't understand what I was saying here in this sentence. What I meant was . . . "
7. "Amy . . . the example I was referring to is in the middle of the essay somewhere. Ahhh . . . a few sentences after the topic sentence in about the third paragraph . . . I think."
8. "You're saying that you think I need more detail about that camping spot my Dad and I chose. I think I'd better write that down."
9. "I liked reading your paper. So where did you go to high school and why did you pick this college?"
10. "I know this is just an early draft, but I was uncomfortable with the word 'delight' in that second sentence, and your third paragraph makes it clear that you need to go over the comma rules."

RESPONDING AND CRITIQUING, EDITING AND PROOFREADING

You've seen in previous chapters that prewriting involves several stages, for example, profiling your reader, writing a purpose statement, and developing strategies for content, organization, and expression. In this chapter and the chapters to follow, you will see that rewriting involves several stages as well. They are (1) responding and critiquing and (2) editing and proofreading.

Although they are all parts of the rewriting process, responding and critiquing are different from editing and proofreading. When you respond to and critique another's work, you are plumbing the depths of the writing for its significance and meaning. You are fishing down deep. When you edit and proofread another's work, you are attempting to catch anything that mars the surface features of the work. You are skimming the surface.

Although in later chapters you will learn about editing and proofreading in more detail, in this chapter you will focus on responding and critiquing to understand the different roles each plays in the rewriting process.

Although responding and critiquing are both attempts to evaluate and assess a piece of writing, there are important differences between them. Although you can respond to a piece of writing at any stage in the writing process, in this text you will use responding to a piece of writing early in the writing process, often after you have produced some preliminary prewriting. Responding is usually a more emotional, experience-based, subjective reaction to the work. Critiquing, which comes later in the writing process after a draft or two has been completed, is a more mental, text-based, objective reaction to the work.

You can understand the difference between responding and critiquing by thinking about your reactions to different movies you've seen. When you leave the theater with a friend, you may hear initial comments such as "I thought Meryl Streep was absolutely stunning in that role" or "The movie made me think of the first time I fell in love" or "When I saw Billy Crystal go flying off that steer, I thought I'd never stop laughing!" Such reactions are like the responding stage of the rewriting process. They are first impressions: emotional, experience-based, and subjective.

On the other hand, as you begin to talk more deeply with your friend, you may find yourself making comments like this: "The cinematography was more dramatic than the dialogue" or "The characters in all these Woody Allen movies are starting to look the same" or "The movie just wasn't as good as the book." These reactions are similar to the critiquing stage of the rewriting process. They require you not just to respond subjectively but to compare, assess, analyze, and explain. They are more mental, more text-based, and more objective.

Your peers can profit from both responding and critiquing. When they hear your responses, they can learn about your emotional, experience-based reactions to their work. When they hear your critiques, they can learn about your mental reactions to their work. Most important, as you learn to improve your abilities to respond and critique, you are learning that reading is not a passive act. Reading is an act in which readers are actively making meaning out of the interaction between their own experiences and the words which appear before them as they experience a text.

METHODS OF RESPONDING

There are many ways to respond to a piece of writing. In fact, responding to the work of other students will help you learn many things about your own subjective preferences and your own emotional reactions to a variety of written texts. As you are introduced to the following methods of responding and as you begin to practice them, remember that when you respond, you are simply attempting to provide a subjective, emotional reaction to what you are reading. You either like it or dislike it. You either respond positively or negatively. You should feel under no pressure to justify your response. You simply observe it and then share it with the writer.

Freewriting

You can respond to a piece of writing by providing the writer with some freewriting of your own. As you respond to what you're reading, simply narrate for the writer what you're experiencing from moment to moment as you read the text.

As you learned in Chapter 4, when you freewrite, you write down anything that comes into your head. These responses may be subjective feelings, comments, questions, associations, interpretations, or related experiences. In the following paragraph, student Aaron Betts introduces an essay on teenage runaways. The scripted words in the left-hand column represent a classmate's freewriting produced in response to Aaron's work.

I can really relate to what Aaron says here because my mother and I fought over piano practicing.

In my case, I actually DID run away. I hid under a bridge near my home, reading comic books and definitely NOT practicing the piano.

I never felt "silly" about running away like Aaron here. I wanted my parents to know how much I hated the piano. I wanted them to take my protests seriously. My running away was not something I took lightly. Having read what Aaron has written, I'm interested in reading more of his thoughts on teenage runaways.

When I was a young boy and my mother and I disagreed over simple issues such as my bedtime or whether I should eat my brussels sprouts, I would threaten to run away. Sometimes I even made it to the end of the driveway; other times I would hide in a closet so my mother might think that I had run away. But I would come out after a few minutes because I felt silly. I was very lucky that my problems were not serious ones. As a result, I eventually grew out of the habit of running away. Some teenage runaways, however, are not as lucky as I was.

Sketching

Sometimes you can share your response to a piece of writing by using not words, but pictures. You'll recall from Chapter 4 the way in which visual representations of ideas—called *branching* and *mapping*—can help you draw out your ideas in the prewriting process. When you use sketching as a way of responding to a writer, you make use of visual methods as well.

In the passages which follow, classmates have recorded their subjective responses to student Marc Gilardi's paragraph on his brother Phil with "faces"—interested, disinterested, and indifferent. Classmates have recorded responses to Jean Landbeck's paragraph on a local bar with check marks: check, check-plus, and check-minus. You can use your imagination to "sketch" a number of creative responses to a piece of writing. One student, for instance, used sketches of traffic signs to respond to a classmate's paragraph, offering advice like "Caution:

Dangerous Intersection," "Slow Down," "Confusing Cloverleaf," "Dead End," and "Smooth Sailing." Experiment with making up some interesting sketches of your own.

1.

When my brother Phil was a teenager, he was a ruthless rebel without a cause, taking his frustrations ☹ *out on anybody or anything. One day while I was still in grade school, Phil was upset with his girlfriend Angela. He felt he had to relieve his anger, so he punched his hand through a window in my 5th* ☺!! *grade classroom. Unfortunately, I was often the target of Phil's anger. He sometimes used me to relieve his daily frustrations. When we watched television together and there was a commercial for Warehouse Paint Center, Phil used to announce, in a deep angry voice, that it was time for the Warehouse "Pain"* ☺! *Center. That meant it was time for him to turn me into Mike Tyson's personal punching* ☺ *bag. Sometimes these beatings took place on a daily basis, my rebellious brother Phil airing his anger as a regular* ☹ *part of his teenage life.*

2.

The wooden floors and paneled walls ✓ *of the bar exaggerate the dim lighting from black and red plastic* ✓+ *lanterns. Four colored television sets are suspended from the ceilings, displaying different* ✓– *shows which can't be heard over the loud* ✓– *music. Three run-down* ✓ *pool tables occupy the northwest corner of the bar, keeping the local leather-jacketed* ✓+ *men amused. Wooden tables are* ✓ *scattered aimlessly about between chairs with ripped* ✓+ *seats and broken backs. Their tops are nicked* ✓+ *from bouncing* ✓+ *quarters and engraved* ✓+ *initials. An aluminum* ✓ *ash tray sits on top of each. Neon beer signs* ✓ *decorate the walls, and a bucking mechanical* ✓+ *bull mimics the bodies* ✓+ *dancing on the raised* ✓ *platform of the dance floor.*

Writing Purpose Statements

Purpose statements are a useful means of responding to a piece of writing. When you use purpose statements, your group asks the writer and his readers to write out a one-sentence purpose statement of the writing. Then you compare your responses.

In the section which follows, you can read the early prewriting effort of student Jeffrey Fina. Then you can read the various purpose statements produced by the writer and his readers and anticipate their usefulness in helping Jeffrey when he rewrites his early draft.

My job consists of working for Food Services in Kettering Dining Hall. Working in the dishroom is a real pain because there's always a mess. Water all over the floor. Food all over your shirt and arms. You have to clean up all the tables and scrape the food from the tray-veyors. But the good part is that there are no supervisors bothering you all the time. The supervisors really bother me. They think they are so different from the other workers. When we go to lunch or dinner, all the workers eat together, but the supervisors eat at the other end of the dining room. Like if they were something exclusive or special. Yesterday, I needed help carrying silverware out to the front, and I asked one of the supervisors to help me. She asked one of the salad bar workers to help me carry the silverware when she could have done it herself. The ironic part is that the "real" boss acts completely different. He helps everyone and eats with the workers. He knows he's the boss, but he doesn't act like he's something special. That's why a lot of people quit working at Kettering Dining Hall.

Purpose statement, Reader #1: The purpose of this paragraph is to explain why the writer hates his job at Kettering Dining Hall.

Purpose statement, Reader #2: The purpose of Jeffrey's writing is to create reader sympathy for the hard time he has at his job.

Purpose statement, Reader #3: The purpose of Jeff's paragraph is to tell why the supervisors at Kettering Dining Hall irritate him so much.

Purpose statement, Writer: I wanted to write a paragraph describing my job and also the way the supervisors—except for my boss—really bug me.

Talking About It #110

Imagine that you are Jeffrey Fina's classmates. Then role-play the parts of the three readers and the writer. Model a group meeting in which a discussion of Jeffrey's draft, based on those purpose statements, takes place.

What issues were addressed in the role playing situation? What help did Jeffrey receive from the group?

REDRAFTING

After you have listened carefully to your classmates, you are ready to write another draft. Below appear several points you can keep in mind whenever you begin another draft of your work.

1. *Review your reader profile and purpose statement.* Decide whether your reader profile and purpose statement continue to seem appropriate. If they do, review them once more to keep them in mind as you rewrite. If they do not, rewrite them in line with your classmates' comments and your own purposes for writing.

2. *Review the notes you made when classmates either responded to or critiqued your draft.* It's important to remember what your readers have said as they responded to your draft. Review your notes as you consider carefully what they have said.

3. *Decide whether the reader responses seem justified.* More often than not, you will agree with your readers' assessments of your work and will find it very helpful. On the other hand, it's important to remember that you're the writer. You have the final say over your work. Ultimately, you're the one that's in control.

4. *Make changes that will enable you to improve your content and/or organization in your next version. Don't worry too much about matters of expression.* Concentrate on the broader, more global issues of content and organization as you begin to produce another draft. You will have time during the editing stage of the writing process to respond to concerns with expression. Issues of sentence structure, grammar, spelling, and others can be dealt with later.

5. *If necessary, go back and do more prewriting.* You'll remember that writing is a recursive process, circling backward as often as it moves forward. If you're having trouble generating more detailed or interesting content, take some time to do more talking, freewriting, looping, branching, mapping, or questioning to stimulate more ideas for your paper. If organization is your biggest problem, reassess your organizational strategies.

6. *Remember that you are writing for a reader, attempting to turn writer-based prose into reader-based prose.* Make a conscious effort to put yourself in your reader's shoes, asking yourself how a reader might respond to what you have written.

7. *Relax and enjoy immersing yourself in the writing process again.*

METHODS OF CRITIQUING

After your fellow student has written another version of his paper, you will read it again. As you begin to read this next draft, you may return to considering your responses once more. However, on this reading it is more likely that you will begin to think more critically about *why* you responded the way you did by scrutinizing the text the student has written even more closely. As you begin to offer reasons for your reactions by referring to what appears in the student's text, you are engaging in the *critiquing* stage of the rewriting process. As you have read in an earlier section of this chapter, critiquing is different from responding because it is more mental, more text-based, and more objective.

As you begin to critique the work of your fellow classmates, it's important to remember that in the critiquing stage of the rewriting process you still do not need to be concerned with word choice or sentence structure or punctuation or any other surface features of the writing. These concerns will be taken up later in the editing and proofreading stage of the rewriting process. Some useful methods for critiquing a text are explained. Allow yourself and your fellow classmates to experiment with a variety of these methods:

1. point/support critiques,
2. writer-based and reader-based critiques,
3. analytical critiques,
4. what's missing critiques,
5. 2 + 2 critiques,
6. CCARD critiques,
7. formal question critiques.

Point/Support Critiques

After you have offered your responses to a text either through freewrites, sketches, or purpose statements, you may choose to critique that text by using the *point/support* system. You will remember that every paragraph needs to make a **point**, embodied in the topic sentence, and that every essay needs to make a **point**, embodied in the thesis statement. A point like a topic sentence or thesis statement helps to organize a text. In addition, you will remember that texts make those points through **support**, those facts, descriptions, examples, reasons, comparisons, and other sources of ideas that make up the content of a text.

When you critique a text using the point/support system, you underline or circle the point and then number the different instances of support provided by the writer. Then the points and their support can serve as a basis of discussion among your classmates to help your fellow writer improve his text. In the following section, student Scott Carney has written the paragraph which appears on the right. His classmate first responded to Scott's text using the freewriting response system on the left. Then Scott's classmate critiqued his text using the point/support system to which you have just been introduced.

I was interested in Scott's topic because my mother is just the opposite: incredibly DISorganized!

I was disappointed at the end of Scott's paragraph because I still don't know exactly how his mother is organized. I felt the need for more understanding of her organizational habits.

POINT

My mother is very well organized. For instance, she holds onto her dearest possession at all times: a

1

schedule book. This contains all her important dates. She is also very orga-

2

nized at work. Her desk is unbelievably well organized. Her study at

3

home is just as well organized as her work office.

Talking About It #111

Imagine that you are one of Scott's fellow classmates using the point/support method for critiquing Scott's work as you answer the questions which follow.

1. Discuss the kinds of things you might say to Scott in order for him to improve his paragraph when he rewrites it.
2. Does Scott have a greater problem with content or with organization? Explain your answer.
3. Suggest specific ways in which Scott can strengthen the content of his paragraph.

Writing About It #112

Use your imagination, pretend that you are Scott, and rewrite Scott's paragraph. Then share your responses with the other students in the class. Which of your versions seems improved? Why or why not?

Writer-Based and Reader-Based Critiques

Often you can critique a piece of writing by identifying the parts of it in which the writer forgot to write for you, the reader. Sometimes a writer forgets to profile the reader. Sometimes the writer forgets that he is trying to fashion reader-based, not writer-based prose. Sometimes the writer forgets that writing isn't like speaking: therefore, he can't expect a reader to act like a listener, jumping in when he needs more clarification or more information. As a writer, he needs to try to anticipate what the reader needs from him because the reader, unlike the listener, is not physically present. Thus, another useful means of critiquing a piece of writing asks the reader to underline or circle parts of a text in which *writer-based prose* appears and then to put question marks over those portions. Using this method, the reader merely circles those parts of the text that fail to satisfy him and which need to be transformed by the writer into *reader-based prose.*

In the following paragraph, a classmate critiques student Katie Harbin's paragraph using this method. The classmate has underlined those parts which need to be rewritten to satisfy the needs of a reader. These underlined portions have also had question marks placed over them. In the left-hand margin, Katie's reader has indicated the information that might be needed to turn this paragraph into more reader-based prose.

What was the bad experience? *Who was the music teacher?* *Why didn't he like you?* *What was your brother's name?* *Why was he so good at music?* *Why weren't you?* *What was so hard about getting to his class on time?* *Why did he give you a hard time?* *Why not?*	I had a bad experience with my music teacher. He just never liked me. Maybe it was because my brother was so good at music and I wasn't. I had trouble with getting to his class on time. He also gave me a hard time because I couldn't participate in marching band.

Talking About It #113

Imagine that you are one of Katie's fellow classmates using the writer-based/reader-based method for critiquing her work as you answer the questions which follow.

1. Discuss the kinds of things you might say to Katie in order for her to improve her paragraph when she rewrites it.
2. Does Katie have a greater problem with content or with organization? Explain your answer. Suggest specific ways in which Katie can strengthen her paper in the next draft.

Writing About It #114

Use your imagination, pretend that you are Katie, and rewrite Katie's paragraph. Then share your responses with the other students in the class. Which of your versions seems improved? Why or why not?

Analytical Critiques

Another way of critiquing a piece of writing makes use of an analytical critique. The *analytical critique* asks you to comment on the writing by analyzing three issues for each of the paragraphs in the piece. Thus, for each paragraph, you ask yourself these three questions:

1. What is the writer doing?
2. How is the writer doing it?
3. Is the writer succeeding?

In the following introductory paragraph, Jay Paris is acquainting his reader with his topic, the Melrose apple, affectionately nicknamed by the writer as "Big Ugly." After you read it, notice that Jay's classmate has provided an analytical critique by answering each of the three questions given.

The first time I ate a Melrose apple was sixteen years ago while standing in the small orchard of John Kalafus, a man who had grown fruit for approximately sixty years. I was there to buy a crate of dessert apples for the woman's auxiliary of the Franklin Square Methodist Church. Mr. Kalafus walked me to a block of semi-dwarfs that were laden with the largest, ugliest produce that I had ever seen. He snipped one from a drooping branch and thrust it toward me. "You better try this," he said. I was not encouraged to put it to my lips. It resembled an off-colored grapefruit, dipped in finger paints. Intersecting the awful yellows, greens and reds were patches of russet, and it was lopsided. "Sedimentary, igneous or meteorite?" I asked Mr. Kalafus. "Bite it," he said. And so I did, cutting through its pitiful skin. In that moment, Big Ugly became Sweet Luscious, and no apple has ever tasted as good.

1. <u>What is the writer doing?</u> *In this paragraph, the writer is introducing his topic, the Melrose apple.*

2. <u>How is the writer doing it?</u> *The writer is doing this by telling a story about the first time he ate a Melrose apple.*

3. <u>Is the writer succeeding?</u> *Yes. I think the writer is succeeding because the story arouses my interest in the topic. All the details about Mr. Kalafus and his orchard are interesting. Descriptive language like "dipped in finger paints" and the use of colors like "yellow" and "russet" makes the introduction come alive. Also the contrast—the writer expects not to like the apple and yet finds out he does—effectively arouses the reader's interest.*

It's important to remember to be specific as you're describing what the writer is doing and how he's doing it and as you explain whether or not you think the writer is succeeding. It's also important to remember to answer all three of the analytical critique questions for each separate paragraph in an essay.

What's Missing Critique

Student drafts often leave things out. Sometimes a student forgets to define an important term. Sometimes a student leaves out important evidence. Sometimes a student fails to make connections between ideas.

The *what's missing critique* attempts to identify those places where gaps need to be filled in, inconsistencies need to be explained, connections need to be made. Students are usually good at spotting what's missing in a piece of writing. If they have trouble, they may like to use the following questions to critique a piece of writing more thoroughly.

What's Missing	Question
Purpose	What is the purpose of the writing?
Introduction	Is the introduction effective? Does it point out the direction that the writing will take?
Conclusion	Is the conclusion effective?
Definition	Are there terms that need to be explained?
Expectations	Does the writing set up any expectations that need to be fulfilled?
Alternatives	Are there alternatives that need to be explored?
Generalizations	Are the general statements made clear? Are they bolstered with specifics?
Clarity	Is there anything that remains unclear?
Explanation	Is there anything that needs to be explained?
Logic	Is it logical? Do the ideas take a logical order?
Connections	Are the parts connected?

Talking About It #115

As a class, read the following student paragraph. Then divide into small groups and critique the paragraph using the "What's missing" questions. Note that not all what's missing questions may be relevant; therefore, you shouldn't feel compelled to respond to every what's missing question.

Video games are also blamed for children's low scores on tests. It is a common belief among parents that video games are addictive. Kathy S., the mother of a fifteen-year-old boy and a thirteen-year-old girl, said her son came home from school and played Nintendo until his father came home from work. The father would then drive Tommy to the mall where the boy would play arcade games. Finally, when Tommy got home, he started his homework. If he finished his homework before 11 p.m., he was rewarded by being allowed to play Nintendo a little longer. Another example is Ruth D., mother of four children between the ages of 12 and 22. All of her children enjoy the games on their computer, but the youngest, who spends up to thirty hours a week on the computer, has become completely antisocial.

2 + 2 Critiques

The 2 + 2 method is another useful method for critiquing student drafts. The method requires readers to come up with the *two most effective qualities* of the writing and the *two most necessary changes* for improving the next draft.

Talking About It #116

As a class, read the following student paper carefully. Then divide into groups and use the 2+2 method for critiquing the text, identifying the two most effective qualities of the writing and the two most needed changes.

Being captain of my varsity soccer team helped mold me into a good leader. For example, it was my freshman year when I became captain. At first, I had to work hard at practices to get the team in shape. This was hard at first because everyone else was an upperclassman, and I had to win their trust. For instance, there was one kid, a senior, who kept giving me a hard time. I suggested to my coach that he should be dismissed from the team, which he later was. This incident shows that I finally won the team's trust.

After this point, everything was going great. I was happy and so was everyone else. But as the season progressed, it seemed as if I was losing the team's trust again. We had just lost two games in a row, and I knew we had to respond with a win. We were scheduled to play our archrival, the Howland Tigers, whom we had never beaten. Game day was tense. But we won, and I had finally proved my leadership qualities once again.

CCARD Critiques

The CCARD critique allows you to focus on several matters as you critique a fellow student's text. CCARD is an acronym for *Clarify, Connect, Add, Rearrange*, and *Delete*. When you critique a text based on the CCARD system, you respond to the following issues:

Clarify	Where does the writer need to clarify the material?
Connect	Where does the writer need to make connections?
Add	Where does the writer need to add more information?
Rearrange	Where does the writer need to rearrange the material?
Delete	Where does the writer need to delete material?

Talking About It #117

As a class, read the following student passage carefully. Then form small groups to use the CCARD critique to identify places where the student needs to clarify, connect, add, rearrange, or delete.

Although I am late for work nearly every day, my boss never minds. I guess you could say I'm his favorite waitress. I never get docked in pay for being late, but all the other girls do. I can come and go as I please. I even get my paycheck first. When it comes to getting the best working schedule, I always get my way. When it's a nice Saturday afternoon and I want the day off, all I need to do is make one call, and—presto!—I'm off! I suppose I'm his pet because I always came to this restaurant from the time I was a baby.

All through my growing up years. My parents were his friends. We ate there every Sunday after church and usually one night during the week. Even if I do get yelled at for forgetting something, I can use my sense of humor to get me out of trouble and bring a smile to my boss' lips.

Formal Questions Critiques

Often teachers make up their own formal questions for critiquing. These methods ask you to respond to a set of questions that reflect certain conventions about writing as they apply to the text you are examining. Teachers exhibit a great variety in the kinds of questions they ask and the issues they wish to explore. However, these formal methods often exhibit broad similarities. Typically, they ask you to respond to questions about content (what you say) and organization (the structure in which you say it), leaving questions about expression (how you say it) to the editing stage of the writing process. The chart below will remind you of the broad issues that often arise when you begin to answer *formal questions* about content and organization.

Content	**Organization**
Quality of content	Beginning
Quantity of content	Middle
	End

When you look at the quality and quantity of the **content** in a work of writing you are critiquing, you ask yourself questions such as "Is the content interesting?" "Is the content sufficient?" "Are there enough examples, facts, reasons, descriptions, comparisons and other sources of content to make the text both interesting and satisfying?" When you look at the **organization** of a work of writing, you ask yourself "Does the beginning contain a thesis statement or topic sentence?" "Does the middle exhibit unity and coherence?" "Does the end provide an appropriate conclusion?"

In the section which follows, you will be introduced to some formal questions for critiquing that will help you focus on the content and organization of your fellow students' texts. Just as responding to a piece of writing was made easier by understanding techniques like freewriting, sketching, and writing purpose statements, so is critiquing made easier by understanding the questions which follow. For instance, formal questions for critiquing paragraphs based on some of the principles you have studied in this text might ask you to read a fellow student's written work and then respond to the following questions:

Critiquing Your Paragraph and Essays

Content

1. Is the quality of the content satisfying? Are the details, facts, reasons, examples, comparisons, and other methods of supporting the ideas interesting? Why or why not? Point to specifics in the text to support your ideas.
2. Is the quantity of the content sufficient? Are there enough details, facts, reasons, examples, comparisons, and other methods of supporting the ideas to make the paragraph satisfying? Why or why not? Point to specifics in the text to support your ideas.
3. What suggestions would you make to the writer for improving the content in the next draft?

Organization

1. If this is an essay, is the beginning of the essay well organized with a thesis statement? Is the introduction interesting and appropriate? If this is a paragraph, is the beginning of the paragraph well organized? Does it contain a topic sentence?
2. Is the middle of the paragraph or essay well organized?
   - a. Is it unified? If this is an essay, does each of the topic sentences support the thesis? If this is a paragraph, does each of the sentences support the topic sentence?
   - b. Is it coherent?
     - i. Are the ideas presented in a logical order?
     - ii. Are the ideas repeated with synonyms or other substitutes?
     - iii. Are the ideas tied together with transitions?
3. Is the end of the paragraph or essay well organized? Is there an appropriate conclusion?
4. What suggestions would you make to the writer for improving the organization in the next draft?

The following paragraph was written by student Ed Papp. Read it carefully and then read over the student review of Ed's paragraph which makes use of formal methods of critiquing it.

Working a deconstruction job was a dangerous summer occupation. Although most of my friends had been employed in construction work and had spent their summer building things, I, on the other hand, spent my summer tearing things down. During June, July, and August, the hottest months of the year, some co-workers and I laboriously destroyed the inside of a formal club/dance hall called Rocky's. First, I began work in early June by swinging an eight pound sledge-axe, breaking up a ceramic tile floor into worthless shards. The process of busting up the floor sent broken and chipped pieces flying through the air, slicing the skin near one of my co-worker's eyes and sending him to the com-

pany nurse. Next, on a hot Tuesday morning in July, another worker, who had been on the job only a few hours, was injured, and my foreman had to call the paramedics. Finally, in August, three of us worked on rickety twelve-foot ladders to remove drywall with foot-long crowbars. We were threatened by dangerous heights, protruding nails, and drywall dust. All of us also harbored the secret fear that the drywall we removed may have contained some unhealthy fire-resistant material: asbestos.

Critiquing Your Paragraphs and Essays

Content

1. Is the quality of the content satisfying? Are the details, facts, reasons, examples, comparisons, and other methods of supporting the ideas interesting? Why or why not? Point to specifics in the text to support your ideas.

> *I found the quality of the content very satisfying. Ed used lots of descriptive details to make his ideas interesting. Some examples of these are "eight-pound sledge-axe," "ceramic tile floor," and "rickety twelve-foot ladders." Ed also uses lots of examples to show how dangerous his job was. He gives the example of busting up the floor on the first day of work, the example of the new worker being sent to the hospital after only a few hours on the job, and the example of the fear of asbestos in the drywall material.*

2. Is the quantity of the content sufficient? Are there enough details, facts, reasons, examples, comparisons, and other methods of supporting the ideas to make the paragraph satisfying? Why or why not? Point to specifics in the text to support your ideas.

> *There is generally sufficient quantity of content in Ed's paragraph. As explained above, Ed uses lots of descriptive details and examples.*

3. What suggestions would you make to the writer for improving the content in the next draft?

> *Although Ed's content is very good, I felt the need for more explanation in his second example, lines 11 to 13. Why were the paramedics called? What happened to the new worker? How was he injured? I was curious to learn more about this, and I hope Ed adds an explanation of this in his next draft.*

Organization

1. If this is an essay, is the beginning of the essay well organized with a thesis statement? Is the introduction interesting and appropriate? If this is a paragraph, is the beginning of the paragraph well organized? Does it contain a topic sentence?

Ed has written a paragraph, and he has included a good topic sentence at the beginning. The topic sentence is, "Working a deconstruction job was a dangerous summer occupation."

2. Is the middle of the paragraph or essay well organized?

a. *Is it unified? If this is an essay, does each of the topic sentences support the thesis? If this is a paragraph, does each of the sentences support the topic sentence?*

Yes. I think this is a unified paragraph. All of Ed's sentences support the controlling idea found in his topic sentence, the idea that his summer job was "dangerous."

b. *Is it coherent? Yes.*

i. Are the ideas presented in a logical order?

Yes. There's a logical order here. Ed begins his paragraph with the dangerous things that happened when he first started in the month of June. Then he moves on to the dangerous things in the month of July, and he finishes with the dangerous incidents in the month of August. He makes use of a logical time order in this paragraph. Very good.

ii. Are the ideas repeated with synonyms or other substitutes?

Yes, I think so. Ed's controlling idea is "dangerous." He uses lots of synonyms for this idea: "slicing the skin," "threatened," "paramedics," "rickety," "secret fear," and "unhealthy." All these substitutes for the idea of danger help make the paragraph coherent.

iii. Are the ideas tied together with transitions?

I think Ed uses plenty of transitions to link his ideas. These are words like "on the other hand," "although," "first," "next," "finally," and "also."

3. Is the end of the paragraph or essay well organized? Is there an appropriate conclusion?

No. I don't think Ed has written a satisfying conclusion. Although this is a very good paragraph, I felt like I was left "hanging" at the end. I think Ed needs a conclusion.

4. What suggestions would you make to the writer for improving the organization in the next draft?

Ed's paragraph is very well organized. However, I think he needs to add a conclusion when he revises it.

The following essay is about student Dorey Butter's experiences as an exchange student in Japan. Read it carefully and then watch the way one of her fellow classmates critiques Dorey's work by making use of formal methods of critiquing.

My first dreams of paper cranes and white rice in the "Land of the Rising Sun" came the summer after seventh grade. My family was asked to host some Japanese students as they traveled through Ohio on their school-sponsored tour of the United States. We hosted two boys that year, and I became very interested in learning about Japanese culture and lifestyles. Visions of kimonos, thongs, and chopsticks became regular daydreams for me when, a year later, I learned that I, too, would travel with my own school group to Japan. Unfortunately, I thought that "bonzai" and "sushi" would be enough vocabulary for my 2-week stay in Japan. I left for Japan unaware that the problem of communication threatened to turn my pleasant dream of Japan into a cultural nightmare.

My flight to Japan was over 15 hours long, and I did not sleep. The attendants were pleasant enough, but they spoke only Japanese. When I got hungry, I rubbed my belly and pointed to my stomach and made motions as if to put food in my mouth. I saw a light go on in an attendant's eyes, and she hurriedly returned from the kitchen with something that instantly killed my appetite: cold sushi and soggy noodles. I tried distracting myself from my hunger by watching a movie about Japanese ninjas, but there were no subtitles, and the only sounds I could understand were the grunts and moans of the fighting Japanese men.

My Japanese family picked me up at the airport, speaking Japanese to me the entire way back to their home, an apartment situated above their family business. Although I politely nodded, smiled, and pretended I understood every word, I had no clue what they were saying to me. But when we arrived at the door to their apartment, I made a huge mistake by crossing over the threshhold without taking off my shoes. I had been wondering why all of the family members had been pointing at my feet and why the mother in particular kept shaking her finger at me as if I were being reprimanded. After I realized I had violated the sacred Japanese custom which required removing the shoes before entering a household, I went to my room, flung myself onto my straw mat, and cried.

My lack of Japanese language skills caused me problems over the simplest matters. When I tore my return airline ticket, I had trouble asking for a piece of Scotch tape. As I had lost my book of stamps on the airplane, I struggled to communicate my need for a postage stamp. At meals, I indicated that I preferred the plain rice to the live squid by pointing. Most embarrassing of all were the times when we were touring the city, and I realized I needed a restroom. Because I knew no words to communicate my distress, I learned to hold my bladder for long periods of time, following my host family members gratefully into the restroom when their bladders were in need of relief.

Although I enjoyed my trip to Japan and the special people and places of this exotic country, my lack of language skills continued to be a troubling problem for me until it was time to leave. Then I could finally say one of the only Japanese words I really knew: "sayonara."

Critiquing Your Paragraphs and Essays

Content

1. Is the quality of the content satisfying? Are the details, facts, reasons, examples, comparisons, and other methods of supporting the ideas interesting? Why or why not? Point to specifics in the text to support your ideas.

> *I think that the quality of this essay is very good. There are many examples of the problems caused by Dorey's lack of communication skills—asking for Scotch tape, understanding a Japanese movie, finding a restroom. The ideas in this essay are very interesting.*

2. Is the quantity of the content sufficient? Are there enough details, facts, reasons, examples, comparisons, and other methods of supporting the ideas to make the paragraph satisfying? Why or why not? Point to specifics in the text to support your ideas.

> *The quantity or number of ideas seems very satisfying. I felt that Dorey used many examples. I didn't feel the need for any more.*

3. What suggestions would you make to the writer for improving the content in the next draft?

> *I wouldn't change much of anything. I'm impressed by the quality and quantity of the content here.*

Organization

1. If this is an essay, is the beginning of the essay well organized with a thesis statement? Is the introduction interesting and appropriate? If this is a paragraph, is the beginning of the paragraph well organized? Does it contain a topic sentence?

> *This is an essay that begins with an introductory paragraph. The introduction is very interesting. It tells how Dorey became interested in going to Japan. With references to "paper cranes," "white rice," "chopsticks," and "kimonos" (lines 1 to 6), she made me interested in reading more about the Japanese culture.*
>
> *In addition, the introduction does contain a thesis statement. It is found in lines 9 to 11. It reads, "I left for Japan unaware that the problem of communication threatened to turn my pleasant dream of Japan into a cultural nightmare."*

2. Is the middle of the paragraph or essay well organized?

a. *Is it unified? If this is an essay, does each of the topic sentences support the thesis? If this is a paragraph, does each of the sentences support the topic sentence?*

> *Because this is an essay, each paragraph needs to have a topic sentence that supports the thesis. In Dorey's case, the point of her thesis*

is that she experienced a "problem of communication." This idea about communication problems should be repeated or reemphasized in her topic sentences. She refers to the communication problem through a topic sentence in her fourth paragraph when she writes, "My lack of Japanese language skills caused me problems over the simplest matters" (lines 29 and 30).

However, Dorey does not appear to have written a topic sentence for either paragraph two or paragraph three. Her essay is not really very well unified until each paragraph has a topic sentence that supports her thesis.

b. *Is it coherent?*

i. Are the ideas presented in a logical order?

Yes. The ideas are presented logically. She uses a kind of time or chronological order to describe the language problems that she faces on the airplane to Japan, at the home of her Japanese hosts, and in the course of her daily life there.

ii. Are the ideas repeated with synonyms or other substitutes?

Yes. The central idea of Dorey's communication problems is repeated with synonyms or substitutes like "no clue," "lack of language skills," "trouble," "distress," and "troubling problem."

iii. Are the ideas tied together with transitions?

The many transitions help give this essay a sense of connection and relatedness. These transitions are words like "unfortunately," "as," "when," "after," "because," "although," "then," and "finally."

3. Is the end of the paragraph or essay well organized? Is there an appropriate conclusion?

I really liked the ending. I thought it was strong and clever. To end with the one Japanese word Dorey does *know—"sayonara," which means "good bye"—seems a fitting and ironic ending.*

4. What suggestions would you make to the writer for improving the organization in the next draft?

Dorey needs to work on unity by providing topic sentences in paragraphs two and three. For paragraph two, she might write something like "The airplane trip to Japan warned me that my lack of language skills would be a serious problem." Paragraph three might contain a topic sentence something like this: "When I arrived in Japan the next day, my lack of communication skills caused me to commit an embarrassing cultural faux pas*."*

REVISING

After you produced some preliminary text, your classmates responded to it and then you redrafted your material. Then your classmates critiqued that next draft, providing you with a number of useful ideas to strengthen your paper. Before you revise your draft one more time, review the points about redrafting outlined for you on page 190.

WRITING ASSIGNMENTS

A. Immerse yourself in the process of producing an essay on any topic of your choosing.

In the first stage of the process, remember to profile your reader, write a purpose statement, and plan strategies for content, organization, and expression before you write. After you have produced some initial efforts, share them with your classmates and ask them to respond to them. Record their reactions in the Writing Assessment Profile.

In your next draft, share your writing with your classmates and ask them to critique it, using one of the methods outlined in this chapter. Record their critiques in the Writing Assessment Profile in the back of this book.

After your classmates have critiqued your work, revise your essay again.

When your revision is finished, write a detailed analysis of the ways in which working through this process has improved your paper.

B. Choose a piece of preliminary writing which you have already written for this course. Pick a partner in the class to work with, and ask this partner to respond to your work, using his choice of the methods outlined in this chapter. Then you will do the same for your partner's paper. Record your partner's responses in the Writing Assessment Profile in the back of this book.

After you have both produced another draft, ask your partner to critique your work, using his choice of the methods outlined in this chapter. Provide the same feedback for your partner.

Then write an essay on what both of you learned about your papers through the responding and critiquing process and what both of you will need to do to improve on your papers in your future drafts.

CHAPTER SIX REVIEW

Writing About It #118

Use your journal to reflect on what you learned in this chapter.

7

Rewriting: Editing and Proofreading

What is the difference between editing and proofreading? How can I become a better editor and proofreader?

When you reach the editing and proofreading stage of the rewriting process, you need to take time out to reward yourself, for you've come a long way. You have engaged in some concentrated prewriting, wearing your creative hat and thinking about your reader, your purpose, and your strategies for content, organization, and expression. You've shared those thoughts with your classmates, who have offered responses to help you improve another draft. After you have done some careful revising, you shared that revision with your classmates, who have donned their critical hats along with you, critiquing your draft with care. In your next revision, you've incorporated their concerns as well as your own. Thus, what you've done so far represents significant amounts of time, effort, energy, and thought. You owe yourself a reward.

After you've walked the dog, enjoyed a soda, or taken a telephone break to talk to a friend, you recognize that you've improved on the content and organization of your piece to the best of your ability. You know it's time to move on to the final stage of the rewriting process: editing and proofreading.

As you move into the editing and proofreading stage, you'll probably have many questions: What, exactly, is editing and proofreading? How are they similar to or different from each other? What are the activities that characterize this stage of the writing process? What do I need to know to become a skillful editor and proofreader? You will learn the answers to these questions and many others as you read this chapter.

A popular bumper sticker advocating involvement on behalf of the environment reads, "Think globally. Act locally." What this slogan means is that in order to solve the environmental problems of the planet, we need to think generally about the fate of the entire earth and act specifically to enhance its survival right in our own back yards. Curiously enough, the same kind of advice applies to writing. In the responding and critiquing stage of the rewriting process, you are thinking "globally" about the broad issues of content and organization; in the editing and proofreading stage, you are acting "locally" in your specific response to the words and sentences you have written.

Think back to what you've learned about writing in earlier stages of this textbook. When you were planning your strategies for writing, you developed preliminary ideas about your content, your organization, and your expression. Content, you'll remember, referred to your subject matter or topic: what you were saying. Organization referred to the arrangement of that material: the way in which you presented it. Expression referred to your language choices, the words and sentences that made up your writing style: how you expressed yourself. In the rewriting stage when you are either responding or critiquing, you are dealing with global matters of content and organization. In the rewriting stage when you are either editing or proofreading, you are dealing with local matters of expression.

Editing and proofreading both deal with your use of words and sentences, but editing involves a greater investment of time and thought than proofreading. Proofreading is the finishing touch. It's like the final coat of shellac on a tabletop that you've been sanding smooth for weeks. It's like erasing that stray smudge of charcoal from the drawing you've been laboring over for days. It's like stitching up the hem of an elegant skirt you've been sewing for hours. Because proofreading is in some ways a less demanding skill than editing, most of this chapter will be concerned with developing your skills as an editor.

In order to produce a piece of writing that is reader-based, you need to edit your work by keeping the needs of your reader in mind. Therefore, you need to understand what readers expect about the way you express yourself in a piece of writing. In general, when you edit your work, you need to understand these two things about your expression: your reader's need for (1) consistency and (2) clarity.

EDITING AND CONSISTENCY

Consistency is a quality you are already familiar with. When things are consistent, they exhibit a stability, a harmony, a uniformity that adds congruency and predictability to them. When children are disciplined in a lovingly consistent way, they develop a sense of stability about what's expected of them. When a novelist creates a book in which the theme, characters, and plot are consistent with one another, the work of fiction exhibits a sense of harmony. When a presidential candidate promotes policies about the economy, the environment, the social climate, and the world order consistent with the nation's ideal of democracy, a sense of uniformity emerges.

Readers expect consistency in what they read. They expect a piece of writing to offer a sense of stability, harmony, and uniformity, and it's a writer's job to give it to them. In order to develop that sense of consistency, writers in the editing stage of the rewriting process need to provide their readers with a sense of consistent (1) point of view, (2) tense, and (3) tone.

Consistency and Point of View

In Chapter 4, you learned that an important part of expression in writing involves deciding on the amount of distance or closeness you wish to achieve with your reader, referred to as **point of view**. You'll remember from the chart on page 122 that first person point of view provides the greatest amount of closeness or intimacy with the reader, that second person point of view offers a less intimate but still friendly relationship with the reader, and that third person point of view represents the most formal and objective relationship of all.

The important thing to remember as you edit your work is that your readers expect you to be *consistent* in your point of view throughout your piece. If you have adopted the subjective and personal first person point of view, your readers will expect you to maintain this point of view throughout your work. They will be confused if you suddenly shift to the more formal or distant third person point of view somewhere in the piece. In that case, you will have violated their need for consistency.

The following paragraph provides an example of this lack of consistency in point of view.

I enjoy my Biology lab more than I ever thought I would. In high school, I was intimidated by my Biology teacher, a recent college graduate who thought he was impressing them with his use of fancy terms like "phylogenesis," "nucleoli," or "double helix." In college, my Biology professor takes time in class to respond to their questions and seems to understand that Biology is every bit as interesting as it is challenging. In addition, I am enjoying what I am learning about the lab equipment. For the first time, I can focus the microscope with precision, seeing things you never could when you were first learning which knob to turn or which slide was under the slide clip. Above all, I am no longer squeamish about dissection, taking delight in my own personal earthworm or crayfish or cat. In college, Biology lab is a class you can really enjoy.

Talking About It #119

With your classmates, discuss the following questions:

1. What point of view did the writer choose at the beginning of this piece? Underline the pronouns throughout the piece which indicate a consistent use of this point of view.
2. Can you identify some places where the writer is inconsistent in the use of point of view?
3. With your classmates, change the inconsistent pronouns to pronouns that will produce consistency of point of view throughout the entire paragraph.

Consistency and Tense

You have seen the way readers expect consistency in point of view. In this section, you will see the way readers expect consistency in a writer's use of tense.

Tense refers to time and is a property of verbs. Only verbs in English can indicate time, pointing out whether something happens in the present, past, future or some other variation of these tenses. Several verbs with their tenses marked are as follows,

runs, grows, is, want, throw	(present tense)
ran, grew, was, wanted, threw	(past tense)
will run, will grow, will be grown, will want, will throw	(future tense)

The important thing to remember is that readers expect writers to be consistent in their use of time. If they begin a piece of writing in the present tense, they expect the writer to continue largely in the present tense throughout the piece. If the writer lapses into past time or future time, the reader will become momentarily confused. The need for consistency will have been violated.

In the following paragraph, the writer begins in one tense but then switches back and forth between different tenses.

Last week I took my driving test for the first time. I signed in at the front desk and present my social security card and temporary driving permit. The testing officer, a stern-looking woman with a badge on her chest, points to the door and told me to meet her out by my car. Once we are in, she signals for me to go through a stop sign, across a heavily traveled intersection, and around a cloverleaf. I thought I had passed with flying colors, for I was driving well, and she makes no marks on the test paper in her lap. When we arrived at the driving station once again, I thought I was finished with the test. Unfortunately, she points out the six red traffic cones in the middle of the parking lot. They are part of the maneuverability test, something I know nothing about. However, I did just fine when I was driving between them, but when I got to the part where I had to back up, I run down all three cones on the right in one smooth turn of the wheel. I saw the officer shaking her head and marking furiously on the test paper. I follow her inside to the desk where she says, "There's more to driving than going forward, young man. Come back next week and try again—after you learn how to back up."

Talking About It #120

Discuss the following questions with your classmates:

1. What tense does the writer of the paragraph begin in? Underline the places where the use of tense remains consistent.
2. Look for places where the writer uses a verb tense that is different from the tense in which the paragraph began.
3. With your classmates, replace the inconsistent verbs with verbs that reflect consistency of time from the beginning to the end of the paragraph.
4. Notice the quoted material at the end of the paragraph. Do you think quoted material needs to be consistent in tense? Why or why not?

Consistency of Tone

As you'll recall from Chapter 4, tone refers to the ambience, atmosphere, or mood of a piece of writing. Think back to your elementary school days and a fight taking place in the schoolyard. Someone rushes for a teacher's help, and as the various voices attempt to explain what happened, some of them take on a sarcastic tone, some of them are whining and weeping, and others are hostile or confused or frightened. Chaos prevails until the teacher begins to speak in a self-assured, respectful, reasonable tone of voice, restoring an atmosphere of calm with experience and maturity.

At this point, you've read the writing of many of your classmates, and you've probably recognized differences in tone as they present their writing for consideration. Some pieces of writing may sound shaky and unsure; others may sound saccharine or sentimental; still others, attempting to impress, may sound pompous or self-important. Often a student establishes a sincere and consistent tone but occasionally lapses into arrogance or sentimentality. Of course, tone can certainly vary based on the purposes of the writer and the needs of the reader. But a suitably calm, respectful, and reasonable tone that projects thoughtfulness and maturity—the teacher imposing reason on the playground—provides the greatest sense of consistency for the reader.

The following are guidelines for establishing a consistent tone in your writing. Read them carefully and then respond to the journal entry which follows.

1. Choose words to fit your reader and purpose.

2. Decide on a level of diction—formal, informal, or casual—and choose words that match that level.

3. Avoid "writing like you talk."
4. Aim for a mature, respectful tone.

Choosing Words to Fit Your Reader and Purpose

Choosing words to fit your reader and your purpose will help you establish a consistent tone, and you will make good choices if you understand both the *denotative* and the *connotative* meanings of words.

When you look a word up in the dictionary, you are given its denotative meaning. The word "fat," for instance, is defined as "having much flesh other than muscle." But words have emotional or connotative power as well. They call up associations or pictures that go beyond their denotative meanings. "Fat" may conjure images of a person in the sideshow in the circus, the members of your sister's Weight Watchers class, or the soft pocket of flesh under the baby's chin.

In addition, many different words can share nearly identical denotative meanings and offer a variety of connotative meanings at the same time. Words such as "pudgy," "stout," or "plump" are defined in similar ways, but the emotional or connotative associations they call up are very different. A word like "cross" can denotatively mean about the same thing as "grouchy," "irritable," "sour," or "crabby," but the connotative meanings of these words vary in important ways.

Because you want to choose words to fit your reader and purpose, it is important that you become aware of the denotative and connotative meanings of words. Did the professor whom you are describing in your essay give the class a "talk" or a "lecture"? Is the senator's plan for economic reform which you are discussing in your economics paper "liberal" or "leftist"? Was the experiment in your chemistry lab on which you are writing a lab report a "flop" or a "failure"? Was the performance by the actress in the play which you are reviewing for your theater class "dramatic" or "histrionic"? The choice depends on your goals and your reader's needs. But the choices are critical.

Talking About It #121

Discuss the following memo with your classmates. It has been written because a boss asked his secretary to respond to his plan to rearrange a crowded and windowless office to accommodate more plants and trees in order to set up a more pleasant work space. As you read it, think about the reader and the purpose and the need to strive for a consistent tone. Then point out any words that might need to be changed because of their imprecise or negative connotations. Offer suitable changes, and then discuss with your classmates why your changes might lead to a more consistent tone.

To: Jim Melko
From: Judy Kauflin
Re: Office Refurbishment
Date: September 16, 1994

This memo offers some ruminations about your plans for appending botanical specimens to our environment.

Although I agree that the office is cheerless and depressing because of the dearth of apertures, I do not think the work area would be improved through your newfangled crusade to lead us back to nature.

The office is currently jam-packed with people and equipment, and revamps incorporating more objects, even lush and green ones, seem simply ludicrous.

I believe that a few variegated framed posters and strategically positioned lighting fixtures would brighten the area without additional clutter.

Besides, we are already overworked. Who would assume the repugnant job of watering the aforementioned greenery?

Deciding on a Level of Diction

When you write, you choose a level of diction that is usually either casual, informal, or formal. In this memo, the word "jam-packed" represents casual diction, the word "agree" represents informal diction, and the word "botanical specimens" represents formal diction. In this memo to her boss, the writer failed to decide on a level of diction and stay there throughout the piece. Had she chosen an informal level of diction from the start and maintained that level throughout, the passage would have been far less jarring, for inconsistent use of levels of diction is disturbing to readers.

Often a writer may begin clearly enough, establishing a definite level of diction from the beginning of the piece. Unfortunately, however, it is easy to slip unintentionally into a different level. Most commonly, as in the following example, students struggle to maintain a consistent level of informal diction, finding that it is all too easy to slip into casual diction.

Dear Professor Chambers,

I am requesting permission to withdraw from your history course, Western Civilization 101. I am enrolled in section 101-05 that meets on Tuesdays and Thursdays from 1:00 to 2:30. I have attached a withdrawal form to this request for your signature.

Unfortunately, I have been having difficulty with the class all semester. I've been flunking tests right and left, and I don't understand a thing I read. I have trouble taking notes on the lectures, and the tutoring I've done hasn't made one bit of difference.

Because Western Civilization is a required course, I plan to retake it in my sophomore year when I have improved my study skills. I am determined to work hard to master this subject when, with your permission, I take it again.

Sincerely,
Lauren Ramers
Lauren Ramers

Talking About It #122

Discuss the following questions by referring to Lauren's letter to Professor Chambers in the passage above.

1. What level of diction did Lauren decide on at the beginning of the letter? How do you know?
2. At what point does she slip into a different level of diction? How do you know? What is the name of this level of diction?
3. Suggest some substitutions for those inconsistent portions of Lauren's letter in order to achieve a consistent level of diction throughout the piece.

Avoiding "Writing Like You Talk"

You'll remember from Chapter 5 that writing is different from speaking. The gestures, slang, and mutterings that are common in everyday speech are missing in writing. In writing, ideas are translated or transformed by means of conventions, for example, paragraphs, topic sentences, transitions, and other techniques. One good way of catching inconsistencies in point of view, tense, and diction is realizing that those inconsistencies often arise when a writer writes "like he talks."

Talking About It #123

With your classmates, look back through the passages presented earlier in this chapter which describe a student's college biology experience, a driving test, a memo to a boss, and a letter to a professor. Read through them carefully again and then find several examples of inconsistencies that occurred because the writer began to write "like he talks."

Aiming for a Mature, Respectful Tone

If you aim for a mature, respectful tone throughout your writing, you will rarely go wrong. You need to respect your subject matter, approaching it in a thoughtful, committed manner. You need to respect your own purposes and goals, working diligently to achieve them. Above all, you need to respect your reader, projecting a mature and respectful tone in your work.

An important cultural issue surrounds the goal of aiming for a mature and respectful tone. This is the issue of sexist language. Becoming aware of sexist language and choosing to avoid its use in your work will help mark you as a maturing and enlightened writer. It will signal your awareness of the subtle powers of language and your willingness to direct your thoughts to the entire human community.

Preferring nonsexist language will also signal a break with the practices of the past. In the not very distant past, when the gender of a noun was unknown, common practice substituted the masculine pronoun "he" for the noun to which it referred. Thus, a writer might write, "A modern doctor understands that he will have to keep up with the pace of changing technology." Because such language practices exert subtle influences on people's attitudes, enlightened writers recognize the importance of avoiding such sexist language. Generally, you can avoid sexist language by making it clear that the noun referent includes both men and women or by using plural pronouns to avoid the sexist implications altogether. As a result, the earlier example could be improved in one of two ways.

Original: A modern doctor understands that he will have to keep up with the pace of changing technology.

Revision (1): A modern doctor understands that he or she will have to keep up with the pace of changing technology.

Revision (2): Modern doctors understand that they will have to keep up with the pace of changing technology.

Although the use of both he and she addresses the problem of sexist language, it also can lead to constructions that are awkward or unwieldy. The following passage demonstrates this kind of awkwardness:

> A modern doctor understands that he or she will have to keep up with the pace of changing technology. He or she will have to read the latest medical journals to learn about the new discoveries in biochemistry that will affect his or her practice. He or she will have to pay close attention to developments in the pharmaceutical industry which introduces new drug treatments for his or her patients almost every day. He or she will need to learn about new equipment like exercise machines and artificial implants and state-of-the-art monitors. As a result, a modern doctor can never stop his or her learning.

The awkwardness of this passage can be avoided by using the plural "doctors" throughout and avoiding the problem posed by use of the singular pronoun.

In addition, as an editor, you should be aware that language practices are changing in other ways as well. Nonsexist titles are increasingly accepted. Thus, "The postman is running behind today" is giving way to "The mail carrier is running behind today." Today's usage prefers "firefighters" to "firemen" and "police officer" to "policeman."

As you strive for consistency in point of view, tense, and tone, remember that consistent use of nonsexist language is an important mark of a mature, respectful style.

Talking About It #124

The following examples present problems in the use of sexist language. Offer solutions to these problems with your classmates, discussing the reasons for your solutions.

1. Many mothers testify to the helpfulness of Parent Effectiveness Training programs.
2. The engineer needs to put in many years of field experience in addition to his classroom training.
3. A journalist has the right to protect his or her sources.
4. A male nurse records the vital signs of each of his patients as part of his morning routine.
5. Businessmen have to be attuned to the slightest changes in the economic forecasts.
6. Every citizen should study the candidates carefully before casting his vote.
7. If mankind devoted more effort to solving the problem of hunger, the problem of war might more readily disappear.
8. For this year's company picnic, the men volunteered to bring the food, and the ladies volunteered to serve on the clean-up crew.

EDITING AND CLARITY

As you've learned in the previous section of this chapter, readers have needs for consistency. They also have needs for clarity. As you develop your editing skills, you will learn that it is not enough to be consistent: you must also be clear.

Lack of clarity is perhaps the biggest complaint offered about the writing of other people. Common responses to problems of clarity include, "I can't understand what you're saying"; "This is confusing"; or "It just isn't clear." The writer is often tempted to blame the reader for what is his or her own lack of clarity. Pointing to the words on the page, the writer exclaims, "But I *said* it right *here*!" or "Can't you read plain *English*?" Writers are often frustrated by the fact that the plain English they've worked hard to produce just isn't so plain.

A famous writer once remarked that writing clearly was a matter of "putting the right words in the right places." Humorous as that remark might be, there's also much truth in it. The problem, of course, is in knowing the right words and the right places to put them in. In a sense, the editing stage of the rewriting process is concerned largely with those two things: the right words and the right places.

In the previous section of this chapter when you studied editing for consistency, you were dealing with the "right words." You were choosing words to convey consistent point of view, tense, and tone. In this section of the chapter when you study editing for clarity, you will be dealing with the "right places," the sentences in which you cast those words. Thus, consistency deals more generally with words; clarity deals more generally with sentences.

Characteristics of Sentence Clarity

When you are editing as part of the rewriting process, you are checking to make sure that your sentences are clear. You will know they are clear when you have worked to achieve three things:

1. simplicity,
2. efficiency,
3. humanity.

Each of these three aspects of sentence clarity will be explained in the following section.

Simplicity

Simplicity is a characteristic of all clear writing. Look at each of the following familiar sentences, noting how clear each is:

> A penny saved is a penny earned.
>
> Smoking causes cancer.
>
> You deserve a break today.

Each of these sentences, of course, is short. But simplicity does not refer only to length, for longer sentences can be clear and direct as well. The following examples are cases in point.

> Ask not what your country can do for you; ask what you can do for your country.
>
> The poet's voice need not merely be the record of man, it can be one of the props, the pillars to help him endure and prevail.
>
> Ninety-nine percent of the people in the world are fools and the rest of us are in great danger of contagion.

The secret to such clear sentences—whether short or long—lies in the writer's ability to separate the wheat from the chaff, the essential from the nonessential. Although short sentences are often marvels of conciseness, skillfully managed long sentences are often remarkable, too. In both cases, their writers have worked to whittle ideas down to their essence, tossing the parings into the wastecan.

There are several reasons why developing writers are reluctant to write simply. First, they often think writing is something of a show, a Fourth-of-July display of words designed to amaze the reader. They forget—or haven't learned—that writing is an act of communication between one mind and another and that a single clear light is worth a thousand fizzling firecrackers. Perhaps they've even had teachers who reward written pyrotechnics, looking less favorably on more humble prose.

Another reason why developing writers struggle with the concept of simplicity is that they're secretly afraid their papers will be too short. This fear surfaces when they don't yet have enough on their minds to write about, so they recast one or two emerging ideas in a dozen different ways, unaware that what they need is fewer words and more thought.

In addition, writers are also reluctant to embrace simplicity because when their words do come, it is only after a long and sometimes bitter struggle, and they are reluctant to let go of a single line. Writing for them is a kind of battle, a matter of blood, toil, tears, and sweat, and they leave the field reluctant to free a single captured word.

Probably the most important reason why simplicity eludes students is that achieving simplicity requires practice. However, aiming for sentence simplicity in the editing stage of the rewriting process will provide you with the kind of practice that leads to mastery.

Simplicity in your sentences can be achieved by carefully pruning extra words away. In your efforts to write more clearly, you can lop off many unnecessary words by removing

1. redundancies,
2. wordy expressions,
3. wordy constructions,
4. wordy clauses and phrases.

Eliminating Redundancies

Redundancies are words that are repeated unnecessarily. They are expressions such as "full and complete," "total annihilation," "personal belief," and others like them. A redundancy gives you more than you need, offering two for the price of one—when one is all that's required. Because redundancies are used so commonly in speech, they are often overlooked in writing. But, once spotted, they are easily corrected by eliminating one or more of the unnecessary words. A few common redundancies have been listed.

completely finish	good benefit
continue on	high degree
fall down	pair of twins
few in number	red in color
final outcome	repeat again
great importance	true fact

Eliminating Wordy Expressions

Wordy expressions should also be eliminated from your writing in the interests of simplicity. Common wordy expressions and their more concise replacements are as follows:

at this point in time	now
because of the fact that	because
concerning the matter of	concerning
due to the fact that	because
in the event that	if
in the near future	soon
on an individual basis	individually

In addition, certain words, particularly the adverbs very, really, quite, and so generally add little but padding to your texts. You should strive to eliminate them as well.

Eliminating Wordy Constructions

Several common English constructions are inherently wordy. You should try to eliminate them whenever possible.

1. *There is; There are; It is*

Students often begin their sentences with "There is," "There are," or "It is." Sometimes these can be sound ways to begin, but more commonly these expressions simply add extra padding to your prose. Notice what happens to the following sentences when these wordy constructions are eliminated.

There are three reasons to explain the start of the Civil War.

Three reasons explain the start of the Civil War.

There are now added attractions at the amusement park.

Added attractions are now at the amusement park.

It is true that cholesterol is found only in animal products.

Cholesterol is found only in animal products.

2. *Creating nouns from verbs and adjectives*

Our bureaucratic and increasingly regulated society is fond of turning verbs and adjectives—the language's most lively, active words—into nouns, the language's most staid and proper part of speech. People who unnecessarily turn verbs and adjectives into nouns create *nominalizations* that may "sound" more important but which carry far less power in their new form than in the original. Some common nominalizations and their original form are as follows:

Verb or Adjective Form	Nominalization
realize	realization
significant	significance
assess	assessment
develop	development
important	importance
decide	decision

To eliminate nominalizations, simply turn the new noun back into its original verb or adjective form or eliminate it entirely as in the following examples:

The significance of the case lay in its development of new judicial procedures.

The case was significant because it developed new judicial procedures.

The realization for the need for development of more housing in the area was recognized by the committee.

The committee recognized the need for more housing in the area.

Eliminating Wordy Clauses and Phrases

In striving for simplicity in your sentences, you need to discover and then eliminate the unnecessarily wordy clauses and phrases which spring up unnoticed when you are writing your drafts. The following editing changes have been made in the interests of simplicity.

~~The reason why~~ the case was dismissed ~~that way was~~ because of lack of evidence.

The case was dismissed because of lack of evidence.

~~Because of the fact that~~ his mother wasn't well, he ~~decided that he had to~~ postpone college for another semester.

Since his mother wasn't well, he postponed college for another semester.

If wordy clauses and phrases cannot be entirely eliminated, often they can be reduced. Clauses can be shortened into phrases and phrases into words. Notice how this is done in the following examples.

The robber, ~~who was carrying a gun,~~ frightened the teller.

The armed robber frightened the teller.

~~During the period of~~ orientation, students are introduced to ~~the various aspects of~~ campus life.

Students are introduced to campus life at orientation.

Talking About It #125

The following letter is not clear because it contains redundancies, wordy expressions, wordy constructions, and wordy clauses and phrases. With your classmates, edit the passage in the interests of simplicity.

Julia Greenwood
112 Amherst Place
Devon, Massachusetts 07795

Robert Winslow
Allstate Insurance Agency
4679 Northcutt Place
Boston, Massachusetts 07991

January 29, 1993

Dear Mr. Winslow,

In the interests of full and complete disclosure, I wish to inform you at this point in time that I was the driver of the 1990 Toyota car cited in the vehicular collision that happened to occur on January 1, 1993 at the time of 2:30 P.M. It is my personal belief that I was in no way responsible for this accident.

In the time previous to when the accident occurred, I had pulled over to the side of interstate highway number 80 and fully stopped my car to help a woman who was signaling for help. In a matter of mere seconds, the realization hit me that her baby infant was having a seizure. Because of that eventuality, I was aware of the great importance of returning back to my car to continue on driving into town to get help. It was during this period while I was driving that my car collided with the hay truck owned and operated by Mr. Baskin, the person whose truck is insured by your company, the Allstate Insurance Company. Mr. Baskin was backing out of a feed mill, and his vision was obscured due to the fact of all that hay sticking out of the back of his truck.

We were very fortunate in that the local area doctor was also at the feed mill, having stopped to apply medical first aid to a mill worker who had injured his pinkie finger. Doctor Nosek made a call contacting the emergency rescue squad, and the infant baby was at that juncture rushed to the local hospital.

Because I was not at fault and Mr. Baskin caused $789.69 worth of serious damage to my car, I want you to completely settle this matter. Please feel free to contact my insurance agent, who works for the Travelers Company, at (805) 936-7809. I am very eager for a final resolution of this claim.

Very sincerely yours,
Julia Greenwood
Julia Greenwood

Efficiency

Another characteristic of clear sentences is *efficiency*. Efficient workers, as you know, get their jobs done in an effective and timely manner. They do what they set out to do. Writers who compose efficient sentences work in the same way; they know what has to be done to be effective; then they do it.

More efficient sentences can be achieved in two ways:

1. by writing sentences which are purposeful,
2. by writing sentences which are ordered.

Efficiency and Sentence Purpose

Students who write purposeful sentences understand about sentence structure. Too often, students simply "write," pouring their words out in a kind of full-speed-ahead approach. That approach usually works well during the prewriting stage of the writing process when the goal is to generate ideas and keep the critical self at arm's length. When it's time to edit, however, those sentences must be shaped and molded to achieve a purpose.

Think of the sentences you produced during prewriting or for your first draft as a kind of cake batter, a substance that promises something delicious but that is yet unformed. When you begin to edit your sentences, striving for efficiency, you need to ask yourself the purpose of what you are baking. Are you aiming for something elaborate and impressive—a wedding cake? Are you aiming for something less fancy—a birthday cake? Or are you aiming for something inherently simple—a cupcake or two for a child's celebration?

Sentences work like that, and the kind of sentence structure you choose depends on the purpose behind the ideas you are trying to express. In order of complexity, the four types of sentence cakes you can bake in English are the following: (1) simple, (2) compound, (3) complex, and (4) compound-complex.

Simple Sentences

A *simple sentence* expresses a single idea. Its structure is diagramed in Figure 7.1.

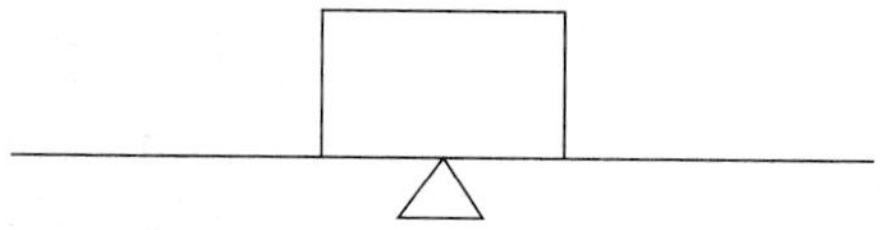

Figure 7.1

An example of a simple sentence follows:

Choosing a computer is difficult.

Compound Sentences

A *compound sentence* expresses two or more simple sentences. The ideas in the simple sentences are equally important. Compound structures join the two simple sentences with connecting words, for example, and, but, or, nor, so, for, and yet. The structure of a compound sentence is diagramed in Figure 7.2.

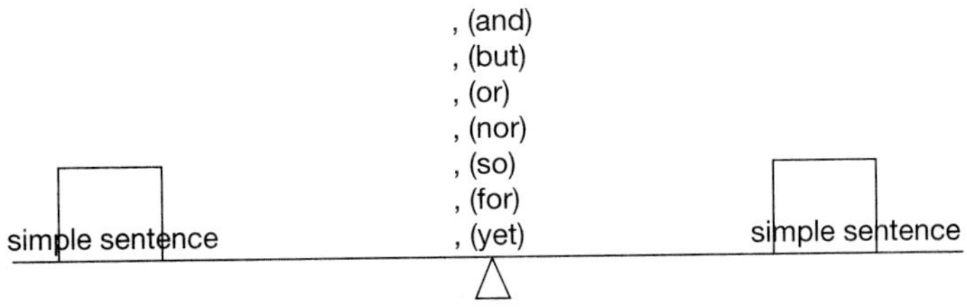

Figure 7.2

An example of a compound sentence follows:

Choosing a computer is difficult, but there are many good ones on the market.

Notice that a comma precedes the connecting word in a compound sentence.

There are two other ways to join compound sentences efficiently. You can (1) use a semicolon or (2) use a semicolon and one of the following special transition words:

also	instead
as a result	meanwhile
consequently	moreover
for example	nevertheless
for instance	on the other hand
furthermore	otherwise
however	therefore
in addition	thus
indeed	
in fact	

The following examples show the way compound sentences can be joined by either a semicolon or a semicolon and one of the transition words.

Choosing a computer is difficult**;** there are many good ones on the market.

Choosing a computer is difficult**; however,** there are many good ones on the market.

Notice that a comma is used after the transition word when parts of a compound sentence are joined in this way.

Using transition words is a particularly efficient way of making your sentences fit your purpose, and your writing will improve if you learn to use them to join ideas. Using transition words is a way of dropping clues to the reader about your train of thought. For instance, if your purpose is to show the way that one idea *results* from another, you might choose a transition word like this:

There are many good computers on the market**; consequently,** choosing a computer is difficult.

If you want, for example, to show that one idea *contrasts* with the other, you might choose a transition word like this:

Choosing a computer is difficult**; on the other hand,** there are many good ones on the market.

Thus, you can make your writing more purposeful by using transitions to guide your reader through the relationships among your ideas.

Complex Sentences

A *complex sentence* expresses two or more ideas. Unlike the compound sentence, however, the two ideas are *not* equally important. In fact, one idea is usually *more* important than the other idea. The more important idea, the main idea, is found in the main or independent clause; the less important idea, the subordinate idea, is found in the subordinate or dependent clause. The structure of a complex sentence is diagramed in Figure 7.3.

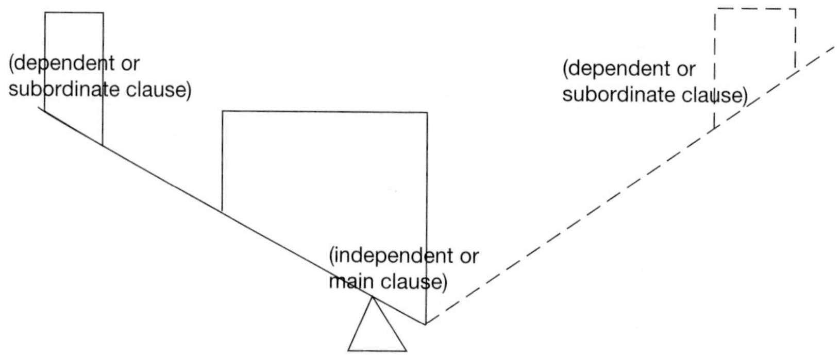

Figure 7.3

Note that the dependent clause or clauses can be attached to either the simple sentence on the left or the simple sentence on the right.

Several examples of complex sentences follow.

If you practice hard, success usually follows.
(dependent clause) (main clause)

The study of biochemistry, **which is a challenging field**, yields
(main clause) (dependent clause)
stunning discoveries.
(main clause)

Because housing starts are up this year, economists are
(dependent clause)
predicting gains for the economy.
(main clause)

You can profit from learning to use the complex sentence structure more frequently. Complex sentences make it easy for you to emphasize one idea over another, suggesting the relative importance of ideas. As your ideas become more sophisticated, so do the sentence structures that contain them. As college will teach you, ideas are never entirely simple. When they become more complicated, you need to be able to emphasize their relative relationships to each other in more efficient ways. The complex sentence allows you to do that.

Notice in the examples that follow that the main clause contains the more important idea and that putting the more important idea in the main clause changes the emphasis of the ideas you are expressing.

Although choosing a computer is difficult, there are many good
(dependent clause) (main clause)
ones on the market.

Although there are many good ones on the market, choosing a
(dependent clause)
computer is difficult.
(main clause)

Notice, too, that when the dependent clause introduces the sentence, it is followed by a comma. However, when the dependent clause comes at the end of the sentence, no comma is used.

Since no one could reach a decision, the issue was tabled for further discussion. (comma)

The issue was tabled for further discussion since no one could reach a decision. (no comma)

Sometimes students think that the name "complex" means that this sentence type is more difficult. Actually, the only real difficulty in mastering the complex sentence is in becoming familiar with the words that signal the dependent or subordinate clause. If you learn the following words with which dependent clauses always begin, you will be well on your way to mastering this efficient sentence type.

Dependent Clause Signals

after	in order that	who
although	since	which
as	unless	whom
as if	until	whose
because	what	that
before	when	
even though	whenever	
how	where	
if	wherever	
	while	

Talking About It #126

With your classmates, join the ideas which follow by using the dependent clause signal suggested. Then discuss with your classmates the way the complex sentence form gives relative weight and emphasis to the ideas. The first example has been done for you.

Example: The Sixth Amendment guarantees a defendant's right to counsel. Poor defendants usually are not as strenuously defended as the rich. (although)

Complex sentence 1: Although the Sixth Amendment guarantees a defendant's right to counsel, poor defendants usually are not as strenuously defended as the rich.

Complex sentence 2: Although poor defendants usually are not as strenuously defended as the rich, the Sixth Amendment guarantees a defendant's right to counsel.

1. I looked over the apples in the store. I was especially hungry. (because)

2. I opened a checking account. I have needed money. (since)

3. Her stand on civil liberties was reported in the newspaper article. I was angry about this. (which)

4. John realized the importance of careful research. John wrote his rough draft. (when)

5. The dog chased the cat. The umbrella stand was broken. (after)

Writing About It #127

Use the ideas in the following paragraph to rewrite it, incorporating several complex sentences.

MTV aired its first video in 1985. Millions of people have spent many hours watching music videos. Music videos have become an integral part of modern pop culture. We should be concerned about their content. Music videos are filled with violence. Music videos are filled with sex. Music videos are filled with advertising. We need to be aware of the messages behind the music.

Writing About It #128

Choose a journal entry or a paragraph from an essay which you have already written. Rewrite it, attempting to express the relationships among ideas with more efficiency through the use of complex sentences.

Compound-Complex Sentences

The final type of sentence structure available to you is the compound-complex sentence. The *compound* part of this structure consists of two or more simple sentences; the *complex* part of this structure consists of one or more dependent clauses. The structure of a compound-complex sentence is pictured in Figure 7.4.

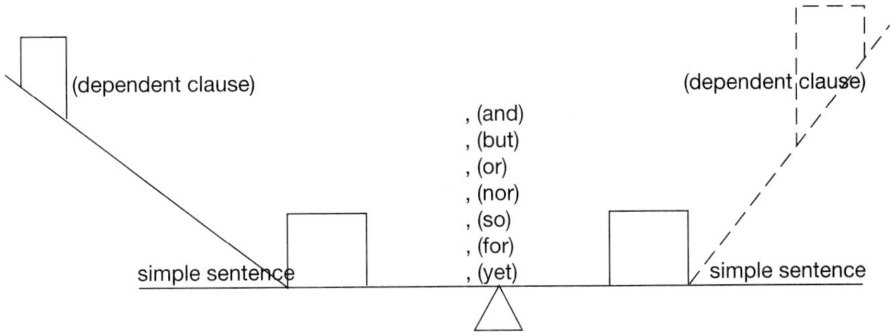

Figure 7.4

Note that the dependent clause or clauses can be attached to either the simple sentence on the left or the simple sentence on the right.

The following compound-complex sentence illustrates this structure.

Although the choice of a computer is difficult, <u>there are many good</u>
(dependent clause) (compound sentence)
<u>ones on the market</u>, **and** a <u>number of knowledgeable professionals</u>
(conjunction) (compound sentence)
can give you sound advice.

You need to be cautious in your use of the compound-complex sentence. Although this sentence type allows you to manage many more ideas than the other two structures, compound-complex sentences can often be quite long. If you find that your compound-complex sentence is becoming too unwieldy, try breaking it down into one or more of the simpler sentence types as in the following example.

After several years of working for the railroad company, Ruthie's grandfather retired to a small farm, and he began a small vegetable garden which he eventually turned into a profit-making enterprise that proved a boon to both himself and the surrounding community.

After several years of working for the railroad company, Ruthie's grandfather retired to a small farm. He began a small vegetable garden which he eventually turned into a profit-making enterprise. This proved a boon to both himself and the surrounding community.

Thus, in editing your sentences for efficiency as part of the rewriting stage of the writing process, remember to fit your sentence structure to your purpose. That way you will make sure that your sentences are effective workers, doing their jobs in the most efficient manner possible.

The following table will guide you as you work to fit your ideas to their most appropriate structure.

Purpose	*Sentence Structure*	*Joining Words*	*Considerations*
To convey a simple idea	Simple	None	One simple idea; conveys a sense of simplicity
To convey two or more simple ideas	Compound	And, but, or, nor, so, for, yet; special transition words	Ideas are equally important; conveys a sense of balance
To convey two or more ideas of relative importance	Complex	Dependent clause signals	One idea more important than the other or others; lends emphasis and weight to ideas; suggests relationships among ideas
To convey two simple ideas and one or more other ideas of lesser importance	Compound-complex	And, but, or, nor, so, for, yet; special transition words as well as dependent clause signals	Two ideas equally important; one or more ideas of lesser importance; may run too long

Efficiency and Sentence Order

Efficient sentences are not only purposeful; they are well ordered. They not only achieve their goals, but they do so in an organized manner. *Order* is important in sentences because a well-ordered sentence makes it easier for the reader to understand what the writer is saying. Note the differences between the following pairs of sentences, one more efficiently ordered than the other.

When I came to Pontiac's village, I saw that the tribes were an easy target, and I swiftly set about to conquer them.

I came, I saw, I conquered.

—Julius Caesar

It is extremely important to preserve democratic governments, to make sure that governments and the people who run them last till the end of time.

Government of the people, by the people, for the people shall not perish from the earth.

—Abraham Lincoln

You are probably familiar with the second quote from Julius Caesar as an illustration of his arrogance, his decisiveness, and his military power. You are probably familiar with the second quote by Abraham Lincoln at Gettysburg as an illustration of his beliefs in democratic ideals and the sacrifices they require. You are probably less familiar, however, with the techniques that give such effective sentences their power.

Sentence Order and Parallel Form

One way in which you can learn to write more ordered and balanced sentences, sentences like those by Caesar and Lincoln, is to practice the principles of parallel form. Essentially, *parallel form* confirms that ideas which are of equal importance are most effectively expressed in the same grammatical structure. For instance, in the following example, the original sentence is revised to express the three equally important ideas as three **to-** phrases:

On the weekend, I plan to work in the garden, and I am also going to tune up the car and perhaps give the dog a bath.

On the weekend, I plan <u>to work in the garden, to tune up the car, and to give the dog a bath</u>.

In the next example, three adjectives have been used to express three equally important ideas.

The sick man, who seemed disoriented, also seemed agitated and downright hostile.

The sick man seemed <u>disoriented, agitated, and downright hostile</u>.

Note that the adjectives have also been arranged in ascending order, from the least disturbing to the most threatening description of the sick man's behavior. The Julius Caesar quote—"I came, I saw, I conquered"—effectively uses this kind of climactic order as well. If arranging your ideas to express climax or importance can achieve your purposes, use it in conjunction with parallel form as another way of achieving an ordered efficiency when you edit your work.

Talking About It #129

Discuss with your classmates the following sentences, noting where they lack the balance called parallel form. Then discuss ways in which these sentences may be rewritten to restore a sense of balance.

1. On the plane he carried a battered briefcase, a broken umbrella, and a novel which was a paperback.

2. My aunt is a nun who possesses the virtues of faith and is patient.

3. In the summer my little brother earns money by walking dogs, babysitting, and he even mows lawns.

4. It was hard to study for the test and also watching my favorite TV show.

5. The boat rocked, the waters churned, and seasickness was something that happened to the entire crew.

6. There was a sense of anticipation, excitement, and even an enthusiastic spirit.

7. Worried, anxious, and full of fear, the young actor paced the floor before the opening curtain.

Order and Placement in Sentences

At the beginnings and endings of sentences Another way in which sentences can be efficiently ordered is by putting various parts of the sentence into their most effective places. As you edit your work, you can learn to use the beginnings and endings of your sentences to achieve your intended effect.

Beginnings and endings are important. When you think back to the movies you've seen, you have a familiar example of the power in beginnings and endings. The beginnings draw you into the story; the endings keep you on the edge of your seat.

Sentences work that way, too. You can increase the efficiency of your sentences by understanding the power of their beginnings and endings. In the following sentence examples, their authors have placed important information—their key ideas—at either the beginning or the end.

> Beginning: We observe today not a victory of party but a celebration of freedom, symbolizing an end as well as a beginning, signifying renewal as well as change.
>
> —John F. Kennedy

End: Even when the path is nominally open—when there is nothing to prevent a woman from being a doctor, a lawyer, a civil servant—there are many phantoms and obstacles . . . looming in her way.

—Virginia Woolf

In the first example, by President Kennedy, the main idea begins the sentence and the rest of the sentence builds on it, supporting it with other words and phrases. Using the beginnings of your sentences in this way allows you to provide initial clarity—and then elaborate on it thereafter. In the second example, by Virginia Woolf, the main idea is held off until the end of the sentence. Using the endings of your sentences in this way allows you to create a sense of anticipation, for the reader must wait for the complete meaning of your sentence to evolve. You should be familiar with both techniques for ordering your sentences for efficiency and for editing your sentences to achieve your intended effects. Understanding the powers of the beginnings and endings of sentences will expand your range of choices.

Talking About It #130

For the following examples, discuss with your classmates whether the writers have placed their most important ideas at either the beginning or the end of the sentence.

1. Shaking the rain from his boots and flinging his coat across the chair, the young man warmed his fingers at the fire.
2. Without the involvement of the people and their awareness of the issues, democratic government cannot flourish.
3. Moses helped the Jewish people build a different kind of culture, a culture whose central meaning was not built around what could be seen but around what was passed on in the Word.
4. He looked out across the valley, the rivers snaking beneath him, the cliffs massing their power, the green hills sweet in the sunlight.
5. At a certian point in the Revolutionary War, well before the defeat of Cornwallis at Yorktown, the tide turned in favor of the young Americans.
6. Machiavelli assumed that many noble virtues might not be compatible, an assumption that angered some and was ignored by many.

Writing About It #131

Look back over some of the sentences you have written in your journal. Rewrite a few of them so that they now present their most important information at the beginning. Choose a few different sentences and rewrite them so that they now present their most important information at the end. Then share those sentences with your classmates.

As you have seen, beginnings and endings of sentences can be used for strategic effect, depending on how you choose to use them to present your ideas.

But we have been looking at those sentences in isolation, as individual expressions of ideas. The fact is that when you are editing your writing, you are often not looking at just one particular sentence: you are looking at that sentence in relationship to the other sentences that are found around it. In most cases, how you decide to structure it will depend on how you want it to function in the paragraph as a whole.

Generally, when you look at a sentence in context—in relation to its neighboring sentences—you will see that the beginnings of sentences often refer back to something in the sentence or sentences that came before it, providing a link or reference or connection or transition to it. Often you will see that the ends of sentences present new information or introduce new ideas into the paragraph. As you look at the following paragraph, about the workings of insects' brains, notice how the beginnings of sentences often relate back to something in a previous sentence and how the ends of sentences often introduce new information.

> Insects' brains are amazingly complex, and research studies by scientists
> (topic)
>
> confirm them as even more complex than we once supposed. First, the insect
> (controlling idea) (old information)
>
> brain, research is finding, is not a solitary organ as it is in humans. Instead, the
> (new information)
>
> insect brain is confirmed as an interconnected system of messenger nerves. These
> (old information) (new information)
>
> messengers run from the insect's limbs and sense organs to the central nerve cord.
> (old information) (new information)
>
> Acting like a railroad conductor, this nerve cord contains knots or ganglia which
> (old information) (new information)
>
> usher the signal along to its proper function. These ganglia regulate functions like
> (old information)
>
> chirping or mating. Thus, with only the ganglia intact, the insect will be able to
> (new information)
>
> chirp or mate—even if the head of the insect is severed from its body.
> (old information) (new information)

Talking About It #132

In the following passage, about changes in the census, identify the topic sentence and controlling idea. With your classmates, identify material that you believe to be old information and material that you believe to be new information. With your classmates, refer to this passage as you discuss whether—in general—old information tends to come at the beginning of sentences and new information at the end.

The nature of the United States census has changed over the years in terms of the citizens included, the collection purposes, the staff required, and the administrative costs. First, the citizens interviewed for the census when it was first taken in 1790 were largely free white males 16 years and older. The citizens interviewed for the 1990 census included all persons without regard to age, sex, gender, race, or ethnic origin. In addition, the purpose of the 1790 census was to determine taxation and representation in the United States government. In 1990, one major purpose was to determine that same issue of representation, but another equally important purpose was to determine a method for allocating federal funds. In 1790, the staff required for compiling the census was fewer than 500 people. In 1990, staffing for the census required the employment of over 300,000 government workers. Finally, the cost for administering the census has also changed over the years, for in 1790 it cost $300,000 to compile the census, but in 1990 it cost $2.6 billion to compile this important and influential document.

Writing About It #133

Look back over some of your previous journal entries and essays. Find a paragraph or two to examine. See if you can rewrite a paragraph or two providing old information at the beginning and new information at the end of sentences. What improvements do you think these changes made in your writing? What difficulties did they cause you?

In the middle of sentences: Modifiers When you are editing your sentences for clarity, it is important to remember to pay attention not just to the beginnings and endings of sentences but to the middle of sentences, too. The phrases, clauses, and words in your sentences need to be arranged in an orderly way so that your reader understands exactly what you mean.

The following example will remind you that modifying or descriptive material is placed close to the word or words it refers to.

The <u>big</u> dog startled the <u>sleeping</u> cat.

If we arranged this sentence so that the underlined modifiers were not close to the words they modified, we might get something like this:

The <u>sleeping</u> dog startled the <u>big</u> cat.

Or:

<u>Sleeping</u> the dog startled <u>big</u> the cat.

As these examples point out, putting modifiers in places other than close to the words they modify leads to either an unintended meaning or total confusion. The solution to either of these problems is to check your sentences to make certain that all modifiers are where they are supposed to be.

In addition, sometimes students forget to include the word being modified in their sentence. Here is an example.

As a young girl, her grandmother told her never to tell a lie and never to trust anyone who did.

Correcting a sentence like this involves adding the modified word to the sentence in its proper place—either within the opening word group or after the opening word group.

When **she** was a young girl, her grandmother told her never to tell a lie and never to trust anyone who did.

As a young girl, **she** was told by her grandmother never to tell a lie and never to trust anyone who did.

The important thing to remember about arranging the middles of your sentences is to make certain that descriptive or modifying material is placed close to the word or words it really refers to.

Talking About It #134

In the following examples, a modifying word, phrase, or clause is misplaced in some way. Decide with your classmates how to restructure the modifier so that an unintended meaning or confusion no longer results.

1. My car almost stalled ten times this morning.
2. Waving tearful good-byes, the ship was filled with boarding passengers.
3. I put hot sauce on the tacos I ate after the movie which was much too strong for my taste.
4. I saw the newspaper headline which reported on the scientist who had discovered a new vaccine for the common cold on the way to the bus.
5. My boyfriend wants to know whether I only love him.

In the following examples, the word being modified has been omitted. Decide with your classmates the possible changes required to make the sentence clear.

1. On the way to work, a green truck swerved into my lane and almost hit me.
2. Being under great pressure, my homework remained unfinished.
3. After spending most of our allowance on candy, our pockets were finally empty.
4. While playing a grueling game of tennis, a phone call interrupted me.
5. Noticing the "Keep Off" signs, a detour was made around the property.

Humanity

You have seen that editing for clarity involves creating prose that is simple and efficient. Now it is time to look at how editing for clarity involves creating prose that is humane as well.

As you mature and grow as a student, you will come to see the way that language can, in subtle ways, rob people of their humanity. When people use phrases that speak of "neutralizing" an enemy or engaging in a "pacification" program, they are using language that obscures the fact that behind those words lies a bloody drama of burned villages, ruined farms, and war-torn refugees. In a less grave example, you might be familiar with legal terminology that talks about "conveying, all and singular estates and interests, rights, titles, claims and other such advantages" instead of using a simple and direct phrase like "I give." If you'll recall the example of the Third Party Designation Notification Form and the government-issue chocolate chip cookie recipe you read about in Chapter 2, you'll quickly remember that such language displays a serious problem, the problem of dehumanizing and thereby diminishing the intimate and important bond between writer and reader.

If you want to make your writing more clear, strive to make it more human. Refuse to hide behind the smokescreen of your own created words. Stand up and be counted. Speak directly to your readers as if they were bending over your shoulder, not dangling from another planet light years away.

Making your writing more human involves visualizing your readers and writing for them. It involves knowing what readers need from you. It involves understanding two essential qualities which all people possess and which all good writing possesses as well. These qualities are

1. strength and
2. imagination.

Humanity and Strength

When you strive for writing that is strong, you attempt to do two things wherever appropriate: (1) put more "people" in the subject position of the sentence and (2) put more strong and "active" verbs in the verb position. Doing these two things will go far to humanize your writing.

In the following sentence examples, the subject is not a person.

1. The building of the bridge across the channel was considered by the engineers.
2. The finest imported ingredients were added to the meal by the cook.
3. Suspension of the student's athletic privileges was decided on by the committee.

If the sentence is edited so that a person is placed up front in the subject position, the resulting sentence is stronger and more "human."

1. The <u>engineers</u> considered building the bridge across the channel.
2. The <u>cook</u> added the finest imported ingredients to the meal.
3. The <u>committee</u> decided to suspend the student's athletic privileges.

Similarly, active verbs give more strength to your prose, and your prose becomes more human if you avoid the use of "being" verbs whenever possible.

A "being" verb—like the familiar "is," "are," "was," "were," "be," or "been"—simply shows that something exists, but it lacks the active power and vibrancy of action verbs such as "shove," "whine," "demand," or "slap." Thus, using active verbs wherever possible will add more strength and humanity to your writing. In the following sentences, the original examples have been given more strength in their revisions by substituting stronger, more active verbs.

Original:

1. His client's right to a jury trial <u>was being waived</u> by the lawyer.

2. The actress' temperamental demands <u>are being found irritating</u> by the other members of the cast.

3. Brilliant plays <u>were made</u> by all the team members, and the fans <u>were cheering</u>.

Revised:

1. The lawyer <u>waived</u> his client's right to a jury trial.

2. The actress <u>irritated</u> the other members of the cast with her temperamental demands.

3. The team members <u>made</u> brilliant plays, and the fans <u>cheered</u>.

Talking About It #135

With your classmates, strengthen the following sentences either by putting a "person" in the subject position or by putting an active verb in the verb position. Then discuss with your classmates whether or not the sentences now seem more humane.

1. Each potential employee is carefully evaluated by the personnel director.
2. The fire was allegedly started in an abandoned building by the arsonist.
3. The date of graduation was announced by the high school principal.

Although writing in many fields is strengthened by placing people in the subject position and active verbs in the verb position, many fields—particularly the sciences—aim for objectivity in their prose. The goal in these fields of writing is to be as objective and *im*-personal as possible. Thus, in such cases, the writer's goal is to focus on things, objects, discoveries, and procedures. These matters—rather than "people"—would naturally find their way into the subject position, and in writing with the goal of objectivity, the use of active verbs might be less important. Again, you need to return to considerations about your reader. Would your reader expect you to be objective and impersonal? Or would your reader expect you to be more subjective? How you answer these and other questions will determine how you respond to concerns about using the subject and verb positions effectively.

Talking About It #136

Discuss with your classmates whether the following passage would be acceptable in the procedure section of a chemistry lab report. If you felt it would be acceptable, explain why. If you felt it would be unacceptable, rewrite it so that it might be more acceptable.

I engaged in the process of testing the pH of various common substances in part one of this experiment which my lab partner and I conducted. Joyce obtained a beaker containing 10 mL of orange juice, the first test solution. I then went up to the professor's desk and obtained strips of both red and blue litmus paper. Then I used a clean stirring rod to transfer a drop of the juice first to a strip of blue litmus paper and then to a strip of red litmus paper. Joyce watched carefully and recorded the color of the litmus paper.

Humanity and Imagination

Another important way of adding humanity to your writing is to use your imagination. No one in the world sees things quite the way you do. No one in the world thinks in quite the way you do. No one in the world expresses ideas in quite the way you do. Because you are unique, you have special gifts to share with others when you write. Allow your imagination to give life to those gifts.

If you worry that your sentences are dull and unimaginative, the editing stage of the rewriting process is a good place to work on making your writing more imaginative and interesting. As you edit, learn to use your imagination to help you (1) avoid cliches, (2) be more concrete, and (3) put more variety into your sentences.

Avoiding Cliches

Cliches are expressions so commonplace that they fail to arouse our interest. You may use cliches fairly frequently in speech, complaining that "it's raining cats and dogs" again or giving a "sigh of relief" when your exam is over, or protesting that you "couldn't care less" what your old girlfriend's new boyfriend looks like.

However, if you rely on cliches to do your writing for you, your reader has been sent a clear signal that you are reluctant to use your own imagination to develop your ideas.

Become familiar with some of the following cliches and try to avoid using them in your writing, preferring your own imaginative word choices instead.

After all is said and done
A thousand times a day
Drop in the bucket
Easier said than done
Hard as nails
In the nick of time
Selling like hotcakes
Short and sweet
To make a long story short
Too close for comfort
Too little, too late
Under the weather
White as a sheet (a ghost, snow, etc.)

Being Concrete

As you have seen throughout this text, one of the traits of good writing is the writer's ability to be specific, exact, *concrete.* When your sentences exhibit convincing amounts of concrete detail, you as a writer have indicated your willingness to use your imagination to set a scene, provide an argument, or tell a story. Your reader will be blessed by reading an account in which you have shared how *you* see things, how *you* explain them, how *you* think about them. You will have learned to rely on the powers of your own imagination to write for a reader. As Natalie Goldberg explains in this passage from *Writing Down the Bones*, "use original detail in your writing."

> Life is so rich, if you can write down the real details of the way things were and are, you hardly need anything else.
>
> Be awake to the details around you..." Okay. I'm at a wedding. The bride has on blue. The groom is wearing a red carnation. They are serving chopped liver on doilies." Relax, enjoy the wedding, be present with an open heart. You will naturally take in your environment, and later, sitting at your desk, you will be able to recall just how it was dancing with the bride's redheaded mother, seeing the bit of red lipstick smeared on her front tooth when she smiled, and smelling her perfume mixed with perspiration.

Incorporating Variety

Variety keeps things interesting. Everyone has experienced the unpleasant feeling of being on a treadmill, walking over the same path again and again, repeating the same predictable, familiar daily routines. Readers, too, long to wander from the familiar pathways, often seeking the unique and unpredictable. If you care about keeping your readers interested in what you write, vary your sentences to keep their walk through your prose lively and interesting.

But incorporating variety into sentences is often a challenge for writers. The challenge can be met, however, by remembering that sentences can be varied in one of three ways: (1) by modifying, (2) by compounding, and (3) by subordinating.

Think back to Sean, the student you met in Chapter 4 who was producing some prewriting about an apple in preparation for the paragraph he needed to write for his biology professor. Let's assume that Sean's first draft included the following paragraph:

> The inside of this apple is very interesting. The inside is made up of flesh and core. The flesh is mostly white and firm. The core is in the center of the apple. The core contains some chambers. There are five chambers in the core. The five chambers are shaped like stars. The chambers contain some seeds. The seeds are dark brown.

You probably noticed that Sean's paragraph—made up of a series of simple sentences—is dull, monotonous, and boring. You are also aware that the editing stage of the rewriting process challenges students—like you and Sean—to create interesting and appropriate sentences. These interesting and appropriate sentences can be achieved through the use of a variety of techniques. When Sean learns to modify his simple sentences in the interests of variety, his sentences become much more interesting. In the following section, you will learn how to achieve sentence variety through modifying, compounding, and subordinating.

Modifying for variety In *modifying for variety*, a writer can use adjectives, adverbs, or phrases (prepositions, infinitives, participles, gerunds) to combine ideas. Some possible combinations are given.

The **white, firm** flesh makes up most of the inside. (adjectives)

Five star-shaped chambers make up the core. (adjectives)

The chambers contain **dark brown** seeds. (adjectives)

The inside is **mostly** made up of flesh. (adverb)

The core is **centrally** located. (adverb)

The chambers **in the core** are shaped **like stars**. (prepositional phrases)

Five chambers exist **to hold dark brown seeds**. (infinitive phrase = to + a verb)

Holding dark brown seeds, five star-shaped chambers, **contained within the core**, occupy the center of the apple. (participle phrase = "ing" form of verb or "ed" form of verb)

Occupying the center of the core is five star-shaped chambers. (gerund phrase = "ing" form of verb used as a noun)

The examples given are only suggested editing changes, for modifiers can be used in a number of different ways to create variety.

Compounding for variety Writers can also make use of compounding to achieve variety in their writing. Compounding is the process of joining similar elements by means of a linking word, often the word "and." Almost any element of the sentence can be compounded to achieve the goal of variety. Words like subjects and verbs can be compounded. Phrases such as prepositional phrases, infinitive phrases, participle phrases, or gerund phrases can be compounded. Even entire sentences can be compounded. Some examples of compounding follow.

The flesh and **the core** make up the inside of the apple. (compounded subjects joined by "and")

The five chambers **are shaped** like stars and **contain** some dark brown seeds. (compounded verbs joined by "and")

The dark brown seeds are located **in the center of the apple** and **within the star-shaped chambers**. (compounded prepositional phrases joined by "and")

The star-shaped chambers appear **to fill the central core** and **to hold the dark brown seeds**. (compounded infinitive phrases joined by "and")

Filling the central core and **holding dark brown seeds**, the star-shaped chambers are the most interesting feature of this apple. (compounded "ing" participle phrases joined by "and")

Shaped like stars and **located in the center of the core**, the chambers hold dark brown seeds. (compounded "ed" participle phrase joined by "and")

Occupying the center of the core and **holding dark brown seeds** are the star-shaped chambers of the apple. (compounded "ing" gerund phrases joined by "and")

The five chambers are shaped like stars, and **they contain the dark brown seeds**. (compounded sentences joined by "and")

The flesh is made up of white firm pulp, but **the core is made up of chambers and seeds**. (compounded sentences joined by "but")

The examples given are only suggested editing changes, for compounding can be used in a number of different ways to create variety.

Subordinating for variety A third way in which ideas can be combined to achieve variety is through subordinating. As you have seen in the earlier part of this chapter on Efficiency and Sentence Purpose (pages 220–226), dependent or subordinate parts of sentences can add sophistication to your writing, for they convey a sense of relationship among your ideas. For instance, a dependent or subordinate word signal such as "because" suggests a cause-effect relationship among your ideas; a word like "after" or "when" suggests time relationships; a word like "although" suggests a qualification or difference. The following sentences result from using subordination in the interest of variety.

Although the majority of the apple is made up of white flesh, the core is made up of five star-shaped chambers containing seeds. (dependent clause signal "although" suggests a difference between the flesh and core)

The flesh, **which is white and firm**, makes up most of the apple.
(dependent clause signal "which" adds additional information about the flesh)

Since the core contains five star-shaped chambers, this part of the apple holds the seeds. (dependent clause signal "since" suggests a relationship between the chambers and the seeds)

The core contains some chambers **that are filled with seeds**. (dependent clause signal "that" adds additional information about the chambers)

These examples are only suggested editing changes, for subordinating can be used in a number of different ways to create variety. Refer to the list of dependent clause signals on page 224 when you wish to use subordination to create variety in your sentences.

Writing About It #137

Return to a paragraph or two from some of the writing you have already produced for this class. Then vary some of your sentences using the methods for creating variety like (1) modifying, (2) compounding, or (3) subordinating. Label the method you used for achieving variety in these new sentences. Then share both your new and old sentences with your classmates.

PROOFREADING

As you come to the end of the editing stage of the rewriting process and enter the proofreading stage, you need to remind yourself that you've come a long way. As you edited the words in your draft for consistency, you looked for problems in point of view, tense, and tone. As you edited the sentences in your draft for clarity, you aimed for simplicity, efficiency and humanity. Because you have done such hard work, it's a good idea to put your draft away for a while before you begin to proofread it. You've been editing it for a long time, and your draft needs some fresh eyes to pick out the surface errors that likely exist.

Proofreading is a kind of final touch that you apply to your revision before you turn it in. It's like the final coat of wax that you give to your car or the final sanding you give to a piece of furniture. To make sure you proofread with skill, remember the following points as you turn your fresh eyes to your draft for its final inspection.

1. *Be aware of your own patterns of error.* Review your Writing Assessment Profile to recall your own personal patterns of error. Knowing these patterns is useful as you begin to proofread, for you can remind yourself to look for the sentence fragments that you are in the habit of writing or the pronoun reference problems that crop up frequently in your essays. Then, once you've identified these trouble spots, make sure to comb your draft carefully for them.

2. *Read your draft out loud—slowly.* Taking the time to read your draft out loud—and very slowly—is probably the best technique you can use for spotting surface errors. As you read, your voice will tend to stumble over sentences that are awkwardly constructed or passages with confusing meanings. If you, working hard to write and then shape these sentences, trip over these awkward sentences, you can be certain that your reader will, too. Reading slowly out loud will also enable you to catch those pesky fragments, comma splices, and run-on sentences that give students so much trouble. As you listen to your voice, you will notice the way it naturally stops or dips at the end of a sentence, reminding you to put periods in appropriate places. As you read slowly, enunciating each word, you will catch those places where you forgot to put the "s"s on the ends of plural nouns or the "ed"s on the past tense endings of verbs. Your voice, you will soon learn, provides even more information to you than your eyes alone.

3. *Be aware of professional tips for proofreading.* Professional copy editors possess several tricks of the proofreading trade. One of them suggests that, if you're drafting on a computer, you need to proofread from both the screen and a printed hard copy. Using your eyes to scan in both media assures you of greater success. Secondly, professional editors know that mistakes tend to "cluster." That is, if you tend to find an error in one line, look carefully for other errors among its neighbors. A third tip is to read the draft backwards, word by word, from back to front. The reading won't make any logical sense, but it will cause you to notice each word in isolation from its fellows and make you more likely to pick up on the missing apostrophes, letter reversals, and usage errors so common to many drafts.

4. *Use a spell-checker.* Today's new computers are nearly all equipped with spell-checking functions, a boon to every writer. Make sure you use your computer's spell-checker or, if you are hand writing your draft, ask a friend to double-check your spelling. You should, at this point, be aware of your own personal spelling demons if you've kept them in your Writing Assessment Profile, so be especially alert to those words in your text. In spite of the helpfulness of modern spell-checking systems, it's important for you to be aware of their limitations. They certainly can't pick out tricky homonym—for instance "to," "too," and "two"—and tell you whether you've properly used them appropriately. Nor can they tell you whether you've properly used tricky words like "affect" and "effect" or "principal" and "principle." It's important for you to remember that the ultimate authority resides with you, not the computer.

5. *Make use of other checking tips.* In the course of this text you have learned many tips about writing. Proofreading is the stage in which you want to use them again—for the final time. For instance, you may wish to review the tips for checking pronoun case on pages 525-527. You can use these tips to help you proofread for pronoun case errors. Remember, too, the "three-step" you perform to check for apostrophe errors (page 500). Similarly, if you're unable to find a comma rule that applies to your situation in a grammar book, recall the comma jingle that says, "When in doubt, leave it out." Perform a unity and coherence check for the last time. Above all, train yourself to remember—and use—the tips you've been taught.

6. *Look things up.* As you proofread, many questions will come to mind. Do you capitalize a season? Where does a question mark go—inside or outside the quotation mark? How do you spell "recommend"—how many "c"s and how many "m"s? You'll need to discipline yourself to look things up, checking your thesaurus, your dictionary, and the appendix at the back of this book for clarification.

7. *Trust your own instincts.* If you sense that a word or passage is weak, it probably is; trust your instincts. Sometimes students shrug off an error when they shouldn't. Some instinct may whisper to them that there's something wrong, but because they can't name the error precisely, they might pass it over, assuming that their instincts aren't reliable. Of course, it helps for you to know the comma rule that says to "use commas after introductory clauses," but you don't need to be able to repeat the precise rule to recognize the signal sent by an out-loud reading when you sensed a comma break might be needed after all those introductory words.

WRITING ASSIGNMENTS

Choose one or several of the writing assignments which follow. As you work through the stages of the writing process, submit your drafts to your classmates for responding and critiquing as well as editing and proofreading.

A. Write an essay with the purpose of evaluating your single greatest editing problem. It might be a problem with consistency. It might be a problem with wordy expressions. It might be a problem with writing purposeful sentences. Once you have decided what your single greatest editing problem is, go back through the drafts of your previous essays. Collect many examples of this type of editing problem. Write them down, identifying the essay in which they occurred. When you have a great deal of information about your own personal editing problem, you are ready to write. Your essay should define your typical problem, give examples of its appearance in our previous essays, explain the reason(s) why you think you make this error, and suggest satisfactory corrections for the errors.

Before you write, spend some time defining your reader and stating your purpose. Think carefully about strategies for content, organization, and expression as well. (Assume for purposes of this paper that your reader will be a fellow classmate.)

B. Write an essay in which you describe the process you currently use to proofread a paper. Evaluate how successful you believe your current process is by referring to specific undetected proofreading errors which have appeared in previous essays. Then explain how several of the proofreading tips which appear on pages 239–241 might be able to help you improve your proofreading. Be specific in your response.

Before you write, spend some time defining your reader and stating your purpose. Think carefully about strategies for content, organization, and expression as well. (Assume for purposes of this paper that your reader will be a fellow classmate.)

C. Look back over this chapter to review the aspects of editing such as consistency (point of view, tense, tone) and clarity (simplicity, efficiency, humanity). Then decide on the three editing aspects likely to lead to the most improvement in your own writing. Write an essay explaining these three aspects and why you think understanding them will help you improve your writing. Back up your choices by referring to specific words, phrases or sentences from your own previous essays.

Before you write, spend some time defining your reader and stating your purpose. Think carefully about strategies for content, organization, and expression as well. (Assume for purposes of this paper that your reader will be a fellow classmate.)

CHAPTER SEVEN REVIEW

Writing About It #138

Use your journal to reflect on what you learned in this chapter.

8

Describing

What is descriptive writing?
How can it help me improve my papers?

WHAT IS DESCRIPTION?

Description is like the air you breathe: so common that you rarely notice it. But you are describing all the time, every day. You describe the car you saw in the dealer's window. You describe the mounds of fruit heaped at the roadside market. You describe the look on your little brother's face as he opens his birthday present.

Novelists and fiction writers make use of description, of course. They describe a heroine's face as she glances in the mirror. They describe the loneliness of the open prairie, the power of a storm at sea, the quiet in the heart of a forest. They describe the way a character walks or gestures or throws back his head to laugh.

Scientists and technicians describe things, too. They describe the inner workings of an airplane engine, the design improvements of a late-model car, the parts of a bicycle which must be assembled.

As a student, you will be asked to use description frequently. Like Sean, the student you met in Chapter 4 who was writing a description of an apple, you might be required by a biology professor to describe something from nature: the compound eye of the grasshopper or the wing structure of a dragonfly. Your art professor might challenge you to describe a well-known painting or your electrical engineering professor might ask you to describe a standard piece of equipment such as a voltmeter. Asking you to make skillful use of description is a common college assignment, for in describing you learn to examine, to experience, to understand what something *is*.

As in every type of writing, descriptive writing requires you to write for a reader, creating reader-based, not writer-based prose. When you describe, you develop content to help your reader understand your subject, often by seeing, hearing, or even smelling it. When you describe, you arrange your content carefully to provide an organized experience of your subject, and you express your ideas in language that heightens and clarifies that experience. All this you do with the aim of communicating with a person who is very important to you: your reader.

SUBJECTIVE AND OBJECTIVE DESCRIPTION

Descriptive writing is usually either *subjective*, conveying a personal or emotional observation, or *objective*, reporting features or characteristics in a factual, nonbiased manner. One of the passages which follows is a subjective description and the other is an objective description.

> The power of the wind was first put to use in a windmill built in Persia in the seventh century. Windmills use sails to develop power, just as waterwheels employ paddles. The classic windmill has four big vertical sails. It works by the principle of the wheel and axle: the force of the wind along the sails produces a stronger driving force at the central shaft. A series of bevel and spur gears then transmit this force, usually to turn a grindstone or to drive a pump. The power of a windmill depends on the speed of the wind on the sails and on the area that the sails present to the wind.
>
> —David Macaulay, *The Way Things Work*

> Out of the mist, one hundred yards away, came *Tyrannosaurus rex*. It came on great oiled, resilient, striding legs. It towered thirty feet above half of the trees, a great evil god, folding its delicate watchmaker's claws close to its oily reptilian chest. Each lower leg was a piston, a thousand pounds of white bone, sunk in thick ropes of muscle, sheathed over in a gleam of pebbled skin like the mail of a terrible warrior. Each thigh was a ton of meat, ivory, and steel mesh. And from the great breathing cage of the upper body those two delicate arms dangled out front, arms with hands which might pick up and examine men like toys, while the snake neck coiled. And the head itself, a ton of sculptured stone, lifted easily upon the sky. Its mouth gaped, exposing a fence of teeth like daggers. Its eyes rolled, ostrich eggs, empty of all expression save hunger. It closed its mouth in a death grin.
>
> —Ray Bradbury, "The Sound of Thunder"

Talking About It #139

Talk to your classmates about the two passages you just read. Which one is a subjective description? Which one is an objective description? Why? Ask someone to serve as recorder and then brainstorm some possible topics for both subjective and objective description.

READER AND PURPOSE IN DESCRIPTIVE WRITING

As in any piece of writing, considering your reader and your purpose is important to effective description. When you begin to think about describing, you need to ask yourself the following questions: Who is my reader? What needs and expectations will he or she have? Will the need be simply to understand the subject I am describing? Or is my reader required to act on my description or to do something based on it? What knowledge about my subject will he or she already possess? What knowledge will I need to provide? What attitudes does he or she hold about my subject? Will I want to change those attitudes or confirm them?

In the descriptive passage we read about the windmill, the writer, David Macaulay, probably made some predictions about his reader. He probably assumed that his reader was a general reader, someone without any great technical knowledge of windmills. He probably predicted that this reader would merely need to deepen the understanding of windmills and to develop a positive attitude about a common energy source that is often taken for granted. On the other hand, if Macaulay's reader had been a farmer wishing to construct a windmill on farm property, the descriptive content might have been very different. If Macaulay's reader were an industrial designer attempting to build an improved dentist's drill, an appliance based on the principles of the windmill, the content of the description might also have been very different.

The writer's purpose also influences a piece of descriptive writing. Before you begin to write, you will need to ask yourself whether you want your description to inform, to entertain, to persuade, or to express yourself. Your description of a tornado heading across the prairie will depend on whether you're a frightened farm hand urging your fellow field workers to head for cover or a meteorologist reporting on wind conditions for the local TV station. In the passage describing Tyrannosaurus rex, Ray Bradbury's purpose was likely to suggest the raw size and power of the dinosaur in order to produce an emotional response in the reader. If Bradbury had intended to report on the animal's anatomy for a team of scientists assembling the skeletal pieces in a local museum, his purpose and thus the resulting description would have been very different.

THE CHARACTERISTICS OF DESCRIPTIVE WRITING

You have seen that descriptive writing can generally be either subjective or objective and that it is greatly influenced by considerations of reader and purpose.

Descriptive writing is also characterized by certain features that mark it as different from other types of writing. Because descriptive writing is so common, it is important for you to become familiar with the characteristics of description which follow.

1. Descriptive writing makes use of concrete detail to characterize people, places, things, and experiences.
2. Descriptive writing often makes use of the senses and imaginative language.
3. Descriptive writing generally attempts to make a single dominant impression.
4. Descriptive writing is usually organized by the collection plan.
5. Descriptive writing makes use of special transition words.

Concrete Detail and Description

Concrete detail makes all writing—particularly descriptive writing—come alive. Without concrete detail, Ray Bradbury's dinosaur would be simply another big, noisy lizard. Add the concrete detail and—presto!—the writer helps us see its "oily reptilian chest," its "pebbled skin," and its "snake neck" coiling.

Professional writers understand the power of concrete detail. In *Writing Down the Bones*, author Natalie Goldberg offers this insight about using specific detail.

> Be specific. Don't say "fruit." Tell what kind of fruit—"It is a pomegranate." Give things the dignity of their names. Just as with human beings, it is rude to say, "Hey, girl, get in line." That "girl" has a name. (As a matter of fact, if she's at least twenty years old, she's a woman, not a "girl" at all.) Things, too, have names. It is much better to say "the geranium in the window" than "the flower in the window." "Geranium"—that one word—gives us a much more specific picture. It penetrates more deeply into the beingness of that flower. It immediately gives us the scene by the window—red petals, green circular leaves, all straining toward sunlight.

But ordinary people make use of concrete detail all the time as well. When you describe what you had for lunch, you can either say "a hot dog" or "a coney with onions, relish, and extra mustard." Which description makes your listener's mouth water, bringing the experience to life? When you bring your car into the shop, you can either tell the mechanic to "fix it" or you can provide specific details, pointing out that "the muffler is noisy, the shocks have gone bad, and the right rear tail light doesn't work." Which description is likely to get you the best service? Will your roommate be more interested when you tell her your boyfriend brought you "flowers" for your birthday—or "a dozen long-stemmed American beauty roses?" Concrete details bring life to everyday descriptions.

In the following passage, columnist Kathleen Stocking uses concrete details to describe her Aunt Myrtle.

Aunt Myrtle provided me with my earliest impressions of Detroit. She was a redheaded woman who had chartreuse Chinese coolies on her what-not shelf and who painted her nails. Aunt Myrtle knew how to play canasta, and once played it with me for a week. "She's from Detroit," my mother said often about Aunt Myrtle. I didn't know what this meant, exactly—that Aunt Myrtle dared to be different because she was from Detroit, or that everyone in Detroit painted their nails and played canasta—but I wanted to find out.

Writing About It #140

Find at least three concrete details that describe Aunt Myrtle in the passage above. Then think of several relatives you know well, jotting down at least three concrete details to describe each of them. When you have finished, share your relative's names and the descriptive details you've provided with the other members of your class by listing them on the board. Then talk with your classmates about which concrete details are most effective, explaining why you think so.

Think of a place that you know well. Then make use of the mapping technique you learned about in Chapter 4 to produce some concrete details about this place. When you have finished, share your place and the descriptive details you've provided with the other members of your class by reproducing your maps on the board. Then talk with your classmates about which concrete details are most effective, explaining why you think so.

Think of an object or "thing" you are familiar with and that is made up of several parts. For instance, a bicycle, a coffee maker, or a childhood toy might be objects that come to mind. Then make use of the branching technique you learned about in Chapter 4 to produce some concrete descriptive details characterizing the object and its various parts. When you have finished, share your object and the descriptive details you've provided with the other members of your class by listing them on the board. Then talk to your classmates about which concrete details are most effective, explaining why you think so.

Description, the Senses, and Imaginative Language

Descriptive writing can help you create an intimate connection with your reader because it often makes use of *the five senses*, enabling your reader not just to see what you're describing but also to feel, taste, smell, and touch it, too. In the following passage from *Cress Delahanty*, by the novelist Jessamyn West, the author makes use of several senses in order to describe an experience for her reader.

[T]he sights and sounds of a beach town on a Sunday afternoon were almost too exciting to be borne. First, there was the strange light touch of the penetrating wind off the sea on her warm inland body. Then there was the constant, half-heard beat of the surf, hissing as it ran smoothly up the sand, thundering as it crashed against the rocks of the breakwater. There were all the smells of salt and seaweed, of fish and water and wind. There were all the human smells too of the hundreds of people who filled the boardwalk: ladies in print dresses smelling like passing gardens; swimmers with their scents of suntan oils and skin lotions; there were the smells of the eating places: of mustard and onions, of hamburgers frying; and the sudden sharp smell of stacks of dill pickles, as brisk in the nose as a sudden unintended inhalation of sea water.

Writing About It #141

Return to the concrete details you produced in thinking about descriptions of your relative, a familiar place, or an object. Try adding a few more concrete details that make use of senses in addition to the sense of sight. Share your new details with your classmates, discussing their effectiveness.

In addition to use of the five senses, descriptive writing often relies on *imaginative language* to create an understanding of its subject for the reader. Imaginative language often involves the use of similes and metaphors to create associations for the reader and bring experiences to life. When a writer uses the word "like" or "as" to create an imaginative association, he or she makes use of a "simile." When a writer creates an imaginative association without using the word "like" or "as," he or she makes use of a "metaphor."

Talking About It #142

Imaginative language prevails in the passage by Ray Bradbury describing the Tyrannosaurus rex. With your classmates, identify the similes and metaphors which appear in this passage.

Writing About It #143

Jot down some similes and metaphors to describe the relatives, the place, or the object you have written about. Then share those similes and metaphors with your classmates, discussing the effectiveness of each.

A Single Dominant Impression

The concrete details that characterize descriptive writing are often directed to the goal of achieving a *single dominant impression* on the reader. In her description of Aunt Myrtle, for instance, Kathleen Stocking used concrete details to create a single impression of her aunt: the way Aunt Myrtle characterized what it meant to be "from Detroit." In his description of Tyrannosaurus rex, Ray Bradbury amassed a greater number of details, but, in spite of the wealth of detail, his descriptive passage still creates only a single dominant impression about the dinosaur: one of great size and strength.

In the following passage, Elting E. Morison describes his great-uncle, George S. Morison, master builder of the Panama Canal. In this passage, the concrete details imply a single dominant impression.

My great-uncle, George S. Morison, one of America's foremost bridge builders, died July 1, 1903, exactly (as he undoubtedly would have said) six years, five months, fourteen days, and six hours before I was born.

He had, like Zeno, a conviction that time was a solid. If he made an appointment to confer with a person at 3:15 P.M., or as he always put it, at 1515 hours, that was when they met. Those who arrived earlier waited; those who came at any time after 1515 never conferred at all.

Talking About It #144

In the passage about George S. Morison, the writer attempts to create a single dominant impression of his great-uncle.

1. What is that single dominant impression? How do you know? What details suggest that single impression to you?
2. Is the single dominant impression explicitly expressed—or is it up to the reader to infer the single dominant impression?
3. Suggest a topic sentence for this passage that conveys the single dominant impression in the controlling idea. Where would you place that topic sentence? At the beginning? At the end? Explain your decision.
4. Do you think this passage is improved by the addition of a topic sentence? Why or why not?

Writing About It #145

Think about the concrete details, the sense impressions, and the imaginative language you have used to describe your relatives. Try now to think of a single dominant impression you'd like to convey about a single relative, and write a topic sentence with a controlling idea that conveys it. Then add to your topic sentence some concrete details, some sense impressions, and some imaginative language to support that controlling idea. Make a chart like the one that appears below to suggest your ideas. Then share your dominant impression and the details that support it with the others in your class.

Topic Sentence: My Uncle Cecil is a saver.
(topic) (controlling idea)

1. Lived through the Depression—times were tough—explains his passion for saving

2. Saves coffee cans, stacking them in a corner of the kitchen like an aluminum Tower of Pisa

3. His shoes scrape across the parlor floor—he's shuffling to add a stray paper clip to his paper clip chain—he's like a rat scuttling behind the wall, hoarding a smelly tidbit of cheese

4. Miscellaneous items. Soda pop rings, rubber bands from the daily newspaper, empty spools of thread

5. Kitchen garbage can—smells of orange peels, coffee grinds, and eggshells—he's saving them to dump out back in his compost heap

6. Seems to save things just for the pleasure of saving them

7. Often puts many of his treasures to good use—walnut shells and corncobs are for the squirrels—wraps gifts in the colorful Sunday comics pages—turns old string into shoelaces

The Collection Plan

You have seen in earlier chapters that writers can organize the content of their writing in one of three ways. They can use the collection plan, the chronology plan, or the connection plan. Descriptive writing generally is organized by means of the *collection plan*. Writers add one detail after another, making sure that they have "collected" enough material to make a single dominant impression on their readers. When you use the collection plan, it's important to decide on the arrangement of the details in your collection. You'll need to make decisions about where the details should be placed in order to achieve the best effect. Do you save your most telling detail for last? Or do you put it near the beginning? These are questions only you, the writer, can answer.

Talking About It #146

Return to the material about Uncle Cecil, the saver. Assume you will be writing a paragraph about Uncle Cecil, making use of the details you have already collected. In using the collection plan for organizing this paragraph, what detail or details would you put first? Why? What detail or details would you put last? Why?

Writing About It #147

Return to the material you have been collecting about your own relative. Assume you will be turning this material into a descriptive paragraph and using the collection plan for organizing it. Now list the order in which you would arrange your details and then share this arrangement with your classmates. Discuss whether or not the arrangement seems effective.

Appropriate Transition Words

Skillful writers take care to guide their readers through their work, leading their readers through their prose with *transition words* like "for instance," "in addition," and "therefore." Descriptive writing often makes use of special transition words to guide the reader. These key transition words that typically guide a reader through a piece of descriptive writing can include the following:

also	for one thing
and	furthermore
as well	in addition
first (second, third, last)	moreover
	what is more

In addition, prepositional phrases are often especially useful in guiding a reader through a work of description. In describing a scene at the beach, for instance, a writer might choose to present details in a certain order: from the horizon line, for instance, up to the sand. In the same way, certain prepositional phrases might guide the reader through the text, phrases such as "at the horizon," "about halfway out," "near the breaking waves," "at the high-tide line," "on the sand," and others that help the reader's eye take in the scene in an orderly fashion from horizon to beach. Or this same writer may decide to arrange details differently, choosing to help the reader's eye pan the scene from left to right and using prepositional phrases like "to the left," "in the middle of the scene," "to the far right," and so on to present details in a meaningful way.

In addition to the transition words listed, the following words and phrases can also help your reader make an organized transition through the scene, picture, or object you are describing.

above	inside
at	nearby
beside	next to
below	on the far side
beyond	outside
from	to the east (south, north, west)
further	to the left (right, center)
here	

Talking About It: #148

As a group, read the following descriptive passage which makes use of the collection plan of organization. Together, suggest some transition words that will help guide your reader through the text.

The boy had been busy all day, and his body showed it. His feet were caked with mud, _________ splotches of mud _________ stained the hems of his jeans, _________ his side pockets were filled to overflowing with goodies like packs of bubble gum and red hots, _________ a nonedible slingshot stuck out of the back pocket of his jeans, its rubber band snapped in two. _________, his face bore silent witness to mischief. There was a bloody scratch on the left cheek _________ a blackening, swelling bruise across the right eye.

As a group, read the following descriptive passage which also makes use of the collection plan for organization. However, this time add appropriate prepositional phrases to guide your reader through the text.

_________, 60 feet above the ground, you had a bird's-eye view of King's Island Amusement Park. _________ were the shops and arcades where you could buy T-shirts and sunglasses, key chains and buttons, and the emergency umbrella in case of rain. _________ was the main section of the park, the place where you could ride the Beast, the King Cobra, the Racer, and the Vortex, each one guaranteed to give you the heart-stopping ride of your life. _________ were the parks and the lagoons where you could eat your picnic lunch at a leisurely pace, free from the noisy riders and jostling crowds, or ride silently on a canoe through the quiet forest.

DESCRIPTION IN COMBINATION WITH OTHER STRATEGIES FOR WRITING

Seldom does a strategy for writing—like description—exist in isolation from other kinds of writing. More typically, description is often interspersed with several different modes. For instance, a travel sketch which largely offers facts and reasons for traveling to a particular place might include a descriptive paragraph detailing a particularly interesting resort hotel. Or a process piece explaining how to view a slide under an electron microscope might include descriptive matter detailing the parts of the microscope or giving a picture of the view the slide presents to the trained eye.

Although you will learn more about narration, a mode of writing that uses chronological order to tell a story or provide a sequence of events, you can easily see the way Natalie Kusz combines description with narration to explain the way a visit to the ocean helped free her of her writer's block.

Kelp pods washed up around my feet, and I stomped on them with tennis shoes to find what was inside. I collected driftwood, and urchins, and tiny pink clam shells dropped by gulls, thin enough to see through and smaller than a thumbnail. When the tide had gone far out, I climbed the bluff back to my cabin and sat writing in front of the window, eating cheese on bread and drinking orange spritzers or tea. The walls and windows there had space in between, and they let in shreds of wind and the arguing of birds and the metal smell of seaweed drying out on the beach. When the tide started back in, I took pen and notebook and sat on a great barnacled rock, letting water creep up and surround me, then jumping to shore just in time.

Using description can be a powerful way of inviting your reader into your text. In the following introductory paragraph from an article called "The Scoop on Ice Cream," writer Lawrence E. Joseph uses description to draw the reader into a piece of writing that is a scientific, factual look at the properties of ice cream.

Take a lick of vanilla ice cream: sweet and cool, as expected, but with little fragrance. Surprising, since vanilla normally has such a distinctive scent. But wait a beat; then suddenly there's the familiar aroma, the one that, if you go back long enough, schoolgirls once used as perfume. That wait was just long enough to allow all hell to break loose inside your mouth. The ice cream is now literally exploding. Air bubbles are bursting from the heat of your tongue. A volatile compound, in this case vanillin, is boiling. Sweet scents are wafting their way up your nasal cavities, where olfactory cells send your brain the belated good news. Take another lick, and touch off another explosion. "Ice cream is virtually the only food we eat frozen, which means that its flavor . . . is only fully released upon melting," explains Arun Kilara, a 43-year-old professor of food science at Penn State and one of the world's acknowledged authorities on ice cream.

Talking About It #149

With your classmates, talk about the instances of concrete detail used to flesh out the descriptions by Kusz and Joseph. Then find some places where the writers made use of sensory experience and/or imaginative language.

A STUDENT USES DESCRIPTION: A FIRST DRAFT

Student Molly Kennedy has been writing a descriptive essay about her grandmother. She submitted an early draft to her classmates, and they responded to it in a number of ways. Some of them made use of freewriting to respond; others sketched their responses; still others wrote purpose statements in response to Molly's paper. Molly read their responses carefully, reviewed her own purposes, and then produced another draft. Her second effort follows.

Many people think that the term "grandmother" means "old." They haven't met my Granny. Although Granny is on the way to ninety, she is up-to-date. She is petite, standing only five feet tall. She's strong and limber. Unfortunately, Granny's feet give her trouble, so she can't wear high-heeled shoes any more. Instead, she copes by wearing high tops in assorted colors. She even wheels around town in a sporty new car.

Unlike many eighty-year-olds, Granny still knows how to have fun. After I made my first communion, Granny came up and gave me a high five—right in front of the priest. Sometimes she invites all her grandchildren over to spend the night, and we have fun then, too. Holidays are especially enjoyable because of Granny's ability to have fun.

Best of all, my Granny is especially close to me. She either stops by my house to visit me or I stop by hers to visit there. Granny loves to have big dinner parties, and she always calls me up to help her out. Since I have been away at college, I have received many letters from Granny. Sometimes she even sends little poems along with the letters. Last week she sent me some post cards that she bought in Paris many years ago. Another way in which Granny and I share a special relationship is that we are bedmates when she comes up to our cottage in the summer. I am Granny's bedmate for two reasons. First, I love it. Second, I am the only one in the family who doesn't mind Granny's snoring. My Granny is a special eighty-three-years young.

—Molly Kennedy

Talking About It #150

Critique Molly's draft using the point/support system explained in Chapter 6. Underline the points Molly makes and then number the instances of support she provides for those points. What changes may Molly need to make in her next draft based on your point/support critique?

Think about the characteristics of descriptive writing which you have just studied: (1) using concrete detail, (2) employing the senses and imaginative language, (3) creating a single dominant impression, (4) making use of the collection plan, and (5) using appropriate transition words. As a group, try to answer the following questions that relate to descriptive writing.

1. Where does Molly use concrete detail? Where could she use some additional concrete detail? Make some suggestions about what she might include.
2. Does Molly employ the senses and imaginative language? Would her description profit from these additions? Make some suggestions about what she might write.
3. Does Molly create a single dominant impression of her Granny? Does she make use of a thesis statement or topic sentences to do this? Make some suggestions about an appropriate thesis statement or appropriate topic sentences to help Molly.
4. Does Molly make use of the collection plan? What makes you think so? Could her plan be strengthened? How?
5. Does Molly use appropriate transition words?

A STUDENT USES DESCRIPTION: A REVISED DRAFT

Molly listened closely to her classmates' comments after they critiqued her work. Here is the draft that she revised in response.

When most people think of the word "grandmother," they think of rocking chairs, nursing homes, and knitting. When I think of the word "grandmother," I think of my Granny, who is 83 years young. My grandmother's body may be old, but it houses an ever-youthful heart. My Granny is modern, fun-loving, and special.

Although Granny is almost 90, she is up-to-date. Although she is petite, standing only five feet tall, she's strong and limber. She stays fit by going to the YMCA twice a week where she swims laps, enjoys the steamy sauna, and gets a massage from the handsome young masseuse. Unfortunately, Granny's feet give her trouble, so she can't wear high-heeled shoes any more. Instead, she copes by wearing Reebok high tops. She has them in red, black, and white. She even wheels around town in a sporty new Mazda.

Unlike many eighty-year-olds, Granny still knows how to have fun. After I made my first communion, Granny came up and gave me a high five—right in front of the priest. Sometimes she invites all her grandchildren over to spend the night, and we sit up late together. The sounds of rattling poker chips, crunching pretzels, and laughing voices make up some of my fondest memories. Furthermore, holidays are especially enjoyable because of Granny's ability to have fun. Every Christmas, Granny, jolly as an elderly elf, puts a lottery ticket in each of our stockings. At Easter she buys colored plastic Easter eggs, filling them with money and then hiding them around her house for us to find.

Best of all, my Granny is special because she is especially close to me. She either stops by my house to visit me or I stop by hers to visit there. Granny loves to have big dinner parties, and she always calls me up to help her out. Together we put out the centerpiece and set the table. Together we cook the dinner, preparing a mustard-glazed ham or a velvety chocolate mousse. Together we clean up the kitchen after the party is over. Since I have been away at college, the mail carrier has brought me many letters from Granny that remind me of how close we are. Sometimes she even sends little poems along with the letters. Last week, for example, she sent me some post cards that she bought in Paris many years ago. They showed drawings of French children who looked like angels. Beside the drawings, Granny penned this inscription: "These dear children remind me of you and your brothers and sisters and how much I adore you all." Another way in which Granny and I share a special relationship is that we are bedmates when she comes up to our cottage in the summer. I am Granny's bedmate for two reasons. First, I love it. Second, I am the only one in the family who doesn't mind Granny's snoring.

Eighty-three is not rocking chairs and canes and dentures when it comes to my Granny. Eighty-three is modern, fun-loving, and special.

Talking About It #151

Molly thought about her own purposes as well as her classmates' critiques when she wrote her revised draft. Talk to your classmates about the specific changes she has made. Do you think her draft has been improved? Why or why not?

WRITING ASSIGNMENTS

A. Write a descriptive essay about a relative in which you employ the characteristics of good descriptive writing: using concrete details, employing the senses and imaginative language, creating a single dominant impression, making use of the collection plan, and using specific transitions. You have already brainstormed many ideas about a relative which you could use in developing this essay, or you could begin again with an entirely new topic.

Before you write, define your reader and your purpose, and do some preliminary planning in the areas of content, organization, and expression. (Assume for purposes of this paper that your reader will be a classmate.)

After you have written your first draft, ask your classmates to respond to it. Then rewrite it, making improvements that consider their responses and your own purposes. Invite your classmates to critique this next draft. After you have written yet another draft in response to those critiques, ask your classmates to make editing suggestions. Finally, proofread and submit your paper.

Record all responses to the drafts of your paper in the Writing Assessment Profile which appears in the back of this text.

B. Write a descriptive essay describing a painting you like or a painting you have studied in an art class. Make sure you employ the characteristics of good descriptive writing: using concrete details, employing the senses and imaginative language, creating a single dominant impression, making use of the collection plan, and using specific transitions.

Before you write, define your reader and your purpose, and do some preliminary planning in the areas of content, organization, and expression. (Assume for purposes of this paper that your reader will be an art teacher or someone who is familiar with this painting.)

After you have written your first draft, ask your classmates to respond to it as if they were an art teacher.

Record all responses to the drafts of your paper in the Writing Assessment Profile which appears in the back of this text.

C. Write a descriptive essay about a piece of equipment commonly used in a science laboratory (a microscope, a Bunsen burner, an oscilloscope, etc.). Make sure you employ the characteristics of good descriptive writing: using concrete details, employing the senses and imaginative language, creating a single dominant impression, making use of the collection plan, and using specific transitions.

Before you write, define your reader and your purpose, and do some preliminary planning in the areas of content, organization, and expression. (Assume for purposes of this paper that your reader will be a science teacher or someone who is familiar with this piece of equipment.)

After you have written your first draft, ask your classmates to respond to it as if they were a science teacher. Then rewrite it, making improvements that consider their responses and your own purposes. Invite your classmates to critique this next draft. After you have written yet another draft in response to those critiques, ask your classmates to make editing suggestions. Finally, proofread and submit your paper.

Record all responses to the drafts of your paper in the Writing Assessment Profile which appears in the back of this text.

D. Write a descriptive essay in which you describe a scene common to a profession (a hospital for a health professional; a soup kitchen for a social worker; a classroom for a teacher; an assembly line for a factory worker). Make sure you employ the characteristics of good descriptive writing: using concrete details, employing the senses and imaginative language, creating a single dominant impression, and using specific transitions.

Before you write, define your reader and your purpose, and do some preliminary planning in the areas of content, organization, and expression. (Assume for purposes of this paper that your reader will be an employee familiar with this workplace.)

After you have written your first draft, ask your classmates to respond to and critique it as if they were an employee familiar with this workplace. Then rewrite it, making improvements that consider their responses and your own purposes. Invite your classmates to critique this next draft. After you have written yet another draft in response to those critiques, ask your classmates to make editing suggestions. Finally, proofread and submit your paper.

Record all responses to the drafts of your paper in the Writing Assessment Profile which appears in the back of this text.

CHAPTER EIGHT REVIEW

Writing About It #152

Use your journal to reflect on what you learned in this chapter.

9
Illustrating

What are some of the characteristics of illustration?
How can using illustration help improve my writing?

WHAT IS ILLUSTRATION?

You use illustration all the time.

"What kind of teachers do you like?" a friend asks you.

"Oh, teachers who know how to be fair. Like Mr. Sample, Miss Fratini, or Mrs. Robinette," you reply.

Or your mother talks to the sales clerk at the garden center. "What kind of flowering plant will grow in the shade?" she asks.

"You'd do best with some impatiens," the clerk replies. "Although you have to water them a lot, they spread very rapidly, and most of our customers are happy to learn that they actually prefer a shady spot."

Or you study the essay question on the final exam for your American History class. "Choose one important Civil War general who exhibited great strengths as well as great weaknesses. In a well-structured essay, explain the impact of those strengths and weaknesses on the outcome of the war."

You chew on the end of your pencil, thinking. You have studied hard for this final, so examples of Civil War generals come quickly to mind. John B. McClellan. Nathan Bedford Forrest. Robert E. Lee. Stonewall Jackson. You think about what you know about several of them, recalling their strengths and weaknesses. Then you begin to write, "Ulysses S. Grant was one of the most important generals of the Civil War. This essay will provide examples of the way his strengths and weaknesses affected the outcome of the war."

In all of the situations mentioned, you were making use of the technique of *illustration* because you were providing examples to explain a point. You cited the examples of Mr. Sample, Miss Fratini, and Mrs. Robinette to underscore your preference for teachers who are fair. The clerk at the garden center provided your mother with the example of the impatiens as an appropriate flowering plant for a shady area. And you gave examples of General Grant's strengths and weaknesses as they affected the outcome of the Civil War.

In your college work, you will often be asked to provide examples or illustrations in your written work. For an art class, you might be asked to provide several examples of what you consider to be a sculptor's best work. In a sociology class, you might be asked to research a significant example of social prejudice. In an education class, you might need to write up a case study of an elementary school student you've been observing this semester, providing many examples of this youngster's learning problems. In a brochure describing your club's activities to prospective members, you might give several examples of the activities in which the club members are involved. Because you will be called on to use illustration so often in your college career, it is important that you become familiar with its characteristics.

CHARACTERISTICS OF ILLUSTRATION

Illustration is characterized by the following qualities.

1. Illustration uses examples to make a point.
2. Illustration uses the collection plan of organization.
3. Illustration makes use of appropriate transition words.

Examples to Make a Point

Illustration uses examples to *make a point*. If you want the essay for your religion class to explain a religious experience that has affected your life, you will need to provide a clear example of it. If you want your engineering lab report to make the point that the oscilloscope is a useful measuring device, you would provide an example or examples to confirm your point. If you want the paper for your introductory architecture class to convince your teacher that prefabricated houses are generally substandard, you will need to provide examples to prove your point.

The following passage from "The Case of Harry Houdini" by Daniel Mark Epstein makes use of the technique of illustration.

> The newspaper accounts are voluminous, and consistent. The mere cataloging of Houdini's escapes soon grows tedious, which they were not, to be sure, in the flesh. But quickly:

the police stripped him naked and searched him thoroughly before binding his wrists and ankles with five pairs of irons. Then they would slam him into a cell and turn the key of a three-bond burglar-proof lock. He escaped, hundreds of times, from the most secure prisons in the world. He hung upside down in a straitjacket from the tallest buildings in America, and escaped in full view of the populace. He was chained hand and foot and nailed into a packing case weighted with lead; the packing case was dropped from a tugboat into New York's East River and ninety seconds later Houdini surfaced. The packing case was hauled up intact, with the manacles inside, still fastened. He was sealed into a paper bag and got out without disturbing the seal. He was sewn into a huge football, in the belly of a whale, and escaped. In California he was buried six feet underground, and clawed his way out. He did this, he did that. These are facts that cannot be exaggerated, for they were conceived as exaggerations. We know he did these things because his actions were more public than the proceedings of Congress, and most of them he performed over and over, so no one would miss the point.

Writing About It #153

In the passage about Houdini, identify the examples used by the author and then discuss the point these examples are designed to illustrate.

Writing About It #154

In your journal, freewrite for 10 minutes or so on one of the following topics, generating some examples to illustrate them.

Movies that are enlightening as well as entertaining
Heroes of the popular culture that are positive role models for children
Pet peeves

The Collection Plan

Like description, illustration is organized using the collection method. Just as description collects a number of specific details to make a point, so does illustration collect one or several examples to make a point. Often the points themselves are also arranged in a special way. The following excerpt explores the importance to animals of an appendage that is largely overlooked—their tails. The writer has arranged this collection of examples in order of importance—from the least important example to the most important example. This is often an effective method for arranging the examples in a collection plan.

Although people do not have tails, in the animal kingdom tails are common—and important. A swimming beaver, for example, can use its tail to steer through water. When danger appears, however, the beaver's tail can be used to slap out a warning signal. A horseshoe crab's tail is also important. If the crab accidentally lands on its back, it flails about in a helpless position; however, it can right itself by poking its long stiff tail in the sand and using it to flip over. Although the tail of the scorpion is famous for its stinger and the poison that it carries, the scorpion is actually dependent on its tail for its very survival. Because it is not very efficient at trapping food, the scorpion would die were it not for its tail. As a matter of fact, the tail enables the scorpion to capture its food by paralyzing it first; then it can feast at leisure on a more cooperative meal.

Appropriate Transition Words

Special words often signal that the illustration mode is being used. These words include the following words and phrases:

a case in point	for example
an example	for instance
an illustration	in particular
another	one such
first (second, third, etc.)	yet another

SUBJECTIVE AND OBJECTIVE ILLUSTRATIONS

Illustrations can generally be of two types: subjective or objective. In a *subjective* illustration, the author presents examples from his own personal experience, creating a closer bond of intimacy with the reader. In an *objective* illustration, the author presents examples from information gathered outside himself, creating more distance between himself and his reader.

In the article which follows, called "The Thrifty Thirties," co-writers Betty Lou Wolfe and Marian Jean Gray use examples from personal experience to recall a thrifty and resourceful mother, circa 1930.

My mother was the most resourceful person I've ever known. She found a use for everything. A broken pair of scissors with one blade made a good letter opener, and an empty tuna can with a little red paint became a candle holder. Mother saved string in balls according to size. When shoelaces broke, they were replaced with string that had been dyed either black or brown. Furthermore, food was never wasted. A pot of beans was many times the special of the week. Breakfast consisted of bread and beans, a bean sandwich was featured for lunch, and beans with corn bread made our supper.

Mother found good use, too, for the cardboard she saved. When shoes wore thin and developed a hole, she placed our foot down on a piece of cardboard and drew around the outside with a pencil. Then she cut this "insole" a little smaller than the outline so it would fit into our shoe. Usually it lasted several days, but if the weather changed, the rain soon dissolved our cardboard soles.

Mother even developed her own penny-saving methods for cosmetics and personal grooming. For deodorant, you splashed cider vinegar under the armpits (the vinegar smell disappeared in a few minutes). For face powder, you used white flour tinted lightly with ground cinnamon. For hair rinse, you used lemon juice in water if you were blonde, vinegar in water if you were brunette. To get an instant shoe shine, you rubbed a small amount of Vaseline on your shoe and then polished with a soft cloth.

[The thesaurus lists several synonyms for "resourceful": "ingenious," "clever," "capable," "imaginative," and "cunning." I recognize only one: "Mother."]

As this essay by Wolfe and Gray points out, subjective illustration draws on personal experience. Objective illustration, on the other hand, does not make use of personal experience. Its origin lies in facts, data, and observations outside the writer. In the objective illustration which follows, professional writer Suzanne Kantra presents an article called "The House that Junk Built" for *Popular Science* magazine. Notice that it is not based on personal experience but on objective research.

You would never know by looking at them, but the building materials in this seemingly ordinary new house already are in their second incarnation. They have been newspapers, old cars, sawdust, soft-drink bottles, polystyrene packing, peanuts—even used computers.

But at the Resource Conservation House, conceived by the National Association of Home Builders Research Center, it is not only "garbage in." There is also almost no garbage out. Unlike most building sites, where nearly all waste is sent to a landfill, an estimated 90 percent of the scrap materials from this Upper Marlboro, Md., house were either recycled or reused on-site.

[The house uses] recycled materials, which today are comparable in cost and quality to those made from virgin materials. The Research Center discovered dozens of such products, including "lumber" that combines plastic grocery bags and used pallets ground into sawdust, ceiling material made from old newspapers, and siding produced from mill waste.

One of the biggest resource-savers was the house's steel frame, made from demolished bridges and junk cars. Unlike wood, says architect Orville Lee, "Steel is always specially cut at the mill," eliminating scraps. At a visit during construction, the mass of glinting steel overhead also provided a striking contrast to the usual wood "stick" framing.

The house's roof ventilation system is formed from recycled plastic soda bottles. As it saves energy by releasing hot attic air in summer, ventilation also prevents rot-causing moisture buildup. The roofing is made from recycled computer housings.

Not all construction waste could be eliminated through planning or using resource-efficient materials, however. [And, of course, one nagging problem remained: what to do with the fast-food wrappers from the Maryland construction crew's meals.]

READER AND PURPOSE IN ILLUSTRATION

As always, when you write an illustration, you are aiming to communicate with a reader by writing reader-based prose. In the attempt, it's important to be clear about both your reader and your purpose.

For instance, let's say you're a business major asked to write a market outlook for a certain product. In this paper you're to evaluate what the prospects are for a certain product's marketability. You decide to study high-tech toys, providing several examples in your paper of high-tech toys that manufacturers are busily investing in. Because this paper is clearly slanted to a business reader, it would only be necessary for you to examine certain market factors affecting sales of the toy: start-up investments, manufacturing costs, season of the year, research and development costs, and competition. Your reader would not need much detailed information about how the toy works or the technology on which it was built.

If, on the other hand, you were enrolled in a computer class as one of the requirements for a business major, you might also find yourself writing about examples or illustrations of high-tech toys. This time, however, your computer science professor would be interested in the way the toys work or the computer program on which they are based or the new technology that led to their development. The point is that who your reader is profoundly influences what you will write.

Your purpose as a writer will also influence the illustrations you use. In the following letter to the editor of *The Artist's Magazine*, Mr. Juve offers fellow artists and readers of the magazine some tips on how to recycle common products in his art studio.

Dear Editor:

I've found several creative ways to recycle polyurethane products in my studio—you know, those indestructible plates and plastic cups you sometimes get at fast-food joints. For instance, the plates make handy paint palettes. In addition, cups are always great to have around the studio, especially the ones with covers. You can blow excess paints or solvents from an airbrush through the straw hole to contain the spray. Also you can reuse plastic film canisters to hold paint or anything you want to keep airtight.

Robert Juve
Mason, GA

Mr. Juve's purpose in writing this letter was simply to let fellow artists in on some helpful hints he'd discovered in his own studio. The helpful hints were presented as a series of examples. Note, too, that his purpose does not mandate the use of formal language, and he can present his examples using casual diction: "you know," "great," "fast-food joints." On the other hand, an article in a scientific journal or a magazine of popular science would approach the problem of recycling everyday materials very differently because the writer's purpose might be more serious or scholarly. In these articles, the writers might also use a number of examples to suggest recycling approaches, but the content, organization, and tone might be very different because of the writer's very different purpose—and reader.

ILLUSTRATION IN COMBINATION WITH OTHER STRATEGIES FOR WRITING

Seldom are any of the strategies—illustration included—used in isolation. Often writers combine various strategies as they compose their essays, articles, and research papers.

In the following paragraph, the author combines illustration with description.

> From the snow-capped peaks of the Rocky Mountains to the cypress-draped swamps of Georgia, America offers scenic beauty that is unequalled in the world. In Arches, Utah, huge red sandstone arches, looking like giant gateways to the sky, show the effects of erosion. Crater Lake in Oregon, formed from the crater of an extinct volcano, is circled by 2000-foot lava walls, and the lake itself is filled with water that sparkles with shades of turquoise, aquamarine, and cobalt blue. The Olympic National Park in Washington contains a rain forest as lush as any in the tropics; it also features glaciers that still actively creep southward and free-ranging elk with yard-wide antlers and tawny coats. Virginia's Shenandoah National Park offers vistas of deep green valleys, winding ridges, and pine-draped slopes. From the swampy bogs of the south to the rocky coasts of Maine, America is alive with natural beauty.

In addition, illustration can often help a writer fulfill another important purpose: providing a method for writing an interesting introduction to a work. A lively or gripping example—or two—can go far to draw the reader into your writing. In the introductory paragraph that follows, notice how the newspaper writer used examples to pull the reader into his subject: the increasingly ruthless nature of juvenile crime.

> A sub-headline called them "The Young and the Ruthless."
>
> There was Kerry Marshall, 17, who shot and killed a woman fish seller when she reached for a knife as he tried to rob her.
>
> There was Richard Caraballo, 17, who shot and killed a taxi driver for demanding to be paid the $7 fare on the meter.
>
> There was Kenyatta Miles, 18, who shot and killed a 15-year-old honor student for a new pair of Air Jordan sneakers.

A STUDENT USES ILLUSTRATION: A FIRST DRAFT

Carol Buechler, a student in a college writing class, has learned a lot from her employment experiences. When given an assignment to write a paragraph about job experiences using the mode called illustration, Carol submitted an early draft to her classmates. They responded to it in a number of ways. Some of them made use of freewriting to respond; others sketched their responses; still others wrote purpose statements in response to Carol's paper. Carol read their responses carefully, reviewed her own purposes, and then produced another draft. Her second effort follows.

At Easter Seals, I saw a fellow employee stealing from the company that employed him. That made a lasting impression on me. During the next summer, I accepted a job at Systems Research Laboratories at Wright Patterson Air Force Base. After completing all the military paperwork required by the job, I stopped to meet my new boss. I felt he had prejudged me. He immediately identified me as another "military brat." I got all the worst jobs from him. This incident helped me cope with a similar problem at Ohio Electronic Engravers. At Progressive Industries, I learned the difference between my evaluation of my work and my supervisor's evaluation. I felt I had done so terribly the first summer that I never considered putting in an application the next year. Much to my surprise, my supervisor called me and offered me a job in the professional photofinishing department.

Talking About It #155

Critique Carol's draft using the writer-based/reader-based system explained in Chapter 6. Underline or circle those parts of her paragraph in which writer-based prose appears, remembering to put question marks over these portions. Then, in the margins or elsewhere, write down the questions that you as a reader still need the writer to answer. What changes may Carol need to make in her next draft based on your writer-based/reader-based critique?

Think about the characteristics of illustration which you have just studied: (1) using examples to make a point, (2) organizing by the collection plan, and (3) using appropriate transition words. As a group, try to answer the following questions that relate to Carol's illustration.

1. What examples does Carol use? Do the examples make a point?
2. Does Carol organize her illustration paragraph with the collection plan? Are all the examples presented in the most effective order?
3. Does Carol use any transition words to make connections in her paragraph?
4. What suggestions would you offer Carol for improving her next draft?

A STUDENT USES ILLUSTRATION: A REVISED DRAFT

The following is Carol's next draft of her paper. In it, she tries to incorporate the responses of her readers as well as her own purposes.

I have never had a "bad" job because I have learned something from every job I have held. At Easter Seals, where I worked as a receptionist, I learned about employee theft. A fellow employee regularly stole money from the petty cash box. He also slipped staplers, rolls of Scotch tape, and boxes of pencils out of the office, hiding the stolen goods under his coat. That kind of dishonest behav-

ior made a lasting impression on me. During the next summer, I accepted a job at Systems Research Laboratories as an engineering assistant on a contract at Wright Patterson Air Force Base. After completing all the military paperwork on the base, I stopped in to meet my new boss, Major Herbert. He knew that my father was also in the military, and he instantly labelled me as just another military "brat" whose employment, he assumed, was the result of some kind of influence peddling. In fact, he was rude enough to say, "I would have preferred someone majoring in engineering at college." In working for Major Herbert, however, I think I proved that my two years in technical school had adequately prepared me for his job, and I made sure he saw my letter of recommendation. It wasn't from my father but from Major Herbert's own supervisor, a man I knew from church. At Ohio Electronic Engravers, where I worked on a noisy factory floor, I coped with a similar problem of prejudice. This time, however, my boss, Mr. Rivers, objected that I was a woman. He told me he felt that this job was not appropriate for a female. I think I showed Mr. Rivers that I could work just as hard as any man and in just as challenging conditions. At Progressive Industries, I learned that I sometimes valued my work differently than my supervisors did. At PI, I struggled to learn to use the photographic equipment in the lab. It was difficult for me. The machines were complicated, and they required an ability to take careful numerical readings and to time processes with great precision. Although I found it very difficult work, I resisted the temptation to quit. In fact, I felt I had done so poorly that I never considered putting in an application for the next year. To my surprise, my supervisor called me personally, offering me an even more challenging job in the photofinishing department. Thus, I may not have liked every job when I held it, but eventually I learned something important from every employment situation I have ever experienced.

Talking About It #156

Carol thought about her own purposes as well as her classmates' critiques when she wrote her revised draft. Talk to your classmates about the specific changes she has made. Do you think her draft has been improved? Why or why not?

WRITING ASSIGNMENTS

A. Do some preliminary library research into the year you were born. Record examples of popular songs, cultural fads, historical events, and other items of interest that characterized your birth year. Write an essay of illustration in which you use examples to characterize different aspects of the year in which you were born.

For this paper, assume that your reader will be your classmates. Your paper will have two purposes: (1) to support your ideas using examples and (2) to provide your reader with sufficient information. Be sure to do some preliminary thinking about content, organization, and expression before you begin to write.

When you have finished your first draft, share your paper with your classmates and invite them to respond to it. After you have rewritten your next draft, invite them to critique it. Finally, rewrite another draft in response to those critiques, asking your classmates to help you edit it.

Record all responses to the drafts of your paper in the Writing Assessment Profile which appears in the back of this text.

B. Imagine that you are planning a dinner party in which your guests will be several famous people. They could be people famous for work in the sciences like Einstein or Newton. They could be people famous for work in the arts like Charles Dickens or William Shakespeare. They could be people famous for religious work like Jesus or Moses or Mother Teresa. After you have done some preliminary prewriting about your choice of guests, write a paper of illustration in which you explain your choice of guests and your reasons for inviting them.

For this paper, assume that your reader will be your classmates. Your paper will have two purposes: (1) to support your ideas using examples and (2) to provide your reader with sufficient information about your interest in your dinner guests. Be sure to do some preliminary thinking about content, organization, and expression before you begin to write.

When you have finished your first draft, share your paper with your classmates and invite them to respond to it. After you have rewritten your next draft, invite them to critique it. Finally, rewrite another draft in response to those critiques, asking your classmates to help you edit it.

Record all responses to the drafts of your paper in the Writing Assessment Profile which appears in the back of this text.

C. Think of several pieces of advice given to you over the years by people you know. For instance, your mother may have said, "A penny saved is a penny earned" many times as you were growing up. Or your Aunt Sylvia might have said, "You're not really dressed until you smile." Do some freewriting to gather several good examples of advice you've been given through the years. Then write a paper of illustration in which you discuss these pieces of advice, relating them to situations in your life when such advice proved to be true—or false.

For this paper, assume that your reader will be your classmates. The purpose of this paper will be to provide examples of advice, relating them to situations in which this advice applied. Be sure to do some preliminary thinking about content, organization, and expression before you begin to write.

When you have finished your first draft, share your paper with your classmates, and invite them to respond to it. After you have rewritten your next draft, invite them to critique it. Finally, rewrite another draft in response to those critiques, asking your classmates to help you edit it.

Record all responses to the drafts of your paper in the Writing Assessment Profile which appears in the back of this text.

D. Every field boasts of its successful achievers. There are achievers in business, achievers in education, achievers in science, achievers in social work, achievers in virtually every walk of life. For your paper of illustration, do some preliminary investigation of the people who are considered achievers in the field you plan to study. Use present-day modern examples. Then write a paper in which you give examples of the achievers in your chosen field, explaining their accomplishments.

For this paper, assume that your reader will be someone who is also interested in working in your chosen field. Your purpose will be to provide enough information to make your achieving subjects appealing to your readers. Be sure to do some preliminary thinking about content, organization, and expression before you begin to write.

When you have finished your first draft, share your paper with your classmates and invite them to respond to it. After you have rewritten your next draft, invite them to critique it. Finally, rewrite another draft in response to those critiques and ask your classmates to help you edit it.

Record all responses to the drafts of your paper in the Writing Assessment Profile which appears in the back of this text.

E. In 1992, *Business Week* magazine named the Best Public Service Projects of the year. Its nominees included the following examples:

PepsiCo, which distributed water and ice, and Pizza Hut, which served 120,000 hot meals, in the days following Hurricane Andrew.

Greyston Corporation which makes upscale desserts and bakery products, hires only the "chronically unemployed," trains them, and pays $7.75 an hour.

IBM, in responding to the Los Angeles riots, is providing $35 million to help train people at 10 centers, several of which will be tailored for the learning-disabled.

Take some time to do some preliminary research into laudable public service projects on your campus, in your neighborhood, in your community, or in your region. Then write a paper of illustration in which you provide examples of noteworthy public service efforts.

For this paper, assume that your reader will be someone tired of the "bad" news that appears regularly in the daily newspaper. Your reader is interested in reading a more positive account of the things that people do. Your purpose will be to provide examples of praiseworthy public service projects explained in order to hearten or encourage your reader. Be sure to do some preliminary thinking about content, organization, and expression before you begin to write.

When you have finished your first draft, share your paper with your classmates and invite them to respond to it. After you have rewritten your next draft, invite them to critique it. Finally, rewrite another draft in response to those critiques, asking your classmates to help you edit it.

Record all responses to the drafts of your paper in the Writing Assessment Profile which appears in the back of this text.

CHAPTER NINE REVIEW

Writing About It #157

Use your journal to reflect on what you learned in this chapter.

10

Using Facts

How can I make use of facts to improve my papers?
Where can I find reliable facts for my writing?

WHY USE FACTS?

The world we live in is based on facts. Daily life is an outpouring of computer printouts, annual reports, scientific findings, government figures. Newspapers, television, and radio provide us with the number of housing starts, the count of dead and wounded, the figure by which crime is up or down this season. Facts convince us to wear our seat belts, stop smoking, eat more fruits and vegetables.

Facts find their way into every conceivable discipline and every walk of life. Anthropologists, psychologists, astronomers, engineers, and social workers collect facts to support their studies. Pilots depend on facts beamed at them from the control tower and the instrument panel. Nurses rely on facts collected from thermometers and blood pressure cuffs. Auto mechanics make use of facts about tire pressure, oil levels, and pressure gauges in order to do their jobs. People make use of all kinds of facts. All the time. Every day.

As you know, human beings differ greatly. Some are Republicans; others are Democrats. Some are Independents; others are indifferent. Some like to drive long luxury sedans; others wouldn't think of traveling in anything other than a fuel-efficient economy car. Some like cats; others like dogs; still others keep pet iguanas. Although human beings share many similarities, differences abound.

Not only do human beings tend to differ, but they tend to disagree. They'll disagree about the competence of the president, about the best route to Chicago, about the virtues of "diet" or "regular" soft drinks. Facts, as a result, serve as a kind of human weather reporting gauge, a barometer around which people can record their individual weather. For instance, the TV weatherman can report a fact: "It is 82 degrees outside." His viewers can arrange their opinions around that fact, offering that 82 is "too hot" or "too cool" or "just right." But they cannot disagree about the fact that, according to objective measurements, it ***is*** 82 degrees outside. Facts provide a common reference point, a common ground.

In fact, facts are the foundation on which our opinions, our knowledge, and our policies are based. Our opinions about our neighbors will depend on facts we infer through their behavior. Our knowledge about the depletion of the ozone layer is the direct result of scientific studies producing facts about the changing nature of this protective planetary shield. Our policies about the economic future of the country are based on interpretations of facts about the work force, national resources, and global markets.

Because we depend on facts to help us through so many aspects of life, we expect our facts to be reliable. Reliable facts are based on reliable evidence. They have the weight of good reporting systems behind them. The evidence may be recorded by a microphone or a microscope, a stream of camera footage or a stream of census figures. The evidence behind a fact may be as varied as the handwritten notes of an interviewer or the behavior of bacteria in a petri dish. But all reliable facts are built on a foundation of reliable evidence.

CHARACTERISTICS OF FACT-BASED WRITING

Because good facts inform good writing, it's important for you to understand the characteristics of effective fact-based writing. The following points can help you.

1. Fact-based writing is based on reliable evidence.
2. Fact-based writing often makes use of a variety of sources.
3. Fact-based writing supports a point.
4. Fact-based writing makes use of the collection plan of organization.
5. Fact-based writing makes use of appropriate transition words.

Reliable Evidence

If you've had the experience of overhearing the latest rumor from someone who's a notorious gossip, you're familiar with the phrase "consider the source." That phrase applies to a writer's fact-gathering efforts as well. The more closely your facts are based on evidence from a reliable source, the more accurate they are likely to be.

Sources for facts abound. You can consult almanacs, encyclopedias, reference books, statistics, research reports, biographies and autobiographies, newspaper and magazine articles, documents, treaties, letters, government records, and other sources. And because potential sources for facts are limitless, it is often difficult for students to understand which source is actually the most reliable source for their facts. Discovering the "best" source actually depends on a number of things: your goals as a writer, the needs of your reader, the resources available on your topic, the accessibility of materials, and other factors.

You can learn something about your own search for good sources of facts by studying an instructive example: a working historian researching a topic of interest. Historians often refer to their sources as either "primary" or "secondary" sources. The term "primary source" refers to documents and other records produced during the period under study. For instance, a historian researching Thomas Jefferson's authorship of The Declaration of Independence would consider the actual document declaring American independence from Britain as a primary source. Other primary sources might be books, diaries, letters, and government records produced during that same period. The term "secondary source" refers to materials prepared later by those who have studied the primary sources. Thus, regarding research on Thomas Jefferson's authorship of The Declaration of Independence, a book of commentary on the nature of that authorship written in the early twentieth century would be considered a secondary source. Historians consider primary sources as the most reliable resource for the facts they wish to know.

In addition, technology is changing notions about primary and secondary sources. A movie or tape recording, potentially important primary sources for a modern topic, would not be considered a primary source for research conducted before the twentieth century since these methods of recording information had not even been invented. Furthermore, many historians currently make use of "oral histories," spoken accounts of important events given by people who were "eyewitnesses" to the history under examination. This is a technique made possible by the accuracy of the tape recorder.

You can think of your own sources as primary or secondary as well, evaluating them as either more important or less important sources of fact.

A Variety of Sources

Although it's possible for you to rely on a single important source of facts for a piece of writing, it's more likely that you will make use of a variety of sources for gathering facts.

As you read the following article by an author interested in business and economic trends, pay close attention to the variety of sources used by the author. The piece is about the declining middle class.

Forget about the simple pleasures of going to work for a nice company and counting on it to be a nurturing, warm family. Not only is corporate loyalty a thing of the past, but the changing economy is shortchanging many young middle-class Americans.

Troy and Linda Marshall of Cleveland are in their early 20s. Both work, caring in shifts for sons Cameron and Cory and daughter Amber. Their income is about half what Troy's father earned in his 20s—while Troy's mother stayed home. Rent payments are challenge enough—they don't know how they'll save enough to buy a house.

The Marshalls are not alone.

The middle class—households with earnings of about $20,000 to $60,000 annually—is where most American workers check in. In headlines describing "America's middle-class meltdown," a *Washington Post* story says that in the 1980s, few escaped poverty, more fell into it—and it's getting worse.

Citing a recent report by the University of Michigan's Panel Study of Income Dynamics, a group that has sampled the nation's earners since 1968, the newspaper says the social change is nothing short of startling. "The boom years of the 1980s were a bust for fully half of all Americans . . . While three out of four Americans could claim to be in the middle class just 15 years ago, barely six out of 10 could make that claim by the end of the 1980s."

"What we are looking at is a permanent proportional decline in the size of the middle class," says economics professor Timothy Smeeding at Syracuse University.

Government census figures agree that the income spread has become less equal over the past two decades. The top one-fifth of earners get almost as much as the other four-fifths put together. That is, the top 20 percent of workers receive 46.6 percent of the pay—nearly one-half of America's payrolls.

Commenting on the shrinking middle class, *Philadelphia Inquirer* investigative reporters Donald L. Barlett and James B. Steele insist the economy favors the privileged, the powerful, and the influential—at the expense of everyone else.

Talking About It #158

With your classmates, discuss the variety of sources cited or quoted in the article about the middle class. Is the article more credible because a variety of sources is used? Explain.

Supporting a Point

Facts support a point, just like descriptions and illustrations do. After you read the following fact-based paragraph closely, decide what point these facts support.

The story of the decimation of a species is probably best told in the events surrounding the blue whale. Even with the most modern equipment, the great blue whale, which sometimes weighs almost a hundred tons, is difficult to kill; but intensive hunting methods gradually reduced the stock from somewhere between 300,000 and 1,000,000 to, at present, somewhere between 600 and 3000. In the 1930–1931 winter season almost 30,000 blue whales were taken. By 1945–1946, less than 10,000 were taken; and in the late 1950s the yearly catch was down to around 1500 per year. By 1964–1965, the total was only 20 whales. In 1965, a ban was placed by the IWC (International Whaling Commission) on killing blue whales. But even after the ban, the hunting of blues continued from land stations by nonmembers such as Brazil, Chile, and Peru.

Talking About It #159

Make note of the facts that are used in the paragraph above. Decide what point the facts are used to support. How do you know?

Writing About It #160

Write a short essay based on imaginary sources. The thesis of the essay will state that the college you are currently attending is undergoing unprecedented growth for a number of reasons. Document the growth and the reasons for it with your imaginary sources. They can be imaginary statistics from the admissions office, imaginary quotes from the president of the university, imaginary comments from students, imaginary records from the financial aid office: you can make up any facts that you'd like. The purpose of the writing experience is to allow you to use a variety of sources to make a point using facts.

Although facts are always used to support a point, sometimes the reader must determine what that point actually is. Carefully study the following paragraph about the Black Death. It was written by historian Barbara Tuchman.

In Paris, where the plague lasted through 1349, the reported death rate was 800 a day, in Pisa 600, in Vienna 500 to 600. The total dead in Paris numbered 50,000 or half the population. Florence, weakened by the famine of 1347, lost three to four fifths of its citizens, Venice two thirds, Hamburg and Bremen, though smaller in size, about the same proportion. Cities, as centers of transportation, were more likely to be affected than villages, although once a village was infected, its death rate was equally high. At Givry, a prosperous village in Burgundy of 1,200 to 1,500 people, the parish register records 615 deaths in the space of fourteen weeks, compared to an average of thirty deaths a year in the previous decade. In three villages of Cambridgeshire, manorial records show a death rate of 47 percent, 57 percent, and in one case 70 percent. When the last survivors, too few to carry on, moved away, a deserted village sank back into the wilderness and disappeared from the map altogether, leaving only a grass-covered ghostly outline to show where mortals once had lived.

Talking About It #161

With your classmates, refer to the passage above to answer the following questions.

1. Is the writer's point made directly or is it implied? How do you know?
2. Do you think the writer's point needs to be made directly? Why or why not?
3. In what way do the facts alone allow the writer to make his or her point? Does this strike you as a good technique for using facts?

Writing About It #162

Use the library to gather some facts. You might amass facts about highway fatalities, tuition costs, auto recalls, or any other topic that interests you. Then write a paragraph based on those facts in which you let the facts speak for themselves as in the paragraph on the Black Death.

The Collection Plan

As with writing that makes use of descriptive details and writing that makes use of examples, fact-based writing typically employs the collection plan for organizing information. Instead of collecting descriptive details or telling examples, fact-based writing collects a series of facts to develop a point.

Often the author will arrange these facts in order of importance—from least important to most important—to create a sense of anticipation or climax in the reader. In the following paragraph about the way that litter threatens animal life, the author has arranged his collection of facts from the least important to the most compelling.

> As we continue to mistake the vastness of our seas for a limitless dump for human waste of every imaginable description, we not only recklessly foul one of our most valuable resources, but are also directly responsible for the death of thousands of marine animals . . . The world's fleet of more than 70,000 merchant vessels dumps at least 450,000 plastic, 300,000 glass, and 4.8 million metal containers into the sea every day. In the digestive tract of a single sea turtle found dead on a beach in Hawaii, medical researchers found a golf tee, a pocket comb, a plastic flower, pieces of monofilament fishing line, part of a bottle cap, an eight-inch square plastic bag, and dozens of other pieces of plastic. Entanglement in six-pack holders and other plastics has contributed to an annual decline of 4 to 8 percent in the fur-seal population of Alaska's Pribilof Islands. Sea turtles regularly mistake plastic bags for the jellyfish that are their favorite food. They die because they can neither ingest anything else nor expel the poisonous material that clogs their digestive systems.

Appropriate Transition Words

Fact-based writing, like descriptions and illustrations, makes use of special transition words to connect ideas for the readers. These transition words are listed as follows:

also	furthermore
and	in addition
another	in particular
as well	moreover
first (second, third, last)	one such

for example	what is more
for instance	yet another
for one thing	

FACT-BASED WRITING IN COMBINATION WITH OTHER STRATEGIES FOR WRITING

Facts are often used in combination with a number of other strategies for writing such as description, illustration, and narration. For instance, in the previous paragraph about the ways in which plastic products endanger ocean animals, facts are combined with illustrations to make a point. The fact which reports injury to 4 to 8 percent of Alaska's fur-seal population has been included as part of an example supporting the idea that plastic pollution in the world's seas is harming the ocean's wild creatures.

The essay which follows appeared in *Newsweek* magazine and is a thoughtful look at the trend of more and more teenagers entering the work force while they go to school. As you read it, notice the abundance of facts used to support the writers' ideas. Notice, too, the way those facts are used in paragraphs of description, illustration, and narration.

Anyone who thinks teenagers spend their afternoons playing hoops, hanging out at the mall—or, for that matter, studying—should meet 18-year-old Dave Fortune of Manchester, N.H. He wakes up at dawn, slurps some strawberry jam for a sugar rush, goes to the high school until 2:30 p.m., hurries home to make sure his little sister arrives safely, changes and goes off to his job at a clothing store. He gets home at around 10:30, does maybe an hour of homework—"if I have any"—and goes to sleep around midnight. The routine begins anew five hours later. Fortune knows he's sacrificed some of his school life for his job. He misses playing soccer and basketball as he did in junior high, and he had to give up a challenging law class because he had so little time for studying. "I have to work," Dave says. "I have to work."

A peek in Fortune's closet suggests otherwise. His back-to-school wardrobe: two leather jackets, six sweaters, 12 pairs of jeans, four pairs of shoes, two pairs of sneakers, two belts, "loads of shirts," and a half-dozen silk pants and shirts that would make a jockey proud. Price tag for the spree (with his store discount): $550.

After-school jobs have become a major force in teen life. More than 5 million kids between 12 and 17 now work, according to Simmons Market Research Bureau. Teens are twice as likely to work as they were in 1950. The change has been fueled by the growth of the service sector after World War II, the rise of the fast-food industry in the 1960s and 1970s and an increase in the number of girls entering the work force. About two thirds of seniors today work more than five hours a week during the academic year.

As political attention focuses on improving the quality of high schools—and producing a highly trained work force better fit for global competition—states have begun restricting the hours teens can work during the school year. In their senior year, about 47 percent of male student workers and 36 percent of females put in more than 20 hours per week at their jobs.

Psychologists and teachers see the strain on students. They have little time for homework, and teachers who regularly watch exhausted students struggling to keep their heads up all too often respond by lowering standards. "Everybody worries why Japanese and German and Swedish students are doing better than us," says Laurence Steinberg, a psychology professor at Temple University. "One reason is they're not spending their afternoons wrapping tacos."

Kids willingly make the sacrifice in part because high school's frenzy of consumerism has grown only more intense. Teens have always coveted thy friends' belongings, but could do little about it when their pockets were empty. But teen earning power increased from S65 billion in 1986 to $95 billion last year, far outpacing inflation and parental income, according to Teenage Research Unlimited, a marketing firm. Teens spent $82 billion in 1991, and have maintained the pace despite the recession. The more money Johnny has, the more he buys.

Some run-of-the-mill purchases by middle-class teens capture the 90210-ish expectations of teen life: Chris Lamarre, who works at a Manchester carpet store, bought his girlfriend a $100 Gucci watch and himself a $600 car stereo. Mary Kane of Olney, Md., spent $1000 of her earnings from Lady Foot Locker to go to Cancun for eight days with her friends. More and more students at Glenbrook South are spending hundreds of dollars to get beepers—not to consummate drug deals, but to retrieve messages from friends. Blame it on peer pressure: when you go out with friends, "you don't want to say, 'I can't do that, I don't have the money'," explains Kirsten Fournier, a senior at Manchester West High.

There are those, of course, who must work. The recession has forced some kids into the labor force to help their parents survive. Teachers, students and social scientists also agree that work can teach discipline, self-respect and efficiency. Some studies show that kids who work moderately actually do better in school than those who don't take jobs at all. Students on the verge of dropping out—or into criminality—can be kept on track by a good job. It can even teach tolerance by forcing them to meet kids of different social cliques.

Nonetheless, educators worry that while the benefits of work have been known for years, a range of problems has been left unexplored. Some are apparent at Pembroke Academy, a public high school near Concord, N.H.:

Vanessa Thompson saw her grades plummet from B's to D's when she increased her schedule last year from 25 to 30 hours a week at a movie theater and Lady Foot Locker. "You either do homework at study hall or it just doesn't get done," she says. Her boss at the shoe store questioned whether she was keeping up with school. "Of course I lied to her because I needed the hours," Thompson says. "School's important but so's money. Homework doesn't pay."

Andrew Cutting points to a small red scar above his right eye, a reminder of what might be called a job-related injury. Last month Cutting was in study hall writing a composition when, midsentence, he fell asleep, slamming his head down on the tip of his pen cap. "It hurt wicked bad," he says. "I felt like an idiot." He was tired from pumping gas at a nearby Mobil station the night before.

Artie Bresby stocks shelves at Shaw's Supermarket. To sustain his job pace, he takes six Vivarin pills (equivalent to about 15 cups of coffee), plus two liters of turbo-charged Mountain Dew.

Ultimately, though, it is neither legislators nor employers who will have to solve the conundrum of teen work. Most parents are proud of their children earning a paycheck but find themselves unaware of the problems their children's jobs can create. All parents want the best future for their kids. Once upon a time, after-school work seemed a perfect way to teach sons and daughters a little something about the real world and reward them with some cash at the same time. Now, for too many teenagers, too much of a wise thing may be squandering that very future.

Talking About It #163

With your classmates, talk about which paragraphs in the article above use facts in order to (1) describe, (2) provide a narrative, and (3) illustrate or give examples.

Another common use for fact-based writing is as an introduction to a longer piece of writing. In the following introduction to an article about heart disease, the author collects facts to inform the reader of the deadly impact of heart disease.

Americans are being stalked by a killer. This killer took the lives of 930,479 citizens in 1990 alone. It accounts for nearly 50% of the deaths from any cause in this country each year. Silently stalking its victims, this murderer of millions costs the nation $117.4 billion a year in treatment and nearly $20 billion a year in lost productivity. This killer is heart disease, and this year's American Heart Association report on America's most deadly ailment offers advice about controlling high blood pressure, managing blood cholesterol levels, and swapping the cigarette habit for exercise. These suggestions, the report suggests, are the only way Americans can take up arms against the killer that would rob them of their lives.

READER AND PURPOSE IN USING FACTS

The way in which you use facts in your writing will again depend on your reader's needs and your purposes as a writer. Let's say, for example, that your reader is a member of the medical community reading a scientific report confirming the recent finding that beta-carotene, a vitamin commonly found in yellow vegetables like carrots and sweet potatoes, is a possible cancer fighter. To satisfy this medical audience, you, as the writer of this report, will likely make use of facts explaining how the study was conducted, what variables might have affected the outcome, and what statistical methods were used to evaluate the accuracy of the study itself. However, let's say you're the writer of a magazine article in a publication for health-conscious consumers. For this readership, you might ignore such statistical facts. Instead, you might emphasize the general findings of the study and provide a list of common foods which are a good source of beta-carotene, a list likely to interest your health-conscious reader. Thus, who your reader is will determine what facts you will use.

Your own purposes will also affect your use of facts. If you are an American automobile manufacturer seeking to persuade Americans to buy American as opposed to foreign cars, you might write an ad campaign emphasizing negative facts about foreign automobiles and promoting more positive facts about

American automobiles. If your purpose as a student in a sports management course is to inform your reader about the increasingly high salaries of professional baseball players, your writing will emphasize different facts than it will if your purpose as a baseball fan is to protest the higher ticket prices at the gate. Therefore, your own purposes will greatly affect how you handle facts in a piece of writing.

In fact, the key to effective use of facts in writing involves an understanding of how to select facts to suit your purposes. The following essay, entitled "Homeless," was built from facts that journalist Anna Quindlen gleaned from her own personal observation of a homeless woman. Read it carefully to determine the way Quindlen uses her facts to serve her purpose.

Her name was Ann, and we met in the Port Authority Bus Terminal several Januarys ago. I was doing a story on homeless people. She said I was wasting my time talking to her; she was just passing through, although she'd been passing through for more than two weeks. To prove to me that this was true, she rummaged through a tote bag and a manila envelope and finally unfolded a sheet of typing paper and brought out her photographs.

They were not pictures of family, or friends, or even a dog or cat, its eyes brown-red in the flashbulb's light. They were pictures of a house. It was like a thousand houses in a hundred towns, not suburb, not city, but somewhere in between, with aluminum siding and a chain-link fence, a narrow driveway running up to a one-car garage and a patch of backyard. The house was yellow. I looked on the back for a date or a name, but neither was there. There was no need for discussion. I knew what she was trying to tell me, for it was something I had often felt. She was not adrift, alone, anonymous, although her bags and her raincoat with the grime shadowing its creases had made me believe she was. She had a house, or at least once upon a time had had one. Inside were curtains, a couch, a stove, potholders. You are where you live. She was somebody.

I've never been very good at looking at the big picture, taking the global view, and I've always been a person with an overactive sense of place, the legacy of an Irish grandfather. So it is natural that the thing that seems most wrong with the world to me right now is that there are so many people with no homes. I'm not simply talking about shelter from the elements, or three square meals a day, or a mailing address to which the welfare people can send the check—although I know that all these are important for survival. I'm talking about a home, about precisely those kinds of feelings that have wound up in cross-stitch and French knots on samplers over the years.

Sometimes I think we would be better off if we forgot about the broad strokes and concentrated on the details. Here is a woman without a bureau. There is a man with no mirror, no wall to hang it on. They are not the homeless. They are people who have no homes. No drawer that holds the spoons. No window to look out upon the world. My God. That is everything.

Talking About It #164

With your classmates, talk about the following questions:

1. What was Anna Quindlen's purpose in writing "Homeless?"
2. How do you think Anna Quindlen defined her reader?

Writing About It #165

Make a list of the facts which Anna Quindlen collected from personal observation and which appeared in her essay. Then make a list of other facts which Quindlen may have noticed in her personal observation of this woman but which did not find their way into this essay. Explain why you think Quindlen chose the facts she did and ignored others.

Collect facts about something or someone based on personal observation. You might choose someone from another culture or something like a battered old car or an animal you've observed at a zoo. Then select key facts to write a paragraph which makes a point about that person or thing or animal. After you have finished, reflect in your journal about why you selected certain facts and ignored others.

Choose a product with which you're either highly satisfied or highly dissatisfied. Possible products might be a telephone, a brand of food, a radio, a brand of tires, a style of shoe, or any other product you can think of. Then record facts and features of that product which are either satisfactory or unsatisfactory to you. Write a paragraph incorporating those facts to support your view of the product as either satisfactory or unsatisfactory.

A STUDENT USES FACTS: A FIRST DRAFT

Student Aaron Betts has been writing a fact-based essay about the Department of Languages at his university. The purpose of Aaron's paper, which will be distributed to prospective language majors, is to provide sufficient information about the Department of Languages such that students considering foreign languages as a major would be aided in their decision by reading what Aaron, a fellow student, has to say.

Aaron has already submitted an early draft to his classmates, and they responded to it in a number of ways. Some of them made use of freewriting to respond; others sketched their responses; still others wrote purpose statements in response to Aaron's paper. Aaron read their responses carefully, reviewed his own purposes, and then produced another draft. His second effort appears below.

I reached the office of Gina King, the department secretary, who greeted me with a smile and a handshake. Behind her was a bulletin board displaying information about international study programs, lectures, and language mini-courses. She pushed a few buttons on the phone and then said, "Your appointment is here to see you, Professor Chiodo." She hung up and then motioned me to a chair. "Dr. Chiodo will be with you shortly."

Just then the door opened, and a dark-haired petite woman walked right over to me and shook my hand, "I'm Andrea Chiodo," she said. "I'm the department chair. Welcome."

"Thank you," I said, feeling instantly at home. "I just came to ask you a few things about the Language Department."

With a whisk of her arm, she ushered me into her office. I soon found out that the atmosphere in the Department of Languages was warm and welcoming. Dr. Chiodo said that she hoped to make a major in a foreign language "relevant." She said that the French professor, for example, had recently added a course in Advanced Commercial French. "The idea is that students today will have to understand the specialized business vocabulary and the specialized syntax used in commercial correspondence. We want to make certain our graduates are prepared for the challenges of international business." Dr. Chiodo also prizes fluency. "Often our graduates find themselves in fast-paced, near-emergency situations requiring fluency. A social worker in a Cuban neighborhood in Miami, a journalist interviewing a witness to a shooting in Beirut, an emergency room nurse working for the International Red Cross in China—all these situations call for a complete command of the language. And we try to provide our majors with that."

I headed down a short corridor on the second floor of Wohlleben Hall, leaving the Department of Languages behind me. The walls were lined with colorful posters from all over the world: Madrid, Paris, Vienna, Hong Kong. The Department of Languages at the University of Dayton attempts to create an atmosphere in which relevance and fluency are two primary goals.

Talking About It #166

Critique Aaron's draft using the analytical critique system explained in Chapter 6. Remember to answer these three questions for every paragraph: What is the writer doing? How is the writer doing it? Is the writer succeeding? What changes may Aaron need to make in his next draft based on your analytical critique?

Think about the characteristics of fact-based writing which you have just studied: (1) using reliable evidence, (2) employing a variety of sources, (3) supporting a point, (4) organizing with the collection plan, and (5) using appropriate transitions. As a group, try to answer the following questions that relate to fact-based writing.

1. *What facts does Aaron use in this essay? What is the source of that evidence? Is it reliable evidence? Why?*
2. *Does Aaron use a variety of sources? Explain.*
3. *Does each of Aaron's paragraphs support a point? Does each paragraph have a topic sentence? Does the entire paper have a thesis statement? Make some suggestions to help Aaron in these areas.*
4. *Does Aaron make use of the collection plan to organize his facts? Is the order in which he presents his ideas effective? Could his plan be strengthened?*
5. *Does Aaron use appropriate transition words?*

A STUDENT USES FACTS: A REVISED DRAFT

Aaron listened closely to his classmates' comments after they critiqued his work. Following is the draft that he revised in response. In it, he tried to incorporate the responses of his readers as well as his own purposes.

I held the red-white-and-blue brochure in my hand. The Dean of Arts and Sciences, Frank Morman, had given me the brochure in his office. "Why Would YOU Want to be a Language Major?" the title read. It was a question I hoped to answer.

As I began to read, I saw that facts about the Department of Languages were set off in boxes: 150 students were currently Language majors at the University of Dayton; an additional 237 students minored in foreign language; 53% intended to become language teachers. In addition, the brochure stated that the Language Department offered both modern languages like French, German, Italian, Russian, and Spanish, and classical languages like Greek and Latin. The department employed thirteen teachers: two full-time professors, two associate professors, five assistant professors, and four lecturers. The brochure reported that the Language Department was growing and that the trend was expected to continue because of the global economy and the pressures on American business to expand internationally. "Why Would YOU Want to be a Language Major?" ended with this sentence: "A second language is as necessary in today's world as familiarity with a computer." Thus, my general introduction to the Department of Languages had begun.

I walked from the Arts and Science building across campus to Wohlleben Hall, headquarters for the Department of Languages. Once I reached the second floor, I saw that the atmosphere in the Department of Languages had an international flair. Walls were lined with colorful posters from all over the world: Madrid, Paris, Vienna, Hong Kong. On the wall behind the secretary's desk was a bulletin board displaying information about international study programs, lectures, and language mini-courses.

Just then the door opened, and a dark-haired petite woman walked right over and shook my hand. "I'm Andrea Chiodo," she said. "I'm the department chair. Welcome."

"Thank you," I said, feeling instantly at home. "I just came to ask you a few things about the Language Department."

With a whisk of her arm, she ushered me into her office, answering my questions without a moment's hesitation. Dr. Chiodo said that there were two goals she wanted to achieve in her department. One goal was for the teachers; the other goal was for the students. "I want the teacher to make language study relevant to the students," she said. "And I want the students to become fluent." Dr. Chiodo stated that the department had recently added a course in Advanced Commercial French. "The idea is that students today will have to understand the specialized business vocabulary and the specialized syntax used in commercial correspondence. We want to make certain our graduates are prepared for the challenges of international business." Dr. Chiodo also stated that she prized fluency. "Often our graduates find themselves in fast-paced, near-emergency situations requiring fluency. A social worker in a Cuban neighborhood in Miami, a journalist interviewing a witness to a shooting in Beirut, an emergency room nurse working for the International Red Cross in China—all these situations call for a complete command of the language. And we try to provide our majors with that." Before I left, Dr. Chiodo gave me a wink and said, "Your survey of the Department of Languages would not be complete without a visit to Herr Oberholzer."

Dr. Chiodo's secretary motioned me down the hall to Room 214. The room number to Herr Oberholzer's office was almost entirely obscured by a collage of pictures of Germany. Munich, Berlin, Hamburg, Dusseldorf and cities less familiar to me were represented. I knocked and entered. Herr Oberholzer gave me a hearty handshake. His office was strewn with stacks of papers to grade, and on a shelf that took up an entire wall, there were knick-knacks with an international flair: a pig wearing a miniature sombrero and a cow standing in a tiny pair of wooden shoes. "Language study here is fun,*" said Professor Oberholzer. "Haven't you heard about my title for my Introductory German course, son? Everybody wanted me to call it German 101. That's too boring. I decided to call it 'Guten Tag I,'" he said. "It's listed like that in the catalog." Another offering of the Language Department that Herr Oberholzer called "fun" is the special travel abroad opportunities. He told me that the Department offered travel abroad to two groups of students: non-majors and majors. The non-majors could choose from a three-site summer option in a variety of sites like Florence, Vienna, Munich, Paris, London, Madrid, and Athens. Majors have a more intensive experience. French majors, for instance, take part in a three-month study program in Paris. Part of their requirement is to speak only French for the entire experience. They also take two courses taught in French at the Sorbonne, and they take a series of field trips to important sites near Paris like Mont Saint Michel, Nice, and Lourdes. Thus, studying in the Department of Languages offers opportunities for enjoyment not available to students in most other majors.*

Another important point Herr Oberholzer made was that the department is interested in helping students learn about the culture in which the language is spoken. He picked up the ceramic pig and took off its sombrero. "A culture is more than just artifacts like this," he said, indicating the sombrero. "It's about a world that's often very different from ours. The planet is changing. We're more of a global society now. If we're to get along, we have to understand our differences. Learning a language is one way of doing just that."

As I quietly closed the door to Professor Oberholzer's office, I thought I had some answers to the question, "Why Would YOU Want to be Language Major?" I had learned some general facts about majoring in a foreign language. I had come to understand that the philosophy of the department stressed relevance and fluency. I saw that studying languages both here and abroad could be fun. Most important, I learned that, in a global society, knowing a language was not a luxury; it was as essential as a passport.

Talking About It #167

Aaron thought about his own purposes as well as his classmates' critiques when he wrote his revised draft. Talk to your classmates about the specific changes he has made. Do you think his draft has been improved? Why or why not?

WRITING ASSIGNMENTS

A. Using Aaron Betts' paper as a starting point, write a fact-based paper on a department on campus that interests you or in which you plan to major. Collect facts from a number of sources—the college catalog, departmental brochures, conversations with students studying in that department, interviews with professors and/or the department chairman. Your research will likely point out the number of students in the major, the number of professors and their educational background and interests, the special opportunities available to students in that major, some course titles, the departmental philosophy, and other items of interest.

For this paper, you are to write for a reader who is considering a major in this department, and your purpose is to provide him or her with as much information as he or she is likely to need in order to reach a decision.

Before you write, draft a reader profile and a purpose statement. Do some preliminary planning about content, organization and expression. When you have finished your first draft, invite your classmates to respond to it, and then revise it once again. Ask your classmates to critique this new draft. After you have considered their critiques, write another draft, inviting your classmates to edit it with you.

Record the various responses to your paper in the Writing Assessment Profile which appears in the back of this text.

B. Using Anna Quindlen's essay as a starting point, collect facts about something or someone based on close personal observation. You might choose someone from another culture, a battered car you've driven, a well-known person in your community, or an animal you've closely observed at a zoo. Then select key facts to write a paper which makes a point about that person or thing or animal.

For this paper, you can assume that your reader is a classmate and that your purpose is to provide him or her with the necessary number of facts sufficient to establish your point about your subject.

Before you write, draft a reader profile and a purpose statement. Do some preliminary planning about content, organization and expression. When you have finished your first draft, invite your classmates to respond to it, and then revise it once again. Ask your classmates to critique this new draft. After you have considered their critiques, write another draft, inviting your classmates to edit it with you.

Record the various responses to your paper in the Writing Assessment Profile which appears in the back of this text.

C. Choose a product with which you're either highly satisfied or highly dissatisfied. Possible products might be a telephone, a brand of food, a radio, a brand of tires, a style of shoe, or any other product you can think of. Then record an abundance of facts and features of that product which are either satisfactory or unsatisfactory.

Using your facts and features, write a paper to convince your reader, a potential consumer of the product, about whether he or she should—or should not—

purchase the product. Remember that your purpose is to influence your reader's purchasing behavior.

Before you write, draft a reader profile and a purpose statement. Do some preliminary planning about content, organization and expression. When you have finished your first draft, invite your classmates to respond to it, and then revise it once again. Ask your classmates to critique this new draft. After you have considered their critiques, write another draft, inviting your classmates to edit it with you.

Record the various responses to your paper in the Writing Assessment Profile which appears in the back of this text.

CHAPTER TEN REVIEW

Writing About It #168

Use your journal to reflect on what you learned in this chapter.

11

Giving Reasons

How can I learn to use reasons effectively?
In what ways can learning to use reasons help my writing?

WHY GIVE REASONS?

Facts, useful as they are, simply aren't enough. Ultimately, you need to make sense of facts. You need to place them in a context. You need to interpret them responsibly in order to use them in an intelligent manner. Facts need to be marshaled in the interests of opinions: to question ideas, to compare or contrast positions, to establish a cause-effect relationship, to reach a solution to a problem. In short, you need to use facts to help you develop compelling reasons for your ideas.

You've already seen the way in which facts can be used in the interests of sound reasoning. For instance, student Aaron Betts provided some facts on the Language Department of his college in Chapter 10. But those facts remain lifeless unless someone makes use of them, manipulating those facts in order to develop a context of reasons to explain them sensibly. Aaron's facts, for instance, have a number of uses. A fellow student could use Aaron's piece in order to give his or her parents reasons for deciding to travel abroad with a university group this summer. Another student could use the facts presented by Aaron in order to offer reasons for choosing to major in a foreign language. A faculty advisor could read Aaron's essay to develop reasons for suggesting that advisees enroll in course offerings in the Language Department. In these ways, Aaron's facts can be used in the interests of reasons.

SUBJECTIVE AND OBJECTIVE REASONS

You are probably well aware that educated people are able to support their ideas and that they do this most commonly by giving reasons. That they do this in a number of contexts, situations, or disciplines is probably less familiar to you. But the fact is that giving reasons is a common and important part of everyday life.

Scientists, for instance, seek to provide reasons for the hibernation of bears or the existence of black holes. Historians attempt to explain why Gandhi gave up his British barrister's garb to wear the peasant robes of a social activist. Literary scholars look into Nathaniel Hawthorne's job in the Salem customhouse to explain the reasons behind his novel *The Scarlet Letter*. Psychologists seek to give reasons for violent behavior, studying the effects of television violence on children.

In the following passage, the writer is attempting to explain why the number of students applying to medical school will soon be on the decline. Note the way the writer uses facts to support reasons, adopting a third person objective point of view.

> By the time the average American medical student becomes a doctor, he or she knows anatomy, physiology, diagnostic procedures, and medical technology. More surprising is that aspiring doctors know something else: that they are deeply in debt. In fact, by the mid-1990s, a private medical school education will cost nearly \$110,000. By the time a young medical candidate graduates, he or she is typically \$85,000 in debt. To make matters worse, financial prospects for medical school graduates have never been so grim. The average salary for an M.D.-in-training during a typical 3-year residency program is about \$30,000 a year, barely enough to support a family with monthly interest payments on hefty school loans. Add to this financial burden the escalating cost of malpractice insurance, payments for the high-tech equipment which must be accessible to a doctor's practice, and the looming health care reform changes, and there's enough motivation to send a bright young man or woman straight into another career path, one more promising financially than medicine now appears to be. For these reasons, the number of talented students applying to medical school is likely to decline.

Outside of specific disciplines like business or humanities or the sciences, ordinary people make use of reasons, too. Shoppers in the local grocery store weigh the nutrient content or the price of their purchases before putting them into the shopping cart. College students in a line at registration have talked to friends, faculty advisors, and upperclassmen in order to develop reasons for enrolling in a particular course. Here, their reasons are not based on scientific investigations, but on personal experience.

In the following passage, a student uses the first person subjective point of view to provide reasons for her decision to switch majors.

There were several reasons why I switched majors from communications to sports management. Although I was originally attracted to communications, particularly photography, I found myself drawn to sports subjects at every turn. I begged the sports editor of our college paper to assign me to cover everything from football games to ping pong tournaments, and when I carried my camera, I found myself working extra hard to capture the rebounding basketball, the superb football pass, the perfectly placed soccer ball. In my spare time, I got involved in intramural sports. I played soccer and hockey every season, missing my involvement in sports when each season ended. I gradually became aware that I felt an excitement in a locker room that I didn't feel in a news room. After I took a sports management course, I knew that I wanted to learn everything I could about training, managing teams, coaching, and building a quality sports program. I realized I could use my communications skills in a context I could enjoy my whole life: athletics. Although I have now traded in my camera for a clipboard, so far I haven't a single regret.

Talking About It #169

With your classmates, explore some potential topics you might write about in which you choose the strategy of giving reasons. Then for each topic, suggest whether your writing would make use of the first person subjective point of view or the third person objective point of view.

READER AND PURPOSE IN GIVING REASONS

As in any writing situation, considerations of reader and purpose are important when you're writing in order to offer compelling reasons.

Let's say you're interested in the law, entertaining thoughts of becoming a police officer or an FBI agent after college. Hearing that there's a prelaw program on campus, you read the college catalog to learn more about it. The college catalog describes the pre-law program as one for "students interested in exploring the possibilities in a law-related career. This may include positions in the criminal justice system, work in local, state, or national law enforcement agencies, or general introductory experience with the legal system in preparation for entering law school." The catalog also states that the program is "rigorous and demanding, mirroring the academic environment students are likely to encounter in law school. Thus, prelaw students are required to attain a 3.0 average each semester in order to be retained in the program."

You decide that the program interests you, and you and several of your friends, who are also interested in criminal justice careers, have enrolled in the prelaw program for the first time. All of you, unfortunately, have been under tremendous pressure to keep up your grades and maintain the required 3.0 average, and you're frustrated. You have also been deeply disappointed in the program. You've noted that the catalog suggests that the program is designed to help students "interested in exploring the possibilities in a law-related career," but so far the program has been clearly geared to those students with an eye on law school after graduation. When you talk to your friends in the student union or the dorm, you find yourselves becoming increasingly angry about the program, and you decide you need to take action to change things.

You and your friends decide to write a letter to the chair of the prelaw department, asking that the grade point requirement be evaluated and that offerings in the program meet the needs of those students who are *not* thinking of becoming lawyers. However, as you begin your collaborative draft of the letter, you realize that who your reader is—the chair of the prelaw department—dramatically affects what you need to say. In establishing your two points—the need for a more realistic grade requirement and course offerings that meet the needs of those not planning on law school—you realize that your chair will want solid reasons for those positions as well as solid facts to back those reasons. The complaints and grumblings of a few unhappy prelaw students, you realize, are unlikely to result in major change. Together, you and your friends recognize that little change can be expected if your reasons and the facts that support them are not compelling.

Together, however, you and your friends then decide on another strategy. You decide to design a survey of all the students in the prelaw program, soliciting their reactions and responses to a number of questions in which you're interested. You spend the time you would have spent drafting a letter to your chair on drawing up a good survey, convinced that the responses you'll elicit will eventually help you build a stronger case.

Two weeks later, you're pleased. Your efforts have paid off. Your survey gives you the reasons and facts you've been looking for. It tells you several things: even the pre-law students headed for law school find the academic requirements too rigorous; your university, which has its own law school, requires only a 2.0 grade point average of its law students each semester; the faculty in the prelaw program contains only one person with any background in criminal justice or police work, and 78 percent of those enrolled in prelaw are not interested in attending law school.

Now when you and your friends get together to draft a letter, you're well prepared. You have good reasons at hand and good facts to support them. You've invested productive effort in assessing your reader, an assessment that has paid off in terms of the facts you've gathered and the reasons you've used to explain them.

However, as you begin writing the draft of your letter to the chair, you and your friends find that you need to be clear about something else: your purpose. You remember from your writing class that most writing purposes involve either informing, persuading, entertaining, or expressing yourself. Together, you and your friends struggle to clarify your purpose as you write this letter, challenged by this difficult and slippery task. You are sure that your purpose is not to entertain the chair or simply to express yourselves to him as you would in a journal or a diary. But you are wrestling with whether or not your letter should attempt to persuade the chair to change the department policy or whether or not you're simply interested in informing the chair that a problem exists. As you immerse yourselves in the writing of the letter, your purpose becomes ever more focused. You decide that persuading the chair to make policy changes is unlikely to come on the heels of your letter. You realize that changes are more likely to come after a gradual process of discussion, investigation, and policy making gets under way. You decide that a persuasive, argumentative tone may alarm your reader, creating unintended disagreement or downright hostility to your ideas and that the time for strong persuasion lies somewhere in the future. Together, you and your friends agree that your initial purpose, for the moment, is simply to inform the chair that certain problems exist, offering reasons and facts on which to base later discussions. Thus, in the writing context of giving reasons, purpose as well as reader are once again of prime importance.

CHARACTERISTICS OF GIVING REASONS

Writing that is intended to give reasons to a reader generally displays the following characteristics:

1. Reasons are used to make a point.
2. Giving reasons requires convincing support.
3. Reasons are organized by means of the collection plan or the connection plan.
4. Appropriate transition words are used to connect ideas.

Reasons to Make a Point

A writer marshals reasons to make a point. As you've seen in the earlier examples, a writer may use facts to make a point about the potential decline in the number of students studying medicine or a writer may use experiences to make a point about a decision to change majors. In the following paragraph, student Kelly Kuhn gives reasons to make a point about why people don't volunteer their time to worthy causes.

> People don't volunteer like they used to, and the list of excuses is familiar to anyone who wishes more people were willing to give the gift of time. Although homelessness, hunger, sexism, drug abuse, and poverty plague our society more deeply than ever, the number of people volunteering to help is on the decline. The reasons people give for their complacency are familiar. "I don't have any extra time," say some. "I don't feel strongly enough about anything to give that much to a cause," say others. Many people feel that donating money is a gift equivalent to the gift of time. "I already donate to my favorite cause. Isn't that enough?" they ask. Others take a more passive stand. "I don't see how one person could make a dif-

ference," they say, shrugging their shoulders. If the spirit of volunteerism is ever to increase, these common reasons for complacency must be dispelled.

As Kelly's paragraph demonstrates, reasons are always marshaled to make a point about a topic.

Reasons and Support

A writer who gives reasons is a writer on the lookout for support. That support can be found in a number of ways. The writer may use facts, examples, descriptions, experiences, and any number of sources in order to give weight and credibility to reasons. Notice the way the following student attempts to provide convincing support.

> The tips I have learned in my writing class about improving my sentences have paid off in better grades. In the first half of this semester, before I began to employ these techniques, I couldn't seem to get higher than a "C" on my compositions. Now I have developed habits for addressing these problems. For instance, I have always had trouble with sentence structure. Because I know that my sentence structure is one of my biggest weaknesses, I look at each sentence carefully as I edit. Unfortunately, I have a habit of beginning each sentence with the same subject again and again, creating monotony in my style. Thus, I try to vary the beginnings of my sentences every now and then to add more interest for the reader. I'll look for places where I can begin with a prepositional phrase or an opening clause or simply a one-word adverb. I also look at the verbs I have chosen. In the past, I was content to use colorless, passive verbs like "is" or "have." Now I try to choose verbs that show action: "assert," "persuade," "confirm." When I proofread, I make use of techniques that have led to improved sentences. I read my paper out loud, emphasizing each word, noticing that my voice often tells me where I've written a run-on sentence. I also read my paper backwards as a way of catching sentence fragments. Using these editing and proofreading techniques, I have seen my grades steadily rise from low Cs to consistent Bs.

The Collection and the Connection Plan

Although you have seen that the most common plan for organizing descriptions or illustrations or facts is the collection plan, when you organize material to give reasons for your ideas, two organizational plans are usually available to you: collections and connections.

The Collection Plan

When you use the collection plan to provide your reader with reasons, you can often rely on lists or enumerations to make your point. In the following essay from *Audubon* magazine, Peter Berle offers the newly elected Clinton administration some reasons for encouraging good stewardship of the nation's federal parks and recreational areas.

> To encourage good stewardship, the new administration needs to make clear that it expects federal land managers to:
>
> (1) Obey the law. Federal agencies need to comply with the law. This is hardly a radical idea. But recent court injunctions, including those against cutting ancient forests in the Pacific Northwest, resulted from judges ruling that federal land stewards had failed to meet their legal responsibilities.
>
> (2) Act as stewards for all Americans—those alive today and those yet to come. Resources on public land are often regarded as the prize of those who extract, lease and sell them. Exploitation can rob the land of qualities important to others. For example, logging along some streams has jeopardized salmon populations. Why should woodcutters be entitled to more of the public treasure than fishermen?
>
> (3) Insist that uses be sustainable and that ecological systems be kept intact. This is the "grandchildren test," and it must apply to recreational as well as commercial uses. Obviously, oil, gas, and mineral extraction cannot pass this test, but when such uses are permitted they must minimize damage and ensure continued biodiversity.
>
> (4) Get the prices right. Below-cost timber sales, below-market grazing fees, oversubsidizing water for agricultural uses, giving away minerals under the 1872 Mining Act—all are policies that waste and misallocate public resources.
>
> (5) Keep the process open. People feel strongly about public-resource decisions. Mistakes are made no matter how good the process. Recent efforts to limit legal challenges of administrative action are shortsighted. The best way to grant access to public resources is to do it right in the first place and allow all parties to seek relief when things go wrong.

The Connection Plan

The previous passage is an example of a writer giving reasons by means of the collection plan of organizing. The author simply piles reason upon reason to make a point.

However, the connection plan is also a common method for presenting material in the interest of giving reasons. In this plan, the writer offers reasons for an occurrence or situation by making connections between a cause and an effect or an effect and a cause. For instance, a writer may wish to write about secondhand smoke and its deadly effects. In this case, the writer uses reasons in order to make connections between secondhand smoke and its tragic consequences. Or perhaps a writer wishes to look at the changed history textbooks used by students today, exploring the causes for these changes. In that case, the writer marshals reasons to make connections between the effect of the changed texts and the causes which brought them about.

The cause and effect or effect and cause method for making connections is a common one, and it is useful to the writer searching to make good use of reasons and facts.

The following newspaper article makes use of the cause and effect method of connecting ideas. It uses facts to link a cause—a California antismoking TV campaign—with an effect—the decline in cigarette smoking in the state.

A voter initiative that established the nation's most ambitious antismoking TV ad campaign hastened the decline of cigarette smoking in California and cost the tobacco industry $1.1 billion in lost sales, a study shows.

An earlier study showed that the $28 million, 18-month TV campaign increased the rate at which smokers quit smoking. The new study is the first to look at the campaign's effect on cigarette sales.

"We have proof that it is a cost-effective campaign," said the study's author, Stanton A. Glantz of the University of California, San Francisco.

Before the campaign, cigarette comsumption was falling by 46 million packs per year in California, Glantz found. During the campaign, from April 1990 to September 1991, cigarette consumption fell at a rate of 164 million packs per year, triple what it had been before.

When the campaign was suspended, the decline in cigarette sales fell to 19 million packs per year, Glantz said.

"We have evidence that an aggressive campaign can reduce tobacco consumption significantly," he said.

The TV ad campaign was mandated by a referendum passed by California voters in 1988 that increased cigarette taxes by 25 cents per pack and required that 20 percent of the tax money be used for smoking cessation programs.

The campaign included commercials that depicted the tobacco industry as greedy and cold-hearted.

In the 3½ years following passage of the referendum, the decline in cigarette sales cost the tobacco industry $1.1 billion.

Dr. Thomas E. Novotny of the Centers for Disease Control and Prevention said the study was a convincing demonstration of the campaign's effectiveness.

Some had suggested that the tax increase itself was responsible for the decline in cigarette consumption, but Novotny disagreed.

"The media campaign had the most immediate impact on behavior," he said.

Glantz addressed that question by looking at smoking rates in neighboring Nevada, which adopted a 25-cent-per-pack tax increase at the same time California did.

In "Dinophilia," which follows, the writer draws connections between effects and causes. Writer James Gorman, drawing on both facts and reasons, begins with effects—the enormous popularity of dinosaurs—and offers several causes to explain this popularity.

This is the year of the dinosaur. To anyone with children it may have seemed that each of the last 10 years was the year of the dinosaur. Nonetheless, Joseph Donnelly, representing the fledgling not-for-profit Dinosaur Society, tells me that in 1993, every company that makes anything for children will be making some kind of dinosaur product.

There are already numerous dinosaur books. The Carnegie Museum of Natural History in Pittsburgh has a new line of scientifically approved dinosaur models . . . , and the Smithsonian Institution puts its dinosaurs out in plush. We already have Designasaurus, the computer game and puzzle. Coming soon will be new dinosaur toys, apparel, stationery, and computer games. My guess is that there will soon be more dinosaurs in North America than there were during the Cretaceous period.

Of course, then they were alive, in all their flesh and blood (lukewarm?), and with their giant, ripping, serrated teeth. Now they're plush or rubber or plastic or digital. But that's not our problem. In fact, nothing about dinosaurs, including their disappearance from the face of the earth, is our problem. And therein, I suspect, lies the reason for their enormous surge in popularity. In an age of environmental anxiety, when contemplation of almost any animal or plant is guaranteed to cause anguish and when every phylum, if not every suborder, has its own charitable organization to play upon our conscience, the dinosaurs are guilt free.

It's important to recognize that not only children have fallen for dinosaurs. Adults read *Jurassic Park.* Adults buy the toys, write the books and computer programs, and film the documentaries for *3-2-1 Contact.* Kids love dinosaurs because they're big, scary, and real, but conveniently dead. So do grownups, but with one important twist. With children the issues are personal, psychological, Oedipal probably. They are fascinated by monsters but don't want to be eaten, and so prefer huge, drooling, extinct tyrannosaurs.

For adults, particularly reality-based professionals with graduate degrees, the fear is entirely different. We know that we're not likely to get eaten by anything as long as we don't go to Glacier National Park and sleep with a salami next to us, or swim off the California coast taunting great white sharks by clapping our flippers and barking. And we learn, as we grow older, that in terms of terrifying interpersonal encounters, monsters are the least of our problems. We know what's really scary. We don't need to look in the mirror at the Bronx Zoo's Great Apes House (labeled World's Most Dangerous Animal) to learn who wreaks the most havoc on earth—us.

Think of an animal. Any animal. The result, if you have any heart at all, will be a wave of guilt. Either we are destroying them and their habitat—whales, manatees, elephants, not to mention spotted owls—or we are eating them by the containership-load—chickens, lambs, tuna. For adults the great thing about dinosaurs is not that they're not going to eat us. It's that we're not going to eat them.

There is no jobs-versus-dinosaurs issue. Dinosaurs don't have a habitat to destroy. You say you'd like to construct a multimillion-dollar petroleum-based mall-amusement park on the site of a former wetland? It won't hurt the dinosaurs. You know why? They're already extinct! And *we didn't do it*! Who cares why they became extinct? The point is that they're gone, and they can't make any demands on us.

People always tend to love things more when they're gone—the passenger pigeon, the great auk, the Mohicans. (Actually, there still are Mohicans, no thanks to the rest of us.) If you think about it, the appeal of dinosaurs is similar to the appeal of pornography—excuse me, erotica. When real sex involving real persons becomes too complicated and dangerous, one can always turn to erotic fantasies. When real animals are too complex, too fragile, too demanding—they want habitat, they want rights, they constantly have to be dusted for fleas—one can always turn to the Saurischia.

In the realm of "biophilia," dinosaurs are fantasy lovers, partners that give everything and ask for nothing. Political action, cutting down on gasoline use, sharing your feelings? Forget it. Dinosaurs are titillating. Disease free. Lords of a fantastic, fully populated, rich and complex ecological system on which our cherished bad behavior cannot possibly have any effect, ever. Eco-popcorn. *Deinonychus Does Dallas*. Now showing everywhere.

Appropriate Transition Words

As with other strategles for writing, giving reasons—whether by means of the collection plan or the connection plan—requires the use of special transition words to lead your reader through your text. The following list presents some transition words to help you when your writing task calls for giving reasons.

also	in addition
and	moreover
as well	now
the cause (reason, etc.)	of course
the effect (result, etc.)	on one hand
first, second, third, etc.	on the other hand
for one thing	then
furthermore	what is more

GIVING REASONS IN COMBINATION WITH OTHER STRATEGIES FOR WRITING

As you have seen, writers are constantly engaged in the process of offering reasons for things. But in offering reasons, writers typically make use of facts, descriptions, and examples to bolster their positions. As you grow and mature as a writer, you'll gain increasing appreciation for the way in which all of the strategies for writing like giving reasons, using facts, employing examples, and offering descriptions interrelate.

In the following passage, written by Anne and Paul Ehrlich, the biologist/ecologists make use of facts, examples, and descriptions in order to support their point: that preserving nature is not incidental but essential to the well being of humanity's spirit.

There are . . . millions of adults who enjoy nature in some way. There are some 8 million bird-watchers in the United States alone. A 1965 outdoor recreation survey found that about 20 million Americans took nature walks and almost 3 million photographed wildlife annually. Keeping aquaria, an activity heavily dependent on the diversity of fishes, is the largest hobby in the country. People fascinated by succulent plants are so common that "cactus rustling" has become a crime in the southwestern United States. And there are enormous numbers of people who keep birds and reptiles as pets. So many people are interested in the wildflowers on Stanford University's Jasper Ridge Preserve that tight controls have had to be established to prevent research areas from being trampled. There are hundreds of nature and conservation centers in the United States. Similar statistics apply to many other countries, where nature hobbies are often even stronger; Winston Churchill and Vladimir Nabokov unashamedly collected butterflies.

Of course, while the total number of people who can visit Antarctica, the plains of East Africa, tropical rainforests, or other exotic places as touring naturalists is large, it still represents a tiny fraction of humanity. But as many millions of backyard bird, bug, and flower watchers have learned, the pleasures of knowing other organisms are not restricted to the well-off. Indeed, how many ghetto children have been thrilled—or could be—by watching a female guppy give birth in a school aquarium? Or by seeing a gorgeous male Siamese fighting fish, ablaze with crimson or blue, build a bubble nest, embrace his mate beneath it, and then catch her fertilized eggs in his mouth and spit them into the nest? Not one encounter with sharks, Killer Whales, lions, rhinos, elephants, chimps, rare butterflies, or army ants in Paul's (Paul Ehrlich, co-author of this piece) lifetime as a field biologist has had the impact of his discovery as a child that a giant silk moth—a Polyphemus—had emerged from a cocoon he had been watching. That is a thrill available to virtually any child at no expense.

But beyond compassion for leopards and baby seals slaughtered for their hides, beyond the naturalist's delight in the millions of diverse lifestyles produced by evolution, there seems to be a deeper feeling for other life forms that runs through all societies. In the West, as naturalist Jim Fowler likes to point out, it can be seen in the use of symbols. Not just in the Mercury Cougar, Ford Falcon, and Audi Fox, but in metaphors and symbols that go far back in history and are perpetuated in such phrases as *a real tiger, lionhearted, brave as a bull, sturdy as an oak, strong as an ox, free as a bird.* It shows up too in national symbols such as the double eagle of Napoleon, the Russian bear, and the American eagle.

People of all cultures seem to feel that they are more "human" in the context of a natural world. This clearly was a factor in the post-World War II rush to the suburbs in the United States. It may well be that contact with nature is essential to human psychological well-being.

Many aspects of human behavior confirm this observation. That the color green is soothing is well known. People try to nurture plants even in the worst city slums, and city dwellers as well as suburbanites often surround themselves with animals—dogs, cats, fishes, birds—as if trying to recapture a time when animals were an everyday part of human existence. Is it any wonder that environmental concerns remain high in the polls even in times of economic distress? Could it be that most people intuitively understand that preserving nature is not just an elitest ploy, but something essential to preserving the spirit, if not the body, of a human being?

Talking About It #170

Discuss with your classmates the following questions about the Ehrlichs's article.

1. State the Ehrlichs's point or thesis and then the reasons which support that thesis.
2. Note places where the Ehrlichs use descriptions to validate their reasons.
3. Note places where the Ehrlichs use examples or illustrations to validate their reasons.
4. Note places where the Ehrlichs use facts to validate their reasons.

Writing About It #171

Write a short paragraph discussing the way in which use of a combination of modes might add strength to writing.

A STUDENT GIVES REASONS: A FIRST DRAFT

Student Jennifer Kline has been working on her application to the Ohio State University School of Social Work. She hopes to be accepted into this program after her graduation from college. In this application, Jennifer marshals a number of reasons to convince the Graduate School Admissions Department of her interest in professional development as a social worker.

Jennifer has shared her early prewriting with her classmates. They responded by freewriting, sketching, or writing purpose statements. She considered their comments as well as her own purposes as she produced this draft of her application, which follows.

The purpose of social work is to help people cope with adversity. Social workers do not solve their client's problems, but they help them acquire the knowledge and skills so that they may be able to do so themselves. The social worker's responsibility is to guide people to a more productive way of life. Those kinds of skills are not just learned in the classroom. They are acquired through hours of practical experience in dealing with all kinds of people. Because that kind of experience is available to me through the Ohio State University College of Social Work, I hope to be admitted to this graduate program. This essay will explain why I'd like to be considered for graduate work.

Having come from a strong Catholic background, I have grown up believing in the importance of service to one's community. I always came away from service projects feeling good about both myself and the person or persons I had helped. In high school, I developed an interest in the work of Dr. Elisabeth Kubler-Ross. Fortunately, I was also able to hear her speak at that time.

In college, I took the usual number of sociology classes like Child Abuse, Social Welfare, Social Services in the Health Field, and even an independent study on Hospice Care, but most important to my developing interest in social work was the practical experience I gained while at college. The summer following my freshman year, I volunteered at Eastway Crisis Services. In my sophomore year, I became interested in the plight of the homeless, so I began volunteering at a local runaway shelter called Daybreak. Through Daybreak, I became involved with Foodshare, a program which transports leftover food from the three dining halls at our university to area homeless shelters. Eventually I became campus coordinator for Foodshare, and I was proud of its efforts as the first such campus program in our area and its use as a model for other area colleges. The summer after my junior year I traveled to the South Bronx with a group of religious brothers from my college, and I became involved in several community service projects such as AIDS awareness, literacy training, and homeless shelter.

One strength I exhibit is compassion. Even as a child, I was always sensitive to other people's feelings and always favored the underdog. My intention in revealing this fact is not to paint a picture of myself as the stereotypical bleeding heart but to express my awareness and concern for the well-being of others. One limitation I possess is that I am somewhat shy. While I find that I do well in social situations, I remain somewhat nervous about them. I am especially anxious among large groups of people with whom I am unfamiliar. Another part of who I am involves my commitment to learning. I have enjoyed my classes in the social sciences, most especially my social work classes.

Because of these and other reasons, I would be proud to be a part of a fine educational program like Ohio State's.

Talking About It #172

Critique Jennifer's draft using the what's missing critique explained in Chapter 6. Recall that the what's missing critique attempts to point out gaps that need to be filled in, inconsistencies that need to be explained, or connections that need to be made. As you look at Jennifer's draft, try to make comments about purpose, expectations, alternatives, generalizations, clarity, connections, explanations, and/or logic.

Think about the characteristics of writing that gives reasons which you have just studied: (1) making a point, (2) marshaling support, (3) organizing with the collection or connection plan, and (4) using appropriate transitions. As a group, try to answer the following questions:

1. What point or points does Jennifer make in her different paragraphs?
2. What kind of support does she offer the reader? Facts? Examples? Experiences? Reasons? Does it seem sufficient?
3. What plan does Jennifer use to organize this application? Collections? Connections?
4. What special transitions words does Jennifer use to connect her ideas?

A STUDENT GIVES REASONS: A REVISED DRAFT

Jennifer listened carefully to her fellow classmates' comments as they critiqued her work. Then she wrote this revised draft in response.

The purpose of social work is to help people cope with adversity. Although social workers do not solve their client's problems, they do help them acquire the knowledge and skills to be able to do so themselves. The social worker's responsibility is to guide people to a more productive way of life. Those kinds of skills are not just learned in the classroom. They are acquired through hours of practical experience in dealing with all kinds of people. Because that kind of experience is available to me through the Ohio State University College of Social Work, I hope to be admitted to this graduate program. I believe that my family background, volunteer experiences, and personality make me a strong candidate for graduate work at Ohio State.

Having come from a strong Catholic background, I have grown up believing in the importance of service to one's community. All through my education in Catholic schools I took part in class service projects such as food drives and visits to local nursing homes. While such projects took place long before I knew what social work was, I always enjoyed them. I always came away from them feeling good about both myself and the person or persons I had helped. In high school, I took a course in Death and Dying, and from this class I developed an interest in the work of Dr. Elisabeth Kubler-Ross, a pioneering figure in the field of death and dying. Fortunately, I was also able to hear her speak at that time, and I was especially impressed by her work with terminally ill AIDS patients. Thus, even before I attended college, I sensed that I would somehow be drawn to social work.

In college, I took the usual number of sociology classes like Child Abuse, Social Welfare, Social Services in the Health Field, and even an independent study on Hospice Care, but most important to my developing interest in social work was the practical experience I gained while at college.

The summer following my freshman year, I volunteered at Eastway Crisis Services. I worked one night a week with patients who had psychological problems ranging from depression to schizophrenia. My duties as a volunteer were to help run group therapy sessions and to help blind and other physically disabled patients participate in these sessions.

In my sophomore year, I became interested in the plight of the homeless, so I began volunteering at a local runaway shelter called Daybreak. At Daybreak, I was responsible for planning several group sessions, and I also took care of some of the paperwork on these sessions, meeting and working with the social workers on the staff there and becoming aware of the many different agencies with which social workers must become familiar. Through Daybreak, I became involved with Foodshare, a program which transports leftover food from the three dining halls at our university to area homeless shelters. Eventually I became campus coordinator for Foodshare, and I was proud of its efforts as the first such campus program in our area and its use as a model for other area colleges.

The summer after my junior year was a very full one. I traveled to the South Bronx with a group of religious brothers from my college, and I became involved in several community service projects such as AIDS awareness, literacy training, and homeless shelter. The highlight of my experience was a full day spent with a social worker as she visited elderly shut-ins living in deteriorated housing developments throughout the Bronx. When I returned from New York, I worked full time as a teacher's aide at the Early Childhood Learning Center, and on Saturdays I worked as an Assistant Activity Director at the Riverside Nursing Home.

My personal characteristics also lend themselves to social work as a career. One strength I exhibit is compassion. Even as a child, I was always sen-

sitive to other people's feelings and always favored the underdog. My intention in revealing this fact is not to paint a picture of myself as the stereotypical bleeding heart but to express my awareness and concern for the well-being of others. One limitation I possess is that I am somewhat shy. While I find that I do well in social situations, I remain somewhat nervous about them. I am especially anxious among large groups of people with whom I am unfamiliar. However, although my shyness is also part of my nature, it is not debilitating, for I am always involved in a number of service activities and feel I am successful at them. Another part of who I am involves my commitment to learning. I have enjoyed my classes in the social sciences, most especially my social work classes. They have led me to pursue a clearer focus as I seek graduate work: an interest in hospital social work, particularly hospice work. In my quest for learning, I have continued to seek out a number of practical experiences in my chosen profession.

Part of the reason I have chosen to apply to Ohio State is that I admire its practical orientation and its emphasis on practical experience. I have followed Ohio State's research efforts on the Columbus homeless program and its new course offerings in the field of hospice care and hospital service; these are both programs I would like to become involved in. I believe that my background, my experiences, and my personality qualify me to become part of such a fine educational program.

Talking About It #173

Jennifer thought about her own puposes as well as her classmates' critiques when she wrote her revised draft. Talk to your classmates about the specific changes she has made. Do you think her draft has been improved? Why or why not?

WRITING ASSIGNMENTS

A. You have already produced some prewriting in response to this chapter on one of the following topics or a topic of your choosing:

The need for a clearer parking policy on campus
The usefulness of a summer job placement program on campus
The importance of more green space on campus
The necessity of a healthier menu in the campus dining facility
The importance of a reliable health center on campus
The usefulness of a social service requirement for graduation on your campus

Make use of this prewriting to write an essay that employs the strategy of giving reasons. Remember that your essay will need to make a point, lend support through facts, examples, experiences, or other methods, be organized according to the collection or connection plan, and make use of transitions.

Before you write, define your reader and your purpose, and do some preliminary planning in the areas of content, organization, and expression. (Assume for purposes of this paper that your reader will be someone reading your essay in your campus newspaper.)

After you have written your first draft, ask your classmates to respond to it. Then rewrite it, making improvements that consider their responses and your own purposes. Invite your classmates to critique this next draft. After you have written yet another draft in response to those critiques, ask your classmates to make editing suggestions. Finally, proofread and submit your paper.

Record all responses to the drafts of your paper in the Writing Assessment Profile which appears in the back of this text.

B. You have already produced some prewriting in response to this chapter on one of the following topics or a topic of your choosing in order to explore the topic using either the cause-effect or effect-cause method of giving reasons.

The effect or cause of increasingly high professional athletes' salaries
The effect or cause of your decision to major in a certain field
The effect or cause of escalating costs for college
The effect or cause of peer pressure
The effect or cause of drunk driving
The effect or cause of poor study habits

Make use of this prewriting to write an essay that employs the strategy of giving reasons through cause-effect or effect-cause. Remember that your essay will need to make a point, lend support through facts, examples, experiences, or other methods, be organized according to the connection plan, and make use of transitions.

Before you write, define your reader and your purpose, and do some preliminary planning in the areas of content, organization, and expression. (Assume for purposes of this paper that your reader will be a classmate.)

After you have written your first draft, ask your classmates to respond to it. Then rewrite it, making improvements that consider their responses and your own purposes. Invite your classmates to critique this next draft. After you have written yet another draft in response to those critiques, ask your classmates to make editing suggestions. Finally, proofread and submit your paper.

Record all responses to the drafts of your paper in the Writing Assessment Profile which appears in the back of this text.

CHAPTER ELEVEN REVIEW

Writing About It #174

Use your journal to reflect on what you learned in this chapter.

12
Narrating

What are the characteristics of narration? How can learning to use narration effectively make me a better writer?

WHAT IS NARRATION?

Narration is as old as humankind and as familiar as life itself. The ancient Greeks passed on their narratives from generation to generation, creating classic epics. The American Indians huddled in their teepees, sharing their legends. The pioneers, heading West, told stories around the campfire, swapping tall tales. Modern television watchers, their eyes glued to their screens, await the next episode of their favorite show. The fellow in the barber chair, the ladies in the check-out line, the players in the locker room whisper story after story, describe incident after incident, recount event after event in a beloved and familiar literary form: the narrative.

Narratives tell a story. You have already read several narratives in this text. As you watched James Thurber struggle to see through a microscope or John Updike's young Harold struggle to swim, you watched narrative unfold. In fact, whenever you are attuned to the unfolding of events, whether fictional events or factual events, you are involved in narrative. When your best friend recounts for you the football game you missed on Friday night, when your chemistry professor explains how to use a Bunsen burner, when a fellow student shares an anecdote about a favorite teacher, when your father tells you the latest joke, you are being exposed to narrative. The form of storytelling called narrative is everywhere.

Narratives are so common that they may go unnoticed by the beginning writer. But if you learn to look carefully at the things you read and write, the mark of narrative is unmistakably present. When you pick up the morning newspaper and read of the political events unraveling in an Eastern European country, you are reading narrative. When you answer an essay question on your Western Civilization exam, tracing the events that led to the French Revolution, you are writing narrative. When you read about Darwin's travels to the Galapagos Islands and the scientific observations he made there, you are reading narrative. When you write a short story about a character and the events through which she progresses, you are writing narrative.

SUBJECTIVE NARRATION

Although narrative always traces events using some kind of chronological order, narrative can generally be classified as either subjective or objective.

Subjective narratives use the first person pronoun "I." They trace events in time as told from the personal point of view of the writer. They convey a sense of intimacy with the reader. A common form of subjective narrative which has served writers for centuries and college students for decades is called the *personal essay.* The personal essay, a kind of subjective narrative, recounts the writer's own unique experience for the reader. In the following essay, college student Juan Angel presents a subjective narrative about his passion to acquire an education and how that passion affected his relationship with his grandmother.

My name is Juan Angel. I am 30 years old, and I was born in Mexico.

As a child, I was alone for most of the time. My father was an alcoholic, and he abandoned my family and me when I was three years old. My mother had to struggle to survive by working from place to place in Mexico. Her good intentions to support me economically were not enough because of low salaries, so she eventually ended up working here in the United States.

I lived with some of my relatives in a little village in Mexico and worked from dawn to sunset and ate sometimes once a day. I felt totally condemned to die of starvation and hard work. My relatives spent the money that my mother sent me, claiming that I was just a child and didn't need it. As a defenseless child, I was innocent, ignorant, and lacked the courage to stand up against the abuse and the injustice. My Gramma, who lived in another little village, couldn't do anything about the oppression I suffered, and she probably didn't even know what was really happening in my life. My relatives covered everything up, and the complaints I made were ignored while my suffering continued to get worse. After five years of being mistreated, humiliated, and abused by my relatives, I decided to put an end to it, and I went to live with my Gramma.

When I moved into my Gramma's house, I started living a new lifestyle. By then, I was eight years old, and I felt for the first time proud of myself because I had made my first big decision in life.

My Gramma had some pigs, so I had to feed them. One day I was feeding them close to a water stream when I saw two boys passing by. They carried some books in their handbags. I saw them every day walking down a grassy road while I fed those pigs. My curiosity grew intensely, and one day I stopped them on their way back home. I asked them what they were doing, and they told me that they were attending school. I wanted to know if they knew how to read, and immediately they started reading and writing to show me. I simply couldn't believe it. When they left, I scratched my head and nodded for a moment, looking toward the sky. I said, "Going to school! That's exactly the next step I have to work on." After I finished feeding those pigs, I went home. While I was walking home, I thought about how I would convince my Gramma to allow me to go to school. I knew it was going to be hard to convince her because there were around twenty boys in the village, and they were not attending school either, except those two whom I admired.

When I talked to her about my decision on going to school, she got very upset, and she immediately thought about who would care for her pigs. I calmed her down by telling her that I would continue feeding them. She didn't accept my proposal at first, so I looked for the two boys and talked to them about my interest in going to school. They encouraged me to leave the house and forget about the pigs; they would help me to go. I thought it was not a bad idea, but I opposed it because my Gramma and I were living alone. In addition, the closest school was two miles away from the village. For those reasons I hesitated to make such a decision. I had spent two years growing pigs and hesitated about my next step.

Finally, I gave up and left my Gramma alone in the house. My friends helped me find a place to sleep in town where the school was, and they gave me some food every day. They took me to the school, and I explained my situation to the principal; to my surprise, his name was Juan, also. He told me that my age (ten years old) wouldn't match the rules of the school. "You're too old," he said. He questioned me for about five minutes, and then he told me to come back the next day. He met with all the teachers, and after some deliberation, they approved my enrollment as a new student. I was excited and happy about my achievement as a ten-year-old boy. On the other hand, I couldn't sleep very well at night because I remembered my Gramma very much. She was desperately looking for me, and she found me after a week. I cried while I explained to her why I had left home. She hugged me very hard, and then she went to talk to the principal about my desire to attend school. I never expected her to talk to the principal, but she did. I have never experienced so much happiness in my life as I did when I was ten years old.

I walked the two miles back and forth to school every day. In addition, I had to feed the pigs early in the morning before I went to school and after I came home from school. I also chopped wood for cooking. I did chores at home as a responsible man in charge of a household. My Gramma and I lived happily for six years while I was in primary school.

After I finished my first six years in school, I had to make another tough decision. I had to leave my Gramma completely alone because the secondary school I wished to attend was in another town about three hours away by bus. A few months before I took off, she began to suffer from an acute pain in her chest. I didn't want to leave her, but I did. I wanted to stay in school as much as I could. I used to visit her every weekend, but sometimes the lack of money made it impossible. When I started my second year in the school, I began to worry about my Gramma's health. Her chest pains were getting worse, and I received a letter in which she said that she missed me very much.

A week later a friend of mine was looking for me at the school. He told me that my Gramma was very sick. I immediately went to see her. She was lying down with a blanket on the floor. When she saw me, she hugged me very hard, and then she began to ask how my school was. I could hardly answer her because my tears ran down my cheeks as never before. She asked me not to cry, but I couldn't stop. She told me to continue in school, and I promised her I would. A few minutes later, she died in my arms, and I felt that everything was torn apart inside me. I thought that I could never overcome the painful experience of losing my Gramma forever.

OBJECTIVE NARRATION

Objective narratives are less intimate or personal than subjective narratives. They are generally written in third person, using a point of view that creates more distance between writer and reader. You will find that objective narratives figure prominently in your college textbooks. You will discover them when you read about historical events or the autobiography of a famous politician or the discoveries that led to a scientific breakthrough.

The following objective narrative, a historical account, tells of the diamond hoax in which famed jeweler Charles Tiffany was once ensnared.

Fortunately for Charles Tiffany, the notoriety of his role in the century's greatest diamond swindle did not survive. In 1872, shortly after they learned of some stunning diamond discoveries that had been made in South Africa, two veterans of the California Gold Rush appeared in San Francisco toting bags of rough diamonds they claimed to have unearthed in Arizona. When news of the "find" leaked, mania to buy stock in their mine quickly reached New York, gripping the likes of General George B. McClellan, August Belmont, and Henry Seligman (whose clan had made a fortune brokering the 1849 gold rush).

But the financiers refused to proceed without Tiffany's opinion of the diamonds. Regrettably, though expert in assessing cut and polished stones, he knew little of rough gems. "They are worth at least $150,000," he judged at a hushed viewing; in exchange for all rights to the claim, the Wall Streeters promptly plied the prospectors with four times that sum. A mining engineer hired on Tiffany's advice endorsed the claim's value after being led blindfolded into the mountains where he found diamonds scattered on the ground.

Only the pride of a government geologist, who had surveyed the region of the purported mine and found no diamonds, undid the fraud. He led a party to the site, which was actually in Utah, and discovered a partly cut diamond among the roughs. It had slipped into the buckets of poor-quality South African stones the plotters had bought in London and salted there. "Most adroit and skillfully managed," opined the *New York Times* of the fraud. "I had never seen a rough diamond before" was all Tiffany could say, having lost $80,000 of his own in the swindle.

A special kind of objective narrative is called a *process narrative* or a "how-to." Generally written in third person but often acceptably written using second person, depending on the level of intimacy the writer wishes to create with the reader, process narratives are familiar to everyone. Your Aunt Bess's cabbage roll recipe is actually a process or how-to narrative. Your roommate's written directions to his family's summer home at the beach is also a process narrative.

Although processes are commonly found in every kind of writing, they are especially familiar in the sciences when a writer is attempting to recount important steps in chronological order. When you write a lab report for your physics class, the scientific procedures you describe are an example of a process narrative. In addition, many scientific or technical magazine articles are devoted to process narratives. They describe the steps in building your own stereo system or in setting up a home office or in understanding how an electronic gadget works. Often such process narratives are accompanied by diagrams or illustrations to help the reader visualize the steps in the process. Such a process narrative from *Consumer Reports* follows.

How a Cellular Phone System Works

The word "cellular" reflects the carving of cities, counties, and rural regions into areas called cells, each of which has its own transmission tower. The towers receive calls via FM radio waves like those your FM tuner receives but at a different frequency, to avoid interfering with your radio.

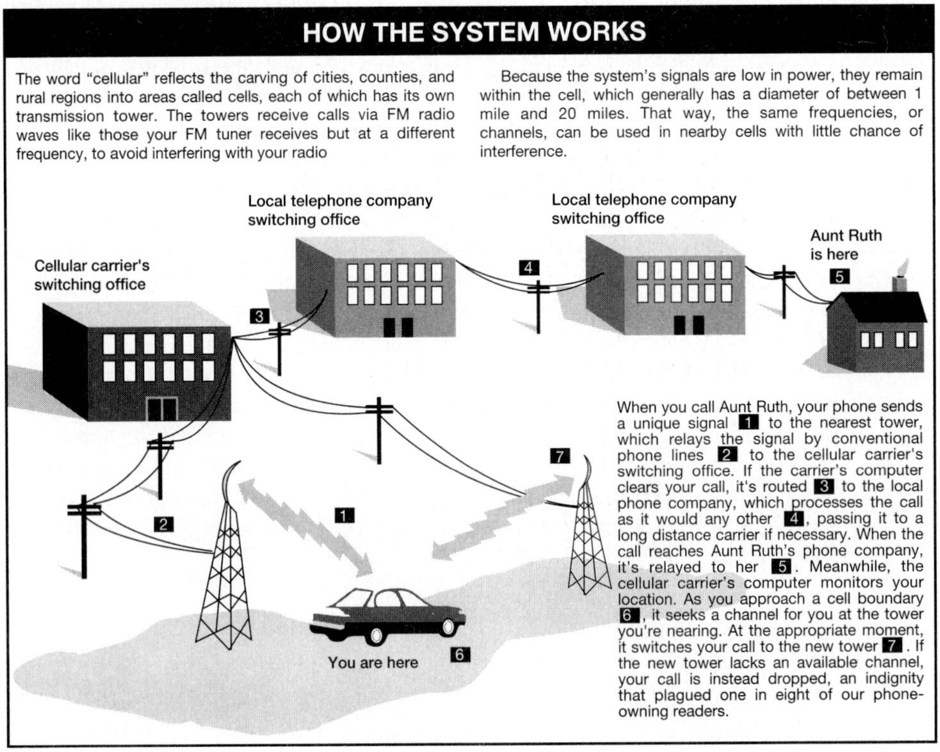

Figure 12.1

Because the system's signals are low in power, they remain within the cell, which generally has a diameter of between 1 mile and 20 miles. That way, the same frequencies, or channels, can be used in nearby cells with little chance of interference.

When you call your Aunt Ruth, your phone sends a unique signal (1) to the nearest tower, which relays the signal by conventional phone lines (2) to the cellular carrier's switching office. If the carrier's computer clears your call, it's routed (3) to the local phone company, which processes the call as it would any other (4) passing it to a long-distance carrier if necessary. When the call reaches Aunt Ruth's phone company, it's relayed to her (5). Meanwhile, the cellular carrier's computer monitors your location. As you approach a cell boundary (6), it seeks a channel for you at the tower you're nearing. At the appropriate moment, it switches your call to the new tower (7). If the new tower lacks an available channel, your call is instead dropped, an indignity that plagued one in eight of our phone-owning readers.

READER AND PURPOSE IN NARRATIVE WRITING

Every writer, including the writer of narrative, needs to consider reader and purpose. It's important to ask, "Who is my reader?" "What does my reader already know?" "What does my reader need to know?" "What is my purpose?" "How can I best achieve it?"

As you know, who your reader is can profoundly influence your text, particularly its content. The following passage contains two sets of directions to a single grocery store, written for different readers. As you read, you will notice that who the reader is has greatly influenced the content of the narrative.

Go west out of your driveway and continue along Honeycreek Drive until you get to Northcutt Avenue. Take a left and then go through three traffic lights until you reach the Wayco River Bridge. After you cross the bridge, turn right on Plaza Boulevard. You'll see the Kroger's in the plaza straight ahead.

Get your bike out of the garage, and head in the direction of Bobby Light's house. At the 7-11 where you buy your bubble gum is a street called Northcutt Avenue. Turn left on that street, heading toward the pet store. Keep going until you reach the bridge. Make sure you get in the special lane for bikers and ride carefully over the bridge. Notice the way your stomach turns over as you coast down the far side of the bridge. Put on your brakes at the bottom of the bridge because the first street you'll see is Plaza Boulevard, and it's easy to spot because there's a Shell station on the corner there. Turn in the direction of the Shell station. Slow down now because the shopping center is very close. The Kroger's is right between the movie theater and the ice cream shop.

Whenever you write a narrative, it's important to think about your reader. If, for instance, your Genetics 432 professor asks you to write a paper tracing the events that led to Charles Darwin's formulation of the theory of evolution, you probably won't need to define terms familiar to her such as "natural selection," "creationism," or "punctuated equilibrium." If you were writing for the novice biology major, on the other hand, such terms might require definition.

Your purpose or purposes as a writer are also worth thinking about. You might want to recount a hilarious occurrence at a Halloween party in order to entertain your friends. You might want to write to your dean, informing her about the inappropriate behavior of a campus police officer which you witnessed during a weekend incident. You might want to persuade your history professor that Charles Dickens, in writing about the French Revolution in *A Tale of Two Cities*, sided with the revolutionaries. You might want to recount the day's events in your journal, wishing only to express yourself through narrative in the pages of your private book.

Thus, your reader and your purpose are important considerations as you begin to create narrative writing.

CHARACTERISTICS OF NARRATION

Because narrative is so common, it's important that you become familiar with its characteristics. These characteristics are listed for you.

1. Narration tells a story or traces events to make a point.
2. Narration presents only certain selected details to make that point.
3. Narration is organized by means of the chronology plan.
4. Narration makes use of appropriate transitions to place events in time.

Narration to Make a Point

It's important to understand that narrative tells a story to make a point. You might tell a story about last night's basketball game, for instance, to make a point about the changes the new coach has made in team strategy. You might tell a story about your experiences with the ferocious dog next door as a way of making a point about your ability to conquer a childhood fear. You might recount an anecdote about a roommate in order to make a point about his legendary messiness.

In all of these examples, narrative serves a point. You may have experienced listening to a child tell a story about something that happened, noticing the way the youngster rambled on and on, indifferent to the need to make a point. You can contrast this tendency with that of a mature writer, for the mature writer understands that narrative serves a point.

Selected Detail

Similarly, writers of narratives share only certain selected details with their readers. Those *selected details* must be observations that contribute to the writer's point. You might be familiar with someone who loves to talk, someone who can bend your ear for extended periods of time or stay on the telephone for hours. Such a person often fails to select the most significant details for sharing, rambling on and on about things that might be irrelevant to you, the listener.

If, for instance, you are enrolled in a psychology seminar and your professor asks you to write a case study of a client with a shoplifting problem, your case study will not recount every incident in which the client went shopping; it will include narratives of only those incidents in which shoplifting occurred.

To focus on your point, often it's useful to answer the journalist's questions—Who? What? When? Where? Why? How?—as they relate to your point. Thus, when you write narratives, try to be selective about the details you present to your reader, choosing only those details which relate to your main point.

The Chronology Plan

In addition, narratives make use of a unique method of organizing content, the *chronology* technique. Unlike the collection technique which you studied in the chapters on description, illustration, and fact-based writing, chronology does not merely list ideas; it arranges them in chronological sequence. Chronology presents events as they occur through time. When using chronology, it's important that you pay close attention to the order of events, for if you fail to present the events in your narrative in chronological order, your reader is often confused. Mixing up the order of events can leave your reader baffled.

Appropriate Transition Words

Certain key transition words can help link the events in your narratives. These words are useful to know, for they guide the reader through your sequence of events. They are words like the following:

after a while	eventually	now
afterward	finally	soon
as	first (second, third, etc.)	then
at last	gradually	until
at present	later	
currently	meanwhile	
during	next	

The following passage is an example of narrative. It was written by Martin Luther King, Jr., the slain civil rights leader.

Not until I entered theological seminary, however, did I begin a serious intellectual quest for a method that would eliminate social evil. In the early 1950s I read Walter Rauschenbusch's *Christianity and the Social Crisis*, a book which left an indelible imprint on my thinking.

After reading Rauschenbusch, I turned to a serious study of the social and ethical theories of the great philosophers. During this period I had almost despaired of the power of love to solve social problems. The turn-the-other-cheek and the love-your-enemies philosophies are valid, I felt, only when individuals are in conflict with other individuals; when racial groups and nations are in conflict, a more realistic approach is necessary.

Then I was introduced to the life and teaching of Mahatma Gandhi. As I read his works I became deeply fascinated by his campaigns of nonviolent resistance. The whole Gandhian concept of *satyagraha* (*satya* is truth which equals love and *graha* is force; *satyagraha* thus means truth-force or love-force) was profoundly significant to me. As I delved deeper into the philosophy of Gandhi, my skepticism concerning the power of love gradually diminished, and I came to see for the first time that the Christian doctrine of love operating through the Gandhian method of nonviolence, is one of the most potent weapons available to an oppressed people in their struggle for freedom. At that time, however, I acquired only an intellectual understanding and appreciation of the position, and I had no firm determination to organize it in a socially effective situation.

When I went to Montgomery, Alabama, as a pastor in 1954, I had not the slightest idea that I would later become involved in a crisis in which nonviolent resistance would be applicable. After I had lived in the community about a year, the bus boycott began. The Negro people of Montgomery, exhausted by the humiliating experience that they had constantly faced on the buses, expressed in a massive act of noncooperation their determination to be free. They came to see that it was ultimately more honorable to walk the streets in dignity than to ride the buses in humiliation. At the beginning of the protest, the people called on me to serve as their spokesman. In accepting this responsibility, my mind, consciously or unconsciously, was driven back to the Sermon on the Mount and the Gandhian method of nonviolent resistance. This principle became the guiding light of our movement. Christ furnished the spirit and motivation and Gandhi furnished the method.

Talking About It #175

Discuss with your classmates the narrative by Martin Luther King, Jr. Use the questions below to guide you.

1. What is the point this narrative attempts to make?
2. Does the writer present only certain selected details to make his point? Explain.
3. Does the narrative make use of time or chronological order? How do you know?
4. Does the narrative make use of special transitions to place events in time? Identify some of these transitions.
5. Is this a subjective or objective narrative? How do you know?
6. Use your imagination to suggest where you think this narrative was likely to have been published. Why do you think so?

NARRATION IN COMBINATION WITH OTHER STRATEGIES FOR WRITING

Although writers often use narrative as the basis for an entire piece of writing, narrative is also commonly found in combination with other types of writing. A travel writer, for instance, might make use of description to convey the exotic beauty of a tropical island in a magazine article. Within that article, however, he might also include a narrative paragraph or section to explain a trip around the island by jeep.

The following passage comes from a *Smithsonian* magazine article written by former astronaut Michael Collins. Notice the way the author skillfully combines the narrative with descriptions and facts.

The little old ladies of Worcester, Massachusetts, who sew and glue pressure suits for the National Aeronautics and Space Administration (NASA) have been good to me. My custom-tailored outfit is about as comfortable as it can be. I slip into it, lock helmet and gloves in place and begin breathing 100-percent oxygen to start the process of purging nitrogen from my system. This is the day John Young and I have been anticipating ever since we were assigned to the Gemini 10 spaceflight six months ago. It's July 18, 1966—launch day.

John is the commander and I'm his copilot. This morning we stayed up until 4 making last-minute preparations, then slept until noon. Now, carrying our portable oxygen containers like attache cases, we leave the ready room at Cape Kennedy and ride in a small van out to the launchpad. Here we enter the grillwork cage of an orange elevator that clatters up the side of the gantry. On top, people help shove us down inside our Gemini capsule, attach parachute harnesses, oxygen and radio connections, shake hands and reverently close the hatches.

Although John and I are alone in our cramped quarters aboard Gemini 10, we're not lonesome, for over the radio comes a continual chatter from people in the nearby blockhouse and from Mission Control in Houston. Down below, our Titan stirs as its two engines swivel back and forth during a final check. We feel a little shudder in the cockpit and then all is still again. Finally comes the ten-second countdown and, clutching an emergency ejection ring between my legs in a death grip, I hold my breath and wait for ignition. There it is! A slight bump and I know we're on our way.

We jerk back and forth a bit as the engines a hundred feet below work to keep us balanced despite gusty winds and sloshing fuel tanks. I can see a tiny patch of blue sky out my window but there is no sensation of speed until a thin layer of cloud approaches. Then—pow!—we burst through it faster than my eye can follow. We really *are* moving out. I begin to feel heavier and heavier, and now a mild fore-and-aft vibration causes the instrument panel to go slightly out of focus. At 50 seconds, we pass the altitude after which we can no longer use our ejection seats and I let go of the ring, my fingers tingling. Noise and vibration smooth out abruptly as we reach supersonic speed and thinner air.

In a minute and 20 seconds, we have accelerated from zero to 1,000 miles per hour and have climbed from sea level to 40,000 feet. As the first-stage tanks empty, we are up over five Gs, which means the pressure we are feeling is five times the normal weight of gravity. Suddenly, as the power shifts to the second-stage engine, I am flung forward in my straps, and the window changes from black to red to yellow. We find out later that the second-stage engine has blasted the top of the first stage, causing an oxidizer tank to explode—without damage to us but creating a spectacular light show visible even on the ground. As quickly as chaos came, order is restored; the second stage hums along quietly, and the window darkens again. Now a heavy hand is pushing on my chest but before I get too uncomfortable there is another lurch—and here we are, hanging in our harnesses, weightless at last. Out the window is the most amazing sight I have ever seen, a glorious panorama of sea and clouds stretching for a thousand miles in a glistening white light. In an instant, our little cubbyhole has been magically transformed. These are not ejection seats, but thrones facing out on the Universe—and we are wealthier than kings.

Talking About It #176

Discuss the passage by astronaut Michael Collins with your classmates. Point out the largely narrative sections of the article. Then point out the descriptive and factual details.

Narratives also make good introductions to longer pieces of writing. A short tale that illustrates a person's character, called an *anecdote*, is actually a brief narrative that can provide insight for the reader about the subject of a piece. For instance, this anecdote by Banesh Hoffmann is the first paragraph in a longer article called "My Friend, Albert Einstein."

He was one of the greatest scientists the world has ever known, yet if I had to convey the essence of Albert Einstein in a single word, I would choose *simplicity*. Perhaps an anecdote will help. Once, caught in a downpour, he took off his hat and held it under his coat. Asked why, he explained, with admirable logic, that the rain would damage the hat, but his hair would be none the worse for its wetting. This knack for going instinctively to the heart of a matter was the secret of his major scientific discoveries . . .

Writing About It #177

Write a short anecdote that illustrates a characteristic of someone you know.

A STUDENT USES NARRATION: A FIRST DRAFT

In the following essay, student Kelly Kuhn is writing a process narrative, which she titles "OSCAR Packs a Suitcase." In it, she attempts to display the characteristics of narration that she learned about in this chapter.

Kelly has shared her early prewriting with her classmates. They responded by freewriting, sketching, or writing purpose statements. She considered their comments as well as her own purposes as she produced another draft of her paper, which follows.

The OSCAR method of packing involves just a few easy steps: Organize, Select a suitcase, Collect items into one place, Arrange large items and breakables, and Roll clothes.

When you select a suitcase, keep in mind the items you'll be packing. If you will be taking only clothes and shoes, a sturdy cloth or leather suitcase will fit your needs. They are lightweight and easy to carry. My mother bought me a bookbag from L.L. Bean last fall, and it works well for carrying my books back and forth to class. If you plan to take a large number of breakable items, you should take a suitcase with a hard outer shell. This will prevent breakage should your luggage be bounced around in transit. One of the Samsonite suitcase commercials shows a piece of luggage being dropped from an airplane and surviving undamaged.

Begin to arrange bulky items in your suitcase. Heavy sweaters or jackets can make up the first layer. Shoes, clocks, shampoo, and other odd-shaped items are next. Visualize how your suitcase looks when you are carrying it. Heavier articles, such as clocks and boots, should be placed where the bottom of your suitcase will be when it is in an upright position. By doing this, you will avoid having the items shift, creasing your clothes when your suitcase is carried. Collect everything into one place. Look at the items in front of you and decide if all of them are necessary. If you know your destination has a wake-up service, you will not need an alarm clock. Personally, I have a great deal of trouble waking up in the morning although most of the members of my family are early risers. Remember to pack as lightly as possible. Any items that may leak (shampoo, lotion, and cologne) should be placed in sealed plastic bags as you prepare to pack.

The last step is to take the remainder of your clothes and roll them. Forget what you may have been told in the past about how rolling clothes puts creases in them. Done properly, rolling actually helps reduce the number of wrinkles you will have. You need to take each article of clothing separately and spread it out on a flat surface. Fold the sleeves in at the seams and carefully flatten or "hand-press" the garment. Start at the top of the garment and begin to roll as tightly as possible towards the bottom. In order to conserve space, you should place these rolled clothes as tightly as possible around the other articles. They can be placed inside stiff dress shoes and may act as a buffer for glass and other fragile items.

If you carefully follow OSCAR's simple steps, you should have no unexpected problems when you arrive.

Talking About It #178

Critique Kelly's draft using the 2 + 2 critiquing method explained in Chapter 6. Recall that the 2 + 2 method points out two of the greatest strengths of the piece as well as two of the greatest weaknesses that need to be addressed in the next draft. Discuss these strengths and weaknesses with your classmates.

Think about the characteristics of narrative writing that you learned about in this chapter: (1) tracing events to make a point, (2) presenting selected details to make that point, (3) organizing with the chronology technique, and (4) making use of appropriate transitions to place events in time. As a group, try to answer the following questions:

1. What events is Kelly tracing? What point do the events serve to make?
2. What are some of the selected details she uses to make that point? Do all of the selected details seem relevant?
3. Does Kelly organize by means of the chronology plan? Are the events recounted in acceptable time order?
4. Has Kelly used appropriate transition words to place events in time?

A STUDENT USES NARRATION: A REVISED DRAFT

Kelly listened carefully to her fellow classmates' comments as they critiqued her work. Then she wrote this revised draft in response.

Going on a camping trip? Staying overnight with a friend? Planning on a weekend at the beach? How many times have you realized that you need to get packed—usually in one hour or less—when you haven't even begun to start? If you learn to use the OSCAR method, you can pack those worries away, for the OSCAR method of packing involves just a few easy steps: Organize, Select a suitcase, Collect items into one place, Arrange large items and breakables, and Roll clothes.

In order to get organized, you must first assess your needs and make a list. It is a good idea to have a list of standard items you always take on trips: toothpaste, toothbrush, pajamas, and so forth. The other items on your list will depend on where you're going and how long you're staying. Keep in mind an item's versatility. A plain white shirt can be dressed up with accessories like a tie or scarf, but it can be made more casual with the sleeves rolled up and a t-shirt underneath. Choosing items based on versatility can help limit the number of things you take. Don't forget to consider any special needs like a swimsuit for a trip to the beach. By making a list, you can organize your thoughts and estimate how much you will be taking.

Once you have thought about what you are bringing, you can select a suitcase. Keep in mind the items you'll be packing. If you will be taking only clothes and shoes, a sturdy cloth or leather suitcase will fit your needs. They are lightweight and easy to carry. If you plan to take a large number of breakable items, you should take a suitcase with a hard outer shell. This will prevent breakage should your luggage be bounced around in transit.

Next, refer to your list and collect everything into one place. Look at the items in front of you and decide if all of them are necessary. For example, if you know your destination has a wake-up service, you will not need an alarm clock. Remember to pack as lightly as possible. At this time, any items that may leak (shampoo, lotion, and cologne) should be placed in sealed plastic bags as you prepare to pack.

Now you may begin to arrange bulky items in your suitcase. Heavy sweaters or jackets can make up the first layer. Shoes, clocks, shampoo, and other odd-shaped items are next. Visualize how your suitcase looks when you are carrying it. Heavier articles, such as clocks and boots, should be placed where the bottom of your suitcase will be when it is in an upright position. By doing this, you will avoid having the items shift, creasing your clothes when your suitcase is carried.

The last step is to take the remainder of your clothes and roll them. Forget what you may have been told in the past about how rolling clothes puts creases in them. Done properly, rolling actually helps reduce the number of wrinkles you will have. You need to take each article of clothing separately and spread it out on a flat surface. Then fold the sleeves in at the seams and carefully flatten or "hand-press" the garment. Next, start at the top of the garment and begin to roll as tightly as possible towards the bottom. In order to conserve space, you should place these rolled clothes as tightly as possible around the other articles. They can be placed inside stiff dress shoes and may act as a buffer for glass and other fragile items.

If you carefully follow OSCAR's simple steps, you should have no unexpected problems when you arrive. Everything will be ready for you to use and nothing will be broken. But before you leave your house, put a quarter in your pocket. That way, should you arrive and realize that you have forgotten something important, you can always call home and have it sent.

Talking About It #179

Kelly thought about her own purposes as well as her classmates' critiques when she wrote her revised draft. Talk to your classmates about the specific changes she has made. Do you think her draft has been improved? Why or why not?

WRITING ASSIGNMENTS

A. Produce some prewriting in response to one of the following topics or a topic of your choosing in preparation for writing a narrative paper. Remember to profile your reader, define your purpose, and develop some preliminary strategies for content, organization, and expression. The suggested topics are as follows:

an important childhood experience,
a trip or journey you have taken,
a riveting incident or event you have witnessed.

Make use of this prewriting to write a narrative essay that demonstrates the characteristics of narrative that you have learned about in this chapter: (1) telling a story to make a point, (2) presenting selected details to make that point, (3) organizing with the chronology technique, and (4) making use of special transitions to place events in time. Assume for purposes of this paper that your reader will be a fellow classmate.

After you have written your first draft, ask your classmates to respond to it. Then rewrite it, making improvements that consider their responses as well as your own purposes. Invite your classmates to critique this next draft. After you have written yet another draft in response to those critiques, ask your classmates to make editing suggestions. Finally, proofread and submit your paper.

Record all responses to the drafts of your paper in the Writing Assessment Profile which appears in the back of this text.

B. Produce some prewriting in preparation for writing a process or how-to narrative. You may describe any process with which you are familiar. Remember to profile your reader, define your purpose, and develop some preliminary strategies for content, organization, and expression.

Make use of this prewriting to write a process essay that demonstrates the characteristics of narrative that you have learned about in this chapter: (1) tracing events to make a point, (2) presenting selected details to make that point, (3) organizing with the chronology technique, and (4) making use of special transitions to place events in time. Assume for purposes of this paper that your reader will be a fellow classmate.

After you have written your first draft, ask your classmates to respond to it. Then rewrite it, making improvements that consider their responses as well as your own purposes. Invite your classmates to critique this next draft. After you have written yet another draft in response to those critiques, ask your classmates to make editing suggestions. Finally, proofread and submit your paper.

Record all responses to the drafts of your paper in the Writing Assessment Profile which appears in the back of this text.

CHAPTER TWELVE REVIEW

Writing About It #180

Use your journal to reflect on what you learned in this chapter.

13

Exploring Problems and Solutions

What techniques can I use to explore problems and solutions?
Will learning to write about problems and solutions improve my written work?

WHAT IS PROBLEM-SOLUTION WRITING?

Problems abound in life. The Congress of the United States wrestles with difficult problems like health care or drug abuse. Scientists struggle to solve the problems posed by AIDS, heart disease, or tuberculosis. The superintendent of your local school district faces problems caused by the escalating cost of education. The manager of the small business down the block wonders how to solve the problem of increased competition from the chain stores springing up all over town. Your parents struggle to decide whether day care or a neighborhood babysitter is the better solution to the problem of what to do with your younger sister and brother while they go to work. You face problems about which career might be best for you, which professor to take this term, whether you want to live in the dorm next year or find an apartment near campus.

But human beings have not been content to dwell on their problems for too long, for they understand that those problems may be solved through their search for solutions. The Congressional hearing, the laboratory experiment, the campaign for a new school levy, the business merger, the new day care center up the street, the decision to take a career interest survey are all attempts at solutions to a number of problems. And those solutions are often incorporated in writing.

The Congressional testimony finds its way into the *Congressional Record* and the daily news; the scientific experiment is recounted in the pages of a scholarly journal; the school levy campaign is explained in news releases and position papers; the business merger is recorded in incorporation documents; the day care center is announced in a press release; and your career interest results are written up by your career counselor. Thus, writing often involves exploring problems and offering solutions for them.

Closely related to problems and solutions are questions and answers. In fact, problems are often first articulated as questions: What can we do about health care? Can we find a cure for AIDS? How can we control the cost of education? What is the best way to combine our business efforts and meet the challenge of competition? Who will care for the children? What career should I choose? As writers search for answers to questions like these, they are using a strategy for writing closely related to formulating problems and exploring solutions.

SUBJECTIVE PROBLEM-SOLUTION WRITING

As in other kinds of writing you have studied, problems and their solutions may be discussed from either a subjective point of view or an objective point of view.

A subjective discussion of a problem and its solution is generally written in the first person, using the pronoun "I." Often, the problem and its solution are based on the writer's personal experience as in the example which follows.

When I was in 9th grade and just beginning high school, our family received news that would change our life. My little sister Lisa, who had just turned 10, was diagnosed with cancer.

Because she had always been healthy and active, I watched in fear as I saw Lisa weaken and change. But all of us hung on to hope, helping her through the biopsies, the chemotherapy treatments, the loss of hair, and the radiation therapy she received at our local hospital. For 18 terrible months while I tried to balance a normal high school life with the abnormal life I was living at home, I wondered whether Lisa would live or die. Five years after Lisa's initial diagnosis, I gratefully listened to her doctor pronounce the words I'd been praying to hear: "Lisa is cured."

That was nearly 10 years ago. Lisa is now a college graduate, a journalism major looking for her first job. She'd like to work on a community newspaper or do public relations work or cover the news for a local television station. She's well-qualified for nearly any kind of communications job. She had a 3.6 average in college and many extracurricular activities. She's a hard worker. I know that if there's a challenge to be met, nobody can meet it better than Lisa because I watched Lisa beat cancer.

But as Lisa applied for job after job and was turned down again and again, I began to think that Lisa was having problems getting a job that went beyond the normal problems any recent college graduate looking for employment experiences.

I listened to Lisa explain what typically happened as she interviewed for nearly every position she had applied for. A pattern seemed to be occurring. After an initial interview at which Lisa expressed enthusiasm for the job and her potential employer expressed enthusiasm for her and her outstanding record, Lisa was called back to discuss a question on her application form. On the form was a box that asked, "Have you ever been treated for a serious disease?" Because Lisa believed in being honest, she always checked "yes." Employer after employer then asked Lisa about her cancer, questioning her about how much her treatments had cost, how frequently she needed medical check-ups, and how her previous medical condition might affect her work if her cancer should recur. Lisa answered all these questions directly, stating that although her treatments were expensive, they had all been paid for, that she hadn't been required to have medical check-ups for the last ten years, and that her doctor had stated that her cancer was not likely to recur. Somehow, at the end of these discussions, Lisa's future employers ended the meeting with a promise to call her back. But they never did.

Because of the pattern I was seeing, I began to think that Lisa was being discriminated against because of her cancer. I decided to talk to my next-door neighbor, Mr. Hart, a prominent lawyer in town. He gave me some very important information, information that might help Lisa solve her problem.

Mr. Hart told me about the Americans with Disabilities Act that was passed by Congress in 1990. As I explained the pattern of behavior that Lisa experienced as she looked for jobs, Mr. Hart nodded his head. He said he thought that Lisa might be a victim of discrimination. He looked over some legal papers and told me that, in his view, Lisa would qualify as a person with a disability under the definition in the Act. The Act defined a disability as a "physical or mental impairment that substantially limits a major life activity" and that the term "disability" even applied to people like Lisa who have only "a record of a substantially limiting impairment." Mr. Hart told me that as long as Lisa qualified under the Act and could perform the essential functions of the job, she could not be discriminated against by a prospective employer because of her disability.

I thought that Lisa should talk to Mr. Hart herself. Being a cancer survivor, Lisa had a potential problem as she began to look for jobs. Having talked to Mr. Hart myself, I thought the solution to her problem might be close at hand. I hoped that learning about her rights under the Americans with Disabilities Act might give Lisa the helping hand, the open door, and—eventually—the office desk she dreamed of!

As you have learned, closely related to the problem-solution strategy for writing is the question-answer mode. Just as problems invite solutions, questions invite answers.

In the following passage, writer Ursula K. LeGuin raises inviting questions.

On the shore, by the sea, outdoors, is that where women write? Not at a desk, in a writing room? Where does a woman write, what does she look like writing, what is my image, your image, of a woman writing? I asked my friends: "A woman writing; What do you see?" There would be a pause, then the eyes would light up, seeing. Some sent me to paintings, Fragonard, Cassatt, but mostly these turned out to be paintings of a woman reading or with a letter, not actually writing or reading the letter but looking up from it with unfocused eyes: Will he never never return? Did I remember to turn off the pot roast? . . . Another friend responded crisply, "A woman writing is taking dictation." And another said, "She's sitting at the kitchen table, and the kids are yelling."

OBJECTIVE PROBLEM-SOLUTION WRITING

Problem-solution writing can also be employed from a more objective point of view. Unlike the two passages you just read, the following article, called "Washing Clothes Can Be a Gas," is not based on personal experience. More objective and impersonal, it begins with a problem and explains its solution using the third person point of view.

In an effort to make doing the laundry, well, not exactly fun, but less environmentally burdensome, a Florida company has developed a laundry system that does away with detergents, hot water—and the rinse cycle, too.

Ozone is the key to the innovative system devised by Tri-O-Clean of Fort Pierce. The versatile gaseous molecule, easily manufactured, consists of three atoms of oxygen, and it can lift all but the heaviest grease out of soiled clothes by breaking down the organic structure of ordinary dirt and grime. It has trouble with lipstick and really heavy industrial grease, but what washing machine doesn't?

The laundry system consists of a series of holding tanks, filters and pumps, as well as an ozone generator and injector. Water combined with ozone flows through clothes, loosening the dirt and breaking down its structure. The decomposed dirt is absorbed into the waste water, which then runs back into a holding tank for reuse. It can be recycled hundreds of times before new water must be added.

"Normally you need three gallons of water to wash a pound of clothing," says Tri-O-Clean managing director Charles W. Pearsall. "With our system, you use one-eighth of that, so think how much water a commercial laundry that washes three million pounds of clothes a year could save."

The system saves energy as well as water because it uses cold water rather than hot—unstable ozone molecules actually dissipate faster in hot water, Pearsall adds.

Current installations include prisons and hotels, with hospitals and nursing homes being added.

As you have seen, the example demonstrates the problem-solution mode from the third person point of view. In the excerpt which follows, the question-answer mode is used. It explores the question of legal ownership in space from the third person point of view.

Who owns the moon? Throughout history, planting a flag in unclaimed territory has meant ownership, and the United States has its flag on the moon.

If several countries own a space station, what is the nationality of a baby born in space?

As the presence of humans in space increases, so must the body of laws governing their actions there . . . Still only a tiny legal field—just 300 of the country's 777,000 attorneys specialize in space law—it draws from a combination of legal disciplines, including international relations, government, and patents and property rights.

CHARACTERISTICS OF PROBLEM-SOLUTION WRITING

Problem-solution writing, like the other strategies you have studied, displays some well-known characteristics. These characteristics are as follows:

1. Problem-solution writing or question-answer writing deals with either a well-defined problem or a well-formed question.

2. Problem-solution writing offers one or several solutions to a problem. Question-answer writing offers one or several answers to a question.

3. Problem-solution writing or question-answer writing makes use of the connection plan of organization.

4. Problem-solution writing or question-answer writing makes use of appropriate transitions.

Each of these four characteristics of the problem-solution strategy is explained in the following section.

A Well-Defined Problem

Successful discussion of problems and their solutions—or questions and their ultimate answers—begins with a well-defined problem or well-formed question. A vague statement of a problem or a too general question invites disaster. Your reader must have no doubt about what your problem or question is, and you must have no doubt about the problem you are trying to solve or the question you are trying to answer. Your statement of the problem or question must be clear because an awkwardly worded problem or weakly articulated question blurs your own focus as you write, setting a poor standard for the paper to come.

To avoid the problems of vagueness or generality, challenge yourself to narrow your problem to a manageable size. No one could expect you to do a competent job of solving the problem of welfare or answering a question about the general social effects of alcohol abuse in a standard essay. On the other hand, a local problem facing the administration of the Women-Infants-and-Children program for meeting the nutritional needs of babies of mothers on welfare might easily be managed in an essay-length piece. Likewise, a question raising issues about local tavern practices and their effect on the underage college drinker might also be reasonably managed within the limitations of an essay.

In addition, you may have to spend considerable effort providing background on your problem for your reader. You will most likely provide this in your introduction, taking the time to inform your reader about your problem so that your reader can share your interest in its solution. Thus, when writing a problem-solution paper, defining your problem well includes providing enough information so that your reader can understand your perspective.

One or Several Solutions

Once your problem or question has been clearly stated, you will need to decide whether your problem has one solution—or several. In the paper you read earlier about Lisa and her difficulty in finding a job, the writer has offered one solution—turning to the Americans with Disabilities Act—for solving the problem. Other problems may suggest more than one solution. A paper on the problem of campus parking might offer several solutions: a reorganization of the parking assignment system, increased patrolling by campus security, a plan to build additional parking facilities, and a restriction of campus driving privileges for first-year students. Thus, this problem paper would offer not just one but several solutions. Likewise, discussing a question effectively might involve one—or several—answers.

The Connection Plan

In most strategies for writing in which relationships between things are being explored, the connection plan is the most common plan of organization. When writers compare and contrast or search for causes and effects or explore problems and questions, they are looking to express the relationships involved: what solutions best solve this problem? What causes a particular result? What answer might be the best response to this question? In what respects is this one thing similar to or different from another?

Typically, when you express your problem or question in your thesis statement, each supporting topic sentence offers a solution or answer, returning again and again to the thesis, making connections between it and the solution or answer being offered. In the following paragraph, student Kate Zimmerman expresses a problem in her introductory paragraph and then connects it with three potential solutions.

Among environmentalists, there's a whole lot of finger-pointing going on, and the finger is usually wagged in the direction of American industry. Blame the industrial conglomerates for polluting our rivers, our air, our landscape, goes the cry. Whether the accusations are right or wrong, the problem of industrial pollution will not be solved without the cooperation of industry. In fact, industries everywhere are helping to fight pollution through new technology, recycling, and alternate resources.

New technology is one solution to America's environmental crisis. First, American automobile industry leaders are working on making electric cars a reality by the year 1998. Ford Motor Company, for example, has developed two new automobile models that will cut down on emissions by 40%. In addition, the Allied Signal Company has started to produce "ozone friendly" refrigerators for supermarkets; these release less chlorofluorocarbons and are reliably cost-efficient. The Robbins Company, a jewelry manufacturing and plating company, is investing in low or no-waste production equipment. Its system makes use of an elaborate closed-loop wastewater treatment and recovery system that saves the company $71,000 a year and recycles water that is 40 times cleaner than average city water.

Recycling is yet another technique used by many industries to help clean up the environment. McDonald's, for instance, has created a solid waste reduction plan to reduce McDonald's waste by 80%. Another company that capitalizes on minimizing waste is Hoechst Celanese. This company, in partnership with Coca Cola, is recycling the two-liter plastic bottle, spending $500 to $600 million to minimize waste pollution. In addition, Xerox and the Scott Paper Company are not only promoting recycling in their advertisements, but they are also reusing and recycling their own products. Scott, in fact, has been honored for planting more trees than it harvests. Furthermore, Safety-Kleen is a company that specializes in recycling contaminated fluids. Its clients are auto body repair shops and dry cleaners, and Safety-Kleen removes and recycles the dirty solvents used in industrial processes.

Finally, industries are looking to alternative resources to fight pollution. In the agriculture industry, for instance, farmers are lessening their dependence on chemical pesticides and fertilizers, making use of natural ecological cycles to improve soil and increase pest resistance. Paper industries are producing more naturally colored paper as opposed to white paper, thereby decreasing the need for chlorine in the paper pulp. In addition, newspapers are doing their part by using soy-based ink instead of ink containing polluting petrochemicals.

Contrary to popular belief, industries make up the major force behind America's major clean-up efforts. Companies all over the United States are searching for ways to be helpful to our natural surroundings. Through new technology, recycling, and alternative resources, they are offering important solutions to our nation's environmental problem.

Talking About It #181

With your classmates, discuss the organization of Kate Zimmerman's problem-solution essay.

1. What is Kate's thesis statement? Where is it found? Does it establish a problem-solution relationship?
2. What are Kate's topic sentences? Do they offer solutions? Do they point back to the problem articulated in the thesis statement?
3. What is Kate's conclusion? How does it sum up the problem and its solutions?
4. Why is Kate's essay an example of the connection plan?

Appropriate Transition Words

A final characteristic of the problem-solution strategy is that this strategy makes use of certain transition words to connect the ideas and establish relationships between a problem and its solutions or a question and its answers. Some of these transition words are listed for you.

above all	in addition
another	indeed
as a result	in fact
consequently	in particular

especially	one such
finally	most important
first (second, third, etc.)	most of all
for example	so
for instance	surely
furthermore	therefore
hence	thus
	yet another

Talking About It #182

With your classmates, identify the special transition words Kate Zimmerman uses in her problem-solution essay.

READER AND PURPOSE IN PROBLEM-SOLUTION WRITING

Considerations about your reader and your purpose play an important role in determining the success of your problem-solution or question-answer strategy. First of all, an important task is to convince the reader of the seriousness of your problem. You must work to get your reader to see your problem like you do and persuade your reader that your problem is worth thinking about. Your reader comes to a piece of writing with a lot of things on his or her mind; your job is to convince your reader that your problem or your question is something to pay attention to. As a result, you must devote considerable effort to the introduction section of your problem-solution papers, for the introduction is the place where you are best able to hook your reader, luring him or her into a shared concern with your problem.

In addition, you must spend some time thinking about who your reader is. For instance, a classroom reader might naturally share your concern with problems that relate to getting good grades or financing a college education or finding a place to park on campus. Other subjects, on the other hand, might be more risky. You'd be asking your classroom reader to stretch to take in your essay about the technical solutions to problems posed by the Challenger explosion or the potential political solutions to the problems raised by the international drug trade. These might be excellent topics for a problem-solution paper, but they will challenge you to think hard about your reader and cast a wider net to pull him in.

You will also need to think about your own purpose in writing a problem-solution or question-answer paper. Are you just trying to inform your reader about a problem and merely suggest potential solutions? Are you trying to convince your reader of the reasonableness of your solutions or the rightness of the answer to your question? Or are you trying to inspire your reader to take some kind of action like signing a petition or writing a Congressional representative? Clarifying your own purposes as a writer will help you focus your efforts more effectively.

PROBLEM-SOLUTION IN COMBINATION WITH OTHER STRATEGIES FOR WRITING

Problems and their solutions are explored for readers in combination with other strategies for writing which you have already studied. As you read about problems and solutions or questions and answers, you will notice the descriptions, facts, examples, narratives, reasons, and other strategies which writers use to make exploration of problems and solutions or questions and answers more effective.

In the following passage from an essay called "Becoming a Doctor," physician Lewis Thomas uses the problem-solution approach to probe the problem posed by doctors of the past, whose real knowledge of disease was quite limited. Jumping off from the ironic quotation, "It is better to have a future than a past," Thomas takes a look at the problem of medical ignorance and its solution.

Early on, there was no such thing as therapeutic science, and beyond the efforts by a few physicians to classify human diseases and record the natural history of clinical phenomena, no sort of reliable empirical experience beyond anecdotes. Therapeutics was a matter of trial and error, with the trials based on guesswork and the guesses based mostly on a curious dogma inherited down the preceding centuries from Galen. Galen himself (c. 130–c. 200) had guessed wildly, and wrongly, in no less than five hundred treatises on medicine and philosophy, that everything about human disease could be explained by the misdistribution of "humors" in the body. Congestion of the various organs was the trouble to be treated, according to Galen, and by the eighteenth century the notion had been elevated to a routine cure-all, or anyway treat-all: remove the excess fluid one way or another. The ways were direct and forthright: open a vein and take away a pint or more of blood at a sitting, enough to produce faintness and a bluish pallor, place suction cups on the skin to draw out lymph, administer huge doses of mercury or various plant extracts to cause purging, and if all else failed induce vomiting. George Washington perhaps died of this therapy at the age of sixty-six. Hale and hearty, he had gone for a horseback ride in the snow, later in the day had a fever and a severe sore thoat, took to his bed, and called in his doctors. His throat was wrapped in poultices, he was given warm vinegar and honey to gargle, and over the next two days he was bled from a vein for about five pints of blood. His last words to his physician were, "Pray take no more trouble about me. Let me go quietly."

Beginning around the 1830s, medicine looked at itself critically, and began to change. Groups of doctors in Boston, Paris, and Edinburgh raised new questions, regarded as heretical by most of their colleagues, concerning the real efficacy of the standard treatments of the day. Gradually, the first example of science applied to clinical practice came somewhat informally into existence. Patients with typhoid fever and delirium tremens, two of the most uniformly fatal illnesses of the time, were divided into two groups. One was treated by bleeding, cupping, purging, and the other athletic feats of therapy, while the other group received nothing more than bed rest, nutrition, and observation. The results were unequivocal and appalling, and by the mid-nineteenth century medical treatment began to fall out of fashion.

The great illumination from this, the first revolution in medical practice in centuries, was the news that there were many diseases that are essentially self-limited. They would run their predictable course, if left to run that course without meddling, and, once run, they would come to an end and certain patients would recover by themselves. Typhoid fever, for example, although an extremely dangerous and potentially fatal illness, would last for five or six weeks of fever and debilitation, but at the end about 70 percent of the patients would get well again. Lobar pneumonia would run for ten to fourteen days and then, in lucky, previously healthy patients, the famous "crisis" would take place and the patients would recover overnight. Patients with the frightening manifestations of delirium tremens only needed to be confined to a dark room for a few days, and then were ready to come out into the world and drink again. Some were doomed at the outset, of course, but not all. The new lesson was that treating them made the outcome worse rather than better.

Talking About It #183

Discuss the passage by Dr. Thomas, using the following questions to guide your discussion.

1. What is the problem Dr. Thomas is dealing with?
2. What facts, examples, descriptions, and other strategies are used to explain the problem? Is the problem explained in sufficient detail?
3. According to Dr. Thomas, what was the solution to this problem? Does Dr. Thomas recommend one solution or several?
4. Describe the connection plan which Dr. Thomas uses to organize this piece. What connections does he establish between the early practices of medicine and the more modern practices? What was the result for medicine of these new discoveries?
5. Identify a few transitions used by Dr. Thomas in this piece.
6. How much space does Dr. Thomas devote to explaining the problem? How much space does Dr. Thomas devote to explaining the solution? Why is so much space given to an explanation of the problem?

Similarly, the question-answer strategy makes use of a combination of methods to achieve its purposes. Writers employing the question-answer technique often draw on the power of other strategies like facts, narratives, reasons, examples, and other methods to pursue questions and their answers. In the passage that follows, father and former principal Richard R. Bradfield raises questions about the way his son Scott has been treated by the social welfare establishment.

Our son, Scott, has two words in his vocabulary—"bye, bye." For him, these words reflect joy, the anticipation of things to come. For me, they invoke a dread I feel daily.

Scott is 27 years old. He has been classified as severely developmentally delayed. He has other medical problems as well.

Ten years ago, I shared Scott's optimism. He was attending a public school in Centerville. He had the services of specialists to foster and enhance his growth.

Speech therapists worked with him on a communication board and helped him with exercises to decrease his excess salivation. Occupational therapists worked with him on putting on his coat and pulling off his socks. Physical therapists created regimens that helped Scott function in spite of cerebral palsy and scoliosis.

The best part was that Scott was accepted in his school. For instance, students in the regular classes used their free time to help handicapped students practice feeding themselves and walking; they helped my son's classmates learn to use a pencil or crayon. In addition, swimming, horseback riding, picnics, nature hikes and other field trips were regular activities.

What happens to people like our son when they get older? What happened to the anticipation and satisfaction I felt 10 years ago when the bus pulled away from our house in Centerville?

When a handicapped person turns 22, he is relegated to whatever the political arena has to offer.

Unlike 10 years ago, Scott now doesn't associate with the average or normal population. As a result, improper behavior—not proper social behavior—is reinforced every day.

Although Scott will never be able to hold down a job, the Montgomery County Board of Mental Retardation and Developmental Disabilities assigned him to pre-vocational training. Pre-vocational, in Scott's case, has meant taking large bolts and hanging them on hooks.

When our son was young, we depended on the Centerville school staff to tell us what transpired during the day. Teachers sent home a daily note, which I read with Scott, so we could share in his efforts and accomplishments. Scott's face would light up, and his laugh repeatedly lifted our spirits.

Today, we have no idea what has gone on while Scott is at the mental retardation board's Calumet Center.

The mental retardation board is responsible for offering and implementing programs and activities for mentally handicapped people older than 22. It is failing to do so in the case of my son and hundreds like him.

First, Scott must ride a bus from one end of the county to the other. The bus ride takes more than an hour, and the long ride is hard on him.

Second, his current placement is haphazard at best. Programming is reactionary, rather than realistic.

Third, many of the people who work directly with our son and other handicapped adults are hired off the street and given titles such as "language specialist" or "body programmer." Calumet Center has no therapists. The lack of true specialists and educators trained in mental retardation means the program is superficial at best.

Furthermore, meaningful programming does not exist at Calumet. A written goal for Scott at one time was to differentiate between hot and cold by using a towel soaked in cold and warm water. Aside from the fact that this activity was meaningless, the goal was abandoned because staff said they didn't have the materials. Individual classrooms are crowded, and signs of a program are absent. Most of the people wander about aimlessly or sit gazing at the floor.

Scott has come home many times with his hands and clothes dirty and disheveled. He has even come home in clothes different from the ones he had on in the morning. At times, his knees have been red-raw from crawling on the dirty floor.

Scott was toilet-trained before he was assigned to Calumet. He isn't now.

My dread comes daily because I must send my son to a place that is our only alternative to an institution.

There are tremendous differences between living in an institution and living at home. Having people care for you out of love, rather than because they get $9 or more an hour, is important.

My wife and I have structured our lives around helping our son; we want him to have the best life possible. But we fear for the future, for the time when we are unable to take care of him.

Since Scott left Centerville schools, he no longer has the opportunity to participate in his community. He is forced to spend meaningless time on a bus, rather than doing something beneficial. He does not have the array of educators who know what he needs and who are able to plan, coordinate, organize, facilitate, and evaluate his progress.

Scott needs the services of specialized therapists. He needs to be close to his home, so we can be there quickly if he becomes ill or is hurt. He needs to come home as clean as he started the day. He needs to be exposed to the normal population to avoid the reinforcement of bad behaviors, such as scratching and screaming. He needs to be in a place that is answerable to those who care the most for him.

Normalization of the family situation should be a major goal for the public entity that is supposed to serve people like Scott.

Space should be made available where it is needed in the least restrictive environment: the community setting.

With a $21-million budget for 1,100 people, there's no excuse for a lack of sound activities and reliable supplies.

Administrators need to be responsive to parents. They need to see that there is a difference between what parents want for their children and what institutionalized care-providers think is best for the people they call clients.

The programs for adults, such as they exist, should not be located in the northwest quadrant of the county, far away from the people they serve.

The effort to integrate mentally handicapped people into the community should not be abandoned when they turn 22.

My son Scott is not a criminal. But under the present scheme of things, he would get a lot more attention and effort if he were.

Our son is a good person. He deserves better.

Talking About It #184

With your classmates, discuss the passage by Richard Bradfield, using the questions to guide your discussion.

1. What is the question or questions Bradfield is asking?
2. What facts, examples, narratives, descriptions, and other strategies are used to explore the question? Is the question explored in sufficient detail?
3. According to Bradfield, what is the answer to this question? Is there one answer—or several?
4. Describe the connection plan which Bradfield uses to organize this piece. What connections does he establish between the early treatment of Scott and

the later treatment of Scott? Why does he establish these connections? What result does Bradfield hope for by establishing these connections?

5. Identify a few transactions used by Bradfield in this piece.
6. How much space does Bradfield devote to explaining the problem? How much space does Bradfield devote to explaining the solution? Why is so much space given to an explanation of the problem?

In addition, using questions is often an ideal way to interest readers in what you are writing. Often a series of sharp, focused questions, used in your introductory paragraph, can draw your reader into your work, creating a sense of anticipation about the material to come. Thus, a skillful use of questions is a technique to add to your developing writing resources.

The following introductory paragraph raises questions to draw the reader into the subject: the link between creativity and madness.

Was the Roman poet Seneca observing accurately when he noted in the first century that "there is no genius without some touch of madness"? Was Aristotle, writing in the fourth century, on target when he asked, "Why is it that men outstanding in the arts are melancholic?" Is it true that the pantheon of artists like Byron, Shelley, and Melville and scientists like Einstein, Huxley, and Alexander Graham Bell could be labeled with the psychiatric disorder called manic depression? Is it true that creativity and mental illness are closely allied? Is there a link between genius and madness? The answer offered in a new book called *The Price of Greatness* by Dr. Arnold M. Ludwig, a professor of psychiatry, is a resounding "Yes."

A STUDENT USES PROBLEMS AND SOLUTIONS: A FIRST DRAFT

In the early draft of the following problem-solution essay, student Josh Porowski is attempting to write a short essay about a solution to the problem of what to do on spring break. Josh has shared his early prewriting with his classmates. They responded by freewriting, sketching, or writing purpose statements. He considered their comments as well as his own purposes as he produced the second draft of his problem-solution paper, which follows.

As spring approached this year, my friends and I had a problem to solve. We didn't want to go to Daytona during spring break.

My friends and I came up with a solution to the problem of what to do over spring break by participating in "Alternative Spring Break" sponsored by Campus Ministry at our college. Our destination? Florida—just like all the other students who headed South. But we didn't land in Daytona. We landed in Homestead where we participated in the disaster relief effort for victims of Hurricane Andrew.

When we got there, we were not alone. Just like our friends who had decided to go to Daytona, we were surrounded by college students. We spent a week helping to pour foundations, hammer up siding, entertain relief-stricken children, and cook for the newly homeless.

Heading back home on Interstate 75, our van passed hundreds of cars filled with college students returning to their campuses after a week-long party. Our party, on the other hand, was returning with something more substantial than a stomachful of beer: a fully satisfied heart.

Talking About It #185

Critique Josh's draft using the writer-based and reader-based critique explained in Chapter 6. Recall that the writer-based reader-based critique asks you to underline the parts that fail to satisfy you, the reader. Then place question marks over those portions that require additional clarification or explanation.

Think about the characteristics of writing that deals with problems and their solutions: (1) a well-defined problem or well-formed question, (2) one or several solutions, (3) the connection plan for organizing, (4) appropriate transition words. As a group, try to answer the following questions:

1. Has Josh defined his problem well? Has he provided enough information to orient the reader to his perspective on the problem?
2. Has Josh offered one or several solutions?
3. Has Josh connected problem and solution by means of the connection plan?
4. Has Josh made use of appropriate transition words to make connections between problem and solution?

A STUDENT USES PROBLEMS AND SOLUTIONS: A REVISED DRAFT

Josh listened carefully to his fellow classmates' comments as they critiqued his work. Then he wrote this revised draft in response.

As spring approached this year, my friends and I had a problem to solve. We didn't want to go to Daytona during spring break. Tony doesn't like the idea of the crowds in Florida. Brian figures that if he wants to drink, he can just stay home. Stewart says he can't afford the hefty price tag Spring Break carries. I don't like the idea of wasting a week on activities that seem completely meaningless. To me, the beer-drinking, sun-worshipping, party-making tradition called spring break is just plain silly.

My friends and I came up with a solution to the problem of what to do over spring break by participating in "Alternative spring break" sponsored by Campus Ministry at our college. CM plugged into a national relief effort that coordinates aid for over 200 relief agencies. Campus Ministry provided a university van, plenty of gas, and shelter in an abandoned school building. Our destination? Florida—just like all the other students who headed South. But we didn't land in Daytona. We landed in Homestead, Florida, to work on the relief effort for victims of Hurricane Andrew.

When we got there, we were not alone. Just like our friends who had decided to go to Daytona, we were surrounded by college students. Homestead was home to over 40 colleges, from Allegheny College in Pennsylvania to Xavier University in Ohio. We spent a week helping to pour foundations, hammer up siding, entertain relief-stricken children, and cook for the newly homeless. Brian and I were proud of our "find." It wasn't a local bar but a thrift store in Oakland Park, Florida where we spied 5-cent loaves of Wonder bread and aging bananas for 10-cents a pound. With a contribution of only a dollar each, our group of twelve volunteers brought home enough bread and bananas to feed five tentfuls of homeless people for nearly a week.

Heading back home on Interstate 75, our van passed hundreds of cars filled with college students returning to their campuses after a week-long party. Our party, on the other hand, was returning with something more substantial than a stomachful of beer: a fully satisfied heart.

Talking About It #186

Josh thought about his own purposes as well as his classmates' critiques when he wrote his revised draft. Talk to your classmates about the specific changes he has made. Do you think his draft has been improved? Why or why not?

WRITING ASSIGNMENTS

A. You have already thoroughly explored a campus problem in Chapter 5 of this text. Use these explorations as a basis for writing about a solution or solutions for this problem. Make sure that your paper demonstrates the characteristics of problem-solution writing that you have learned about in this chapter: (1) a well-defined problem or well-formed question, (2) one or several solutions, (3) the connection plan for organizing, (4) special transition words. You may change or revise your original problem section in any way you wish. Assume for purposes of this paper that your reader will be a classmate.

After you have written the draft containing your solutions, ask your classmates to respond to it. Then rewrite it, making improvements that consider their responses as well as your own purposes. Invite your classmates to critique this next draft. After you have written yet another draft in response to those critiques, ask your classmates to make editing suggestions. Finally, proofread and submit your paper.

Record all responses to the drafts of your paper in the Writing Assessment Profile which appears in the back of this text.

B. Produce some prewriting in response to one of the following topics or a topic of your choosing in preparation for writing a problem-solution paper. Remember to profile your reader, define your purpose, and develop some preliminary strategies for content, organization, and expression. Remember that it will be important to provide sufficient background information in your introductory explanation of your problem.

The problem of pollution on campus
The problem of campus parking
Problems with the grading system
The problem of time management
The problem of study skills
The problem of dishonest politicians
The problems with pets
Problems with the weather
Problems with money
Problems with child-raising
Problems balancing work and school
Problems attaining a balanced diet
The problems of raising teenagers

Make use of this prewriting to write a problem-solution essay that demonstrates the characteristics that you have learned about in this chapter: (1) a well-defined problem or well-formed question, (2) one or several solutions, (3) the connection plan for organizing, (4) special transition words. Assume for purposes of this paper that your reader will be a fellow classmate.

After you have written your first draft, ask your classmates to respond to it. Then rewrite it, making improvements that consider their responses as well as your own purposes. Invite your classmates to critique this next draft. After you have written yet another draft in response to those critiques, ask your classmates to make editing suggestions. Finally, proofread and submit your paper.

Record all responses to the drafts of your paper in the Writing Assessment Profile which appears in the back of this text.

CHAPTER THIRTEEN REVIEW

Writing About It #187

Use your journal to reflect on what you learned in this chapter.

14

Comparing and Contrasting

Why is learning to compare and contrast important to me as a writer? What techniques contribute to an effective comparison-contrast paper?

WHAT IS COMPARISON AND CONTRAST?

You compare and contrast things every day. Because you are a consumer, you have probably found yourself making comparisons at the record store, at the pop machine, at the supermarket. Do you want the cassette tape or the CD? Should you choose a diet or a regular soft drink? Do you purchase the regular size or the giant economy brand?

In making decisions, you also compare and contrast things of more lasting importance. Should you attend a four-year or a two-year college? Do you want a quiet family wedding or a big celebration? Would a major in business offer you more career opportunities than a major in education?

In college, comparison and contrast is a strategy your teachers will often ask you to employ to help you understand things more thoroughly. Comparing and contrasting helps you perceive similarities and differences, evaluate information, weigh and consider alternatives. Your education professor, for instance, may ask you to compare traditional preschool philosophies of education with non-traditional Montessori preschool philosophies. Your engineering professor may ask you to contrast differing laboratory procedures. Your biology professor may ask you to compare and contrast a species of crustacean. Your business professor may ask you to contrast the marketing strategies of competing companies. In all these situations, you are being asked to compare and contrast in order to deepen your understanding of the subjects under investigation.

When you compare, you focus on the similarities between things; when you contrast, you focus on differences. Because comparing and contrasting is a strategy that can strengthen your understanding significantly, this chapter will help you develop your skills in this area.

SUBJECTIVE AND OBJECTIVE COMPARISONS AND CONTRASTS

Sometimes writers use comparison and contrast to develop personal topics. They might contrast their mother with their father. They might contrast their family's holiday traditions with the family traditions of their spouse. They might compare their own childrearing practices with the childrearing practices of their parents. They might compare their college study habits with the study habits they practiced in high school.

In these cases, they develop their ideas using the subjective "I" point of view, creating intimacy and closeness with their readers. In the following paragraph, a student focuses on the differences between two high school teachers.

> Mr. Arndt, my 11th grade History teacher, and Mrs. Myers, my 12th grade History teacher, had two entirely different styles of teaching. Mr. Arndt ran a tight classroom. Typically dressed in a no-nonsense bow tie, his beard neatly trimmed, Mr. Arndt recorded each new grade in his grade book according to a finely tuned system: red ink for major tests, blue ink for quizzes, and pencil for homework assignments. With Mr. Arndt, I learned history by the book. He covered every chapter in *America: Our Heritage*, my classroom text, in exact chronological order. I proceeded from Plymouth Rock to Viet Nam by means of a neat, orderly process, answering Prereading questions and Postreading questions at the beginning and the end of every chapter. With Mr. Arndt, history was a long, orderly march in single file order. Mrs. Myers, on the other hand, was easygoing and relaxed. Often she dashed into the classroom just as the bell rang, her scarf flying out behind her, her hair tousled and blown. Her desk was a jumble of essays, magazines, notes, and paperweights. Often Mrs. Myers's grade was a simple check mark at the top of a paper, and occasionally she misplaced an essay or a make-up test. She largely abandoned her textbook, using *Newsweek* and *Time* magazines for reading material instead. Each of Mrs. Myers's classes was a lively but often circular discussion in which Constitutional rights, political policy, and democratic institutions always figured. Mrs. Myers could jump from the civil rights movement to the Boston Tea Party in the course of an hour, challenging me to think about the great issues of history that recurred over time. With Mrs. Myers, unlike Mr. Arndt, history was a circular process that wrestled with themes to which Americans returned again and again. Mr. Arndt and Mrs. Myers were entirely different teachers, and, curiously, I managed to learn important things about history from them both.

Writers also make use of comparisons and contrasts in a more objective, impersonal way. In college you will make particular use of objective comparisons and contrasts in a variety of disciplines. Whether you are comparing two varieties of plant life, two historical figures, or two political philosophies, you will most generally be writing in third person, adopting this more objective, dispassionate point of view.

In the following example, authors Amato and Partridge make use of comparison-contrast as well as the third person point of view to deflate some of the myths about vegetarians.

> Stereotypes about vegetarians are generally uncomplimentary. It is widely held, for example, that vegetarians are health nuts, members of bizarre religious cults, hippies, or other fringe-dwellers. But our research reveals that most vegetarians today are practical and sensible members of the social mainstream; increasing numbers, in fact, are academics, business people, doctors, lawyers, and other professionals, as well as skilled tradespeople. Vegetarians are also seen as ascetic, skinny, weak, and anemic. However, we show that most vegetarians experience better than average health and typically live physically active, and demanding, lives. Finally, vegetarians are often seen as superficial trend-followers, ready to jump on the latest bandwagon. In contrast, we find that deeply held convictions underlie the diets of most vegetarians.

Writing About It #188

To get a feel for both subjective and objective comparisons and contrasts, write a paragraph in which you compare two family members, two teachers, or two friends using the first person point of view. Then write a paragraph in which you compare the same two people using the third person point of view. Discuss with your classmates your experience in shifting between first and third person point of view.

READER AND PURPOSE IN COMPARING AND CONTRASTING

As in the other writing strategies you have studied, you must consider your reader and your purpose as you begin to write using the strategy of comparing and contrasting.

It's important for you to define your reader before you begin. For instance, let's imagine that your American literature professor is giving an exam on which he has asked you to compare the way two nineteenth century writers—Ralph Waldo Emerson and Henry David Thoreau—lived out their belief in Transcendentalism, a spiritual orientation that both writers espoused. In answering this question, it would be important for you to make sure not to spend much time comparing the books they published or the education they had acquired. In meeting the needs of your reader, it would be most important for you to talk about the way they *lived*. In addition, in commenting through comparison on the way both men lived, it would be important to discuss only those life events that reflected their belief in Transcendentalism. Thus, considering what your reader asks from you, particularly in the comparison-contrast essay question, is of vital importance.

Your purpose as a writer is also important. Comparisons and contrasts can differ widely, depending on your purpose. Sometimes a writer can compare and contrast simply to point out similarities and differences; in this case, by simply explaining how things are like or unlike. Sometimes, however, a writer compares and contrasts in order to evaluate or judge; in this case, similarities and differences are pointed out to decide which philosophy is more realistic, which political system is more just, which alternative is more humane. For instance, a business major might write a paper comparing and contrasting capitalism and socialism with the purpose of simply explaining similarities and differences to the reader. However, that same student might also write a paper which attempts to evaluate or judge which economic system is more realistic or just or humane. In such a case, this student would be comparing and contrasting to serve two very different purposes: explanatory and evaluative.

CHARACTERISTICS OF COMPARISON AND CONTRAST

Comparison and contrast as a strategy displays definite characteristics.

1. Effective comparison and contrast makes use of appropriate subjects.
2. Effective comparison and contrast compares appropriate features.
3. Effective comparison and contrast makes use of the connection plan of organization.
4. Effective comparison and contrast makes use of appropriate transition words.

In the section that follows, you will explore these four characteristics.

Appropriate Subjects

Effective comparisons or contrasts begin in appropriate subjects. Finding an appropriate subject is not as easy as it appears, for arriving at an appropriate subject to compare or contrast involves a process of selection. For instance, let's assume that you are attempting to write a paper of comparison and contrast and that you have focused very generally on the subject of sports figures. You have a vague notion that you'd like to compare or contrast major figures in sports. As you begin to do some prewriting, you find that you'll have to become a lot more narrow and focused. You realize, as you focus and narrow, that appropriate subjects must exhibit some natural bases for comparison. Thus, you reject a comparison of a major football player—for instance, Jim Brown—with a major basketball player such as Michael Jordan: you realize that the differences between the two sports are too great to offer a basis for meaningful comparison. As a result, you decide to narrow your focus to basketball, deciding to compare two basketball greats, Michael Jordan and Magic Johnson. Once you begin to prewrite, however, you realize that even this more narrowed topic is too broad because both Jordan and Johnson have rich personal and professional histories that offer a number of possibilities for comparison and contrast. In wrestling with this issue of an appropriate subject and struggling to select and choose, you have recognized the first requirement of effective comparisons and contrasts.

In the paragraph that follows, writer Murray Ross has attempted to narrow the two very broad topics of baseball and football appropriately.

As a pastoral game, baseball attempts to close the gap between the players and the crowd. It creates the illusion, for instance, that with a lot of hard work, a little luck, and possibly some extra talent, the average spectator might well be playing; not watching. For most of us can do a few of the things the ball players do: catch a pop-up, field a ground ball, and maybe get a hit once in a while. Chance is allotted a good deal of play in the game. There is no guarantee, for instance, that a good pitch will not be looped over the infield, or that a solidly batted ball will not turn into a double play. In addition to all of this, almost every fan feels he can make the manager's decision for him, and not entirely without reason. Baseball's statistics are easily calculated and rather meaningful; and the game itself, though a subtle one, is relatively lucid and comprehensible.

As a heroic game football is not concerned with a shared community of near-equals. It seeks almost the opposite relationship between its spectators and players, one which stresses the distance between them. We are not allowed to identify directly with Jim Brown any more than we are with Zeus, because to do so would undercut his stature as something more than human. The players do much of the distancing themselves by their own excesses of speed, size and strength. When Bob Brown, the giant all-pro tackle says that he could "block King Kong all day," we look at him and believe. But the game itself contributes to the players' heroic isolation. As George Plimpton has graphically illustrated in *Paper Lion*, it is almost impossible to imagine yourself in a professional football game without also considering your imminent humiliation and possible injury. There is scarcely a single play that the average spectator could hope to perform adequately, and there is even a difficulty in really understanding what is going on. In baseball what happens is what meets the eye, but in football each action is the result of eleven men acting simultaneously against eleven other men, and clearly this is too much for the eye to totally comprehend. Football has become a game of staggering complexity, and coaches are now wired in to several "spotters" during the games so they can find out what is happening.

Talking About It #189

With your classmates, discuss how Ross has appropriately narrowed the two very broad topics of baseball and football.

Appropriate Features

Once you find an appropriate subject, you must then wrestle with the second requirement of effective comparison-contrast: finding appropriate features of this subject to compare and contrast. Although you probably haven't thought much about it, you are used to comparing the features of things. When you go to the grocery store and decide whether to buy the 6-pack of pop or the liter bottle, you mentally weigh the features of the two products. You think about the taste, the cost, even the effect on the environment of your purchase of plastic or cans. When you consider these factors, you are comparing appropriate features.

Likewise, when you begin to compare and contrast in a writing assignment, you must decide what features you want to compare, and those features must be relevant to your overall discussion of your topic and your purpose. In attempting to compare and contrast appropriate features, it is often helpful to make a list. For the paper about Michael Jordan and Magic Johnson, for instance, the student has made a list of the potential features he can compare.

Michael Jordan v. Magic Johnson

1. career successes
2. pre-professional experiences
3. playing styles
4. family life
5. attitudes about basketball

In selecting appropriate features, the student must also consider his purpose. Is he attempting to simply explain the basketball playing styles of Jordan and Johnson? Or is he trying to evaluate the playing styles of Jordan and Johnson in order to convince the reader that one of these is more exciting? Is he attempting simply to compare the career successes of Jordan and Johnson in order to inform the reader of them? Or does he want to persuade the reader that one of the careers is simply more impressive than the other?

Talking About It #190

For each of the following topics, list with your classmates some appropriate features to compare or contrast:

Your classroom teacher and another classroom teacher whom many of your classmates know

One student in your class and another student in your class

One method of writing a paper practiced by a student in your class and another method of writing a paper practiced by another student in your class

The study habits of one student in your class and the study habits of another student in your class

The career choice of one student in your class and the career choice of another student in your class

For each of these topics, decide how your final drafts would differ if your purpose in one paper was explanatory and your purpose in the other paper was evaluative.

The Connection Plan

When you are using the comparison/contrast strategy for your writing, you make your points by means of the connection plan. Through connecting, you point out relationships between the features of your topic, helping your reader see how they are similar or different.

There are two kinds of connection plans available to you when you compare and contrast. These are (1) the block connection plan, and (2) the point-by-point connection plan.

In order to see the way in which the block plan and the point-by-point plan work, let's take an example from the pages of *Psychology Today*. In a recent issue of that magazine, psychologist Lynne Kahle, Ph.D., observes a new psychological phenomenon, a phenomenon she calls the "psychology of limitations." Kahle observes that the behavior of modern consumers is very different from the behavior of consumers in the past. In drawing up her portrait of the modern consumer, she sets up features to compare and contrast.

Then	**Now**
Value being well-respected	Value self-respect
Money can buy happiness	Money buys quality products
Conspicuous consumption	Unpretentious consumption
Envy of possessions	Satisfied with quality
Possessiveness	Products are means to ends
Nongenerous	May or may not be generous
Expensive means quality	Purchases should be practical
"Lifestyles of the Rich and Famous"	"Consumer Reports"

In the passages which follow, the writer has made use of Kahle's chart. Notice the way the writer organizes this material by either the block plan or the point-by-point plan.

1. In the recent past, consumption was conspicuous. The whole world watched as consumers bought their Cadillacs, their Seiko watches, their beachfront properties. In fact, the figure on the price tag was considered to indicate quality; "you get what you pay for" was the motto of these conspicuous consumers. Underlying these practices were certain assumptions: that being well respected was related to how much money was made and

that how much money was made was an indicator of happiness. Thus, the family with an income in the six figures, a hefty retirement plan, stock options, and a vacation home was the family the neighbors respected. Furthermore, this family was counted entirely happy, for the amount of happiness was directly proportional to the amount of disposable income.

Today, however, consumers disdain such pretensions. They prefer to purchase quietly, privately, out of the public eye, indifferent to brand names and advertising ploys. This more modern consumer understands that price may or may not be an indicator of quality. These consumers have experienced enough broken appliances and automobile recalls to know that things have a way of breaking down—no matter what they cost. The attitudes of these consumers are completely different from their previous counterparts. They reject the notion that money and respect have anything to do with each other, believing that self-respect is a matter of personal honesty and integrity, not personal income. The person who behaves well, not the neighbor who earns the most, is the person who is respected. In addition, this consumer, who understands the limitations of consumption, knows that money doesn't purchase happiness; it purchases only goods and services.

2. In the recent past, consumption was conspicuous. The whole world watched as consumers bought their Cadillacs, their Seiko watches, their beachfront properties. Today, however, consumers disdain such pretensions. They prefer to purchase quietly, privately, out of the public eye, indifferent to brand names and advertising ploys. In addition, consumers in the past considered the figure on the price tag to be an indicator of quality; "you get what you pay for" was their motto. In contrast, more modern consumers understand that price may or may not be an indicator of quality. They have experienced enough broken appliances and automobile recalls to know that things have a way of breaking down—no matter what they cost. Furthermore, the greatest difference between modern consumers and consumers of the past lies in the assumptions on which their practices are based. In the past, it was assumed that being well respected was related to how much money was made. Thus, according to this view, the family with an income in the six figures, a hefty retirement plan, stock options, and a vacation home was the family the neighbors respected. Modern consumers, however, reject the notion that money and respect have anything to do with each other, believing that self-respect is a matter of personal honesty and integrity, not personal income. In this view, the person who behaves well, not the neighbor who earns the most, is the person who is respected. Another difference in attitude is that, in the past, this same wealthy family was assumed to be entirely happy, for wealth was also equated with happiness. Today, the attitude of the modern consumer is completely different from that of his or her previous counterpart. Clearly this consumer, who understands the limitations of consumption, knows that money doesn't purchase happiness; it purchases only goods and services.

Talking About It #191

With your classmates, identify which of the pieces has been developed by the block method and which of the pieces has been developed by the point-by-point method.

With your classmates, chart the features of both the block and the point-by-point plan in an outline.

Describe for each other the technique used in developing a comparison/contrast by either the block plan or the point-by-point plan.

Writing About It #192

Think of a topic suitable for comparison and contrast. Then write two paragraphs, one of which develops the topic by means of the block method, another of which develops the topic by means of the point-by-point method.

Appropriate Transition Words

The comparison-contrast strategy often makes use of special transition words to guide the reader to the connections being made. These special words are as follows:

also	however
although	in contrast
as well	in the same way
be that as it may	likewise
both (neither)	nevertheless
but	on the contrary
even though	on the other hand
both (neither)	similarly
but	whereas
	yet

In the passage which follows, Carol Berkenkotter reports on the findings of researchers Linda S. Flower and John R. Hayes. The investigators have studied the relationship between novice and expert writers and novices and experts in similar problem-solving fields, for example, mathematics, physics, and chess-playing. As you read, note the special transition words used to compare and contrast these findings.

> The findings in all of these areas point to a common conclusion: whether the problem solver is a writer, a musician, a physicist, or a chess player, experts appear to have an arsenal of strategies which will direct them toward a . . . solution. Novices, on the other hand, most often rely on trial and error. A novice chess player, for example, might randomly try a variety of moves in a chess problem; an expert, in contrast, will employ a powerful strategy, such as "try to control the center of the board," drawing from long-term memory a pattern which matches the configuration on the board. Similarly, novice writers when given a composing task will simply begin writing while thinking aloud, hoping for the "right" sentence that will carry them through the whole written draft. Expert writers, like expert chess players, are able to draw strategies from long-term memory which put them in "control of the board." These strategies involve setting and resetting goals, generating ideas, exploring their relationships, and finally connecting them in some kind of analytic framework aimed at a specific reader.

Talking About It #193

With your classmates, identify the special transition words in this passage. What purpose do these transitions serve?

Return to the passages about consumers in the past and consumers in the present written by both the block or the point-by-point plan. Identify the special transition words in each passage. Which passage makes use of more transition words—the passage using the block method or the passage using the point-by-point method? Why?

COMPARISON-CONTRAST IN COMBINATION WITH OTHER STRATEGIES FOR WRITING

When you make use of the comparison-contrast strategy, you point out similarities and differences. You do this by making use of many of the other strategies you have already studied: by describing, providing examples, using facts, giving reasons, telling stories, and employing other methods. In the following passage, the writer is comparing and contrasting dollar bills with dollar coins in order to persuade the reader of the need for the dollar coin.

The U.S. Mint should rethink its position on dollar bills and switch to the manufacturing of dollar coins instead. Most Americans would rather switch to coins than fight the battle that comes with using dollars. Nearly everyone has experienced the frustration of attempting to place a dollar bill in a vending machine only to have the machine reject this wrinkled paper. A dollar coin, on the other hand, won't face that kind of rejection. In addition, old bills often appear unsightly and worn, and, even though they are perfectly good, perfectly legal tender, people are often reluctant to give—or accept—them for purchases. A dollar bill has a life span of no more than 17 months; coins, in contrast, live for at least 30 years. An even stronger reason to favor the coin is the cost savings to the government. The Federal Reserve Board estimates that between $395 and $500 million could be saved each year through the use of dollar coins and their correspondingly lower production costs. Proponents of dollar bills argue that lower costs are irrelevant if nobody uses the dollar coin, citing the miserable failure of the Susan B. Anthony dollar coin as a case in point. However, it is clear that the "Susie B" failed through some serious design flaws: it looked too much like a quarter. A smartly designed new dollar coin could be colored gold, not silver, to distinguish it from other coins and place it squarely in a proud tradition to which it rightly belongs: right up there with the Indian head penny and the Kennedy half dollar.

Talking About It #194

With your classmates, discuss the different strategies—such as descriptions, facts, examples, reasons—that the writer of this comparison/contrast piece makes use of.

A STUDENT USES COMPARISON AND CONTRAST: A FIRST DRAFT

In this first draft of the following comparison-contrast essay, student Julia Hurley, whose military family has lived all over the world, is attempting to write about the differences between Easter as it is celebrated in the United States and Easter as it is celebrated on the island of Cyprus. Julia has shared her early prewriting with her classmates. They responded by freewriting, sketching, or writing purpose statements. She considered their comments as well as her own purposes as she produced a first draft of her comparison-contrast, which follows.

Religion in Cyprus is very important, and Easter is the most religious holiday of the entire year. Forty days before Easter, people go to church every evening. Then three nights before Easter Day, Mass is held at midnight. The priest leads a procession through the streets, blessing everybody. An icon of Jesus Christ is held up. People then kiss the icon and pass under it. At midnight, on the Eve of Easter, people embrace their neighbors and say, "Christos Anesti," which means "Christ has risen"; the reply given is "Alithos Anesti," meaning, "truly he has." Sparklers are then lit, and cannons are fired at dawn to start the holy day.

In the States, more emphasis is placed on dinner, which is traditionally ham, while in Cyprus, two types of cakes are made to portray Easter. The first is called "Flaouna." The second cake is a dry white cake where a penny is placed in the dough; whoever picks the slice with the penny will have good luck for the entire year. This is a very old custom throughout the island. In the States, there is no special dish or tradition that everybody follows. Each community or family has its own little habits.

One thing which is common between the two cultures is the egg and the Easter Bunny. In both Cyprus and the States, people color eggs, but the uses for the eggs are entirely different. In the States, eggs are colored and then hidden so the children must "hunt" for them. Once they are found, they can either be eaten or thrown away. However, in Cyprus, the eggs are taken after the Easter lunch and are cracked in a game. The Easter Bunny and baskets with chocolate eggs are more significant in the States than they are in Cyprus.

Talking About It #195

Critique Julia's draft using the CCARD critique explained in Chapter 6. Recall that the CCARD critique asks you to clarify, connect, add, rearrange, and delete. Try to respond to the following questions as you critique Julia's paper.

1. Where does the writer need to clarify material?
2. Where does the writer need to make connections?
3. Where does the writer need to add more information?
4. Where does the writer need to rearrange the material?
5. Where does the writer need to delete material?

Think about the characteristics of writing that compares and contrasts: (1) appropriate subjects, (2) appropriate features, (3) the connection plan, and (4) appropriate transitions. As a group, try to answer the following questions.

1. Does Julia make use of appropriate subjects for comparison-contrast?
2. Does Julia compare and contrast appropriate features of her subjects? What are these features?
3. Does Julia effectively make use of the connection plan for organizing her work? Does she make use of a block plan or a point-by-point plan? Explain.
4. Does Julia make use of appropriate transition words to link the ideas she is comparing and contrasting?

A STUDENT USES COMPARISON AND CONTRAST: A REVISED DRAFT

Julia listened carefully to her classmates' comments as they critiqued her work. Then she wrote this revised draft in response.

Sometime in early April, spring comes to Cyprus, a tiny Greek island in the Mediterranean Sea where I lived when my father, an Air Force officer, was transferred to the American base there. In Cyprus, spring carries a special freshness in the air. Flowers are awakening; sunsets are displaying their vivid colors. In Cyprus in spring, celebration is in the air, and the holiday that marks the highlight of this time of celebration is the holy day of Easter. Of course, beautiful springs and Easter Sunday arrive in the United States, too. However, the ways in which Easter is celebrated in the United States and on the island of Cyprus are very different.

Unlike the United States, religion in Cyprus is very important, and Easter is the most religious holiday of the entire year. In the United States, Christmas gets most of the religious attention, and Easter is a relatively insignificant holiday by comparison. Many American churches, certainly not all of them, offer Good Friday services at noon, and most worshippers pack the churches on Easter Sunday. However, once the choir stops singing and the Easter lilies are carried away, the American celebration of Easter is essentially over. In contrast, in Cyprus, the religious celebration of Easter is honored for weeks. Forty days before Easter, people go to church every evening. Then three nights before Easter Day, Mass is held at midnight. On this occasion, the churches are so full that people have to stand outside and listen to the ceremony over speakers. Meanwhile, everybody holds candles and prays in the cool spring air. After an hour or so, the priest leads a procession through the streets, blessing everybody. An icon of Jesus Christ is held up. People then kiss the icon and pass under it. At midnight, on the Eve of Easter, people embrace their neighbors and say, "Christos Anesti," which means "Christ has risen"; the reply given is "Alithos Anesti," meaning, "truly he has." Sparklers are then lit, and cannons are fired at dawn to start the holy day. Such an ongoing and emotional celebration of Easter does not occur in the United States.

Another difference between the two countries is seen in the types of food that accompany an Easter celebration. In the States, more emphasis is placed on the Easter dinner. Traditionally this consists of baked ham and a number of side dishes, none of which is a vital part of the Easter tradition. In the States, there is no special dish or tradition that everybody follows. Each community or family has its own little habits. In contrast, in Cyprus, two types of cakes are made to celebrate Easter in a special way. The first is called "Flaouna," which is similar to a dry cheesecake with raisins; it is made into small pies. The second cake is a dry white cake with a penny placed in the dough; whoever picks the slice with the penny will have good luck for the entire year. These penny cakes are a very old custom throughout the island. Thus, traditions surround Easter foods more thoroughly in Cyprus than they do in the United States.

Another difference between Cyprus and the United States involves the way in which the traditional Easter egg is treated by the two cultures. In both Cyprus and the States, people color eggs, but the uses for the eggs are entirely different. In the States, eggs are colored and then hidden so that children must hunt for them. Once they are found, the eggs can either be eaten or thrown away. However, in Cyprus, the eggs are not hidden and hunted. They are taken after the Easter lunch to be cracked in a traditional game. The game requires partners. The eggs of both partners are held in the hand so that only the tip shows. The object is to try to break the other's egg with just one strike. The winner is the person whose egg does not crack. Therefore, an important difference between Easter in Cyprus and Easter in the United States relates to different cultural practices involving the Easter egg.

Differences between cultures abound, but those differences are what makes the world interesting. In terms of religious practices, Easter foods, and practices involving the Easter egg, the celebration of Easter in the United States and of Easter in Cyprus points out the world of difference between the two countries.

Talking About It #196

Julia thought about her own purposes as well as her classmates' critiques when she wrote her revised draft. Talk to your classmates about the specific changes she has made. Do you think her draft has been improved? Why or why not?

WRITING ASSIGNMENTS

Produce some prewriting in response to one of the following topics or a topic of your choosing in preparation for writing a comparison-contrast paper. Remember to profile your reader, define your purpose, and develop some preliminary strategies for content, organization, and expression. It is especially important that you decide whether your comparison-contrast paper will be explanatory or evaluative.

Two bosses you have worked for

Two different sports teams

Two commercials for the same kind of product like perfume, running shoes, toothpaste, etc.

Two characters in a TV show

Two works of art about the same general subject

Two people doing the same kind of work: two doctors, two teachers, two cashiers, two secretaries

Two jobs you have held

Attending a four-year college vs. attending a two-year college

Going to school full time or going to school part time

One possible career in your major vs. another possible career in your major

Choosing a formal wedding v. choosing to elope

Attitudes you held about child-rearing before you had children

Study habits you engaged in before you came to college

Behavior people engaged in before and after they became aware of environmental concerns

Your attitudes toward a controversial subject that have changed over time

Things that are important to you now v. things that were important to you in the past

The past behavior of a close friend or family member as opposed to the present behavior of that same close friend or family member

Make use of this prewriting to write a comparison-contrast essay that demonstrates the characteristics that you have learned about in this chapter: (1) choosing appropriate subjects for comparison-contrast, (2) comparing appropriate features of the chosen subjects, (3) making use of the connection plan through the block or point-by-point method, (4) using special transition words. Assume for purposes of this paper that your reader will be a classmate.

After you have written your first draft, ask your classmates to respond to it. Then rewrite it, making improvements that consider their responses as well as your own purposes. Invite your classmates to critique this next draft. After you have written yet another draft in response to those critiques, ask your classmates to make editing suggestions. Finally, proofread and submit your paper.

Record all responses to the drafts of your paper in the Writing Assessment Profile which appears in the back of this text.

CHAPTER FOURTEEN REVIEW

Writing About It #197

Use your journal to reflect on what you learned in this chapter.

15

Classifying

What does the strategy called "classifying" involve? How can I learn to use it successfully in my writing?

WHAT IS CLASSIFICATION?

Imagine a world in which you enter the library to look for a book only to find the books have been lined up in random order. Or a world in which you wheel your cart through the grocery store to find the products displayed in a haphazard manner. Or a world in which you enter your Chemistry class to engage in a discussion of chemical reactions—without benefit of the periodic table of the elements. Of course this world is only imaginary because the real world could not be run without classification systems. We need them to organize our libraries, our grocery stores, our very knowledge of the world.

You are classifying whenever you sort things into groups or types to make sense of the jumble of the world. Life would be far too confusing without the Library of Congress system of cataloging books, without the phyla describing the animal kingdom, without the yearly calendar for organizing your daily life.

Classification is an aid to understanding. When you classify, you gain a greater appreciation for the similarities and differences among groups. For example, the Motion Picture Association of America's Classification and Ratings System categorizes movies based on categories, for example, G, PG, PG-13, R, and NC-17. Understanding those classifications gives the potential movie viewer a way to predict the level of sex and/or violence in the film and whether or not the film would be suitable for children. Such a classification system serves an important purpose.

READER AND PURPOSE IN CLASSIFICATION

In college, you are often called on to classify things in writing. If your reader is a history professor, you might be asked to look at prerevolutionary France and sort out for discussion the three classes or estates existing at the time: the church, the aristocracy, and the peasants. If your reader is an aeronautical engineering professor, you might be asked to classify the different roles necessary for a successful NASA space mission; in that case, you would attempt to classify the types of workers, for example, scientists, technicians, engineers, astronauts, ground crew, Mission Control specialists, and other groupings that work together to assure a successful space launch. If your reader is an English professor, you might be asked to classify the types of students on campus in order to suggest the variety of people who attend your college; you might begin to write about the part-time students, the athletes, the Greeks, the co-op students, the international students, and various other groups on campus. Each of these classifications would need to shed light for your reader on your general topic: prerevolutionary France, successful space missions, and student groups.

Your purpose is an important force behind the success of a classification paper. In fact, how you decide to classify the subjects under discussion will depend almost entirely on your purpose. Do you want to present your reader with a serious discussion classifying the characteristics of full-time and part-time students on your college campus, or do you want to present your reader with a humorous look at those two categories of students? Do you want to classify textbooks in your school system into groups such as traditional or interactive in order to effect adoption of a particular kind of textbook for the students? Do you want to inform your reader about the important characteristics of the political classifications called Democrat and Republican, or do you want to treat those classifications with scathing sarcasm? Thus, when you use the strategy of classification, your purpose will be very important.

In fact, when you write a paper based on classification, you should plan to devote some significant part of your introduction to explaining your purpose. Explaining your purpose in the introduction will quickly orient your reader to the rationale behind your classification system. In the following excerpt, the author has used classification to discuss the various engineering disciplines. However, an introduction that establishes an orienting purpose has been omitted. As you read it, think about what the author's purpose might have been.

Electrical and electronic engineering is a supercharged field this decade. Jointly it is a broad discipline that includes, among other things, computer software design, cellular communications, artificial intelligence, laser technology, robotics, and biomedical technology. Although some industries that attract huge numbers of EEs are shedding jobs (aerospace, defense, computer manufacturing, telecommunications), the outlook is good because EEs have their fingers in the sockets of leading-edge industries across the economic spectrum.

Mechanical engineering graduates are the general practitioners of the profession and as such have the flexibility to move in and out of thriving job areas as the need arises. A main function of MEs is to design power-producing machines, such as jet engines, as well as power-using machines, such as air-conditioning and drilling equipment. Anti-lock brake systems and upgrading pumps in oil refineries are other ME interests. Manufacturing engineering mechanizes the nation's factories, designing and operating the requisite computers and robots. Industrial engineering is in the same family but focuses on production rather than on design.

Civil engineering will grow as the nation spends billions of dollars tackling our decaying bridges, leaking sewer systems, worn-out roads, and other infrastructure projects. As rebuilding begins, look to state and local governments to create a strong demand for these graduates. The decade opened with a soft job market for civil engineers, but by the time you get out of college, it should be quite good. On college campuses, some civil engineers concentrate on environmental subjects and some even take a degree in the discipline.

Environmental engineering deals with the ever-growing mountains of material we discard, air pollution, ground water contamination, workplace accidents, and exposure to dangerous conditions. As the laws to keep the planet green grow, so do the numbers of environmental engineers. About half go to consulting firms; the rest go to government regulatory agencies or to private industry. Although you can major in environmental engineering, large numbers come into the field from mechanical and chemical engineering. Until supply catches up with demand, this is a white hot field.

In the early 1990s only about half the number of graduates in chemical engineering rolled off the line, compared to the number graduated in the early 1980s. Their dwindling ranks, plus their ability to fill in for petroleum engineers, should keep the job offers coming. CEs chiefly work for chemical manufacturers, oil and gas companies, engineering construction companies, and, to an increasing extent, environmental companies.

Aerospace engineering is in a slump it won't shake quickly. While commercial aerospace is doing well, there are not enough employers to compensate for the dwindling jobs in the defense portion of the industry.

Engineering as a profession looks better at its front door than at its back door. Industry may race after new college graduates, but its treatment of older engineers is brutal. The 45-year-old engineer who loses a job may find it nearly impossible to compete with younger engineers who are paid less. Heaven help the 60-year-old.

A shortage of engineers may or may not develop but there probably won't be a shortage problem. Job descriptions traditionally are elastic; when there aren't enough engineers, technicians do more work. Academic standards are relaxed.

The strength of science and engineering is fundamental to this nation's quality of life. If engineering declines as an attractive career choice, we're all in trouble.

Talking About It #198

With your classmates, attempt to determine the purpose or purposes in the classification passage about engineering. Choose a recorder to write your opinions on the board. Why is a clear purpose important to a successful classification piece?

Writing About It #199

In your journal, attempt to write an introduction to the article about the engineering disciplines. Your introduction should incorporate some of the points you made about purpose in the Talking About It discussion. When you have finished, read your introductions to the other students in your class.

In your journal, jot down some ideas for subjects that might profit from a deeper understanding if explored by the strategy of classification.

SUBJECTIVE CLASSIFICATION

Writers make use of classification to discuss personal, subjective reactions to the world. They may write about their perception of the differences between planners and procrastinators, morning people and night people, the types of waiters or waitresses they have experienced, the types of comic strips they love—or hate.

In the following essay, writer Judith Viorst classifies friendships in order to explore the broader subject of what it means to be a friend.

Women are friends, I once would have said, when they totally love and support and trust each other, and bare to each other the secrets of their souls, and run—no questions asked—to help each other, and tell harsh truths to each other (no, you can't wear that dress unless you lose ten pounds first) when harsh truths must be told.

Women are friends, I would have said, when they share the same affection for Ingmar Bergman, plus train rides, cats, warm rain, charades, Camus, and hate with equal ardor Newark and Brussels sprouts and Lawrence Welk and camping.

In other words, I once would have said that a friend is a friend all the way, but now I believe that's a narrow point of view. For the friendships I have and the friendships I see are conducted at many levels of intensity, serve many different functions, meet different needs and range from those as all-the-way as the friendship of the soul sisters mentioned above to that of the most nonchalant and casual playmates.

Consider these varieties of friendship:

1. Convenience friends. These are the women with whom, if our paths weren't crossing all the time, we'd have no particular reason to be friends: a next-door neighbor, a woman in our car pool, the mother of one of our children's closest friends or maybe some mommy with whom we serve juice and cookies each week at the Glenwood Co-op Nursery.

Convenience friends are convenient indeed. They'll lend us their cups and silverware for a party. They'll drive our kids to soccer when we're sick. They'll take us to pick up our car when we need a lift to the garage. They'll even take our cats when we go on vacation. As we will for them.

But we don't with convenience friends ever come too close or tell too much; we maintain our public face and emotional distance. "Which means," says Elaine, "that I'll talk about being overweight but not about being depressed. Which means I'll admit being mad but not blind with rage. Which means I might say that we're pinched this month but never that I'm worried sick over money."

But which doesn't mean that there isn't sufficient value to be found in these friendships of mutual aid, in convenience friends.

2. Special-interest friends. These friendships aren't intimate, and they needn't involve kids or silverware or cats. Their value lies in some interest jointly shared. And so we may have an office friend or a yoga friend or a tennis friend or a friend from the Women's Democratic Club.

"I've got one woman friend," says Joyce, "who likes, as I do, to take psychology courses. Which makes it nice for me—and nice for her. It's fun to go with someone you know and it's fun to discuss what you've learned, driving back from the classes." And for the most part, she says, that's all they discuss.

"I'd say that what we're doing is *doing* together, not being together," Suzanne says of her Tuesday-doubles friends. "It's mainly a tennis relationship, but we play together well. And I guess we all need to have a couple of playmates."

I agree.

My playmate is a shopping friend, a woman of marvelous taste, a woman who knows exactly *where* to buy *what*, and furthermore is a woman who always knows beyond a doubt what one ought to be buying. I don't have the time to keep up with what's new in eyeshadow, hemlines, and shoes and whether the smock look is in or finished already. But since (oh, shame!) I care a lot about eyeshadow, hemlines and shoes, and since I don't *want* to wear smocks if the smock look is finished, I'm very glad to have a shopping friend.

3. Historical friends. We all have a friend who knew us when . . . maybe way back in Miss Meltzer's second grade, when our family lived in that three-room flat in Brooklyn, when our dad was out of work for seven months, when our brother Allie got in that fight where they had to call the police, when our sister married the endodontist from Yonkers and when, the morning after we lost our virginity, she was the first, the only, friend we told.

The years have gone by and we've gone separate ways and we've little in common now, but we're an intimate part of each other's past. And so whenever we go to Detroit we always go to visit this friend of our girlhood. Who knows how we looked before our teeth were straightened. Who knows how we talked before our voice got unBrooklyned. Who knows what we ate before we learned about artichokes. And who, by her presence, puts us in touch with an earlier part of ourself, a part of ourself it's important never to lose.

"What this friend means to me and what I mean to her," says Grace, "is having a sister without sibling rivalry. We know the texture of each other's lives. She remembers my grandmother's cabbage soup. I remember the way her uncle played the piano. There's simply no other friend who remembers those things."

4. Crossroads friends. Like historical friends, our crossroads friends are important for *what was*—for the friendship we shared at a crucial, now past, time of life. A time, perhaps, when we roomed in college together; or worked as eager young singles in the Big City together; or went together, as my friend Elizabeth and I did, through pregnancy, birth and that scary first year of new motherhood.

Crossroads friends forge powerful links, links strong enough to endure with not much more contact than once-a-year letters at Christmas. And out of respect for those crossroads years, for those dramas and dreams we once shared, we will always be friends.

5. Cross-generational friends. Historical friends and crossroads friends seem to maintain a special kind of intimacy—dormant but always ready to be revived—and though we may rarely meet, whenever we do connect, it's personal and intense. Another kind of intimacy

exists in the friendships that form across generations in what one woman calls her daughter-mother and her mother-daughter relationships.

Evelyn's friend is her mother's age—"but I share so much more than I ever could with my mother"—a woman she talks to of music, of books and of life. "What I get from her is the benefit of her experience. What she gets—and enjoys—from me is a youthful perspective. It's a pleasure for both of us."

I have in my own life a precious friend, a woman of 65 who has lived very hard, who is wise, who listens well; who has been where I am and can help me understand it; and who represents not only an ultimate ideal mother to me but also the person I'd like to be when I grow up.

In our daughter role we tend to do more than our share of self-revelation; in our mother role we tend to receive what's revealed. It's another kind of pleasure—playing wise mother to a questing younger person. It's another very lovely kind of friendship.

6. Part-of-a-couple friends. Some of the women we call our friends we never see alone—we see them as part of a couple at couples' parties. And though we share interests in many things and respect each other's views, we aren't moved to deepen the relationships. Whatever the reason, a lack of time or—and this is more likely—a lack of chemistry, our friendship remains in the context of a group. But the fact that our feeling on seeing each other is always, "I'm *so* glad she's here" and the fact that we spend half the evening talking together says that this too, in its own way, counts as a friendship.

(Other part-of-a-couple friends are the friends that came with the marriage, and some of these are friends we could live without. But sometimes, alas, she married our husband's best friend; and sometimes, alas, she *is* our husband's best friend. And so we find ourself dealing with her, somewhat against our will, in a spirit of what I'll call *reluctant* friendship.)

7. Men who are friends. I wanted to write just of women friends, but the women I've talked to won't let me—they say I must mention man-woman friendships too. For these friendships can be just as close and as dear as those that we form with women. Listen to Lucy's description of one such friendship:

"We've found we have things to talk about that are different from what he talks about with my husband and different from what I talk about with his wife. So sometimes we call on the phone or meet for lunch. There are similar intellectual interests—we always pass on to each other the books that we love—but there's also something tender and caring too."

In a couple of crises, Lucy says, "he offered himself, for talking and for helping. And when someone died in his family he wanted me there. The sexual, flirty part of our friendship is very small, but *some*—just enough to make it fun and different." She thinks—and I agree—that the sexual part, though small is always *some*, is always there when a man and a woman are friends.

It's only in the past few years that I've made friends with men, in the sense of a friendship that's mine, not just part of two couples. And achieving with them the ease and the trust I've found with women friends has value indeed. Under the dryer at home last week, putting on mascara and rouge, I comfortably sat and talked with a fellow named Peter. Peter, I finally decided, could handle the shock of me minus mascara under the dryer. Because we care for each other. Because we're friends.

8. There are medium friends, and pretty good friends, and very good friends indeed, and these friendships are defined by their level of intimacy. And what we'll reveal at each of these levels of intimacy is calibrated with care. We might tell a medium friend, for example,

that yesterday we had a fight with our husband. And we might tell a pretty good friend that this fight with our husband made us so mad that we slept on the couch. And we might tell a very good friend that the reason we got so mad in that fight that we slept on the couch had something to do with that girl who works in his office. But it's only to our very best friends that we're willing to tell all, to tell what's going on with that girl in his office.

The best of friends, I still believe, totally love and support and trust each other, and bare to each other the secrets of their souls, and run—no questions asked—to help each other, and tell harsh truths to each other when they must be told.

But we needn't agree about everything (only 12-year-old girl friends agree about *everything*) to tolerate each other's point of view. To accept without judgment. To give and to take without ever keeping score. And to *be* there, as I am for them and as they are for me, to comfort our sorrows, to celebrate our joys.

Talking About It #200

As you learned earlier in this text, dividing a subject into groups by means of classification can help you understand that subject more deeply. With your classmates, discuss the following questions which related to Judith Viorst's essay:

1. What is the general subject of Viorst's essay? In what specific ways does she use classification in order to discuss this subject? Do the classifications help you understand her general subject in more depth? Why or why not?
2. Reread Viorst's introduction. What is its purpose? Does it help you as a reader in any way? Reread Viorst's conclusion. What is its purpose? Does it help you as a reader in any way?

Take a general topic like "education" or "childhood experiences" or "parents" or "families." Then with your classmates brainstorm these topics on the board. Finally, once you have explored one or several of them in some detail, think of ways of classifying this information in preparation for a future paper.

Writing About It #201

Refer to Judith Viorst's essay on friendship as you attempt to come up with some other categories of friendship in your journal. Use examples of the friends you have known to flesh out your categories.

Use the information you have brainstormed and categorized from the Talking About It section above in order to do some freewriting on the topic of education or childhood experiences or parents or families.

OBJECTIVE CLASSIFICATION

When writers wish to make use of classification in a less personal, more objective manner, they will describe their system of classification from the third person point of view. You can recognize these types of classifications in your geology textbook when you read about the types of rock like sedimentary, igneous, and metamorphic or in your psychology textbook when you read about the types of defense mechanisms such as projection or paranoia or reaction formations. In the following excerpt, the third person point of view is adopted to explain to a reader and potential pig-purchaser about the various types of pigs.

> Pigs have long been the victims of a poor image, reputed to be unclean, unfriendly, and overall, uncouth. Let's face it, their name is reserved for the most despicable of people. Happily for pig owners, none of these rumors is true. Given the chance . . . , pigs may be the cleanest of all farm animals. They even make great pets. They will stand by your side for hours emitting love grunts as you scratch them. Pigs are truly the sweethearts of the barnyard.
>
> With pigs, there is no one outstanding breed. Your choice will be based on personal preference and what is available in your location . . . While certain breeds may have their own advantages and disadvantages, any well-bred pig is suitable for raising and consumption . . . Here are the common breeds of swine:
>
> - *American Landrace*: This swine is the American version of the Danish hog that has made the Danes famous for their fine hams and bacon. They are white or pink with floppy ears and a long, lean body.
> - *Chester White*: A large, white hog with a medium snout and floppy ears.
> - *Hampshire*: This hog is quite popular in the Northeast and quite easy to take care of; it is a good pig for beginners. It is black with erect ears and a white band around the front of the body and fore-legs and, sometimes, white on the rear feet. It is a good hog for southern climates because its darker coloration makes it less susceptible to sunburn.
> - *Yorkshire*: This is a very popular breed and easy to keep. Yorkshires are pink or white, sometimes with black spots, and have erect ears. This is the best breed . . . if you plan to go into breeding because they have large litters and are good mothers.

CHARACTERISTICS OF CLASSIFICATION

Classification, like the other strategies for writing you have studied, demonstrates certain characteristic features. In order to make sure that your classification papers succeed, try to remember the following points:

1. Classification requires a clear principle or basis for grouping.
2. Classification makes use of convincing support.
3. Classification makes use of an organization based on the connection plan.
4. Classification employs appropriate transitions.

A Clear Principle for Grouping

A classification requires a rationale. When you have articulated clear principles for grouping, you are well on your way to a convincing classification system.

Will you classify cars based on the principle of fuel efficiency? Or safety? Or stylistic features? These decisions, of course, will largely depend on your purpose.

Your purpose and your ability to provide a clear basis for grouping are closely related. It's important that you spend some time early in the writing process thinking about your own purposes. Do you want to arrange elements of a teenager's diet into appropriate food groups like breads, proteins, and dairy products in order to inform teens about the elements of a sound diet? Or do you wish to group these foods in order to persuade growing teenagers that a certain diet is better suited to teenagers than to adults? Do you want to tell your readers about the different categories of rock music so that they are informed about the choices available to them when they enter the record store? Or do you want to persuade those readers that a certain type of music is more enjoyable than another? Such questions regarding purpose will help you generate sound principles for grouping.

It's also important that your groupings are made clear to your reader. It's not very helpful if the categories overlap each other, for the reader may become confused. If overlap does occur, the overlap must be explained or the system must be adjusted. For example, could Viorst's classifications of friends also include relatives? Because it's important to keep category boundaries clear, classifications are sometimes numbered, as in the Judith Viorst article about friendship; sometimes they are set off by different type or by typographical "bullets" as in the article about pigs which you have read. Such graphic features are not required, but they do help keep the writer's groups separate from each other, thus promoting understanding in the reader. If you decide that numbering or bulleting or using graphic features will help your reader, these are legitimate techniques at your disposal.

In addition, in formulating your features or groupings, it often helps for you to think about whether you are writing a two-part classification or a classification based on three or more groups. If you choose a two-part classification, you typically discuss a single factor that distinguishes two groups. For instance, a classification discussing the two categories of people called introverts and extroverts might be arranged around the single factor that distinguishes them: their sociability. On the other hand, a classification involving more than two groups might make use of additional subcategories in order to provide a thorough understanding for your reader. For example, a classification paper grouping colleges as either expensive, middle-range or relatively inexpensive might consider factors in addition to outright costs in order to explore the subject of the price of a college education in depth. Such a classification might need to account for opportunities for campus employment, financial aid practices, the availability of internship programs and other factors that impinge on overall cost. Thus, in looking at the features you must isolate in order to classify effectively, it's often helpful to understand whether your classification system is made up of either two-part or multipart groupings.

Once your purpose has been clarified and your groups established, then you can make the basic features of your classification scheme clear to your reader by writing an effective introduction. In the following paragraph from "The Three New Yorks," writer E.B. White introduces his essay by making the basic features of his classification very clear—right from the start:

> There are roughly three New Yorks. There is, first, the New York of the man or woman who was born here, who takes the city for granted and accepts its size and its turbulence as natural and inevitable. Second, there is the New York of the commuter—the city that is devoured by locusts each day and spat out each night. Third, there is the New York of the person who was born somewhere else and came to New York in quest of something.

A clear principle for grouping requires thought on your part. You must look at the ways in which a subject can be divided. You must account for inconsistencies. You must figure out your purpose. You must determine the needs of your reader. In writing a classification paper, you must take many things into account. However, once you do, you are well on your way to writing a satisfactory paper based on classification.

Convincing Support

As in the other strategies for writing which you have studied, thorough support for your ideas is important. You must support your groupings using facts, examples, reasons, descriptions and any other techniques at your disposal.

In the following essay called "The Plot Against People," writer Russell Baker makes use of convincing support to defend his thesis that inanimate objects exist to "defeat (people)," offering three categories of objects to justify his belief.

> Inanimate objects are classified into three major categories—those that don't work, those that break down and those that get lost.
>
> The goal of all inanimate objects is to resist man and ultimately to defeat him, and the three major classifications are based on the method each object uses to achieve its purpose. As a general rule, any object capable of breaking down at the moment when it is most needed will do so. The automobile is typical of the category.
>
> With the cunning typical of its breed, the automobile never breaks down while entering a filling station with a large staff of idle mechanics. It waits until it reaches a downtown intersection in the middle of the rush hour, or until it is fully loaded with family and luggage on the Ohio Turnpike.
>
> Thus it creates maximum misery, inconvenience, frustration and irritability among its human cargo, thereby reducing its owner's life span.
>
> Washing machines, garbage disposals, lawn mowers, light bulbs, automatic laundry dryers, water pipes, furnaces, electrical fuses, television tubes, hose nozzles, tape recorders, slide projectors—all are in league with the automobile to take their turn at breaking down whenever life threatens to flow smoothly for their human enemies.

Many inanimate objects, of course, find it extremely difficult to break down. Pliers, for example, and gloves and keys are almost totally incapable of breaking down. Therefore, they have had to evolve a different technique for resisting man.

They get lost. Science has still not solved the mystery of how they do it, and no man has ever caught one of them in the act of getting lost. The most plausible theory is that they have developed a secret method of locomotion which they are able to conceal the instant a human eye falls upon them.

It is not uncommon for a pair of pliers to climb all the way from the cellar to the attic in its single-minded determination to raise its owner's blood pressure. Keys have been known to burrow three feet under mattresses. Women's purses, despite their great weight, frequently travel through six or seven rooms to find hiding space under a couch.

Scientists have been struck by the fact that things that break down virtually never get lost, while things that get lost hardly ever break down.

A furnace, for example, will invariably break down at the depth of the first winter cold wave, but it will never get lost. A woman's purse, which after all does have some inherent capacity for breaking down, hardly ever does; it almost invariably chooses to get lost.

Some persons believe this constitutes evidence that inanimate objects are not entirely hostile to man, and that a negotiated peace is possible. After all, they point out, a furnace could infuriate a man even more thoroughly by getting lost than by breaking down, just as a glove could upset him far more by breaking down than by getting lost.

Not everyone agrees, however, that this indicates a conciliatory attitude among inanimate objects. Many say it merely proves that furnaces, gloves and pliers are incredibly stupid.

The third class of objects—those that don't work—is the most curious of all. These include such objects as barometers, car clocks, cigarette lighters, flashlights, and toy train locomotives. It is inaccurate, of course, to say that they never work. They work once, usually for the first few hours after being brought home, and then quit. Thereafter, they never work again.

In fact, it is widely assumed that they are built for the purpose of not working. Some people have reached advanced ages without ever seeing some of these objects—barometers, for example—in working order.

Science is utterly baffled by the entire category. There are many theories about it. The most interesting holds that the things that don't work have attained the highest state possible for an inanimate object, the state to which things that break down and things that get lost can still only aspire.

They have truly defeated man by conditioning him never to expect anything of them, and in return they have given man the only peace he receives from inanimate society. He does not expect his barometer to work, his electric locomotive to run, his cigarette lighter to light or his flashlight to illuminate, and when they don't, it does not raise his blood pressure.

He cannot attain that peace with furnaces and keys and cars and women's purses as long as he demands they work for their keep.

Talking About It #202

With your classmates, discuss the classification scheme Baker has made use of. What is his purpose in writing this essay? How has he grouped his subject? Does he make the groupings clear to you? How? Has Baker provided convincing support for his ideas? Explain.

The Connection Plan

Writers using the strategy of classification often make use of the connection plan for organizing this material. Rather than simply collecting ideas, the writer of a classification essay needs to detail connections or relationships between the various groupings. Often, the writer must point out similarities or differences, or explain inconsistencies or contradictions. Using the connection plan, the writer moves between his or her thesis and his or her categories and back and forth within and among categories to establish ideas. Sometimes it is helpful to make a chart to organize the ideas within categories. An arrangement that lists Category 1, Category 2, Category 3, and so forth as well as the supporting details that relate to each category can often help you keep track of the material you are trying to connect.

Talking About It #203

With your classmates, discuss the way Russell Baker connects his ideas using the connection plan. Find specific examples of the way in which he moves back and forth among and within his categories. Find specific examples of the way in which he attempts to explain contradictions or inconsistencies in his categories.

Together generate a chart of Baker's categories that might help to organize a classification paper. Then list the details or features that might be used to support each category.

Appropriate Transition Words

As in the other strategies you have studied, classification also makes use of special transition words for connecting ideas. Some of these words appear in the following list.

above all	however
also	if
as a result	in addition
because	in contrast
besides	in fact
but	likewise
certainly	no doubt
consequently	of course
especially	on the other hand
first (second, third, etc.)	perhaps

for example	similarly
for instance	since
for one thing	therefore
granted that	thus

Talking About It #204

Look back over the Viorst piece and the Baker piece to identify transitions used by the authors.

CLASSIFICATION IN COMBINATION WITH OTHER STRATEGIES FOR WRITING

As in the other strategies for writing you have studied, classification makes use of descriptions, examples, facts, reasons, comparisons, contrasts, and other techniques to accomplish its purposes. The following essay by writer Jami Bernard of the *New York Daily News* takes a look at the ideas of romance that abound in American musicals.

Disney's *Snow White and the Seven Dwarfs* is back in theaters—as it has been every few years since it was made in 1937—just in time to mess up a new generation of little girls.

What could be so subversive in this charmingly rendered animated fable? Is it the theme of rivalry between daughter and evil stepmother? Is it the anxiety over eating nonorganically grown apples?

No—it's that darn song, *Someday My Prince Will Come*, eminently hummable, ennobling the virtues of passivity and pre-determined happy endings. Snow White doesn't have to kiss a lot of toads before finding her prince (although she does kiss all seven dwarfs on their bald pates, heigh-ho). She has merely to wait prettily, because someday her prince will come, someday she'll find her love.

That song sets up little girls for a lifetime of feverish romantic expectations that don't easily mix with the jungle out there that is the modern dating scene.

The romantic songs that women sing in movie musicals have always had a profound effect on their target audience—impressionable girls who learn to sigh with yearning before they are old enough to understand just what it is that awaits them somewhere over the rainbow.

Smart women, foolish love songs. Here are some of the ideas women harbor about romance, and here are the memorable movie songs that gave them grist for the mill:

Passive Love: Someday My Prince Will Come, etc. Future romantic happiness is your birthright (are we not all princesses?) if you wait patiently for the right guy to awaken your senses with a kiss. While waiting, lie there like a lump; nothing more is required of you until it's time to choose the bridesmaids' color scheme.

Virtuous Restraint: When heartbreak gets you down, it is time to gird your loins against men. Here's the advice from *Flower Drum Song* (1961), as if it fools anyone: "Love, look away, love, look away from me. Fly when you pass my door. Fly and get lost at sea!"

Transformational Love: Ann-Margret in *Bye Bye Birdie* (1963), wearing capri pants and a midriff blouse as if expecting trouble, and hoping to ride off into sexual awakening on the back of an Elvis clone's motorcycle: "Drink champagne as though it were water . . . daddy dear, you won't know your daughter! I've got a lotta livin' to do!"

Noble Suffering: Just as surely as fish gotta swim and birds gotta fly, "I'm gonna love one man till I die, can't help lovin' dat man of mine," as per *Show Boat* (1951). Not only that, but "He can come home as late as can be, home without him ain't no home for me." This is the theory of love as endurance test.

Hygienic Love: Man trouble is nothing that a little styling mousse can't solve in *South Pacific* (1958). "I'm gonna wash that man right outta my hair"—repeat twice—"and send him on his way!" The trouble is that once you have found him, you never let him go.

But hey, what's love got to do with it?

Talking About It #205

What other strategies for writing—in addition to classification—does Bernard employ in this essay? Can you point to facts, descriptions, illustrations, or other techniques for conveying her ideas about music and romance?

With your classmates, identify several modern songs that support Bernard's categories—in addition to the musical songs identified in the piece.

With your classmates, brainstorm a long list of modern songs dealing with love. Identify different categories from those identified by Bernard and suggest the songs that support those categories.

With your classmates, brainstorm a long list of popular songs dealing with subjects *other* than romance. Try to identify different categories for classifying their subject matter.

Writing About It #206

Choose some of the categories you developed in Talking About It #205—or any other categories on subjects that interest you—and write a classification paper based on them.

A STUDENT USES CLASSIFICATION: A FIRST DRAFT

In the early draft of the following classification essay, student Kelly Kuhn is attempting to use classification to group the various roles which a babysitter plays. Kelly has shared her early prewriting with her classmates. They responded by freewriting, sketching, or writing purpose statements. She considered their comments as well as her own purposes as she produced the first draft of her classification, which follows.

When one assumes the role of a babysitter, one must play a variety of roles.

One of the more obvious responsibilities of a babysitter is acting as a parental source of love. Children need to feel secure because their parents have left them in the care of a stranger.

After one has gained the children's trust, the children often begin to confide their problems, and a babysitter must act as a psychologist. Problems may need to be talked about with a nonfamily member who is closer to the children's own ages.

Children love playing games, and a babysitter must be ready to mediate in another role—as referee. In order to avoid fights, the sitter must be prepared to make fair decisions.

Even in play, children get hurt, and a babysitter needs to know basic nursing skills. A sitter should be able to treat minor injuries so the children's health is never in danger.

Planning healthy meals for finicky eaters is the role of a nutritionist. Serving children easy to prepare, well-balanced meals is important.

Eventually, the children are put in bed and fall asleep. The babysitter then becomes a housekeeper. All of the messes the children make must be cleaned and toys put away.

The babysitter must never be so involved in one role that the part of security officer is overlooked. The children's safety is all-important, and a sitter is responsible for their protection. The number of the police department should be kept by the phone in case of an emergency.

Invariably, outsiders will telephone or come to the door and a babysitter must serve as the receptionist. Messages must be clear and complete so that the parents are able to return them.

Thus, being a babysitter requires the flexibility to assume many roles.

Talking About It #207

Critique Kelly's draft using the point/support technique explained in Chapter 6. Recall that the point/support critique asks you to identify the points made by the thesis statement and the topic sentences and then identify the support offered for each of these. Try to respond to the following questions as you critique Kelly's paper:

1. What is the point embodied in Kelly's thesis? Is there an interesting introduction to the paper which leads to the thesis?
2. What are the topic sentences which support the thesis?
3. What evidence is used to support each topic sentence? Is the evidence interesting? Is it sufficient?
4. What is Kelly's conclusion? Does it adequately sum up the paper?
5. What does Kelly need to do when she revises this draft in order to produce a more interesting paper?

Think about the characteristics of writing that make use of classification: (1) a clear principle or basis for grouping, (2) convincing support, (3) a connection plan, (4) appropriate transitions. As a group, try to answer the following questions.

1. Does Kelly make use of a clear principle or basis for grouping? What is her purpose? Is it clear? Does she use a two-part or multipart system for classifying?
2. What are the categories Kelly chooses to explore her topic? Does Kelly offer convincing support for each of her categories? Why or why not?
3. Does Kelly make use of a connection plan? How do you know? Does she explain how any of her categories overlap or account for any inconsistencies?
4. Does Kelly make use of appropriate transitions to explain and connect her ideas?

A STUDENT USES CLASSIFICATION: A REVISED DRAFT

Kelly listened carefully to her fellow classmates' comments as they critiqued her work. Then she wrote this revised draft in response.

Jean-Paul Sartre, a French philosopher, explained that as we go through life, we play many different roles. Our definition of who we are depends on what role we are playing at that moment. Some roles are more complex than others, however. The role of a babysitter, for example, requires a sitter to assume a number of roles. She must be a parental substitute, a recreation director, a health professional, and a housekeeper.

One of the most obvious roles of a babysitter is acting as a parental substitute. In this role, the sitter offers the children love, helping them feel secure when their parents have left them in the care of a stranger. However, the sitter isn't simply given love; she must earn it. By offering words of encouragement, reading stories, and speaking kindly to the children, she eventually earns the children's love. In time, the children will seek hugs from the caregiver, asking to be tucked into bed and requesting a good-night kiss. When a sitter performs these actions, she is acting in the role of parental substitute, and the children forget their parents are gone.

Another role closely associated with the parent substitute role is that of psychologist. After gaining the trust of the children, the sitter might find that they begin to confide their problems, and a babysitter learns to listen like a psychologist. Problems at school or with siblings may simply need to be talked about with a nonfamily member who is closer to the children's own ages. More serious problems of physical or mental abuse and neglect require special attention and even outside help.

A second role which a babysitter must assume is that of recreation director. Children love playing games, and a babysitter must be ready to suggest and participate. She ought to be able to suggest team sports like kickball with the neighborhood children, softball in the backyard, and volleyball with a clothesline as a makeshift volleyball net. She also should know age-appropriate games. A skilled recreation director must know that a four-year-old likes to play tag, that a six-year-old likes jumping rope, and that a ten-year-old likes tetherball. Closely related to the role of recreation director is that of referee. Children often don't know the rules of a game or are tempted to cheat. In order to avoid fights, the sitter-referee must be prepared to decide which rules apply or to mediate arguments with swift justice. She should know that the age differences between children sometimes give an unfair advantage to one of them. As referee, the sitter should decide if the rules need to be modified or an advantage given to one child in order to make the game fair to all. Thus, recreation director and referee are closely allied roles.

Another clear role that a babysitter plays is that of health professional. Even in play, children get hurt, and a babysitter needs to know basic nursing skills as she plays the role of nurse. Sometimes a bruise may simply need to be kissed. Often a scratch may need to be cleaned and a band-aid applied. A more serious injury may need a doctor's attention. (The number where the parents can be reached, therefore, should be placed beside the phone in case of an emergency.) A sitter should be able to treat minor injuries so the children's health is never in danger. In addition, a sitter in the role of health provider must act as a nutritionist as well as a nurse. She must plan healthy meals for the most finicky of eaters. The meals must be easy to prepare and well-balanced. The sitter/nutritionist must deal competently with the question of snacks. Should the children be given any snacks at all? What is a healthy snack? Are there any food allergies that must be taken into account? In addition to the role of nutritionist, another role related to that of health provider is that of hygienist. Although a babysitter in the role of nurse takes care of specific injuries and illnesses and a babysitter in the role of nutritionist takes care of specific food issues, as a hygienist a babysitter provides for general matters of hygiene. Thus, she makes sure that the children have clean hands and faces before and after eating. She also makes sure the children have brushed their teeth and washed their faces before going to bed. Sometimes parents ask for the children to be given a bath, another basic hygiene practice. Thus, the role of health professional is a multifaceted one.

Another role assumed by every babysitter is that of housekeeper. Part of the job of keeping house well involves keeping a house secure. The children's safety is all-important, and a sitter-housekeeper is responsible for their protection. She should make sure all doors and windows are securely locked. She should listen for outside noises and investigate unusual circumstances. She should keep the number of the police department by the phone in case of an emergency. Another part of keeping house involves serving as a kind of receptionist. Invariably, outsiders telephone or come to the door, and a babysitter must know how to handle them. There should be a clear understanding between the sitter and parents about who should be told that the parents are gone. Messages must be clear and complete so that the parents are able to return them. Another part of the housekeeper role comes into play after the children are put into bed and fall asleep. As a housekeeper, the babysitter cleans up the messes the children have made and puts their toys away. She does the dishes and the kind of light straightening up that is appreciated by tired parents. In such ways, the babysitter fulfills the role of housekeeper.

Parental substitute, recreation director, health professional, and housekeeper: these are some of the major roles a babysitter fills. There are minor roles, however, which a babysitter must also serve. These are roles like warden, teacher, even zoologist. In fact, the roles and responsibilities of a good babysitter may seem endless; however, it is this constant juggling of roles that makes babysitting such an enjoyable and challenging job.

Talking About It #208

Kelly thought about her own purposes as well as her classmates' critiques when she wrote her revised draft. Talk to your classmates about the specific changes she has made. Do you think her draft has been improved? Why or why not?

Think about the characteristics of writing that make use of classification: (1) a clear principle for grouping, (2) convincing support, (3) organization based on the connection plan, (4) appropriate transitions. As a group, discuss the ways in which Kelly's revision now more clearly displays these characteristics.

WRITING ASSIGNMENTS

Produce some prewriting in response to one of the following topics or a topic of your choosing in preparation for writing a classification paper. Remember to profile your reader, define your purpose, and develop some preliminary strategies for content, organization, and expression.

Comic strips

Magazines targeted for a certain type of reader (women's magazines, sports magazines, children's magazines, health and/or nutrition magazines, etc.)

Newspaper columns of a certain type (advice, political, horoscopes, business, gardening, home improvement, etc.)

Rock groups

Classified advertisements

Movies

Books

Sports fans

Names (birth names, nicknames, family names, etc.)

Parents

Families

Education

Cars

Friends

Teachers

Make use of this prewriting to write a classification essay that demonstrates the characteristics you have learned about in this chapter: (1) a clear principle or basis for grouping, (2) convincing support, (3) a connection plan, (4) appropriate transitions. Assume for purposes of this paper that your reader will be a fellow classmate.

After you have written your first draft, ask your classmates to respond to it. Then rewrite it, making improvements that consider their responses as well as your own purposes. Invite your classmates to critique this next draft. After you have written yet another draft in response to those critiques, ask your classmates to make editing suggestions. Finally, proofread and submit your paper.

Record all responses to the drafts of your paper in the Writing Assessment Profile which appears in the back of this text.

CHAPTER FIFTEEN REVIEW

Writing About It #209

Use your journal to reflect on what you learned in this chapter.

16
Analyzing

What are the characteristics of analysis?
How can I use them to improve my writing?

WHAT IS ANALYSIS?

It's a cold, wintry morning, and you've finished your cereal, straightened your apartment, and grabbed your books, intent on getting to class. You head for your car, snap on the seat belt, and turn your key in the ignition. Nothing happens. You try again. No result. At that point, the point at which you are challenged to break down an issue in order to understand it, you are engaged in the strategy called *analysis*.

Turning the key in the ignition once again, you begin to analyze what you know about the system for starting a car. Do you have enough gas in the gas tank? Could it be the starter? Is your battery dead? Fortunately for you, a college friend with a jumper cable lives in the next apartment complex. You call him, and he connects the wires and cables between his battery and yours. Gratefully, you hear the comforting sound of your engine kicking over, and you make it to class on time with only seconds to spare. Your ability to analyze has paid off for you.

Analysis is concerned with relationships and looks at those concerns in a special way. When you analyze, you divide things into parts, probing the way the parts in a system relate to each other to make up the whole. For instance, in figuring out why your car wouldn't start, you divided what you knew about the starting mechanism of a car, breaking your information down into working parts like the gas tank, the battery, and the ignition. A computer technician facing a malfunctioning computer would similarly have to understand how the parts were related to the whole in order to analyze the current problem with the system. A teacher faced with a student doing poorly in his or her class would have to understand the relationships inherent in the classroom situation in order to analyze whether the learning problem stemmed from the student, the curriculum, the teaching style, the classroom setting, or some combination of these system components.

People employ analysis to understand situations every day. Your professor analyzes the goals of his or her physics course, including them for you in his or her course syllabus. Your sister, who works as a dietitian in a local hospital, analyzes the nutritional needs of the diabetic patients on the ward in order to create a proper diet for them. Your brother analyzes the job description for an internship advertised through his campus employment office, deciding on the basis of his analysis whether or not he might qualify for the job. Your Aunt Dorothy samples a new chicken entree in a local restaurant and then tries to analyze the ingredients so that she can duplicate it at home. You analyze your reader and your purpose before you begin to write the sociology paper which has recently been assigned in order to produce a work that will be satisfying to you and to your professor. Thus, analysis is a strategy people make use of all the time.

Analysis is a skill you will be called on again and again in college, for analysis helps you understand the nature of things, their function and their structure. When you analyze a poem, an architectural design, a painting, a musical performance, a social problem, a laboratory observation, a historical movement, a business challenge, or any other topic, you break it down into manageable parts in order to understand.

SUBJECTIVE ANALYSIS

Sometimes students will be asked to analyze an issue or problem or situation from a personal perspective. They may be asked to analyze the experiences affecting their success at college, to analyze the factors contributing to a productivity problem at work, to analyze why their tennis swing is off. Such analyses require the first person or subjective point of view. In the following essay, student Brian Sotire uses analysis to understand something very important to him: his golf game.

I am a golf-aholic. I admit it. I live, breathe, eat, and sleep golf, and I've done so for years. When I was a child, my Dad used to buy a bucket of balls and take me out for an afternoon at the local driving range. As a teenager, I caddied at the country club in town, often substituting for a player who hadn't shown up. In high school, I earned a letter in golf after my sophomore year. But golf is not an easy sport. I have learned from experience that only 90% of all golfers can break 100 in 18 holes and that being in that top 10%, my ultimate goal, depends on two things: patience and practice.

Years ago I learned that perfecting my golf game required patience. The golf swing is very complex; even a small mistake caused me to hit a bad shot. For instance, I had a bad habit that required patience to break. I was swinging my club perfectly, but right before hitting the ball, I would lift my head. Consequently, I didn't hit the ball flush, and the shot didn't go very far. In addition, when I was a younger player, my lack of patience affected my golf game. If I made a mistake on the course, I immediately got angry, and my whole game collapsed. When I got angry, my muscles tensed up, my golf swing was off, and, worst of all, my concentration was destroyed. As I practiced patience in controlling my anger, my golf game improved.

Practice has been another key to improving my golf game. Through practice, practice, practice, I learned to drive the ball off the tee, hit the ball out of the fairway or rough, chip a ball onto the green, and putt the ball on the green into the hole. It was never easy, but there was no way around practicing. In addition, I found that practicing with a purpose resulted in the greatest benefits for me. For example, when I wanted to improve my putting, I began by putting balls close to a hole and then working to sink the putts in consistently. Once that purpose had been accomplished, I moved the ball farther away from the hole and practiced longer putts. Practicing in this purposeful way helped me build consistency and minimize mistakes.

Golf looks easy when you look at Arnold Palmer or Lee Trevino on TV. When you look at me on the local links, you're looking at a golfer who has improved his game only through patience and practice.

Talking About It #210

Refer to Brian Sotire's essay about his golf game as you discuss the following questions with your classmates.

1. How has Brian used analysis in writing this essay? Is the analysis made clear in a thesis statement? Is the analysis carried out through topic sentences?
2. Why is this a subjective analysis? What would Brian have to do to turn this into an objective analysis?
3. Choose a recorder and brainstorm some possible topics for analysis, breaking down those topics into their component parts. You might like to begin with the following suggestions for analysis: the diet of a college student, the factors leading to success in a particular course, the challenges facing students in a particular major.

Writing About It #211

Think about some of the topics you have brainstormed using analysis. Then freewrite for a page or two in your journal on any one of them.

OBJECTIVE ANALYSIS

In college, it is very likely that you will use the strategy of analysis in a number of your classes. You may be asked to analyze the political situation in Eastern Europe following the dismantling of the Berlin Wall, the chemical elements in a laboratory solution, the factors in a successful marketing strategy, the themes in a musical symphony. In these and similar situations, your professor would expect your analysis to be presented from the third person objective point of view.

In the following excerpt, Jacqueline Berke uses analysis to explain what she means by "The Qualities of Good Writing."

The first quality of good writing is *economy*. In an appropriately slender volume entitled *The Elements of Style*, authors William Strunk and E.B. White stated concisely the case for economy: "A sentence should contain no unnecessary words, a paragraph no unnecessary sentences, for the same reason that a drawing should have no unnecessary lines and a machine no unnecessary parts. This requires not that the writer make all his sentences short or that he avoid all detail . . . but that every word tell." In other words, economical writing is *efficient* and *aesthetically satisfying*. While it makes a minimum demand on the energy and patience of readers, it returns to them a maximum of sharply compressed meaning. You should accept this as your basic responsibility as a writer: that you inflict no unnecessary words on your readers—just as a dentist inflicts no unnecessary pain, a lawyer no unnecessary risk. Economical writing avoids strain and at the same time promotes pleasure by producing a sense of form and right proportion, a sense of words that fit the ideas that they embody—with not a line of "deadwood" to dull the reader's attention, not an extra, useless phrase to clog the free flow of ideas, one following swiftly and clearly upon another.

Another basic quality of good writing is *simplicity*. Here again this does not require that you make all your sentences primerlike or that you reduce complexities to bare bone, but rather that you avoid embellishment or embroidery. The natural, unpretentious style is best. But, paradoxically, simplicity or naturalness does not come naturally. By the time we are old enough to write, most of us have grown so self-conscious that we stiffen, sometimes to the point of rigidity, when we are called upon to make a statement in speech or in writing. It is easy to offer the kindly advice "Be yourself," but many people do not feel like themselves when they take a pencil in hand or sit down at a typewriter. Thus during the early days of the Second World War, when air raids were feared in New York City, and blackouts were instituted, an anonymous writer—probably a young civil service worker at City Hall—produced and distributed to stores throughout the city the following poster:

Illumination
is Required
to be
Extinguished
on These Premises
After Nightfall

What this meant, of course, was simply "Lights Out After Dark"; but apparently that direct imperative—clear and to the point—did not sound "official" enough; so the writer resorted to long Latinate words and involved syntax (note the awkward passives "is *Required*" and "to be *Extinguished*") to establish a tone of dignity and authority. In contrast, how beautifully simple are the words of the translators of the King James Version of the Bible, who felt no need for flourish, flamboyance, or grandiloquence. The Lord did not loftily or bombastically proclaim that universal illumination was required to be instantaneously installed.

Simply but majestically "God said, Let there be light: and there was light. . . . And God called the light Day, and the darkness he called Night."

Most memorable declarations have been spare and direct. Abraham Lincoln and John Kennedy seemed to "speak to each other across the span of a century," notes French author Andre Maurois, for both men embodied noble themes in eloquently simple terms. Said Lincoln in his second Inaugural Address: "With malice towards none, with charity for all, with firmness in the right as God gives us the right, let us strive on to finish the work we are in . . ." One hundred years later President Kennedy made his Inaugural dedication: "With a good conscience our only sure reward, with history the final judge of our deeds, let us go forth to lead the land we love. . . . "

A third fundamental element of good writing is *clarity*. Some people question whether it is always possible to be clear; after all, certain ideas are inherently complicated and inescapably difficult. True enough. But the responsible writer recognizes that writing should not add to the complications nor increase the difficulty; it should not set up an additional roadblock to understanding. Indeed, the German philosopher Wittgenstein went so far as to say that "whatever can be said can be said clearly." If you understand your own idea and want to convey it to others, you are obliged to render it in clear, orderly, readable, understandable prose—else why bother writing in the first place? Actually, obscure writers are usually confused, uncertain of what they want to say or what they mean; they have not yet completed that process of thinking through and reasoning into the heart of the subject . . .

Talking About It #212

With your classmates, discuss the following questions about Berke's essay.

1. How does Berke use analysis to break down her topic: the qualities of good writing?
2. What other strategies does Berke use to support her ideas?
3. Do you agree with Berke's analysis? Would you add other qualities? Delete any of hers?

Writing About It #213

In your journal, discuss whether you agree or disagree with Berke's three qualities of good writing. Give reasons, examples, or other information to support your view.

Write out your own analysis of "the qualities of good writing." Support your analysis in detail from your experiences as a writer and a reader.

READER AND PURPOSE IN ANALYSIS

Readers analyze differently. Their analysis invariably depends on their own perspective. For example, if a downturn in the economy occurs, a reader who is an economist might be interested in analyzing the market forces behind the slump; a reader who is a sociologist might attempt to analyze the social consequences of the change; and a reader who is a psychologist might want to analyze the psychological consequences of the event. As a writer, it will be important for you to understand the likely perspective of your reader in order to produce an analysis that responds to his or her orientation.

In addition, how you analyze will also depend on your own purposes as a writer. For instance, let's say your literature professor has asked you to analyze a particular poem. How you choose to analyze will depend on your purpose. Will you analyze the poem based on its use of poetical devices such as alliteration and metaphor and meter and form? Or will you analyze its themes in order to suggest the ways in which it reflects the poet's philosophy? Thus, how you define your purpose will affect how you approach your analysis.

In addition, in considering your reader and your purpose, it is helpful to remember to keep your analysis sufficiently manageable. Often students attempt to analyze an idea that is too complex or too broad to tackle in the course of a short paper. For instance, if a student attempted to analyze the broad problem of homelessness, he or she might find that dealing with contributing factors like illiteracy, the lack of low income housing, drug abuse, economic forces, unemployment, human service policies, and other issues. Handling so many issues would make it difficult to do justice to the topic in the course of a typical paper. This student might want to analyze just one of those factors in order to manage the analysis more successfully.

CHARACTERISTICS OF ANALYSIS

You should become familiar with the characteristics of analysis, discussed in the section that follows, in order to assure that the analyses you write are clear and convincing. Analysis seeks to attain these goals:

1. Analysis makes use of clear divisions or parts.
2. Analysis employs convincing support.
3. Analysis is organized with the connection plan.
4. Analysis makes use of appropriate transitions.

Clear Divisions or Parts

Because analyzing a work requires you to understand a subject more deeply by dividing it into parts, those parts or divisions must be made clear to your reader. The divisions must also be kept separate from one another; they should not overlap. Keeping your divisions clear and separate will keep your reader from becoming confused.

In the following passage, writer and artist Bill Tilton uses analysis to help his reader identify and solve the problems artists often encounter in using space effectively.

Space

A too-shallow picture plane is a . . . common weakness . . . in many works. Achieving a believable impression of depth on a two-dimensional surface is one of the primary challenges you face. The first requirement for success is good drawing skills—specifically, the ability to depict mass, shape and form convincingly. You also need to consider the placement of objects and know how to use light and shadow, how to manipulate values and edges, and how to capitalize on advancing and receding color. Here are some tips that may help you tackle space:

Placing shapes. You can create a certain degree of depth just by overlapping the shapes in your drawing so that some are clearly in front of or behind others. Putting objects on an angle—instead of a straight-on or profile view—provides another opportunity to show depth. Consider a house portrait and the difference in perspective between a full-front view that shows a single, flat facade, and a three-quarter view that includes the side of the house.

Adding light and shadow. Shadow alone will often define your subject and give it dimension. Shadows help you develop an illusion of weight and mass. The light planes define and contrast with the shadow areas to complete the perception of dimension.

Managing edges. Simply by emphasizing or de-emphasizing edges, you can add an impression of space. Soft, lost edges give the illusion of a surface that's turning away from the viewer, adding roundness to the image.

Putting value and color to work. Value describes the brightness or darkness of colors—and generally, the brighter the color, the more prominent it appears, while the darker and duller the color, the more it recedes from the viewer. In a similar vein, warmer colors (reds and oranges, for instance) come forward while cooler colors (blues or violets) move back. You can accentuate these characteristics by putting strong contrasts (of color or value) in the foreground while gradually reducing contrasts as you move deeper and deeper into the background.

Talking About It #214

With your classmates, discuss the way Tilton has used analysis in order to explore the subject of space. Why has he highlighted divisions like "Placing shapes" and "Adding light and shadow?" Do you find this a useful or effective technique? Why?

Convincing Support

When you analyze a topic by dividing it into parts, convincing support for each division is required. In the following essay called "Sexism in *Sports Illustrated*," student Alicia Ivory provides an example of the kind of support that is required in an analytical essay.

Sexism in *Sports Illustrated*

"Hey, boys, want to go to the Louisville baseball game?" my father would ask. "I have a few extra tickets to the Cincinnati Reds game. Could you guys use them?" my uncle would ask. "How about all the guys getting together and going to the Xavier basketball game? It could be the boys' day out," my neighbor would ask. Even over Thanksgiving turkey, sports is the topic in my house, but I am never invited into the conversation. Whatever season, whatever sporting event, whatever athlete is being discussed, this is the way it is in my family. I am the only girl with three brothers, and my uncles, neighbors, and friends of my family always call upon the males first when it comes to sports. Throughout my life I have been overlooked as a female sports fan, and now *Sports Illustrated* is continuing the tradition.

In researching the October 8, 1990 issue of *Sports Illustrated*, it is quite obvious that this is a magazine for male sports fans only. The October 8, 1990 issue confirms through its advertisements, its writers, and its articles that *Sports Illustrated* pays little attention to the female sports fan.

The 41 advertisements in the October 8, 1990 issue of *Sports Illustrated* are highly focused on men. The ads depict cowboy hats, Army reserve recruiters, trucks, and football players swilling Coke. The clothing ads seem especially designed for men only. In a Lee jeans ad, a female reader could assume that Lee jeans are only made for men because only men are shown wearing Lee jeans in the ad; no women or girls appear. In a Brittania ad, the scene is set with a man standing in his Brittania outfit in front of a little league baseball team. Two inferences can be made from this ad. First, the ad suggests that Brittania is a clothing line only for men. Secondly, it suggests that only men can be little league coaches. Another interesting example of sexism in this issue of the magazine is related to the male-oriented ads for *Sports Illustrated* itself. The October 8, 1990 issue offers readers an opportunity to buy posters of professional athletes. Only three professional sports are represented by these posters: baseball, football, and basketball. None of these sports, at least in the United States, includes women on a professional level, and the posters on sale are only of men. No opportunity exists for a sports fan to purchase a poster of a favorite female athlete.

However, of the 41 ads in the October 8 issue, seven do contain references to women, but the ads unfortunately depict women in a demeaning way. For example, in a J.C. Penney ad for Stafford Executive clothing on page 113, a man is modeling the clothes, while a woman is hanging on to him, her back to the camera as she embraces the man. Thus, although a woman does appear in this ad, she is pictured in a submissive role. Another ad, one for diamonds, also makes use of a woman. The woman is standing in a swimsuit; water is splashing all around her, and she is wearing a diamond necklace. Such an ad places the female in a peculiar situation. Any female with half an ounce of sense would not take the chance of dropping an expensive diamond necklace into the water of a swimming pool. This kind of ad does not show women in a positive light.

Furthermore, in the October 8 issue, out of the fourteen writers of articles for this issue, only one female writer appears. In addition, the one article that is written by a female journalist is actually co-written by a man. Thus, in actuality, only half of one of the articles in the entire magazine is written by a woman. Two conclusions may be drawn from this fact. First, it is possible to conclude simply that *Sports Illustrated* does not regularly assign women to write its stories. Second, it is possible to conclude that *Sports Illustrated* editors believe women are not as well equipped to cover athletics as men.

Another factor suggesting that *Sports Illustrated* ignores the interests of women is that the sixteen articles in the October 8 issue are almost exclusively about males. A lead article, entitled "A Boost from the Rocket," is about Roger Clemens's return to baseball action. Another, called "Out of the Running," talks about how the NFL rushing games have been slipping. A couple of exceptions do exist to this male-dominated mentality. Two articles do include references to women. One is about sports call-in shows and the other is about the Breeders' Cup. These articles mention that sports call-in shows do respond to women callers and that the sport of horseracing can include female jockeys. In the back of the magazine a feature called "Faces in the Crowd" appears. This column presents the athletic accomplishments of people around the country. In this issue, six sports achievers are mentioned, and two of them are women: Heidi Mason, a 12-year-old who won the world's record for landing a 34-pound African pompano off the coast of Miami, and Darci Mix, 15, an award-winning shortstop/secondbase "man" from San Diego. The other four men are noted for achievements in canoeing, football, golf, and wrestling. The two women featured take up less than one-third of half of a back page in the magazine.

I am not a male basher. I am a female sports fan. But I feel that the advertisements, the authors, and the articles in the October 8 issue of *Sports Illustrated* exclude women from its readership. Women do have an interest in sports, and they would read *Sports Illustrated* if the magazine covered sports events and figures of interest to them. I believe that by featuring advertisements, writers, and sports events of interest to women readers, the editors of *Sports Illustrated* can not only avoid the charge of sexism but sell more magazines as well.

Talking About It #215

With your classmates, discuss the following questions about Alicia Ivory's paper.

1. What is Alicia's thesis? Where is it found?
2. How does Alicia introduce her topic? Do you find it effective?
3. How does Alicia use analysis to support her thesis?
4. Are the divisions of her analysis clear? Why?
5. Is Alicia's support for her ideas thorough and convincing? Explain.

Writing About It #216

In your journal, write a response to Alicia's article. Do you agree with her? Disagree? What weaknesses can you spot in her essay? Are there any assumptions behind what she writes that you disagree with?

The Connection Plan

The connection plan is often used for organizing an analysis. Analysis does not simply collect ideas as in the strategies of description or illustration or using facts. Analysis does not present ideas in time or chronological order like narrative. Analysis makes connections between the parts of its subject in order to understand the entire subject more clearly. Thus, a connection plan can point out those relationships most effectively.

In using the connection plan, a writer typically relates divisions or parts to the subject as a whole, returning again and again to the way in which the parts or divisions impact on the main topic. In Alicia Ivory's paper on sexism in *Sports Illustrated*, for instance, the writer returns again and again to the way in which advertisements, writers, and articles reflect a sexist bias in the magazine, making connections between the divisions of her topic and the topic as a whole.

Appropriate Transition Words

Because writers of analysis are making connections between the divisions of their subject and their subject as a whole, appropriate transition words are needed to help the reader make connections among these relationships. Such special transition words are as follows:

also	for example
although	for instance
and	furthermore
another	however
as well	in addition
because	one such
but	since
first (second, third, etc.)	therefore
	thus

ANALYSIS IN COMBINATION WITH OTHER STRATEGIES FOR WRITING

As in the other strategies for writing you have studied, analysis often exists in combination with other strategies like illustration or description or question/answer or classification. In the following excerpt from "What to Listen for in Music," American composer Aaron Copland uses analysis and other writing strategies to examine the ways in which we listen to and appreciate a piece of music.

We all listen to music according to our separate capacities. But, for the sake of analysis, the whole listening process may become clearer if we break it up into its component parts, so to speak. In a certain sense we all listen to music on three separate planes. For lack of a better terminology, one might name these: (1) the sensuous plane, (2) the expressive plane, (3) the sheerly musical plane. The only advantage to be gained from mechanically splitting up the listening process into these hypothetical planes is the clearer view to be had of the way in which we listen.

The simplest way of listening to music is to listen for the sheer pleasure of the musical sound itself. That is the sensuous plane. It is the plane on which we hear music without thinking, without considering it in any way. One turns on the radio while doing something else and absentmindedly bathes in the sound. A kind of brainless but attractive state of mind is engendered by the mere sound appeal of the music.

You may be sitting in a room reading this book. Imagine one note struck on the piano. Immediately that one note is enough to change the atmosphere of the room—proving that the sound element in music is a powerful and mysterious agent, which it would be foolish to deride or belittle.

There is no need to digress further on the sensuous plane. Its appeal to every normal human being is self-evident. There is, however, such a thing as becoming more sensitive to the different kinds of sound stuff as used by various composers. For all composers do not use that sound stuff in the same way. Don't get the idea that the value of music is commensurate with its sensuous appeal or that the loveliest sounding music is made by the greatest composer. If that were so, Ravel would be a greater creator than Beethoven. The point is that the sound element varies with each composer, that his usage of sound forms an integral part of his style and must be taken into account when listening. The reader can see, therefore, that a more conscious approach is valuable even on this primary plane of music listening.

The second plane on which music exists is what I have called the expressive one. Here, immediately, we tread on controversial ground. Composers have a way of shying away from any discussion of music's expressive side. Did not Stravinsky himself proclaim that his music was an "object," a "thing," with a life of its own, and with no other meaning than its own purely musical existence? This intransigent attitude of Stravinsky's may be due to the fact that so many people have tried to read different meanings into so many pieces. Heaven knows it is difficult enough to say precisely what it is that a piece of music means, to say it definitely, to say it finally so that everyone is satisfied with your explanation. But that should not lead one to other extreme of denying to music the right to be "expressive."

My own belief is that all music has an expressive power, some more and some less, but that all music has a certain meaning behind the notes and that that meaning behind the notes constitutes, after all, what the piece is saying, what the piece is about. This whole problem can be stated quite simply by asking, "Is there a meaning to music?" My answer to that would be, "Yes." And "Can you state in so many words what the meaning is?" My answer to that would be, "No." Therein lies the difficulty.

Simple-minded souls will never be satisfied with the answer to the second of these questions. They always want music to have a meaning, and the more concrete it is the better they like it. The more the music reminds them of a train, a storm, a funeral, or any other familiar conception the more expressive it appears to be to them. This popular idea of music's meaning—stimulated and abetted by the usual run of musical commentator—should be discouraged wherever and whenever it is met. One timid lady once confessed to me that she suspected something seriously lacking in her appreciation of music because of her inability to connect it with anything definite. That is getting the whole thing backward, of course.

Still, the question remains, How close should the intelligent music lover wish to come to pinning a definite meaning to any particular work? No closer than a general concept, I should say. Music expresses, at different moments, serenity or exuberance, regret or triumph, fury or delight. It expresses each of these moods, and many others, in a numberless variety of subtle shadings and differences. It may even express a state of meaning for which there exists no adequate word in any language.

But whatever the professional musician may hold, most musical novices still search for specific words with which to pin down their musical reactions. That is why they always find

Tchaikovsky easier to "understand" than Beethoven. In the first place, it is easier to pin a meaning-word on a Tchaikovsky piece than on a Beethoven one. Much easier. Moreover, with the Russian composer, every time you come back to a piece of his it almost always says the same thing to you, whereas with Beethoven it is often quite difficult to put your finger right on what he is saying. And any musician will tell you that that is why Beethoven is the greater composer. Because music which always says the same thing to you will necessarily soon become dull music, but music whose meaning is slightly different with each hearing has a greater chance of remaining alive.

Themes or pieces need not express only an emotion, of course. Take such a theme as the first main one of the *Ninth Symphony*, for example. It is clearly made up of different elements. It does not say only one thing. Yet anyone hearing it immediately gets a feeling of strength, a feeling of power. It isn't a power that comes simply because the theme is played loudly. It is a power inherent in the theme itself. The extraordinary strength and vigor of the theme results in the listener's receiving an impression that a forceful statement has been made. But one should never try to boil it down to "the fateful hammer of life," etc. That is where the trouble begins. The musician, in his exasperation, says it means nothing but the notes themselves, whereas the nonprofessional is only too anxious to hang on to any explanation that gives him the illusion of getting closer to the music's meaning.

Now, perhaps, the reader will know better what I mean when I say that music does have an expressive meaning but that we cannot say in so many words what that meaning is.

The third plane on which music exists is the sheerly musical plane. Besides the pleasurable sound of music and the expressive feeling that it gives off, music does exist in terms of the notes themselves and of their manipulation. Most listeners are not sufficiently conscious of this third plane. . . .

Professional musicians, on the other hand, are, if anything, too conscious of the mere notes themselves. They often fall into the error of becoming so engrossed with their arpeggios and staccatos that they forget the deeper aspects of the music they are performing. But from the layman's standpoint, it is not so much a matter of getting over bad habits on the sheerly musical plane as of increasing one's awareness of what is going on, in so far as the notes are concerned.

When the man on the street listens to the "notes themselves" with any degree of concentration, he is most likely to make some mention of the melody. Either he hears a pretty melody or he does not, and he generally lets it go at that. Rhythm is likely to gain his attention next, particularly if it seems exciting. But harmony and tone color are generally taken for granted, if they are thought of consciously at all. As for music's having a definite form of some kind, that idea seems never to have occurred to him.

It is very important for all of us to become more alive to music on its sheerly musical plane. After all, an actual musical material is being used. The intelligent listener must be prepared to increase his awareness of the music material and what happens to it. He must hear the melodies, the rhythms, the harmonies, the tone colors in a more conscious fashion. But above all he must, in order to follow the line of the composer's thought, know something of the principles of musical form. Listening to all of these elements is listening on the sheerly musical plane.

Let me repeat that I have split up mechanically the three separate planes on which we listen merely for the sake of greater clarity. Actually, we never listen on one or the other of these planes. What we do is to correlate them—listening in all three ways at the same time. It takes no mental effort, for we do it instinctively.

In a sense, the ideal listener is both inside and outside the music at the same moment, judging it and enjoying it, wishing it would go one way and watching it go another—almost like the composer at the moment he composes it; because in order to write his music, the composer must also be inside and outside his music, carried away by it and yet coldly critical of it. A subjective and objective attitude is implied in both creating and listening to music.

What the reader should strive for, then, is a more *active* kind of listening. Whether you listen to Mozart or Duke Ellington, you can deepen your understanding of music only by being a more conscious and aware listener—not someone who is just listening, but someone who is listening *for* something.

Talking About It #217

With your classmates, discuss the following questions about composer Copland's piece.

1. What is Copland's topic? How has he divided it by using analysis? Are the divisions clear?
2. What personal beliefs of Copland about listening to music does each of these divisions reflect? Explain those personal beliefs. Do you agree with them?
3. What other strategies does Copland use in addition to analysis? Why?
4. Refer to Copland's conclusion and point out similarities between the writer's process and the musician's process.

Writing About It #218

Listen to a piece of music of your choice either in the classroom or at home. Then analyze that piece of music in terms of what you listen for and appreciate in it. When you have finished, share your responses with your classmates. Discuss whether your analyses reflect any of Copland's concerns about what to listen for in music.

A STUDENT USES ANALYSIS: A FIRST DRAFT

In the following essay, student Lynn Darby is writing an analysis of her favorite movie, *Beauty and the Beast*. In it, she attempts to display the characteristics of analysis that she learned about in this chapter.

Lynn has shared her early prewriting with her classmates. They responded by freewriting, sketching, or writing purpose statements. She considered their comments as well as her own purposes as she produced a first draft of her paper, which follows.

I am what you would call a Beauty and the Beast *fanatic. To me,* Beauty and the Beast *is simply the best movie I have ever seen. The characters, the songs, and the themes caught my interest when I first saw it, and they have held it for years.*

Beauty and the Beast *offers the viewer some very unusual characters. There is Lumiere, a candlestick, who keeps trying to romance the French maid, a feather duster. There is Cogsworth, a clock and butler, who blames Lumiere when anything in the household goes wrong. Mrs. Potts is another unusual character. Mrs. Potts's son Chip, a tea cup, is always trying to find out what his mother means when she whispers about the relationship between Belle and the Beast. The most interesting characters of all are the two major characters, Belle and the Beast. Belle is from a small French town where the villagers think she is very unusual because she likes books more than the town's good looking bachelor. The Beast, who was turned into a horrible monster by a beautiful enchantress, is another unusual character.*

Beauty and the Beast *has themes that appeal to everyone. The theme of a daughter's undying love for her father is something that everyone can relate to. The theme of learning to love and be loved in return is also a very important theme. The theme of developing the courage to change is the most important theme. The Beast has to develop a kinder manner and also work up enough courage to tell Belle that he loves her. These themes are often revealed through the music. Songs like "Something There" show Belle and the Beast working through their developing feelings for each other.*

The soundtrack from Beauty and the Beast *appeals to people of all ages. The movie starts with "Bonjour," a song in which Belle is introducing the audience to the different people in her French village. In this song, the audience first meets the town's good-looking bachelor, Gaston. All of the girls in the town drool over this young man. Another song, "Be Our Guest," is the one Lumiere sings to Belle while she is eating. In this song the audience meets the Beast's staff which by a magic spell has been turned into household items. Mrs. Potts sings the theme song, "Beauty and the Beast," while the Beast and Belle are dancing together near the end of the movie. The men of the village sing another song, "Kill the Beast," while they march off to the Beast's castle to kill him before he comes to their village to kill them and take their children.*

Do you like a movie that has unusual characters? What do you think of a movie that has themes that you can relate to? Do you like a movie that has some very good songs? Then I suggest you go and see the movie Beauty and the Beast *as soon as you get the chance.*

Talking About It #219

Critique Lynn's draft using the formal questions method suggested in Chapter 6. With your classmates, respond to the following questions about Lynn's paper:

Content

1. Is the quality of the content satisfying? Are the details, facts, reasons, examples, comparisons, and other methods of supporting the ideas interesting? Why or why not? Point to specifics in the text to support your ideas.

2. Is the quantity of the content sufficient? Are there enough details, facts, reasons, examples, comparisons, and other methods of supporting the ideas to make the writing satisfying? Why or why not? Point to specifics in the text to support your ideas.
3. What suggestions would you make to Lynn for improving the content in the next draft?

Organization

1. Is the beginning of the essay well organized with a thesis statement? Is the introduction interesting and appropriate?
2. Are the beginnings of the paragraphs well organized? Do they contain topic sentence?
3. Is the middle section of the essay well organized?
   a. Is it unified?
   b. Is it coherent?
4. Is the end of the essay well organized? Is there an appropriate conclusion?
5. What suggestions would you make to Lynn for improving the organization in the next draft?

Think about the characteristics of analysis that you learned about in this chapter: (1) clear divisions or parts, (2) convincing support, (3) the connection plan, (4) appropriate transitions. As a group, try to answer the following questions:

1. What are the divisions or parts into which Lynn has divided her analysis? Do these divisions make sense? Are the divisions clear? Why or why not?
2. Has Lynn thoroughly supported her ideas? Why or why not?
3. Has Lynn made adequate connections among her ideas using the connection plan?
4. Has Lynn made use of appropriate transitions? Identify them.

A STUDENT USES ANALYSIS: A REVISED DRAFT

Lynn listened carefully to her classmates' comments as they critiqued her work. Then she wrote this revised draft in response.

I am what you would call a Beauty and the Beast *fanatic. My bedroom looks like a Goodwill store specializing in* Beauty and the Beast *memorabilia. On my desk is a collection that includes a notebook, memo pad, folder, pens and pencils, and a pad of stickers from the movie. On my bed rest two dolls—one of Belle, the movie's heroine, and one of the Beast, the movie's hero. On my wall are even two movie posters advertising the movie. To me,* Beauty and the Beast *is simply the best movie I have ever seen. The characters, the themes, and the songs of this classic tale caught my interest when I first saw it, and they have held my attention for years.*

Beauty and the Beast *offers the viewer some very unusual minor and major characters. One delightful minor character is Lumiere, an animated candlestick, who keeps trying to romance the French maid, a feather duster. Another is Cogsworth, a clock who serves as a butler. Cogsworth blames Lumiere when anything in the household goes wrong. For instance, when Belle can't sleep because she says she has never spent the night in an enchanted castle, Cogsworth angrily assumes that Lumiere has revealed the secret about the enchanted nature of the mansion. Mrs. Potts is another unusual minor character. She is a tea pot and a housekeeper who tries to keep the Beast in line and make him act like a gentleman so that he and Beauty can fall in love. Mrs. Potts's son Chip, a tea cup, is always trying to find out what his mother means when she whispers about the growing relationship between Belle and the Beast. Although the minor characters add humor and interest to the story, the most intriguing characters are the two major characters, Belle and the Beast. Both characters are unique and admirable. Belle is from a small French town; the villagers are right to think her unique, for she prefers books to the town's good looking bachelor. She is also devoted to her father and has a personality open enough to be willing to see the good qualities in a ferocious and ugly Beast. The Beast, who was turned into a horrible monster by a beautiful enchantress, is another unusual character. He is admirable in his attempts to overcome his inability to love and to break the spell that holds his castle through his friendship with Belle. Thus, both minor and major characters contribute to the movie's appeal.*

The themes in Beauty and the Beast *are enduring and appealing. A daughter's undying love for her father is an important theme in the movie. Belle, for instance, risks her life crossing through a dark and dangerous forest in order to find her father. When she arrives at the Beast's castle, Belle risks her life again by trying to rescue her father from the Beast's dungeon. The theme of developing the courage to change is another important theme. The Beast has to develop a kinder manner and also work up enough courage to tell Belle that he loves her, things he finds very difficult to do. Most important of all is the theme that involves learning to be loved and love in return. Although faced with many obstacles to overcome, as the movie develops, both Belle and the Beast learn to give and receive love. Related to this theme of learning to love is the message that real love comes without any strings attached. When the Beast allows Belle to leave him and go back to her father, he shows that he loves her unconditionally, for the Beast now understands that true love does not involve placing unreasonable demands on the freedom of the beloved.*

The soundtrack from Beauty and the Beast *appeals to people of all ages, and this music helps develop the characters and the themes. The opening song, "Bonjour," introduces the audience to Belle and the people who live in her tiny French village. The song establishes her character as someone uninterested in the superficial good looks of the town's most eligible bachelor, Gaston. Although all of the girls in the town drool over this young man, the next song, "Gaston," shows this bachelor in a less than favorable light. As the song reveals, this conceited man is the "size of a barge," mostly "biceps" and "brawn." Another lively and witty song is "Be Our Guest." Sung to Belle as she is served dinner at the Beast's enchanted castle, this song establishes the magical nature of the Beast's castle and introduces Belle to the Beast's household staff. In this entertaining song, the forks dance, the candlesticks twirl, and the serving dishes do the can-can. In the song "Something There," the blossoming love between Beauty and the Beast is revealed. Belle sings, "there's something there that wasn't there before" as testimony to her feelings for the Beast. When Mrs. Potts sings the theme song, "Beauty and the Beast," near the end of the movie, it is clear that the Beast and Belle love each other deeply and that both have learned how to change and how to develop courage.*

Characters, themes, music: Beauty and the Beast *has it all. In the words of its theme song, it is a "tale as old as time," a classic that appeals not just to me, but to viewers of every age and circumstance.*

Talking About It #220

Lynn thought about her own purposes as well as her classmates' critiques when she wrote her revised draft. Talk to your classmates about the specific changes she has made. Do you think her draft has been improved? Why or why not?

WRITING ASSIGNMENTS

Produce some prewriting in response to one of the following topics or a topic of your choosing in preparation for writing an analysis paper. Remember to profile your reader, define your purpose, and develop some preliminary strategies for content, organization, and expression:

An analysis of your current diet

An analysis of area pizza parlors

An analysis of fast foods with which you are familiar

An analysis of a popular consumer product such as running shoes or soft drinks

An analysis of a current movie you have seen

An analysis of a current rock group you have heard

An analysis of a current work of art you have viewed

An analysis of a single artist's style

An analysis of a television show you are familiar with

An analysis of a current or previous job you have held

An analysis of your current academic situation

An analysis of a current sports situation

An analysis of a challenging or difficult part of your life

Make use of this prewriting to write an analysis essay that demonstrates the characteristics of analysis that you have learned about in this chapter: (1) clear divisions or parts, (2) thorough support, (3) a connection plan, (4) appropriate transitions. Assume for purposes of this paper that your reader will be a classmate.

After you have written your first draft, ask your classmates to respond to it. Then rewrite it, making improvements that consider their responses as well as your own purposes. Invite your classmates to critique this next draft. After you have written yet another draft in response to those critiques, ask your classmates to make editing suggestions. Finally, proofread and submit your paper.

Record all responses to the drafts of your paper in the Writing Assessment Profile which appears in the back of this text.

CHAPTER SIXTEEN REVIEW

Writing About It #221

Use your journal to reflect on what you learned in this chapter.

17

Collaborating

What is involved in working well with others?
Why is collaboration important?
How will learning to collaborate now help me in the future?

WHAT IS COLLABORATION?

At this point in *Writing for a Reader*, you're already familiar with collaboration, for you've been consulting with other people about your writing in all of the chapters in this text. You, your classmates, and your teacher have helped each other in the prewriting and rewriting stages of the writing process. You've offered suggestions, criticisms, insights, and responses. You've discovered that collaborating with others not only aids the writing process itself; it also invariably leads to an improved final product.

When you engage in collaboration, however, you involve yourself in a process of production very different from the way writing has been conceived of historically. Traditionally, writing is portrayed as a solitary, lonely act engaged in by an isolated individual writer. When you collaborate, involving others in the writing process, you may feel uneasy or uncomfortable, for when you cooperate with others in the writing process you forego the tradition of working alone and instead establish a new tradition—that of working together.

Writing About It #222

In your journal, attempt to define "collaboration" as it applies to the writing situation. Try out several different definitions. Then, when you have finished, share your responses with your classmates. Together decide which definitions seem most accurate.

In your journal, discuss your attitudes about collaborating. What do you like about it? Dislike? Why? Share your responses with your classmates.

In your journal, offer some reasons why learning to collaborate might be important. Offer some ideas about collaboration in the workplace or in an educational institution. If you have experienced any situations that have called on you to collaborate, either on the job or in school, describe them. When you have finished, share your responses with your classmates.

HOW DO YOU COLLABORATE?

Most people can offer reasons for *why* collaboration is important, but they have difficulty understanding *how* it's done.

Collaborating is a skill, and, like any skill, it has to be learned. As with any skill, you will learn to be a better collaborator with practice and experience.

Writing About It #223

Because learning any new skill—including collaboration—is often difficult, spend some time writing in your journal about the challenges posed by collaborative writing. It might help to think about those challenges in two ways: (1) challenges presented by the work and (2) challenges presented by the people doing the work.

Talking About It #224

On the board, list some of the ideas from your journal under two headings: (1)Work Challenges and (2) People Challenges. After you have listed some ideas under each heading, discuss how practice and experience with collaboration might help you overcome some of those challenges.

When you are first learning to become collaborative writers, it's often helpful to refer to some guidelines for meeting the challenge of learning *how* to collaborate. As you become more skilled at writing with others, you will develop guidelines of your own that can be added to this list.

1. *Design a strategy for handling the collaborative project.* The strategy may include stating goals, designating leaders for various tasks, dividing up the work, and setting timetables and deadlines. Since each project will require different considerations, each project will usually require its own unique set of strategies for completing the work.

2. *Remember that collaboration is often a balancing act.* You will need to balance the needs of the work and the needs of the people engaged in the work. You will need to balance the importance of creativity against the importance of practicality. You will need to balance the need to lead with the need to follow. You will need to balance individual goals and group goals.

3. *Learn to tolerate a reasonable amount of conflict.* Balancing important but often competing interests can create tension and conflict. Learn to expect conflict and then work to resolve it.

4. *Understand that different collaborative groups often have different collaborative styles.* Some groups work in a linear fashion; they are goal-oriented and focused on the final product. Other groups work in a more circular fashion; they are more focused on the process itself. Both kinds of groups can accomplish important work.

5. *Monitor the group's progress as you engage in the process of collaboration.* You can create any kind of monitoring activity that suits the needs of the group and the collaborative situation. You might produce logs or progress reports or individual and group process sheets. But it's important for the progress of the group itself to be charted in some way.

6. *Review your group purposes at several intervals during the collaborative process.* It is helpful to remind the group of its purposes and its audience or audiences throughout the process of working together.

7. *Cultivate a group attitude of respect.* Respect is important in cooperative work. You need to respect the individuals in your group. You need to respect the requirements of the work. You need to respect the processes of the group itself.

WRITING ASSIGNMENTS

The following collaborative writing assignments are designed to build your collaborative writing skills. They will require two or more people to cooperate to produce one or more texts. Choose a cooperative writing assignment that interests you. As you work on your assignment, follow the guidelines for successful group work that appears before this section.

A. Imagine that your group is involved in an elementary classroom teaching situation. As a group, produce the following documents:

1. *A document that describes the learning problem of one particular child in one particular class. Use description, narration, facts, examples, or any other strategy to document this learning problem. Title the document appropriately, and devise a written method for monitoring your group's process as it engages in producing this document.*

2. *A document that details what happens in a meeting held with the child's classroom teacher, the school principal, and the teacher who serves as a tutor to children with special learning problems. At the meeting, suggestions are made about how to address the child's learning problems. Title the document appropriately, and devise a written method for monitoring your group's process as it engages in producing this document.*
3. *A letter sent from the classroom teacher to the child's parent detailing the steps the school will be taking to address the child's learning problem. Devise a written method for monitoring your group's process as it engages in producing this document.*

B. Find an "environmental" problem on your campus. It may be an ugly eyesore on campus or another problem such as the problem of what to do with leftover food in the cafeteria or how to recycle used paper on campus. As a group, produce the following documents:

1. *A document that discusses the problem. Use description, narration, facts, examples, or any other strategy to document this environmental problem. Title the document appropriately, and devise a written method for monitoring your group's process as it engages in producing this document.*
2. *A letter to the university official responsible for dealing with this problem. In your letter, make use of your discussion of the problem in convincing this official to hold a meeting with your group to discuss this problem. Devise a written method for monitoring your group's process as it engages in producing this document.*
3. *A document that details what happens in a meeting between this university official and the members of your group. At this meeting, suggestions are made about how to address this environmental problem. Title the document appropriately, and devise a written method for monitoring your group's process as it engages in producing this document.*
4. *A follow-up letter from the group to the university official which documents the group's experience at the meeting and refers to future plans for solutions to the problem. Devise a written method for monitoring your group's process as it engages in producing this document.*

C. Contact several friends of members of your group to investigate their first-year experiences at college. Prior to contacting these friends, however, decide on the aspects of the first-year experience you are interested in soliciting information about. These aspects might include adjustment issues, financial challenges, course work, or any other area your group wishes to investigate. As a group, produce the following documents:

1. *A questionnaire sent to each of the friends your group has decided to contact and designed to elicit the information you have decided to study. The questionnaire should also be filled out by each of the members of your group. Title this document appropriately, and devise a written method for monitoring your group's process as it engages in producing this document.*
2. *A compilation of the responses to the questionnaire presented in a reader-accessible format. Title this document appropriately, and devise a written method for monitoring your group's process as it engages in producing this document.*

3. *A formal report that makes use of the material gleaned from the questionnaires and which catalogues the similarities and differences among first-year experiences as reported by various students. Title this document appropriately, and devise a written method for monitoring your group's process as it engages in producing this document.*
4. *A letter to a younger brother or sister who is thinking about attending college in another year or two. This letter should offer an informal account of the challenges inherent in the first year of college as detailed by the information gleaned from the questionnaires. Devise a written method for monitoring your group's process as it engages in producing this document.*

D. Work with a group in which all of the group members are enrolled in the same course, for example, History, Biology, or Speech. As a group, produce the following documents:

1. *A complete and well organized set of class notes on a particular unit of study. The notes must be compiled as a group and they should be presented in a format that will make them easy to study from. Title this document appropriately, and devise a written method for monitoring your group's process as it engages in producing this document.*
2. *A set of at least three essay questions likely to occur on a major test on that particular unit. Devise a written method for monitoring your group's process as it engages in producing this document.*
3. *Three essays that represent a model response to those three essay questions. Title these documents appropriately, and devise a written method for monitoring your group's process as it engages in producing these documents.*
4. *A reference handbook entitled "How to Study Successfully" in (Name of Course). Devise a written method for monitoring your group's process as it engages in producing this document.*

E. Imagine that you are in charge of a program to attract more students of a certain type to your college (adult women, minorities, international students, co-op students). As a group, produce the following documents:

1. *A document which describes all of the special interests and programs already in existence on your campus to meet the needs of such students as well as a description of all the special interests and programs which you can assume will be instituted on your campus to meet the needs of these students by the time they arrive on campus. Title this document appropriately, and devise a written method for monitoring your group's process as it engages in producing this document.*
2. *A form letter from the admissions office inviting this targeted group of students to learn more about your college and soliciting their participation in an informational meeting to discuss the opportunities available to them at your college. Devise a written method for monitoring your group's process as it engages in producing this document.*
3. *A handout to provide to these prospective students at that informational meeting. The handout should respond to the concerns most likely to be raised by these students at that meeting and should offer a brief but complete response to them.*

4. *A formal proposal to the dean of your college who is responsible for this population of students. This proposal should cite the need for a new employee position to handle the students admitted under this special program. The proposal should suggest the job skills, education, and duties required of this new employee. It should also persuade the dean of the worth of your proposal. Title this document appropriately, and devise a written method for monitoring your group's process as it engages in producing this document.*

F. Imagine that you are a group of campus entrepreneurs looking to launch a new campus-related business venture. In conceptualizing your venture, as a group produce the following documents:

1. *A document which is a list of potential business ventures. Title this document appropriately, and devise a written method for monitoring your group's process as it engages in producing this document.*
2. *A document which is a description of a meeting in which the potential business ventures are discussed. The description should cite the advantages and disadvantages of each potential project. Title this document appropriately, and devise a written method for monitoring your group's process as it engages in producing this document.*
3. *Name your business venture, design letterhead for it, and then write three letters soliciting financing from three different sources. Devise a written method for monitoring your group's process as it engages in producing this document.*
4. *A wealthy campus alumnus is interested in investing heavily in the start-up costs of your business. Write a letter from this alumnus to your group. The letter should suggest why he's interested, how he plans to help, and what he expects in return for his investment. Devise a written method for monitoring your group's process as it engages in producing this document.*
5. *Write a formal proposal to this alumnus in which you detail aspects of your company business. These aspects can include issues such as your company's goals, market strategies, operation, expenses, and staffing. Title this document appropriately, and devise a written method for monitoring your group's process as it engages in producing this document.*

G. A professor on campus has just published a book and has asked your group to help promote its sale. As a group, produce the following documents:

1. *A letter from the professor to your group asking for help with promotion. Devise a written method for monitoring your group's process as it engages in producing this document.*
2. *A document which is a description of a meeting in which your group discusses various ways of helping promote the professor's book. Title this document appropriately, and devise a written method for monitoring your group's process as it engages in producing this document.*
3. *A formal proposal to the professor in which your group outlines the various strategies you've devised for marketing the book. Title this document appropriately, and devise a written method for monitoring your group's process as it engages in producing this document.*

4. *A publicity biography of the professor and a brief description of the book to be sent to the professor's publisher for publicity purposes. Title this document appropriately, and devise a written method for monitoring your group's process as it engages in producing this document.*
5. *A review of the professor's book for a professional journal. Title this document appropriately, and devise a written method for monitoring your group's process as it engages in producing this document.*
6. *A review of the professor's book in a local newspaper. Title this document appropriately, and devise a written method for monitoring your group's process as it engages in producing this document.*

H. Your group has been assigned to do a historical project about your college. You are to contact alumni in each decade of the last 50 years to share memories about what it was like to attend your college in their generation. Prior to contacting these alumni, however, decide on the aspects of their college experience you are interested in soliciting information about. These aspects might include social life, studies and majors, athletic events, memorable faculty members, or any other area your group wishes to investigate. As a group, produce the following documents:

1. *A questionnaire sent to each of the alumni your group has decided to contact and designed to elicit the information you have decided to study. Each member of your group should also fill out this questionnaire. Title this document appropriately, and devise a written method for monitoring your group's process as it engages in producing this document.*
2. *A compilation of the responses to the questionnaire presented in a reader-accessible format. Title this document appropriately, and devise a written method for monitoring your group's process as it engages in producing this document.*
3. *A formal report that makes use of the material gleaned from the questionnaires and which catalogues the similarities and differences between alumni experiences and the current experiences of students in your group. Title this document appropriately, and devise a written method for monitoring your group's process as it engages in producing this document.*
4. *A letter to each of the alumni participating in your study thanking them for their help and providing a short overview of your group's findings. Devise a written method for monitoring your group's process as it engages in producing this document.*

CHAPTER SEVENTEEN REVIEW

Writing About It #225

Use your journal to reflect on what you have learned in this chapter.

A

A Short Course in Grammar

Although the text of *Writing for a Reader* covers many grammatical conventions, particularly in Chapter 7 on Rewriting: Editing and Proofreading, this appendix presents additional concerns which may be of use to the student. This Short Course in Grammar, which is not intended to be exhaustive, provides supplemental information about grammatical conventions in three general areas: (1) Conventions About Sentences, (2) Conventions About Verbs, and (3) Conventions About Pronouns.

CONVENTIONS ABOUT SENTENCES

In Chapter 5, you learned about writing conventions: the customary or expected ways of doing things. Two important conventions govern readers' expectations about sentences: (1) *readers expect sentences to be complete* and (2) *readers expect sentences to respect the rules of punctuation.*

Readers Expect Sentences to Be Complete: The Problem of Sentence Fragments

As you will see, one of the most important conventions about sentences is that, for the most part, your readers will expect your sentences to be complete. A sentence is considered complete if it (1) contains a subject and a verb and (2) expresses a complete thought.

In the following table, note the reasons why the examples are *not* complete sentences.

	Subject	Verb	Complete Thought
1. When the game ended.	X (game)	X (ended)	?
2. But left the other rider behind.	?	X (left)	?
3. The boy who had delivered papers to make extra money.	X (boy/who)	X (had delivered)	?
4. In the middle of the river next to the barge.	?	?	?
5. To find my Toyota in the parking lot.	?	?	?
6. Helping people with new work skills.	X (helping) (people)	?	?
7. That I had been wondering about.	X (I)	X (had been wondering)	?

In examples 1 to 7, you noticed that sentences can be incomplete by either failing to include a subject, failing to include a verb, failing to express a complete thought, or failing to include one or more of these essentials. In these situations, the incomplete sentence is called a *fragment.*

As you know, the word "fragment" implies a "piece" or "part" of something. A fragment suggests that something is missing. If you look back to the table, you will see that the most *common* characteristic of a sentence fragment is that it fails to express a complete thought. Something is missing. The sentence is incomplete.

Developing writers sometimes write sentence fragments. Most likely fragments appear because the writer has not learned a dependable system for identifying them. One of the most reliable systems for detecting fragments is reading your sentence out loud. If you read your paper out loud—and read it backwards, from the end to the beginning—you are also more likely to detect those pesky fragments. Reading your sentences out loud from back to front keeps your eye from making connections between sentences that aren't really there.

If you have read your paper out loud from back to front and are still stumped by a particular sentence, submit it to the "bus stop test." The bus stop test asks you to repeat the "sentence" you have written and ask, "If a stranger came up to me at the bus stop and repeated only these words, would I know what he or she meant?" Try out the bus stop test on the first example given. Say, "If a stranger came up to me at the bus stop and said, 'When the game ended,' would I know what he or she meant?" Clearly, the answer is "no." When a bus stop test question receives an answer of "no," then you can be fairly certain you've written a sentence fragment.

Correcting sentence fragments is easy. It's a matter of taking your incomplete piece or sentence part and making it complete. You do that in one of two ways: (1) by attaching the fragment to some other group of words in your paragraph or (2) by adding words to make the incomplete part complete.

Practicing What You Have Learned

A. The following paragraph contains many sentence fragments. Try identifying the fragments by reading the paragraph out loud and backwards or by using the "bus stop test."

Original: Because I often procrastinate. I have trouble sitting down to study. Fiddling with my books. Down the hall to get a snack. Make a telephone call to a friend. Sitting in a comfortable chair and watching TV instead of reading my book. When I finish my procrastinating. I know it's time to study.

B. Now correct the fragments in the paragraph in "A." Discuss with your classmates whether you corrected the fragments by (1) adding words to make the incomplete part complete or (2) attaching the fragment to another sentence in the paragraph.

C. Return to the seven sentence fragments you studied on page 390. Correct them by adding words to make the incomplete part complete.

D. Find several examples of sentence fragments in your own or your classmates' writing. Put them on the board and identify what's missing—a subject, a verb, or a complete thought. Then correct each of the sentence fragments you've studied.

Readers Expect Sentences to Respect the Rules of Punctuation: The Problem of Run-Ons and Comma Splices

Punctuation marks are to readers what road signs are to drivers. They signal places where readers are to stop, slow down, register a question, mark a change in speakers, prepare for a list, or note other directions from the writer.

In Chapter 5 you learned about the ways in which speaking and writing are different. One important difference is that speakers do not need to make use of punctuation. To emphasize a point, they may raise their voices. To indicate a question, they may raise their eyebrows. Writers, on the other hand, need punctuation marks to give readers these kinds of signals.

In the following section, you will learn about two marks of punctuation that writers use for signaling the end of a sentence to their readers: (1) the period and (2) the semicolon.

One of the most important "rules of the road" says that the end of a sentence is marked by a period. Thus, the period is the sentence equivalent of the stop sign. It is the place where your complete thought comes to an end. It is the place where you momentarily stop before continuing on into the next sentence. It is the place where, should you fail to come to a complete stop, your reader will feel the urge to pull you over to the side of the road and write out a ticket.

Periods are generally misused in one of two ways. Either the writer (1) fails to stop at all or (2) fails to come to a complete stop. Both problems in the use of the period are similar to problems that occur when people fail to observe a stop sign. Just as a period occurs at the intersection of different sentences, a stop sign appears at the intersection of two or more roads. You are probably familiar with drivers who have run through an intersection, barreling right on through the stop sign, failing to apply the brakes in any way. The sentence equivalent of that failure-to-stop situation is called a *run-on-sentence*.

Run-On Sentences

A run-on sentence misuses the period by failing to use it altogether. In the following example, note where the run-on occurs.

*Although I had my house painted last summer, the paint started peeling right awa**y a**fter several weeks I decided to call the painter and ask for my money back.*

In the revised version of that run-on sentence, the intersection has been signaled by the mark of punctuation which indicates a full and complete stop: a period.

*Although I had my house painted last summer, the paint started peeling right awa**y. A**fter several weeks I decided to call the painter and ask for my money back.*

Run-on sentences tend to occur more often after the following words:

then	I	this
next	you	that
there	he, she, it	
	they	

Original: My little sister chased the rabbi**t i**t was too quick for her.
Revised: My little sister chased the rabbi**t. I**t was too quick for her.

Be careful when your sentence contains one of these words.

Comma Splices

In a second kind of "intersection" problem, the writer puts on the brakes but fails to come to a full and complete stop. You are probably familiar with this kind of driver who slows down at a stop sign but neglects to stop completely. The sentence equivalent of this kind of driving situation is called a *comma splice*. Here the writer uses a comma at the intersection instead of the required period.

The wedding was the most sentimental ceremony I have ever attende**d, t**he bride wore her grandmother's dress, and the groom wore his grandfather's pocket watch.

In the example which follows, the comma splice has been corrected by appropriately using the period.

The wedding was the most sentimental ceremony I have ever attende**d. T**he bride wore her grandmother's dress, and the groom wore his grandfather's pocket watch.

The same technique you learned for detecting sentence fragments (when too little has been included in a sentence) can be used for detecting run-ons and comma splices (when too much has been included in a sentence). This is the technique of reading out loud. If you learn to read out loud, slowly and deliberately, your voice can catch what your eye can miss. Listening for the drops in your voice as you reach the natural intersections in your writing will help you identify the stopping points in your run-ons and comma splices.

Practicing What You Have Learned

The following sentences either fail to stop at the intersection of two sentences or fail to come to a complete stop. Label them as either run-ons or comma splices.

	Run-On	*Comma Splice*
1. In the past many people worked to produce the necessities of life, today they work to produce the luxuries.		
2. Top models earn millions of dollars for their work even the average model brings home a six-figure salary.		
3. The 1990 Census was a marvel of organized statistics-gathering, hundreds of thousands of households were surveyed for information.		
4. Improved education leads to a better understanding of substance abuse the result is a reduction in the overall incidence of drug, alcohol, and tobacco abuse.		
5. There are many systems in place to help people with emergencies should you need sudden help, dial 911.		

Correcting Run-Ons and Comma Splices

There are several ways to correct a run-on or a comma splice at the intersection of two sentences: (1) use a period and a capital letter, (2) use a comma and a conjunction, (3) use a dependent word signal, (4) use a semicolon, (5) use a semicolon and a connecting word.

Period and Capital Letter

As you have seen from the previous examples, the first and easiest way to correct run-ons and comma splices is to use a period at the intersection and begin the next sentence with a capital letter.

Original Run-On: The automobile creates cheap transportation for millions of people it also creates expensive destruction of the environment for the entire planet.

Original Comma Splice: The automobile creates cheap transportation for millions of people, it also creates expensive destruction of the environment for the entire planet.

Corrected Run-On and Comma Splice: The automobile creates cheap transportation for millions of peopl**e. It** also creates expensive destruction of the environment for the entire planet.

Comma and a Conjunction

As you learned in Chapter 7, Editing and Proofreading, compound sentences are created by joining two simple sentences with a comma and a connecting word: *and, but, or, nor, for, so* and *yet*. These connecting words can join run-ons and comma splices at appropriate intersections as in the following examples. Remember to place the comma *before*—not after—the conjunction.

Revised Run-On and Comma Splice: The automobile creates cheap transportation for millions of peopl**e, but** it also creates expensive destruction of the environment for the entire planet.

You should be aware that writers commonly punctuate compound sentences incorrectly. Often they will use a comma before a conjunction that is merely joining *parts* of a sentence rather than an *entire* sentence as in the following example:

Original: Jenny thoroughly enjoys playing basebal**l, a**nd softball as well. (The comma before the "and" is incorrect.)

Revised: Jenny thoroughly enjoys playing basebal**l, and** she enjoys playing softball as well. (The comma before the "and" is correct.)

Dependent Word Signals

When you studied sentences in Chapter 7, you learned that complex sentences are signaled by a dependent word (page 224). You can correct both run-ons and comma splices by connecting them with an appropriate dependent word signal.

Revised Run-On and Comma Splice: **Although** the automobile creates cheap transportation for millions of peopl**e, i**t also creates expensive destruction of the environment for the entire planet.

Remember that when the dependent word signal *introduces* the sentence, as in this example, the dependent part of the sentence is followed by a comma; when the dependent word signal comes at the *end* of the sentence, the dependent part of the sentence does *not* require a comma.

Revised Run-On and Comma Splice: The automobile creates expensive destruction for the entire plane**t al**though it also creates cheap transportation for millions of people. (no comma)

Semicolon

An appropriate use of the semicolon can also correct run-ons and comma splices. Semicolons are used in the same way as periods: to connect two complete sentences. Unlike the period, however, the sentence following the semicolon does not require a capital letter.

Generally, semicolons are used to join sentences containing ideas that are closely related to each other in thought.

The automobile creates cheap transportation for millions of peopl**e; i**t also creates expensive destruction of the environment for the entire planet. (closely related thought)

The automobile creates cheap transportation for millions of peopl**e. W**hen a consumer chooses an economy car, the daily cost of transportation is reduced even further. (not a closely related thought)

Semicolon and a Connecting Word

In addition, using a semicolon and a connecting transition word can also correct problems with run-ons and comma splices. A list of these special connecting transition words appears on page 221. When one of these words is used to join two sentences, the semicolon and connecting words are followed by a comma as in the following examples.

The automobile creates cheap transportation for millions of peopl**e; however,** it also creates expensive destruction of the environment for the entire planet.

It is important to pay close attention to these connecting words. When they actually join sentences together, the semicolon, the connecting word, and the comma are required. When these connecting words merely interrupt the flow of the sentence—without providing the function of joining the sentences—they require commas, not a semicolon:

> The automobile creates cheap transportation for millions of people; it also creates**, however,** expensive destruction of the environment for the entire planet.

Note that connecting words can be used after periods to begin a sentence as well.

> The automobile creates cheap transportation for millions of people**. H**owever, it also creates expensive destruction of the environment for the entire planet.

Practicing What You Have Learned

Review the run-ons and comma splices from page 393. Then correct each of them in five different ways. Compare your solutions with your classmates.

CONVENTIONS ABOUT PUNCTUATION

Readers expect writers to escort them through a text, acting as a kind of tour guide. The way in which writers provide such guidelines is through punctuation. Punctuation can point out things in the text for the reader, telling the reader that "over here is a list" or "over there is a phrase interrupting the flow of thought" or "over yonder is a passage spoken by someone else." Punctuation is, therefore, an important guide to meaning.

Many conventions or commonly agreed-on ways of doing things govern the use of punctuation. In this next section, you will learn about the conventions that govern the following familiar marks of punctuation: (1) the semicolon, (2) the colon, (3) the quotation mark, (4) the apostrophe, and (5) the comma.

Punctuating with Semicolons

As you have seen, semicolons can help correct run-ons and comma splices, and they can be used in conjunction with a special connecting word to join two sentences together. In addition, semicolons help writers express clear divisions between items in a series, especially when those items themselves contain commas. Consider the differences between the original example and the revised version.

> *Original*: The board members represented a number of areas: Phoenix, Arizona, Paducah, Kentucky, Edinboro, Pennsylvania, and Kansas City, Missouri.

Revised: The board members represented a number of areas: Phoenix, Arizon**a; P**aducah, Kentuck**y; E**dinboro, Pennsylvani**a;** and Kansas City, Missouri.

Punctuating with Colons

A colon announces, "Sit up and take notice of what follows." In the case of the colon, what follows is typically one of two things: (1) a list or (2) a significant word, phrase, or explanation.

Please bring the following items to the picni**c: k**etchup, mustard, hot dogs, paper plates, and plastic cups. (a list)

The teacher put a finger across her lips and spoke one wor**d:** "Silence." (significant word)

It's important to remember that what *precedes* the colon should be a complete sentence. The following example, therefore, would be incorrect.

Original: Tom Cruise has acted in many movies **such as:** *Top Gun, Cocktail, Far and Away,* and *A Few Good Men.*

Revised: Tom Cruise has acted in many movie**s:** *Top Gun, Cocktail, Far and Away,* and *A Few Good Men.*

This kind of mistake can usually be avoided if students remember that colons typically *replace* phrases like "the following," "as follows," "such as," "like," and "for example." In fact, using such a phrase *plus* a colon is actually redundant. Notice the way each of these original versions has been revised.

Original: I am postponing college until the fall for reasons **such as:** money, time, and family responsibilities.

Revised: I am postponing college until the fall for these reasons: money, time, and family responsibilities.

Original: Steven Spielberg directed many popular movies like **the following:** *E.T., Star Wars, Return of the Jedi,* and *The Empire Strikes Back.*

Revised: Steven Spielberg directed many popular movie**s:** *E.T., Star Wars, Return of the Jedi,* and *The Empire Strikes Back.*

Practicing What You Have Learned

Punctuate the following sentences correctly by either adding or omitting marks of punctuation. Add or remove words if necessary to make your meaning clear.

1. I am most afraid of things such as: dogs, spiders, and thunderstorms.
2. To soothe the symptoms of the common cold, do things like: take aspirin, drink liquids, keep warm.

3. Thomas Wolfe wrote several memorable works of fiction and poetry as follows: *Look Homeward, Angel, A Stone, A Leaf, A Door: Poems*, and *You Can't Go Home Again.*
4. Our high school awarded several superlatives; Jayne Lutz, Most Athletic, Howard Fain, Most Intellectual, Joyce Rutledge, Most Personality, and Ben Pobuda, Most Likely to Succeed.
5. Marigolds keep out unwanted garden pests; like aphids and spider mites and mealybugs.

Punctuating with Quotation Marks

Writers often need to show readers that the words they're reading belong to someone other than the writer. For instance, they may want to show a reader that dialogue is taking place between speakers. They may want to show a reader that material from another source is being used. In these and other situations, writers make use of conventions about punctuating with *quotation marks* to indicate these different speakers.

Quotation marks, like socks, always come in pairs. Writers make use of either double quotation marks—" "—or single quotation marks—' '. The following are some typical uses of single and double quotation marks:

1. Bruce asked, **"W**hy do we have to go to the mall again**?"**

2. Bruce said that he didn't want to go to the mall again.

3. "**A** lie stands on one leg**,"** wrote Benjamin Franklin**, "b**ut the truth stands on two**."**

4. Historian Arthur M. Schlesinger, Jr. told the 1992 graduating class**, "D**o not lose that wonderful confidence in yourselves, in your own experience, instinct and outlook**."**

5. Teresa sai**d, "D**o you believe he shouted **'Fire!'** in a crowded theater**?"**

6. Was it Emerson who said**, "A** foolish consistency is the hobgoblin of little minds"**?**

Notice in example 1 that if the first word of quoted material begins a sentence, it is capitalized; it is treated, therefore, like the beginning of any other sentence.

It is also important to notice the difference between material that is directly quoted and material that is indirectly quoted. Only direct quotes, as in example 1, receive quotation marks. As in example 2, material that is only indirectly quoted and does not reproduce the exact words of the speaker does not require quotation marks.

If the quotation is divided or interrupted by other words, as in example 3, capitals are not required after the interruption unless a new sentence begins there.

Punctuation marks before and after quotation marks often give writers trouble, but the general rule—illustrated in examples 1, 3, 4, and 5—is a simple one: punctuation marks—like periods, commas, question marks, and exclamation points—come *before* the quotation mark. This is true whether the quoted material comes at the beginning or the end of the sentence.

One exception to the general rule that other punctuation marks come *before* quotation marks occurs when the sense of the entire passage, which includes quoted material, requires a different mark of punctuation from the quoted passage. Example 6 illustrates this situation. Here the final question mark is placed outside the quotation to indicate that the sense of the entire passage is different from that of the quoted material.

Quotation marks are also used to indicate the titles of short works. A "short work" generally refers to a song title, a magazine or newspaper article, a TV program, a poem, or a book chapter. Knowing that certain titles require quotation marks and other titles require italics or underlining, writers are often rightfully confused about whether to put a title in quotes or whether to underline it. An easy rule-of-thumb is to remember that longer, more major works—like an entire book or an album or a magazine or a newspaper—require italics but that shorter works within those longer works—like a book chapter or a newspaper article or a single poem in a volume of poetry—are noted with quotation marks.

Single quotation marks are not as common as double quotation marks. Single quotation marks usually indicate quoted material within an already-quoted passage as in example 5.

Practicing What You Have Learned

Practice your skills with quotation marks by punctuating the following examples where needed.

1. The Rime of the Ancient Mariner is one of Samuel Taylor Coleridge's best-known poems.
2. Bob said I am going to the library to study.
3. Bob said he was going to the library to study.
4. Fellow teachers said the workshop speaker we have important work to do.
5. If Ralph says groovy one more time said Donna I'm going to scream.
6. Professor Hans Morgan, a noted Shakespearean scholar writing about Hamlet in British Heritage magazine, says, Polonius's line—to thyself be true—is the most familiar line in all of Shakespeare.
7. Professor Hans Morgan, a noted Shakespearean scholar, says that Polonius's line—to thyself be true—is the most familiar line in all of Shakespeare.
8. Who was it that originally spoke the lines about blood, toil, tears, and sweat?
9. I'm planning on majoring in philosophy said Georgia and I'm not going to let my father talk me out of it.
10. My favorite song on the Beatles's Sgt. Pepper's Lonely Hearts Club Band album is Yellow Submarine.

Punctuating with Apostrophes

Often writers need to indicate that a letter has been left out or that someone "owns" or "possesses" something. These two situations require the use of the *apostrophe.*

An apostrophe is a tricky little critter. It looks like one half of a single quotation mark:'. Because apostrophes are so small and require persistence to catch, writers often fail to notice missing apostrophes in their work. If they resolve to proofread carefully, they can often pick out places where apostrophes have been left out.

A contraction is a shortened version of a word or words. Apostrophes appear in contractions to indicate what letters have been omitted from the shortened version. You should be aware of the fact that contractions are often considered unacceptable in both informal and formal writing. Some typical examples of contractions are as follows:

you are	=	you're
here is	=	here's
who is	=	who's
they are	=	they're
it is	=	it's

Sometimes these forms are confused with similar-sounding possessive forms like *your, whose, their,* and *its*. It's important to remember that these possessive forms do NOT require an apostrophe. The best way to avoid such confusion is to use sound techniques for checking contractions and possessives.

Checking Your Contractions

A good way to catch apostrophe errors is to circle all the contractions in your paper. Then read the sentences in which contractions occur out loud, inserting all the omitted letters for which the apostrophes stand. If the sentence makes sense when read that way, you can be sure you've used your contractions appropriately. If the sentence does not make sense when read that way, make the necessary corrections. For instance, in checking the following sentence, you would first circle the contractions.

> If it's possible, you're to stay an extra hour for basketball practice, for they're practicing especially hard for the upcoming game.

Next, read the sentence out loud in the following way.

> If (IT IS) possible, (YOU ARE) to stay an extra hour for basketball practice, for (THEY ARE) practicing especially hard for the upcoming game.

Because the sentence makes sense when read that way, you have likely used your apostrophes correctly.

Checking your Possessives

A good way to check for correctness in your use of possessive pronouns is to circle all the possessives that appear in your paper. Next, remind yourself that possessives generally modify neighboring nouns, and then draw an arrow to the nouns they modify. Finally, remember that possessives do NOT require apostrophes. If your possessive includes apostrophes, try reading what you've written as if the missing letters had been included. If your possessive does *not* include apostrophes, try reading it as if it did. Such a reading will point out either your appropriate or inappropriate use of apostrophes. The following example explains this process for you.

> If you're coat is left on the rack too long, its likely someone will steal it.
>
> If you're coat (noun) is left on the rack too long, its likely (not a noun) someone will steal it.
>
> If (YOU ARE) coat is left on the rack too long, (IT IS) likely someone will steal it.
>
> Revision: If your coat is left on the rack too long, it's likely someone will steal it.

Checking for Apostrophes with "S"

As you have seen, apostrophes allow you to make use of the "short cut" called contractions. Apostrophes also offer you another "short cut" when you need to indicate ownership or possession. If you didn't have apostrophes to use, you would spend a lot of time writing things like, "The car *of the boy* was hit by the truck *of the farmer*." It's a lot more efficient to write, "The boy's car was hit by the farmer's truck." The apostrophe allows you to do this.

When you want to indicate ownership by singular nouns or pronouns, simply add an apostrophe and an *-s* to the end of the noun or pronoun.

> The boy**'s** jacket and the girl**'s** mittens were discovered in the lost and found.
>
> Someone**'s** troubles are nobody**'s** business.

When you want to indicate ownership by plural nouns, add an apostrophe and an -**s** if the noun does not end in -**s**. If the noun *does* end in -**s**, add only the apostrophe.

> The wome**n's** room and the me**n's** room were located side by side.
>
> The dieter**s'** conference was held in the governor**s'** ballroom.

Writers often have trouble with apostrophes which show plural possession. However, using the following three-step process to check for the appropriateness of your apostrophes will usually yield good results.

Step 1: Ask, "Who owns it?" Write this word down.

Step 2: Ask, "Does the owner end in "-*s*?" Give a "yes" or "no" answer.

Step 3: If the answer is "yes," place the apostrophe *after* the "-*s*." If the answer is "no," place the apostrophe *before* the "-*s*."

Example: Does the brothers barber shop quartet always sound that good?

Step 1: "Who owns it?" brothers

Step 2: "Does the owner end in "-*s*?" "Yes."

Step 3: Place the apostrophe *after* the "-*s*."

brother**s'** barber shop quartet

Practicing What You Have Learned

Make any necessary changes in the following sentences to reflect appropriate use of apostrophes.

1. At the Grimes family reunion, you're plate is heaped with an abundance of home-cooked food.
2. The hostesses menus were judged by the visiting chef's.
3. They're Bible reading quoted Jesus words exactly.
4. Its an idea who's time has come.
5. She's got a good idea for a new childrens' toy.
6. Most of the citizens votes reflected a concern for their elders health care.

Punctuating with Commas

The comma is a deceptively simple-looking mark of punctuation—,—which complicates writers' lives enormously. For some reason, a number of irrational practices surround the use of the comma. Sometimes writers confess that they write a paper and then go back and put all the commas in, sprinkling commas like someone liberally salting a piece of meat. Sometimes they note that they put in a comma in every place where you'd take a breath, equating punctuating with breathing.

Although sometimes these practices can result in accurate use of the comma, more useful is the little jingle governing comma use: "When in doubt, leave it out." The fact is that students tend to *over*use rather than *under*use the comma. A useful guide, then, would be to use a comma only when you're certain a comma is required.

Only a handful of situations actually require the use of a comma. These situations are as follows:

1. compound sentences,
2. introductory material,
3. interrupting material,
4. series,
5. formal conventions.

Commas and Compound Sentences

You have already studied the compound sentence in Chapter 7. You will remember, therefore, that the comma is used before a joining word such as *and, but, or, nor, for, yet*, and *so* when it joins the two parts of a compound sentence as in the following example:

> A baby robin is a voracious eater**, and** its parents spend the majority of each day satisfying its enormous appetite.

You will also remember that the comma follows special transition words when compound sentences are joined with a semicolon.

> A baby robin is a voracious eater**; consequently,** its parents spend the majority of each day satisfying its enormous appetite.

Commas and Introductory Material

When introductory material comes at the beginning of a sentence, the introductory material—either a word, phrase, or clause—is set off by a comma.

> Astonishe**d,** the young boy carefully recorded the number of times the male robin returned to the nest. (introductory word)
>
> In the course of a single spring mornin**g,** the male robin returned over twenty times to the chicks in the nest. (introductory phrases)
>
> Because baby robins are voracious eater**s,** their parents spend the majority of each day satisfying their chicks' enormous appetites. (introductory clause)

Commas and Interrupting Material

Sometimes words, phrases, or clauses are inserted into a sentence, interrupting the main flow of thought. In these situations, commas are placed around the interrupting material. You can check to make sure you have true interrupting material by reading the sentence out loud *without* the interrupting material. If the sentence still makes sense when read with the interrupting material left out, the interrupting material needs to have commas placed around it.

The baby robins**, a common species,** were born in early spring.

The baby robins**, which looked like five pairs of open beaks,** chirped incessantly.

The baby robins**, however,** refused food offered by the researcher.

Commas and Series

A very common use of the comma occurs between three or more items that are given as a series.

The baby robins **chirped, gulped, and swallowed** their food.

The male robin brought **gum wrappers, newspaper scraps, and long strings of twine** back to the nest.

It's important to remember that three items are required, not two.

Original: The baby robins gulped, and swallowed their food.

Revised: The baby robins gulped and swallowed their food.

Although some writers often declare that the comma before the final "and" is optional, it is a generally safer practice to include the comma before the final "and." A comma before the final "and" in the following example makes it clear that the series contains five colors rather than four.

The baby robins were an assortment of colors: tan, yellow, peach, brown, and white. (five colors)

The baby robins were an assortment of colors: tan, yellow, peach, brown and white. (four colors)

CONVENTIONS ABOUT VERBS

In written English, certain conventions also govern the use of verbs. These conventions fall into three general areas:

1. conventions about consistency,
2. conventions about tense,
3. conventions about agreement of subject and verb.

Conventions About Consistency

You have already seen in Chapter 7 that readers expect the verbs they read to convey consistency of time. Readers become confused when a writer switches tenses, flitting between past and present, for instance, or making use of some other disconcerting combination. Review the material on pages 208–209 in Chapter 7 to remind yourself about the convention of consistency, for keeping tenses consistent is one of the most common problems writers experience with using verbs.

Conventions About Tense

In English, time can be expressed in a variety of ways. You can express an idea which is occurring in the present. You can express an idea which was completed in the past. You can express an idea which will occur in the future. In spite of the fact that English verb tenses provide writers with a variety of ways of expressing time, the verb choices that reflect these expressions of time often confuse writers. However, once writers master expressions of time represented by verb choices, they quickly appreciate the shades of meaning about time that these choices provide for them.

In the following paired examples, you can notice the way that different verb tenses allow you to be more precise about describing relationships in time.

1. John mowed the grass this afternoon.
John has been mowing the grass this afternoon.

2. By the time the rain stopped, John had been soaked to the skin.
The rain stopped, and John was soaked to the skin.

3. By the time we arrived at the convention center, the governor stopped speaking.
By the time we arrived at the convention center, the governor had stopped speaking.

4. I read *War and Peace* last summer.
I have been reading *War and Peace* all summer long.

Practicing What You Have Learned

In the four pairs of sentences, discuss with your classmates the differences in time relationships indicated by the changes in verbs.

Principal Parts and Tense

You can learn to manage these changes in verbs by understanding the building blocks that characterize every English verb. Each verb has four parts called "principal parts." These four parts are the "building blocks" used to make up all the verb forms available to you in English. Changes of time are indicated by changing verb forms and/or by using auxiliaries like *had*, *will*, *have*, or some other helping verb. These principal parts are expressed in the following table:

Present	jump	convince
Past	jump**ed**	convince**d**
Past participle	jump**ed**	convince**d**
Present participle	jump**ing**	**con**vinc**ing**

In English there are three kinds of tenses available for expressing time. These are (1) the simple tenses, (2) the perfect tenses, and (3) the progressive tenses. Look at the following table to help you understand the name of the tense, an example of its use, and an explanation of its purpose.

Name of the Tense or Tenses	*Example*	*Purpose*
Simple tenses		Indicates simple past, present, or future time relationships
Present	I talk on the phone to my friends before supper.	Simple present time; uses present principal part; indicates what is happening now
Past	I talked to my professor about my grade.	Simple past time; uses past principal part; ends in -d or -ed; indicates what happened
Future	I will talk to my professor about my grade.	Simple future time; uses helping verb "shall" or "will" with present principal part; indicates what will happen
Perfect tenses	Made up of a past participle plus a helping verb	Indicates that something has been completed in the present, past, or future
Present perfect	I have talked about that issue with my friends many times.	Indicates something that began in the past but that continues or will continue into the present; uses the helping verb "has" or "have" with the past participle
Past perfect	I had talked to the professor about my struggles in the course before I received my failing grade.	Indicates the earlier of two past actions; uses the helping verb "had" with the past participle
Future perfect	Before my grade report comes to the house, I will have talked to my parents about my struggles in that course.	Indicates the earlier of two future actions; uses the helping verbs "will have" or "shall have" with the past participle
Progressive tenses		Indicates something that is or was or will be ongoing; uses an "-ing" present participle plus a form of "be"

Present progressive	I <u>am talking</u> on the phone right now.	"Am," "is," or "are" plus the present participle; indicates something ongoing in the present
Past progressive	I <u>was talking</u> for a long time after supper.	"Was" or "were" plus the present participle; indicates something ongoing in the past
Future progressive	I <u>will be talking</u> to several faculty members next week about changing majors.	"Will be" plus the present participle; indicates something ongoing in the future
Perfect progressive tenses		Uses an "-ing" verb form, a form of "be," and either "has," "have," "had," or "will have" to indicate the length of time in which something is, was, or will be ongoing
Present perfect progressive	I <u>have been talking</u> on the phone before supper all semester.	Uses "has been" or "have been" plus the present participle
Past perfect progressive	I <u>had been talking</u> about my problems with the course since the first day of class.	Uses "had been" plus the present participle
Future perfect progressive	By the time I finally declare a new major, I <u>will have been talking</u> about changing majors for over a year.	Uses "will have been" plus the present participle

Practicing What You Have Learned

In order for you to learn to appreciate the different qualities of time which the English verb tenses allow you to express, look at each of the pairs of sentences. Then label the tenses used as either a simple tense, a perfect tense, or a progressive tense. After you have labeled each tense, discuss with your classmates the different shades of meaning offered by the different verb tenses.

1. a. The president of the university announced that he investigated the need for new faculty contracts before he committed to a salary increase.
   b. The president of the university announced that he had investigated the need for new faculty contracts before committing to a salary increase.
2. a. Laura called from her friend's house and said that she took the baby to the sitter around 3 o'clock.
   b. Laura called from her friend's house and said that she had taken the baby to the sitter around 3 o'clock.
3. a. This spring Mary is planting several fruit trees to improve that bare spot on her lawn.
   b. This spring Mary will be planting several fruit trees to improve that bare spot on her lawn.
4. a. By the time she finally gets a job, Sue Ann will have spent nearly $100 on resumes.

b. By the time she finally gets a job, Sue Ann will spend nearly $100 on resumes.

5. a. I studied business for nearly three years before I realized I was more interested in science.
   b. I had studied business for nearly three years before I realized I was more interested in science.
6. a. The car just stopped at the light when the ambulance siren went off.
   b. The car had just stopped at the light when the ambulance siren went off.
7. a Kevin has been wondering about the truthfulness of that insurance claim for years.
   b. Kevin wondered about the truthfulness of that insurance claim for years.
8. a Brian was excited about his new job until he received his first pay check.
   b. Brian had been excited about his new job until he received his first pay check.
9. a I am planning to bring my lunch to work every day this week.
   b. I plan to bring my lunch to work every day this week.
10. a. Matt had learned to ride a bike by the time he entered first grade.
    b. Matt learned to ride a bike by the time he entered first grade.
11. a. I had been working diligently until last week's test.
    b. I was working diligently until last week's test.
12. a. Harold spent 10 dollars a week on junk food before he went on a diet.
    b. Harold had been spending 10 dollars a week on junk food before he went on a diet.

Standard and Irregular Verbs

As you can see from many of the examples given, most English verbs change tense or time by changing their principal parts in predictable ways. For instance, the verb "move" indicates changes in time by adding a "-d" to the present participle part, and the verb "walk" indicates changes in time by adding an "-ed" to the present principle part.

Present	move	walk
Past	move**d**	walk**ed**
Past participle	move**d**	walk**ed**
Present participle	mov**ing**	walk**ing**

Verbs which indicate changes in time by adding "-d" or "-ed" to the present principal part are called *regular verbs*. Because most of the verbs in English indicate changes in time by adding "-d" or "-ed" to the present principal part, most English verbs are regular verbs.

Unfortunately for writers, many English verbs do not indicate changes in time in this way. Their principal parts aren't consistent. For instance, the verbs "break" and "see" change their forms in a number of ways:

Present	know	see
Past	knew	saw
Past participle	known	seen
Present participle	knowing	seeing

Because these verb forms change in highly irregular ways, these verbs are called *irregular verbs*. The only way to make certain that you're using an irregular verb appropriately is to check the dictionary or the list which follows.

Irregular Verbs

Present Tense	*Past Tense*	*Past Participle*
am, is, are	was, were	been
arise	arose	arisen
awake	awoke, awaked	awoke, awaked
become	became	become
begin	began	begun
bleed	bled	bled
blow	blew	blown
break	broke	broken
bring	brought	brought
build	built	built
burn	burned, burnt	burned, burnt
burst	burst	burst
buy	bought	bought
catch	caught	caught
choose	chose	chosen
come	came	come
cost	cost	cost
cut	cut	cut
deal	dealt	dealt
dig	dug	dug
dive	dived, dove	dived
do	did	done
draw	drew	drawn
dream	dreamed, dreamt	dreamed, dreamt
drink	drank	drunk
drive	drove	driven
eat	ate	eaten
fall	fell	fallen
feel	felt	felt

Present Tense	*Past Tense*	*Past Participle*
fight	fought	fought
find	found	found
fly	flew	flown
forget	forgot	forgotten, forgot
freeze	froze	frozen
get	got	gotten, got
give	gave	given
go	went	gone
grow	grew	grown
have	had	had
hear	heard	heard
hide	hid	hidden
hurt	hurt	hurt
keep	kept	kept
know	knew	known
lay (put, place)	laid	laid
lead	led	led
lend	lent	lent
let (permit, allow)	let	let
lie (recline)	lay	lain
lose	lost	lost
make	made	made
mean	meant	meant
meet	met	met
mistake	mistook	mistaken
prove	proved	proved, proven
put	put	put
raise (force up)	raised	raised
read	read	read
ride	rode	ridden
ring	rang	rung
rise (get up)	rose	risen
run	ran	run
say	said	said
see	saw	seen
send	sent	sent
set (put, place)	set	set
sew	sewed	sewn, sewed
shake	shook	shaken
shine	shone, shined	shone, shined
shoot	shot	shot

Present Tense	*Past Tense*	*Past Participle*
shrink	shrank, shrunk	shrunk, shrunken
sing	sang	sung
sink	sank	sunk
sit (be seated)	sat	sat
sleep	slept	slept
slide	slid	slid
slink	slunk	slunk
speak	spoke	spoken
spin	spun	spun
spring	sprang	sprung
stand	stood	stood
steal	stole	stolen
sting	stung	stung
strike	struck	struck, stricken
swear	swore	sworn
swim	swam	swum
swing	swung	swung
take	took	taken
teach	taught	taught
tear	tore	torn
tell	told	told
throw	threw	thrown
understand	understood	understood
wake	woke, waked	waked, woken
wear	wore	worn
weep	wept	wept
win	won	won
wind	wound	wound
wring	wrung	wrung
write	wrote	written

Practicing What You Have Learned

Refer to the list of the principal parts of the irregular verbs to fill in the appropriate verb form in the following sentences:

1. Mother had ______________ the heavy pot on the stove before she served supper. (set)
2. Uncle Ben ______________ the window to let in some fresh air. (raise)
3. Mrs. Sanders ______________ very highly about the curriculum at that college. (speak)
4. The campers ______________ at dawn to the smell of frying bacon. (awake)

5. By the time the doctor appeared, the baby had ____________ feverish for several hours. (feel)
6. Marian ____________ the book on the table. (lay)

Tense and Dialect Forms

Dialect refers to the special way language is used in a particular region or community. American language is made more rich, interesting, and colorful by the presence of these many dialects. However, speakers of a community dialect need to be aware that their dialect follows different conventions from the standard English of the businesses and professions. Many of these dialect differences apply especially to verbs. For instance, the following verb forms are often used by speakers of a regional dialect.

He do his work without any help.
They be late for the meeting.
This radio don't work.
She have a cold today.
They has set the table for supper.
We ain't coming in until the game is over.

People who use community dialects need to remember some of the common patterns of difference between their dialects and standard written English. Often, dialect speakers fail to put an "**-s**" on the third person singular form of the verb or the "**-ed**" on the past tense form of the verb as in the following examples.

Dialect	**Standard**
She run after her dog.	She runs after her dog. (Third person singular form)
He work a 10 hour shift yesterday.	He work**ed** a 10 hour shift yesterday. (past tense form)

Another common difference between speakers of regional dialects and speakers of standard English is in the use of the verbs **do, have**, and **be**. Notice the difference between the dialect form and the standard form for each of these verbs.

Present Tense

Dialect

I (be or is, has, does)	we (be, has, does)
you (be, has, does)	you (be, has, does)
he/she/it (be, have, do)	they (be, has, does)

Standard

I (am, have, do)	we (are, have, do)
you (are, have, do)	you (are, have, do)
he/she/it (is, has, does)	they (are, have, do)

Past Tense

Dialect

I (were, has, done)	we (was, has, done)
you (was, has, done)	you (was, has, done)
he/she/it (were, have, done)	they (was, had, done)

Standard

I (was, had, did)	we (were, had, did)
you (were, had, did)	you (were, had, did)
he/she/it (was, had, did)	they (were, had, did)

Practicing What You Have Learned

For each of the following pairs, label the sentence as either a standard or dialect form of the verb. For the dialect form, tell whether it demonstrates a problem with (1) lack of "-s" on the singular third person form, (2) lack of "-ed" on the past tense form, (3) use of the verb "be," (4) use of the verb "have," (5) use of the verb "do." When you have finished, check your answers with a fellow classmate.

"-s" *"-ed"* *be* *have* *do*

1. a. Harold have no idea why he missed the bus.
   b. Harold has no idea why he missed the bus.
2. a. That fresh apple pie sure smell good.
   b. That fresh apple pie sure smells good.
3. a. Aunt Martha shops right until closing time.
   b. Aunt Martha shop right until closing time.
4. a. Yesterday Frank got a ticket because he park his car in a No Parking zone.
   b. Yesterday Frank got a ticket because he parked his car in a No Parking zone.
5. a. My little brother be five years old today.
   b. My little brother is five years old today.
6. a. Brenda does all her homework before she watches TV.
   b. Brenda do all her homework before she watches TV.
7. a. That church service last all morning.
   b. That church service lasts all morning.

8. a. Joey passed out the literature at last night's meeting.
   b. Joey pass out the literature at last night's meeting.
9. a. Mary don't really try her best in that class.
   b. Mary doesn't really try her best in that class.
10. a. Their son have a chance for a college scholarship.
    b. Their son has a chance for a college scholarship.

Conventions About Agreement of Subject and Verb

When singular subjects are matched with singular verbs, they are said to "agree." When plural subjects are matched with plural verbs, they are also said to "agree." In English, subjects and verbs are expected to be in agreement as in the following examples.

The girl sings in the choir on Sunday.
(singular subject) (singular verb)

The girls sing in the choir on Sunday.
(plural subject) (plural verb)

In these examples, notice the endings on the subjects and verbs and their appearance in the following table.

	Subject	Verb
Singular (one)	*girl*	*sing***s**
Plural (more than one)	*girl***s**	*sing*

Practicing What You Have Learned

Take some time getting used to the singular and plural subject and verb forms by completing the table with any word choices you wish.

	Subject	Verb
Singular (one)	parent	
Plural (more than one)		climb

Singular (one)	everyone	
Plural (more than one)	sisters	
Singular (one)		predicts
Plural (more than one)	teachers	
Singular (one)	player	
Plural (more than one)		eat
Singular (one)	nobody	
Plural (more than one)		match
Singular (one)	tuba	
Plural (more than one)		annoy
Singular (one)		lasts
Plural (more than one)	concepts	

The "S" Solution

From these examples, it may now be clear that singular subjects do not end in "**s**," but that singular verbs do. Conversely, plural subjects do end in "**s**," but plural verbs do not. Although there are some often frustrating exceptions, in most situations you can assume that either the subject or the verb will end in "**s**." You will generally not find both the subject and the verb with an "s" ending. The fact that, in most cases, an "s" appears on either the subject or the verb but not on both is called the *"S" Solution.*

The "S" Solution and Indefinite Pronouns

The "s" solution makes it easier for you to deal with indefinite pronouns. *Indefinite pronouns* are the "-one," the "-body," and the "-thing" words. A list of the indefinite pronouns follows:

-one words	*-body words*	*-thing words*	*miscellaneous*
one	nobody	nothing	each
someone	somebody	something	either
anyone	anybody	anything	neither
everyone	everybody	everything	

Because indefinite pronouns used as a subject of a sentence never end in "s," the "s" solution tells you that the verb which needs to agree with the indefinite pronoun subject will end in "**s**."

Practicing What You Have Learned

In the following sentences, choose the correct verb for the indefinite pronoun subjects based on the "s" solution:

1. Everybody (talks, talk) about changing the curriculum, but nobody ever (makes, make) the necessary changes.
2. Each of the boys (has, have) a jacket hanging in the hall closet.
3. Everything about that political plan of action (sounds, sound) suspicious.
4. Either of the children (needs, need) recognition from the teacher, but neither of them (seems, seem) likely to receive it.
5. Everyone (believes, believe) that a new alcohol policy is long overdue.

As you have seen, the "s" solution can often help you work out subject-verb agreement problems. There are special circumstances, however, in which you need to use the "s" solution with care. These special circumstances involve (1) reversed-order sentences and (2) intervening words.

The "S" Solution and Reversed-Order Sentences

As you know, most English sentences present the subject first and the verb second. In reversed-order sentences, the subject follows the verb. Although there are many situations in which the subject follows the verb, sentences that begin with "there" or "here" and sentences that are questions dependably signal that the subject will be following the verb. In these cases, the "s" solution still applies, but when the predictable subject-verb order has been reversed, you need to be especially careful to identify the subject correctly.

There are three tools essential for the gardener.
(verb) (subject)

Here are the final reports you requested.
(verb) (subject)

Where are the packages to be delivered?
(verb) (subject)

In the cafeteria are two serving lines.
(verb) (subject)

Practicing What You Have Learned

In the following examples, identify the reversed-order subject, and then choose the appropriate verb based on the "s" solution.

1. There (is, are) three steps to solving this puzzle.

2. Beside the stream (was, were) empty pop bottles left by lazy campers.
3. Which (is, are) the questions most likely to be on the test?
4. Here (is, are) the manuals which you requested.
5. In the library (is, are) the materials for your research paper.
6. Occupying the lawn (was, were) groups of angry picketers.

The "S" Solution and Intervening Words

Another situation that calls for care occurs when groups of words come between the subject and verb. Writers are often tricked by those intervening words into thinking that a word in the intervening word group is the subject of the sentence. A good way to avoid those tricks is to draw a line through the intervening word group in order to see the true subject of the sentence more clearly. The following examples illustrate this technique for you.

> The price ~~of the coats~~ (has, have) been reduced.
> (subject) (intervening words)
>
> Each ~~of the students~~ (needs, needs) more time in the lab.
> (subject) (intervening words)

Practicing What You Have Learned

In the following sentences, strike through the intervening words, and then choose the appropriate verb.

1. The glasses on the shelf in the kitchen (is, are) to be used for the party.
2. My professor, along with the entire class of students, (is, are) planning to go on the field trip.
3. The plumbing fixtures in that old house (needs, need) replacing.
4. Jupiter, as well as its orbiting moons, (was, were) the subject of Mark's report.
5. The athletes, who wanted to be represented at the meeting, (is, are) sending a representative to substitute for them.

The "S" Solution and Compound Subjects

The "s" solution does not really apply in the case of compound or double subjects. When a sentence contains compound subjects joined by the word "**and**," common sense dictates that the verb will be plural; it will therefore not end in "s," even if the double subjects do not end in "s" either.

> A sister and a brother (is, are) usually supportive of each other once each becomes an adult.
> (double subjects)

Note that the pronoun "both" always takes a plural verb.

Both (is, are) usually supportive of each other once each becomes an adult.

If the double subjects are connected by paired connectors like *either/or, neither/nor*, or *not only/but also*, the "s" solution *does* apply, and the verb will agree with the subject which is placed closer to the verb.

Either the coach *or* his assistants (is, are) rethinking the game plan for Friday night. (double subjects; "assistants" closer to verb)

Neither the students *nor* the teacher (approves, approve) of the curriculum changes. (double subjects; "teacher" closer to the verb)

Practicing What You Have Learned

In the following sentences, choose the correct verb, and then explain the compound subject situation that governs your choice.

1. Not only the government but also the citizens (profits, profit) from an expanded tax base.
2. Tobacco and alcohol (is, are) two substances which are heavily taxed.
3. Fuel efficiency and a compact body (is, are) two characteristics of gas-saving automobiles.
4. Either John or his parents (is, are) planning on attending the reception.
5. The kitchen and the family room (is, are) the two most heavily traveled rooms in the house.
6. Both of the mechanics (detects, detect) a problem with the carburetor.

The "S" Solution and Special Words

Certain special words or combinations of words need special consideration. When these special words are used, the "s" solution may or may not apply.

For instance, the following words usually require a singular verb, even though they end in "**s**": news, athletics, mathematics, statistics, physics. In addition, titles also take singular verbs.

Physics (is, are) a subject that explains everyday phenomena.
The Three Musketeers (is, are) Alexandre Dumas' most famous book.

When the words who, which, and that are used as subjects, their verbs are chosen according to the "s" solution, but those choices are based on the word to which who, which, and that refers.

I like a car <u>that</u> (<u>handles</u>, handle) easily.
("car"—word to which "that" refers)

I like cars <u>that</u> (handles, <u>handle</u>) easily.
("cars"—word to which "that" refers)

Practicing What You Have Learned

Choose the appropriate verb based on considerations of the special words used in each sentence.

1. Statistics (is, are) a basic requirement for all psychology majors.
2. This kind of music is not for a listener who (enjoys, enjoy) peace and quiet.
3. *World of our Fathers* (traces, trace) the immigrant experience.
4. The news from the correspondents in East Asia (is, are) optimistic.
5. The Presidency is not a job for politicians who (deals, deal) poorly with criticism.

CONVENTIONS ABOUT PRONOUNS

Pronouns stand in for nouns. They take their place. Thus, the pronoun "he" may take the place of the noun "boy," and the pronoun "they" may stand in for the noun "neighbors." Pronouns are a help to writers, for they keep writers from having to repeat nouns unnecessarily. It would be awkward and unnecessary to have to write sentences like "Father hoped Father's new job would be a challenge to Father." Instead, pronouns allow us to write, "Father hoped <u>his</u> new job would be a challenge to <u>him</u>."

In spite of the shortcut pronouns offer writers, pronouns often offer problems as well. Developing writers typically have trouble with pronouns, and their problems generally fall into four areas.

1. Problems with pronoun reference
2. Problems with pronoun agreement
3. Problems with pronoun case
4. Problems with pronoun point of view

Problems with Pronoun Reference

As you have seen, pronouns stand in for nouns. Thus, because they are a kind of substitute, the noun or word the pronoun is substituting for—called the *referent* or *antecedent*—must be clear. Problems with pronouns often occur because of troubles with referents. Typically, however, problems in pronoun reference occur in only two ways: (1) the pronoun does not refer to a specific word or (2) the pronoun refers to more than one word.

Practicing What You Have Learned

A. The following sentences demonstrate problems in pronoun reference. After you read each sentence, decide whether the pronoun reference problem occurs because (1) the pronoun does not refer to a specific word or (2) the pronoun refers to more than one word. Then rewrite the sentence to solve the pronoun reference problem. The first example has been done for you.

Problem	*(1) No Specific Reference*	*(2) More Than One Reference*	*Solution*
1. After Joe hit Johnny, he cried for hours.		X	After Joe hit Johnny, Johnny cried for hours.
2. Although Susan longs to become a chemist, I have never enjoyed it.			
3. Kathy told Ellen that her face had broken out right before the prom.			
4. Our professor does not grade on the curve, and it frustrates me.			
5. The reporter asked many questions about the candidate's views on abortion which were objectionable.			
6. The old people lunched on sandwiches and fruit; afterwards, they threw them to the birds.			
7. I hold down two jobs; this is difficult for me.			
8. In Harper Lee's novel, she captures the racial atmosphere in a Southern town.			
9. The officer told Henry that he would be going to court.			
10. A tuition hike was being proposed, but they forgot to inform the students.			

B. After you have reviewed these problems and their solutions, hold a class discussion to determine the pronoun reference "rules" that solve problems when (1) no specific reference appears or (2) more than one reference appears.

C. Look back through your writing for examples of problems with pronoun reference. Share them with the class and determine whether the problems arise because there is (1) no specific referent or (2) more than one referent. Then correct those problems by referring to the "rules" you suggested in **B.**

Problems with Pronoun Agreement

Problems with pronoun agreement are only a little different from problems with pronoun reference. You have seen that pronoun reference problems occur when the referent is unclear—either because no referent has been provided or because more than one possible referent appears.

In a problem of pronoun agreement, however, the referent is nearly always clear: it is the pronoun that is the problem. Thus, with a reference problem, the focus is on the noun referent; with an agreement problem, the focus is on the pronoun substitute.

Because pronouns need to agree with their referents in number (singular or plural) and gender (masculine, feminine, or neuter), a referent noun like "squirrel" would call for a substitute pronoun like "it" or "its" because "squirrel" requires a pronoun that is singular in number and neuter in gender. As a result, pronoun and referent are said to be in "agreement."

In addition, certain words cause special problems with pronoun agreement. These words are called indefinite pronouns, and they are always treated as singular in number. The indefinite pronouns are easy to remember because most of them end in the suffix "one" or "body." The indefinite pronouns appear in the following list.

each	one	nobody
either	everyone	everybody
neither	someone	somebody
	anyone	anybody

Indefinite pronouns cause special problems for students for two general reasons: (1) indefinite pronouns are often followed by a prepositional phrase containing a noun and (2) the gender to which the indefinite pronoun refers is often unclear.

When the indefinite pronoun is followed by a prepositional phrase containing a noun, writers are often confused. A sentence like the following can be perplexing:

Either of the solutions has (its, their) share of difficulties.

Students may think that their choice of pronoun should be determined by the noun "solutions" which appears in the prepositional phrase rather than by the indefinite pronoun "either." However, they can guard against this possibility by crossing out the prepositional phrase which follows the indefinite pronoun and choosing the singular pronoun.

Either (~~of the solutions~~) has (its, their) share of difficulties.
(indefinite pronoun) (prepositional phrase) (singular pronoun)
(takes a singular pronoun)

A second example offers more practice with this often confusing construction.

Neither ~~of the boys~~ did (his, their) chores today.
(indefinite pronoun) (prepositional phrase) (singular pronoun)
(takes a singular pronoun)

Another reason why indefinite pronouns cause confusion is that the gender to which the indefinite pronoun refers is often unclear. For instance:

Anyone in line for a promotion must turn in (his, her, their) application today.

A sentence like this is rightfully confusing. Because "anyone" is an indefinite pronoun, it typically requires a singular pronoun like "his." This choice might be technically accurate, especially if it refers to employees in an all-male working environment, but what if that workplace also includes females? In that case, a reasonable response might be something like the following:

Anyone in line for a promotion must turn in his or her application today.

Even if this solution seems to solve one problem, another problem crops up. A solution like this calls attention to the very problem it attempts to solve. Thus, although this awkward construction may avoid the problem of neglecting the females in the workforce, it calls undue attention to the mixed-sex situation at the same time. In cases like this, it is often preferable to recast the sentence in this way:

Anyone in line for a promotion must turn in their application today.

Because this solution violates the traditional rule that indefinite pronouns like "anyone" take a singular, an even better solution is to avoid the "anyone" problem altogether. This can be done by replacing "anyone" with a more concrete noun. A solution like this is often preferable.

Employees in line for a promotion must turn in their application today.

Practicing What You Have Learned

The following examples demonstrate problems with pronoun agreement. Underline the pronoun problem and then choose an appropriate substitute. In some cases, several different substitutes may be appropriate. After you have finished, discuss with your classmates whether the agreement problem arises because of a general pronoun problem or because of an indefinite pronoun problem. Then share your answers with your classmates.

1. A student should always be aware of their course options.
2. A daily newspaper should be concerned about the interests of their readers.
3. Each of the secretaries is responsible for (her, their) own correspondence.
4. I never have to give up my passion for music, for I have dozens of CDs to remind me of them.
5. Everyone who fails to wear his seat belt will be subject to a stiff fine.
6. Anyone who is a devoted athlete should faithfully do their exercises.
7. The hurricane warnings were so serious that it led to evacuation of the entire area.
8. One of the youngsters damaged their roller blades.
9. Everyone in the course plans to turn in their research papers at the end of the semester.
10. Each of the sorority pledges is working hard at their community service projects.

Problems in Pronoun Case

Because pronouns, like verbs, are changeable creatures, they give writers a lot of trouble. One of the areas of frustration relates to the fact that pronouns change their form depending on what role they are playing in a sentence. These changes in pronoun form are what is meant by pronoun case.

Actually, the case forms of pronouns are familiar to most English speakers. They are divided into two types: (1) subject pronouns and (2) object pronouns. These subject and object pronouns are listed for you.

Subject Pronouns	*Object Pronouns*
I	me
we	us
you	you
he	him

she	her
it	it
they	them
who	whom

It's important for you to know which pronoun form to use. In one sentence, the correct pronoun form might be an "I." In another, the correct pronoun form might be a "me." In another place, the correct pronoun might be "who," yet in another place the correct pronoun might be "whom." How do you choose?

Case decisions are based on how the pronoun is used in the sentence. Thus, the subject pronouns are used for subject-related situations in which the pronoun functions as the subject of the sentence or as a subject complement as in the following examples:

(**We,** Us) are going to the circus when it comes to town. (**We** is the subject of the sentence.)

It was (**they,** them) who reported the crime to the police. (**They** is the subject complement after the linking verb "was.")

The object pronouns are used for object-related situations in which the pronoun functions as the direct object, the indirect object, or the object of a preposition. The following examples make use of object forms of the pronoun.

Bonnie asked (he, **him**) to the game. (**Him** is the direct object of the sentence.)

The class gave (she, **her**) the gift. (**Her** is the indirect object of the sentence.)

At the concert the Simpsons sat with (they, **them**). (**Them** is the object of the preposition "with.")

Thus, in addition to knowing the actual forms of the subject and the object pronouns, you must be familiar with how the pronouns are being used in sentences. A guideline to the pronoun uses follows:

Subject Pronouns	*Object Pronouns*
subject	direct object
subject complement	indirect object
	object of the preposition

Checking Pronoun Case

Three useful methods exist for checking pronoun case: (1) the two-step method, (2) the strike-through method, and (3) the who/whom method.

The Two-Step Method

The two-step method is easy to learn and will help you make reliable choices about pronoun case. In the first step of this method, you find out how the pronoun is being used in the sentence. In the second step, you choose the pronoun from the proper column on the previous list. The following exercise will help you practice this two-step method.

Practicing What You Have Learned

For each of the following sentences, first identify the way the pronoun is being used in the sentence, and then choose from the given list the proper pronoun. The abbreviations stand for Subject (S), Subject Complement (SC), Direct Object (DO), Indirect Object (IO), and Object of the Preposition (OP).

Example	*Use in Sentence*					*Correct Case Form*
	Subject Pronouns		*Object Pronouns*			
	S	*SC*	*DO*	*IO*	*OP*	
1. The greatest share of the work on the project was assumed by (she, her).						
2. John and (I, me) played stickball in the alley as children.						
3. The committee had selected Fernando and (he, him) for the award.						
4. Their parents gave (they, them) complimentary tickets to Friday's basketball game.						
5. Lucille observed that it was (they, them) who broke the rules.						

The Strike-Through Method

Another method, called the *strike-through method*, will help you choose your pronouns correctly. This method is especially useful when a pronoun is combined or paired with another word. It involves striking out the part of the pair that is not a pronoun. Striking through the part that is not a pronoun helps make the proper case of the pronoun clear.

> Although they both competed successfully in the tournament, ~~Sylvia and~~ (**she**, her) disliked the way it had been organized.

The most difficult part for ~~Charlene and~~ (I, **me**) was the opening scene.

The Who/Whom Method

Writers often have trouble making decisions about "who" and "whom." Should they choose the subject pronoun "who?" Or should they choose the object pronoun "whom?"

If they practice the who/whom method, the choices are usually clearer. The who/whom method tells writers to isolate the word group in which the "who" or "whom" appears and then substitute "he" for "who" and "him" for "whom." Once the separation and substitution are completed, then read the sentence aloud with either the he-substitute or the him-substitute. Isolating, substituting, and reading in this way usually leads the writer to the proper choice.

Example:	The high grade goes to the person (who, whom) has worked the hardest.
Isolate:	. . . (who, whom) has worked the hardest.
Substitute:	. . . (he) has worked the hardest.
	OR . . . (him) has worked the hardest.
Read:	**He** has worked the hardest.
Correct Case Form:	**He = Who**

Practicing What You Have Learned

The following sentences will give you practice in either the strike-through method or the who/whom method. Choose the proper case forms, and then identify the method you used for choosing them.

1. The local elementary school hired both Leon and (I, me).
2. (Who, Whom) the committee selects faces a tough job next year.
3. At the family reunion, we listened to stories told by my grandmother and (she, her).
4. The local disc jockey, (who, whom) plays at most area events, is appearing on television this weekend.
5. After Jerome and (he, him) scored the last two baskets, the game was all but finished.
6. The president consulted the board members, most of (who, whom) disagreed with his proposal.

Pronoun Consistency and Point of View

In Chapter 7, Editing and Proofreading, you learned that an important part of clear writing involves keeping pronoun point of view consistent. You should refer to pages 207–208 to remind yourself of the importance of honoring your reader's need for a consistent point of view.

B

Writing Assessment Profile

CHAPTER 1: THE CHALLENGE OF WRITING
ASSIGNMENT:

Prewriting comments

Responding comments

Critiquing comments

Editing comments

Proofreading comments

CHAPTER 2: WRITING FOR A READER
ASSIGNMENT:

Prewriting comments

Responding comments

Critiquing comments

Editing comments

Proofreading comments

CHAPTER 3: PREWRITING: YOUR READER AND YOUR PURPOSE ASSIGNMENT:

Prewriting comments

Responding comments

Critiquing comments

Editing comments

Proofreading comments

CHAPTER 4: PREWRITING: PLANNING YOUR STRATEGY ASSIGNMENT:

Prewriting comments

Responding comments

Critiquing comments

Editing comments

Proofreading comments

CHAPTER 5: FROM SPEAKING TO WRITING ASSIGNMENT:

Prewriting comments

Responding comments

Critiquing comments

Editing comments

Proofreading comments

CHAPTER 6: REWRITING: RESPONDING AND CRITIQUING ASSIGNMENT:

Prewriting comments

Responding comments

Critiquing comments

Editing comments

Proofreading comments

CHAPTER 7: REWRITING: EDITING AND PROOFREADING ASSIGNMENT:

Prewriting comments

Responding comments

Critiquing comments

Editing comments

Proofreading comments

CHAPTER 8: DESCRIBING ASSIGNMENT:

Prewriting comments

Responding comments

Critiquing comments

Editing comments

Proofreading comments

CHAPTER 9: ILLUSTRATING
ASSIGNMENT:

Prewriting comments

Responding comments

Critiquing comments

Editing comments

Proofreading comments

CHAPTER 10: USING FACTS
ASSIGNMENT:

Prewriting comments

Responding comments

Critiquing comments

Editing comments

Proofreading comments

CHAPTER 11: GIVING REASONS
ASSIGNMENT:

Prewriting comments

Responding comments

Critiquing comments

Editing comments

Proofreading comments

CHAPTER 12: NARRATING ASSIGNMENT:

Prewriting comments

Responding comments

Critiquing comments

Editing comments

Proofreading comments

CHAPTER 13: EXPLORING PROBLEMS AND SOLUTIONS ASSIGNMENT:

Prewriting comments

Responding comments

Critiquing comments

Editing comments

Proofreading comments

CHAPTER 14: COMPARING AND CONTRASTING ASSIGNMENT:

Prewriting comments

Responding comments

Critiquing comments

Editing comments

Proofreading comments

CHAPTER 15: CLASSIFYING
ASSIGNMENT:

Prewriting comments

Responding comments

Critiquing comments

Editing comments

Proofreading comments

CHAPTER 16: ANALYZING
ASSIGNMENT:

Prewriting comments

Responding comments

Critiquing comments

Editing comments

Proofreading comments

CHAPTER 17: COLLABORATING
ASSIGNMENT:

Prewriting comments

Responding comments

Critiquing comments

Editing comments

Proofreading comments

Bibliography

AUGUSTINE, DOROTHY, AND WINTEROWD, W. ROSS. (1986). Speech acts and the reader-writer transaction. In Bruce T. Petersen (ed.), *Convergences: Transactions in Reading and Writing*, Urbana, IL: NCTE, pp. 127–148.

BATKER, CAROL, AND MORAN, CHARLES. (1986). The reader in the writing class. In Thomas Newkirk (ed.), *Only Connect: Uniting Reading and Writing*, Upper Montclair, NJ: Boynton/Cook Publishers, pp. 198–208.

BEACH, RICHARD, AND LIEBMAN-KLEINE, JOANNE. (1986). The writing/reading relationship: Becoming one's own best reader. In Bruce T. Petersen, (ed.), *Convergences: Transactions in Reading and Writing*, Urbana, IL: NCTE, pp. 64–81.

BERKENKOTTER, CAROLE. (1981). Understanding a writer's awareness of audience. *College Composition and Communication, 32,* 388–389.

BERKENKOTTER, CAROLE. (1982). Writing and problem solving. In Toby Fulwiler and Art Young (eds.), *Language Connections: Writing and Reading Across the Curriculum.* Urbana, IL: NCTE, pp. 33–44.

BERKENKOTTER, CAROLE. (1984). Student writers and their sense of authority over texts. *College Composition and Communication, 35*(3), 312–319.

BERNHARDT, STEPHEN. (1986). Seeing the text. *College Composition and Communication, 37,* 66–78.

BERTOFF, ANN E., AND STEPHENS, JAMES W. (1988). *Forming, Thinking, Writing (2nd ed.).* Portsmouth, NH: Boynton/Cook.

BIRNBAUM, JUNE CANNELL. (1986). Reflective thought: The connection between reading and writing. In Bruce T. Petersen (ed.), *Convergences: Transactions in Reading and Writing*. Urbana, IL: NCTE, pp. 30–45.

BRANDE, DOROTHEA. (1981). *Becoming a Writer.* Los Angeles: J. P. Tarcher.

BRANNON, LIL, AND KNOBLAUCH, C. H. (1982). On students' rights to their own texts: A model of teacher response. *College Composition and Communication, 33*(2), 157–166.

BRANSFORD, J. D., AND JOHNSON, M. K. (1973). Considerations of some problems of comprehension. In W. G. Chase (ed.), *Visual Information Processing*. NY: Academic Press.

BRITTON, JAMES, et. al. (1975). *The Development of Writing Abilities, 11-18*. Schools Council Research Series. London: Macmillan Education.

BROWN, HUNTINGTON. (1966). *Prose Styles: Five Primary Types*. Minneapolis: The University of Minnesota Press.

BRUFFEE, KENNETH. (1984). Collaborative learning and the 'conversation of mankind.' *College English, 46*, 635–652.

BURKLAND, JILL N., AND PETERSEN, BRUCE T. (1986). An integrative approach to research: Theory and practice. In Bruce T. Petersen (ed.), *Convergences: Transactions in Reading and Writing*. Urbana, IL: National Council of Teachers of English, pp. 189–202.

CHRISTENSEN, FRANCIS, AND CHRISTENSEN, BONNIEJEAN. (1978). *Notes Toward a New Rhetoric: Nine Essays for Teachers (2nd ed.)*. NY: Harper & Row.

CLARK, BEVERLY LYON. (1985). *Talking about Writing: A Guide for Tutor and Teacher Conferences*. Ann Arbor: The University of Michigan Press.

CLARK, IRENE. (1985). *Writing in the Center: Teaching in a Writing Center Setting*. Dubuque, Iowa: Kendall/Hunt.

CLIFFORD, JOHN. (1981). Composing in stages: The effects of a collaborative pedagogy. *Research in the Teaching of English, 15*, 37–53.

COLLINS, ALLAN, AND GENTNER, DEDRE. (1980). A framework for a cognitive theory of writing. In Lee W. Gregg and Erwin R. Steinberg (eds.), *Cognitive Processes in Writing*. Hillsdale, NJ: Lawrence Erlbaum Associates.

CUNNINGHAM, FRANK J. (1985). Writing philosophy: Sequential essays and objective tests. *College Composition and Communication, 36*(2), 166–172.

DICK, JOHN A. R., AND ESCH, ROBERT M. (1985). Dialogues among disciplines: A plan for faculty discussions of writing across the curriculum. *College Composition and Communication, 36*(2), 178–182.

DOUGHERTY, BARBEY N. (1986). Writing plans as strategies for reading, writing, and revising. In Bruce T. Petersen (ed.), *Convergences: Transactions in Reading and Writing*, Urbana, IL: NCTE, pp. 82–96.

EDE, LISA. (1984). Audience: An Introduction to Research. *College Composition and Communication, 35*(2), 140–153.

EDE, LISA. (1987). New perspectives on the speaking-writing relationship: Implications for teachers of basic writing. In Theresa Enos (ed.), *A Sourcebook for Basic Writing Teachers*. NY: Random House: pp. 318–327.

EDE, LISA, AND LUNSFORD, ANDREA. (1984). Audience addressed/audience invoked: The role of audience in composition theory and pedagogy. *College Composition and Communication, 35*(2), 155–171.

EDE, LISA, AND LUNSFORD, ANDREA. (1990). *Singular Texts/Plural Authors: Perspectives on Collaborative Writing*. Carbondale & Edwardsville: Southern Illinois University Press.

EDEN, RICK, AND MITCHELL, RUTH. (1986). Paragraphing for the Reader. *College Composition and Communication, 37*(4), 416–430.

ELBOW, PETER. (1973). *Writing without Teachers*. NY: Oxford University Press.

ELBOW, PETER. (1981). *Writing with Power: Techniques for Mastering the Writing Process*. NY: Oxford University Press.

ENOS, TERESA (ed.) (1987). *A Sourcebook for Basic Writing Teachers*. NY: Random House.

FAIGLEY, LESTER, AND HANSEN, KRISTINE. (1985). Learning to write in the social sciences. *College Composition and Communication, 36*(2), 140–149.

FALK, ANNE. (1982). What every educator should know about reading research. In Toby Fulwiler and Art Young (eds.), *Language Connections: Writing and Reading Across the Curriculum*. Urbana, IL: NCTE, pp. 123–137.

FARRELL, THOMAS J. (1977). Literacy, the basics and all that jazz. *College English, 38*, 443–459.

FISH, STANLEY. (1970). Literature and the reader: Affective stylistics. *New Literary History* 2, *1*, 123–162. In J. P. Tompkins (ed.), *Reader Response Criticism*. Baltimore: Johns Hopkins University Press, pp. 70–100.

FLESCH, RUDOLPH. (1949). *The Art of Readable Writing*. NY: Harper & Row.

FLESCH, RUDOLPH. (1979). *How to Write Plain English: A Book for Lawyers and Consumers*. NY: Harper & Row.

FLOWER, LINDA. (1979). Writer-based prose: A cognitive basis for problems in writing. *College English, 41*, 19–37.

FLOWER, LINDA. (1988). The construction of purpose in writing and reading. *College English, 50*(5), 528–550.

FLOWER, LINDA. (1989). *Problem-Solving Strategies for Writers, (3rd ed.)*. NY: Harcourt Brace Jovanovich.

FLOWER, LINDA, AND HAYES, JOHN R. (1980). The dynamics of composing: Making plans and juggling constraints. In Lee W. Gregg and Erwin R. Steinberg, (eds.), *Cognitive Processes in Writing*. Hillsdale, NJ: Lawrence Erlbaum Associates, pp. 31–50.

FLOWER, LINDA, AND HAYES, JOHN R. (1981). A cognitive process theory of writing. *College Composition and Communication, 32*, 365–387.

FLOWER, LINDA, AND HAYES, JOHN R. (1981). Plans that guide the composing process. In Carl H. Frederiksen and Joseph F. Dominic, (eds.), *Writing: The Nature, Development, and Teaching of Written Communication. Volume 2: Writing: Process, Development and Communication*. Hillsdale, NJ: Lawrence Erlbaum Associates, pp. 39–58.

FLOWER, LINDA, HAYES, JOHN R., AND SWARTS, HEIDI. (1980). *Revising functional documents: The scenario principle*. Document Design Project Technical Report #10. Pittsburgh: Carnegie-Mellon University.

FLYNN, ELIZABETH. (1984). Students as readers of their classmates' writing: Some implications for peer critiquing. *Writing Instructor, 3*, 120–128.

FRANCOZ, M. J. (1979). The logic of question and answer: Writing as inquiry. *College English, 41*, 336–339.

FREDERIKSEN, CARL H., AND DOMINIC, JOSEPH F. (eds.). (1981). Introduction: Perspectives on the activity of writing. *Writing: The Nature, Development, and Teaching of Written Communication, Volume 2: Writing: Process, Development and Communication*. Hillsdale, NJ: Lawrence Erlbaum Associates, pp. 1–20.

FREDERIKSEN, CARL H., AND DOMINIC, JOSEPH F. (1981). *Writing: The Nature, Development, and Teaching of Written Communication, Volume 2: Writing: Process, Development and Communication.* Hillsdale, NJ: Lawrence Erlbaum Associates.

FREISINGER, RANDALL. (1982). Cross-disciplinary writing programs: Beginnings. In Toby Fulwiler and Art Young (eds.), *Language Connections: Writing and Reading Across the Curriculum.* Urbana, IL: NCTE, pp. 3–13.

FULWILER, TOBY. (1982). The personal connection: Journal writing across the curriculum. In Toby Fulwiler and Art Young, (eds.), *Language Connections: Writing and Reading Across the Curriculum.* Urbana, IL: NCTE, pp. 15–31.

FULWILER, TOBY. (1992). Provocative revision. *The Writing Center Journal, 12*(2) (Spring), 190–204.

FULWILER, TOBY, AND YOUNG, ART (eds.) (1982). *Language Connections: Writing and Reading Across the Curriculum.* Urbana, IL: NCTE.

FULWILER, TOBY, AND JONES, ROBERT. (1982). Assigning and evaluating transactional writing. In Toby Fulwiler and Art Young (eds.), *Language Connections: Writing and Reading Across the Curriculum.* Urbana, IL: NCTE, pp. 45–56.

GEBHARDT, RICHARD. (1980). Teamwork and feedback: Broadening the base of collaborative writing. *College English, 42,* 69–74.

GEISLER, CHERYL. (1991). Reader, parent, coach: Defining the profession by our practice of response. *Reader: Essays in Reader-Oriented Theory, Criticism, and Pedagogy*, 25, pp. 17–33.

GEORGE, DIANA. (1984). Working with peer groups in the composition classroom. *College Composition and Communication, 35*(3), 320–326.

GERE, ANNE RUGGLES. (1987). *Writing Groups: History, Theory, and Implications.* Carbondale, IL: Southern Illinois University Press.

GIBSON, WALKER. (1966). *Tough, Sweet and Stuffy: An Essay on Modern American Prose Styles.* Bloomington and London: Indiana University Press.

GREENBERG, KAREN L. (1987). Research on basic writers: Theoretical and methodological issues. In Theresa Enos, (ed.), *A Sourcebook for Basic Writing Teachers.* NY: Random House, pp. 187–207.

GREENHALGH, ANNE M. (1992). Voices in response: A postmodern reading of teacher response. *College Composition and Communication, 43*, 401–410.

GREGG, LEE W., AND STEINBERG, ERWIN R. (eds.). (1980). *Cognitive Processes in Writing.* Hillsdale, NJ: Lawrence Erlbaum Associates.

GRIMM, NANCY. (1986). Improving students' responses to their peers' essays. *College Composition and Communication, 37*, 91–94.

HAIRSTON, MAXINE. (1986). Using nonfiction literature in the composition classroom. In Bruce T. Petersen, (ed.), *Convergences: Transactions in Reading and Writing.* Urbana, IL: NCTE, pp. 179–188.

HALPERN, JEANNE W. (1984). Differences between speaking and writing and their implications for teaching. *College Composition and Communication, 35*(3), 345–357.

HARRIS, MURIEL. (1989). Composing behaviors of one- and multi-draft writers. *College English, 51*(2), 174–191.

HARRIS, MURIEL. (1992). Collaboration is not collaboration is not collaboration: Writing center tutorials v. peer-response groups. *College Composition and Communication, 43,* 369–383.

HARTWELL, PATRICK. (1985). Grammar, grammars, and the teaching of grammar. *College English, 47,* 105–127.

HATLEN, BURTON. (1986). Old wine in new bottles: A dialectical encounter between the old rhetoric and the new. In Thomas Newkirk, (ed.), *Only Connect: Uniting Reading and Writing*. Upper Montclair, NJ: Boynton/Cook Publishers, pp. 59–86.

HAYS, JANICE N. (1983). The development of discursive maturity in college writers. In Janice N. Hays, (ed.), *The Writer's Mind: Writing as a Mode of Thinking*. Urbana, IL: NCTE, pp. 127–144.

HAYS, JANICE N. (ed.). (1983). *The Writer's Mind: Writing as a Mode of Thinking*. Urbana, IL: NCTE.

HILLOCKS, GEORGE, JR. (1986). *Research on Written Composition: New Directions for Teaching*. National Conference on Research in English, ERIC.

HOLT, MARA. (1992). The value of written peer criticism. *College Composition and Communication, 43,* 384–392.

HUFF, ROLAND, AND KLINE, CHARLES R. JR. (1987). *A Contemporary Writing Curriculum: Rehearsing, Composing, Valuing*. NY: Columbia University Press.

HULL, GLYNDA. (1987). Constructing taxonomies for error (or Can stray dogs be mermaids?). In Theresa Enos, (ed.), *A Sourcebook for Basic Writing Teachers*. NY: Random House, pp. 231–244.

JOBST, JACK. (1982). Audience and purpose in writing. In Toby Fulwiler and Art Young (eds.), *Language Connections: Writing and Reading Across the Curriculum*. Urbana, IL: NCTE, pp. 57–76.

JONES, LINDA KAY. (1977). *Theme in English Expository Discourse*. Lake Bluff, IL: Jupiter Press.

KALMBACH, JAMES, AND POWERS, WILLIAM. (1982). Shaping experience: Narration and understanding. In Toby Fulwiler and Art Young, (eds.), *Language Connections: Writing and Reading Across the Curriculum*. Urbana, IL: NCTE, pp. 99–106.

KANTOR, KENNETH J., AND RUBIN, DONALD L. (1981). Between speaking and writing: Processes of differentiation. In Barry M. Kroll and Roberta J. Vann, (eds.), *Exploring Speaking-Writing Relationships*. Urbana, IL: NCTE.

KINIRY, MALCOLM, AND STRENSKI, ELLEN. (1985). Sequencing expository writing: A recursive approach. *College Composition and Communication, 36*(2), 191–202.

KROLL, BARRY M. (1984). Writing for readers: Three perspectives on audience. *College Composition and Communication, 35*(2), 172–185.

KROLL, BARRY M., AND SHAFER, JOHN C. (1978). Error analysis and the teaching of composition. *College Composition and Communication, 29,* 243–248.

KROLL, BARRY M., AND VANN, ROBERTA J. (eds.). (1981). *Exploring Speaking-Writing Relationships*. Urbana, IL: NCTE.

LINDEMANN, ERIKA. (1987). *A Rhetoric for Writing Teachers (2nd ed.)*. NY: Oxford University Press.

LUNSFORD, ANDREA A. (1987). Politics and practices in basic writing. In Theresa Enos, (ed.), *A Sourcebook for Basic Writing Teachers*. NY: Random House, pp. 246–258.

MADIGAN, CHRIS. (1985). Improving writing assignments with communication theory. *College Composition and Communication, 36*(2), 183–189.

MALLONEE, BARBARA, AND BREIHAN, JOHN R. (1985). Responding to students' drafts: Interdisciplinary consensus. *College Composition and Communication, 36*(2), 213–231.

MCCLEARY, WILLIAM J. (1985). A case approach for teaching academic writing. *College Composition and Communication, 36*(2), 203–212.

MCGUIRE SIMMONS, JO ANN. (1984). The one-to-one method of teaching composition. *College Composition and Communication, 35*(2), 222–229.

MEYER, BONNIE J. F. (1979). *Research on Prose Comprehension: Applications for Composition Teachers. Research Report No. 2, Prose Learning Series.* Department of Educational Psychology, College of Education. Tempe, AZ: Arizona State University.

MEYER, BONNIE J. F. (1982). *Prose Analysis: Purposes, Procedures, and Problems. Research Report No. 11. Prose Learning Series.* Department of Educational Psychology, College of Education. Tempe, AZ: Arizona State University.

MEYER, BONNIE J. F. (1982). Reading research and the composition teacher: The importance of plans. *College Composition and Communication, 33*(1), 37–49.

MEYER, BONNIE J. F., YOUNG, CAROLE J., AND BARTLETT, BRENDAN J. (1989). *Memory Improved: Reading and Memory Enhancement Across the Life Span Through Strategic Text Structures.* Hillsdale, NJ: Lawrence Erlbaum Associates.

MITCHELL, FELICIA. (1992). Balancing individual projects and collaborative learning in an advanced writing class. *College Composition and Communication, 43*, 393–400.

MURRAY, DONALD. (1982). Teaching the other self: The writer's first reader. *College Composition and Communication, 33,* 140–147.

NEWKIRK, THOMAS. (1984). Direction and misdirection in peer response. *College Composition and Communication, 35*(3), 301–311.

NEWKIRK, THOMAS, (ed.). (1986). *Only Connect: Uniting Reading and Writing.* Upper Montclair, NJ: Boynton/Cook Publishers.

NOLD, ELLEN W. (1981). Revising. In Carl H. Frederiksen and Joseph F. Dominic, (eds.), *Writing: The Nature, Development, and Teaching of Written Communication, Volume 2: Writing: Process, Development and Communication.* Hillsdale, NJ: Lawrence Erlbaum Associates, pp. 67–79.

NORTH, STEPHEN. (1982). Training tutors to talk about writing. *College Composition and Communication, 33,* 434–441.

ODELL, LEE. (1976). Question-asking and the teaching of writing. *The English Record.* Vol. 27. Buffalo, NY: New York State English Council.

ONG, WALTER J., S.J. (1971). *Rhetoric, Romance and Technology: Studies in the Interaction of Expression and Culture.* Ithaca and London: Cornell University Press.

ONG, WALTER J., S.J. (1975). The writer's audience is always a fiction. *PMLA, 90*, 9–21.

PARK, DOUGLAS. (1975). Analyzing audiences. *College Composition and Communication, 37*, 478–488.

PARK, DOUGLAS. (1975). The meanings of "audience." *College English, 44,* 249.

PARKER, ROBERT. (1985). The "language across the curriculum" movement: A brief overview and bibliography. *College Composition and Communication, 36*(2), 173–177.

PERL, SONDRA. (1979). The composing processes of unskilled college writers. *Research in the Teaching of English, 13*, 317–336.

PERL, SONDRA. (1980). Understanding composing. *College Composition and Communication, 31* (December), 363–369.

PETERSEN, BRUCE T. (ed.). (1986). *Convergences: Transactions in Reading and Writing.* Urbana, IL: NCTE.

PFISTER, FRED R., AND PETRICK, JOANNE F. (1984). A heuristic model for creating a writer's audience. *College Composition and Communication, 35*(2), 213–220.

PICKETT, NEIL ANN. (1984). Achieving readability through layout. *Teaching English in the Two-Year College, 10*(2), 154–156.

POLLARD, RITA H. (1991). Another look: The process approach to composition instruction. *Journal of Developmental Education, 14*(3), 30–32.

REDISH, JANICE. (1989). Writing in organizations. In Myra Kogen, (ed.), *Writing in the Business Professions.* Urbana, IL: NCTE, pp. 97–124.

REIGSTAD, THOMAS J., AND MCANDREW, DONALD A. (1984). *Training Tutors for Writing Conferences.* Urbana, IL: NCTE.

RONALD, KATHARINE. (1986). The self and the other in the process of composing: Implications for integrating the acts of reading and writing. In Bruce T. Petersen, (ed.), *Convergences: Transactions in Reading and Writing.* Urbana, IL: National Council of Teachers of English, pp. 231–245.

ROSE, MIKE. (1983). Remedial writing courses: A critique and a proposal. *College English, 45*, 109–128.

ROSENBLATT, LOUISE M. (1983). *Literature as Exploration (4th ed.).* NY: Modern Language Association.

ROTH, ROBERT G. (1987). The evolving audience: Alternatives to audience accommodation. *College Composition and Communication, 38*, 47–55.

SALVATORI, MARIOLINA. (1983). Reading and writing a text: Correlations between reading and writing patterns. *College English, 45*, 657–666.

SCHWARTZ, MIMI. (1983). Revision profiles: Patterns and implications. *College English, 45*, 549–558.

SELZER, JACK. (1984). Exploring options in composing. *College Composition and Communication, 35*(3), 276–284.

SEVERINO, CAROL. (1992). Rhetorically analyzing collaboration(s). *Writing Center Journal, 13*(1), 53–64.

SHAUGHNESSY, MINA. (1977). *Errors and Expectations,* NY: Oxford University Press.

SHOR, IRA. (1977). Reinventing daily life: Self-study and the theme of work. *College English, 39*, 502–506.

SIMMONS, JO AN MCGUIRE. (1984). The one-to-one method of teaching composition. *College Composition and Communication, 35*, 222–229.

SMITH, FRANK. (1988). *Understanding Reading: A Psycholinguistic Analysis of Reading and Learning to Read (4th ed.).* Hillsdale, NJ: Lawrence Erlbaum Associates.

SMITH, ROCHELLE. (1984). Paragraphing for coherence: Writing as implied dialogue. *College English, 46*, 8–21.

SOMMERS, NANCY. (1979). Revision strategies of student writers and experienced adult writers. *College Composition and Communication, 30*, 275–278.

SOMMERS, NANCY. (1982). Responding to student writing. *College Composition and Communication, 33*(2), 148–156.

SPEAR, KAREN. (1988). *Sharing Writing: Peer Response Groups in English Classes.* Portsmouth, NH: Boynton/Cook Publishers.

STERNGLASS, MARILYN S. (1981). Assessing reading, writing, and reasoning. *College English, 43*, 269–75.

STERNGLASS, MARILYN S. (1986). Writing based on reading. In Bruce T. Petersen, (ed.), *Convergences: Transactions in Reading and Writing*. Urbana, IL: NCTE, pp. 151–162.

STOTSKY, SANDRA. (1979). Teaching the vocabulary of academic discourse. *Journal of Basic Writing, 2*(3), 15–39.

TATE, GARY, AND CORBETT, EDWARD P. J. (1988). *The Writing Teacher's Sourcebook (2nd ed.).* NY: Oxford University Press.

TOULMIN, STEPHEN. (1964). *The Uses of Argument.* NY: Cambridge University Press.

TROYKA, LYNN QUITMAN. (1986). Closeness to text. In Thomas Newkirk (ed.), *Only Connect: Uniting Reading and Writing*. Upper Montclair, NJ: Boynton/Cook Publishers.

TROYKA, LYNN QUITMAN (1986). Perspectives on legacies and literacy in the 1980s. *College Composition and Communication, 33*, 252–261.

WALL, SUSAN. (1982). In the writer's eye: Learning to teach the rereading/revising process. *English Education, 14*, 12.

WALVOORD, BARBARA E. FASSLER. (1986). *Helping Students Write Well: A Guide for Teachers in All Disciplines (2nd ed.).* NY: MLA.

WALVOORD, BARBARA E., AND MCCARTHY, LUCILLE P. (1990). *Thinking and Writing in College: A Naturalistic Study of Students in Four Disciplines*. Urbana, IL: NCTE.

WALZER, ARTHUR E. (1985). Articles from the California divorce project: A case study of the concept of audience. *College Composition and Communication, 36*(2), 150–159.

WAUTERS, JOAN K. (1988). Non-confrontational critiquing pairs: An alternative to verbal peer response groups. *Writing Instructor, 7*, 156–166.

WHITE, EDWARD M. (1984). Post-structural literacy criticism and the response to student writing. *College Composition and Communication, 35*(2), 186–195.

WIENER, HARVEY. (1986). Collaborative learning in the classroom. *College English, 48*, 52–61.

WILKINSON, A. M. (1985). A freshman writing course in parallel with a science course. *College Composition and Communication, 36*(2), 160–165.

WILLIAMS, JOSEPH M. (1989). *Style: Ten Lessons in Clarity and Grace (3rd ed.).* Glenview, IL: Scott Foresman & Company.

WINTEROWD, W. ROSS. (1986). *Composition/Rhetoric: A Synthesis.* Carbondale: Southern Illinois University Press.

YOUNG, ART. (1992). College Culture and the Challenge of Collaboration. *Writing Center Journal, 13*(1), 3–15.

YOUNG, R. E., BECKER, A. L., AND PIKE, K. L. (1970). *Rhetoric: Discovery and Change.* NY: Harcourt, Brace & World.

Index

A

B

C

D

E

N

O

P

Q

R

S